INDEPENDENCE IN CENTRAL AMERICA AND CHIAPAS
1770–1823

INDEPENDENCE IN
Central America and Chiapas
1770–1823

Edited by AARON POLLACK

Translated by NANCY T. HANCOCK

UNIVERSITY OF OKLAHOMA PRESS : NORMAN

This book was first published in Spanish as *La época de las independencias en Centroamérica y Chiapas. Procesos políticos y sociales* (2013) by Instituto de Investigaciones Dr. José María Luis Mora.

Library of Congress Cataloging-in-Publication Data
Names: Pollack, Aaron, editor. | Hancock, Nancy T., translator.
Title: Independence in Central America and Chiapas, 1770–1823 / edited by Aaron Pollack ; translated by Nancy T. Hancock.
Other titles: Epoca de las independencias en Centroamerica y Chiapas. English.
Description: Norman : University of Oklahoma Press, [2019] | Translation of: La epoca de las independencias en Centroamerica y Chiapas : procesos politicos y sociales. | Includes bibliographical references and index.
Identifiers: LCCN 2018034185 | ISBN 978-0-8061-6279-9 (paperback : alk. paper)
Subjects: LCSH: Central America—History—To 1821. | Chiapas (Mexico)—History—19th century. | Self-determination, National—Central America—History—19th century. | Central America—Social conditions—18th century. | Chiapas (Mexico)—Social conditions—18th century. | Central America—Politics and government—18th century. | Chiapas (Mexico)—Politics and government—18th century.
Classification: LCC F1437 .E6613 2019 | DDC 972.8/03—dc23
LC record available at https://lccn.loc.gov/2018034185

The paper in this book meets the guidelines for permanence and durability of the Committee on Production Guidelines for Book Longevity of the Council on Library Resources, Inc. ∞

Copyright © 2019 by the University of Oklahoma Press, Norman, Publishing Division of the University. Manufactured in the U.S.A.

All rights reserved. No part of this publication may be reproduced, stored in a retrieval system, or transmitted, in any form or by any means, electronic, mechanical, photocopying, recording, or otherwise—except as permitted under Section 107 or 108 of the United States Copyright Act—without the prior written permission of the University of Oklahoma Press. To request permission to reproduce selections from this book, write to Permissions, University of Oklahoma Press, 2800 Venture Drive, Norman, OK 73069, or email rights.oupress@ou.edu.

CONTENTS

List of Maps   vii

Preface to the English Edition   ix

Acknowledgments for the Spanish Edition   xi

By Way of Introduction to Central American Independence:
A Historical and Historiographical Overview, *by Aaron Pollack*   1

PART I. CONCEPTS, CEREMONIES, SYMBOLS, AND NETWORKS: CONTINUITIES AND CHANGE

Representing Sovereignty in Oath-Taking Ceremonies:
The Kingdom of Guatemala, 1790–1812, *by Sajid Alfredo Herrera Mena*   37

The Costa Rican Concordia Compact, 1821–1823: A Constitutionalist Perspective on Independence, *by Pablo Augusto Rodríguez Solano*   57

Theaters of Power in 1821: Swearing Loyalty to Independence in the Province of Guatemala, *by Xiomara Avendaño Rojas*   81

Bourbon Reforms and Enlightenment in Chiapas, 1758–1808, *by Christophe Belaubre*   103

PART II. REBELLION AND REPRESSION

Local Powers and Popular Resistance in Nicaragua, 1808–1813, *by Elizet Payne Iglesias*   133

Totonicapán, 1820: One of the Tips of the Iceberg? *by Aaron Pollack*   158

The Myth of Bustamantine Terror, *by Timothy Hawkins*   187

Glossary   213

Bibliography   217

List of Contributors   243

Index   247

MAPS

Ecclesiastical divisions of the Kingdom of Guatemala, ca. 1810   **xiii**

Kingdom of Guatemala, ca. 1810   **xiv–xv**

Intendancy of Chiapas, ca. 1810   **xvi**

Guatemala and Sonsonate, ca. 1810   **xvii**

Intendancy of San Salvador, ca. 1810   **xviii**

Intendancy of Comayagua, ca. 1810   **xix**

Intendancy of León, ca. 1810   **xx**

Gobernación of Costa Rica, ca. 1810   **xxi**

PREFACE
TO THE ENGLISH EDITION

English-language publications have generally given less attention to Central American history than to the histories of other Latin American regions, and the contributions to this volume help to remedy that situation. The Central American and Central Americanist authors included here have revised and updated, in greater or lesser degree, the Spanish versions of the chapters originally published in *La época de las independencias en Centroamérica y Chiapas. Procesos políticos y sociales* (2013), thereby offering a sense of the different perspectives present in Central American historiography that treats the independence period and the decades preceding it.

I thank the authors for their eagerness to support this project, their willingness to update texts, and their accompaniment in the translation process. This book would not have been published without the moral support and tenacity of Brian Connaughton and the financial support for the translation offered by the research project "Centroamérica y Chiapas: La independencia y sus secuelas político-sociales," funded by the Mexican National Council on Science and Technology (SEP-CONACYT CB-153658) under his direction. Alessandra Jacobi Tamulevich at the University of Oklahoma Press has consistently demonstrated faith in the importance of producing an English version of this volume and enormous patience throughout the process of translation and publication. I greatly appreciate the interest shown by the University of Oklahoma Press in making these texts available to an English-speaking audience and its ongoing commitment to Central American history.

ACKNOWLEDGMENTS FOR THE SPANISH EDITION

The "Centroamérica y Chiapas: La independencia y sus secuelas político-sociales" research project, financed by the Mexican National Council for Science and Technology (CONACYT) and coordinated by Brian Connaughton, has been fundamental to the publication of this text. The initial proposal for the publication of a book that would present some of the contemporary trends in the study of the process of independence in Central America and Chiapas came out of conversations with Mario Vázquez Olivera. Although he was unable to participate as an editor of this volume, as had originally been planned, his input has been fundamental to several phases of the work.

The publication of this book has been aided by the individual contributions of a number of different people. I thank all the authors for their texts and their patience, especially Elizet Payne Iglesias, whose careful and wide-ranging suggestions on maps have notably improved their content and presentation.

Interns Gabriela Guerrero Álvarez, Andrea López Ortiz, Esaú Juvenal Ramírez Hernández, and Maribel Rivas Vasconcelos made important contributions that facilitated different aspects of the creation of this book, and I am grateful to them for their work. I am particularly grateful to Priscila Melo, who did fine work in the editing of the entire text. Marel Hernández Quiñones showed great perseverance, ability, patience, and a fine sense of humor during the mapmaking process, all of which I am thankful for.

At the Mora Institute a group of people allowed this book to be published: I express my sincere appreciation to Research Director María Cristina Sacristán Gómez; to Lourdes Roca y Ortiz, the coordinator of the Urban, Regional, and International Studies and History Department; to Yolanda Martínez and Gustavo Villalobos Revelo of the Department of Publications; and to Sergio Morales Marín and Yéssica Estrada Flores of the office of the Assistant Manager of the Department of Publications.

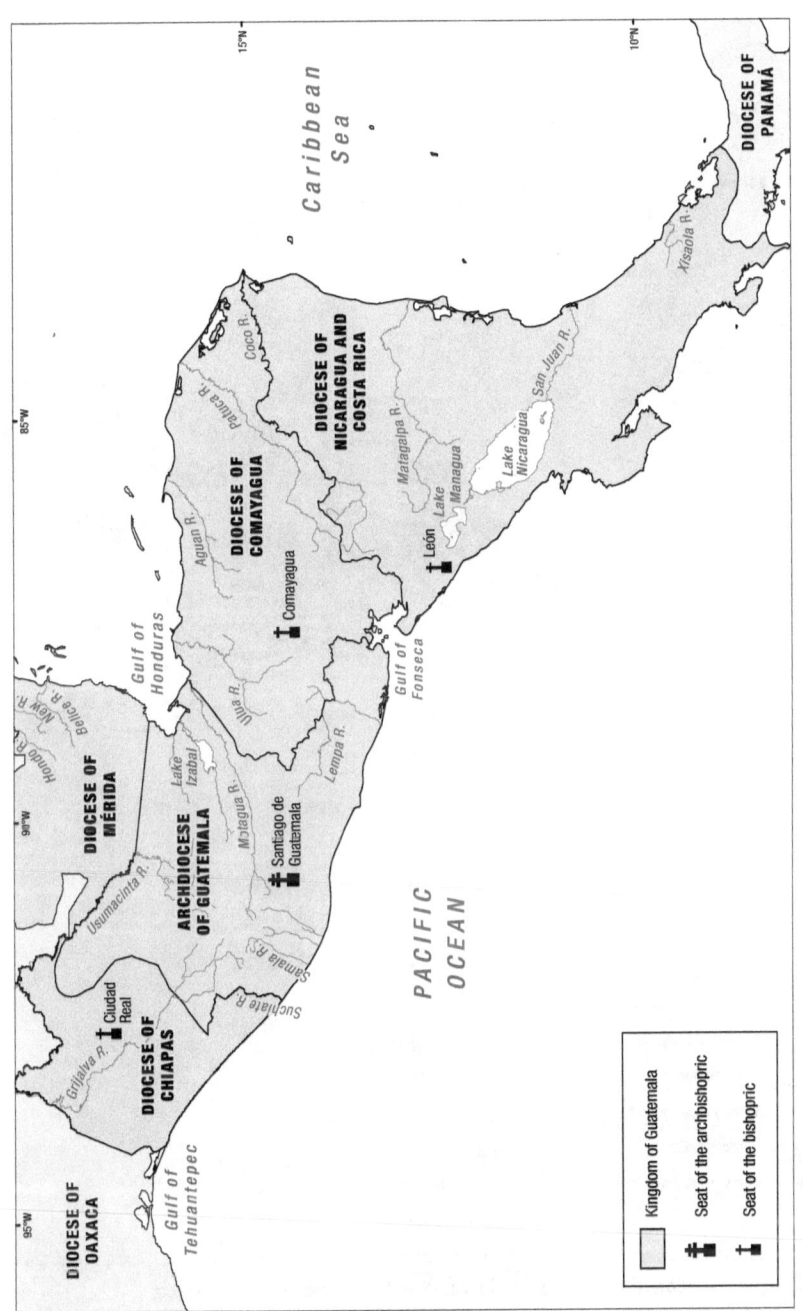

Ecclesiastical divisions of the Kingdom of Guatemala, ca. 1810. Cartography by Erin Greb, based on map by Marel Hernández Quiñones.

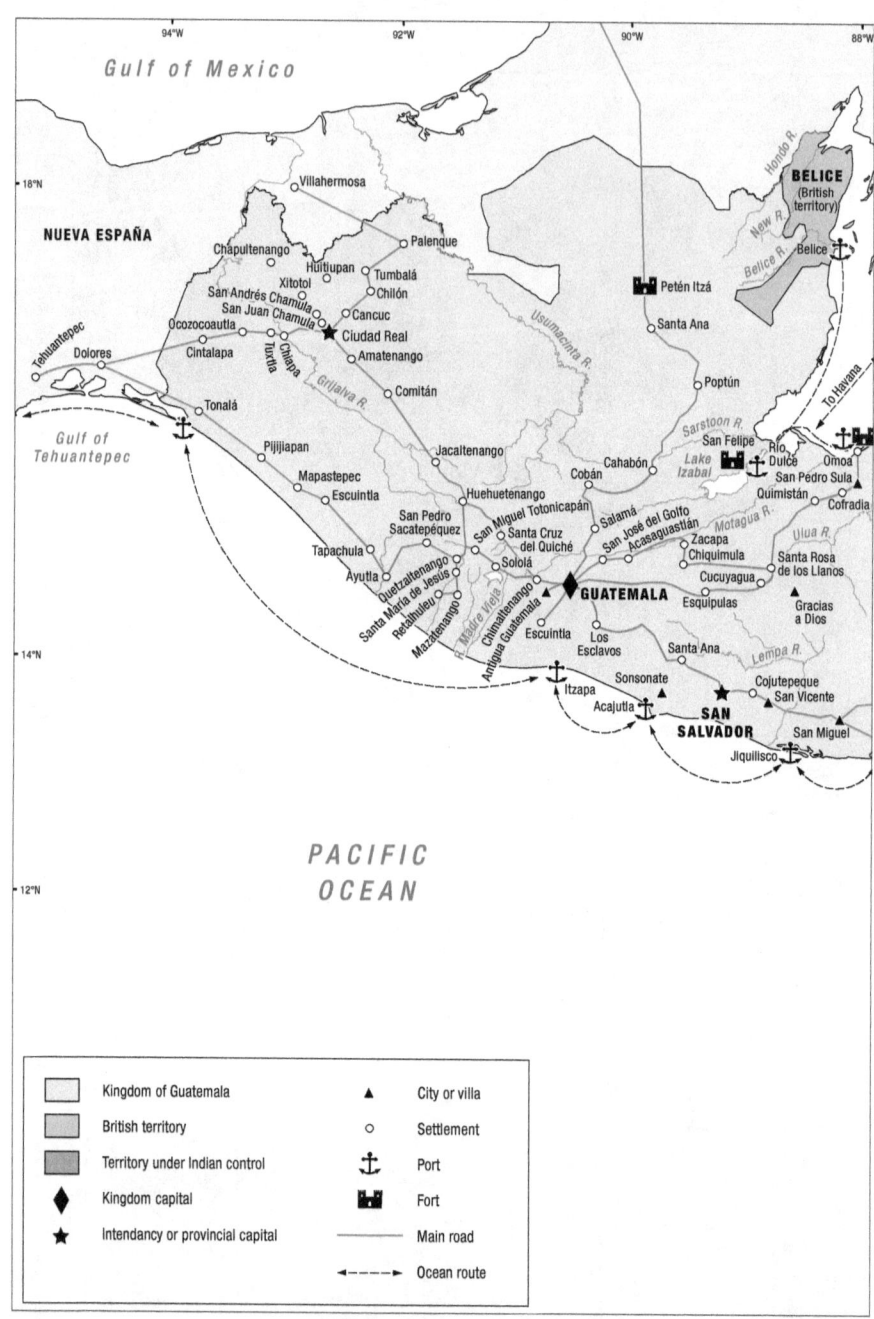

Kingdom of Guatemala, ca. 1810. Cartography by Erin Greb, based on map by Marel Hernández Quiñones.

xv

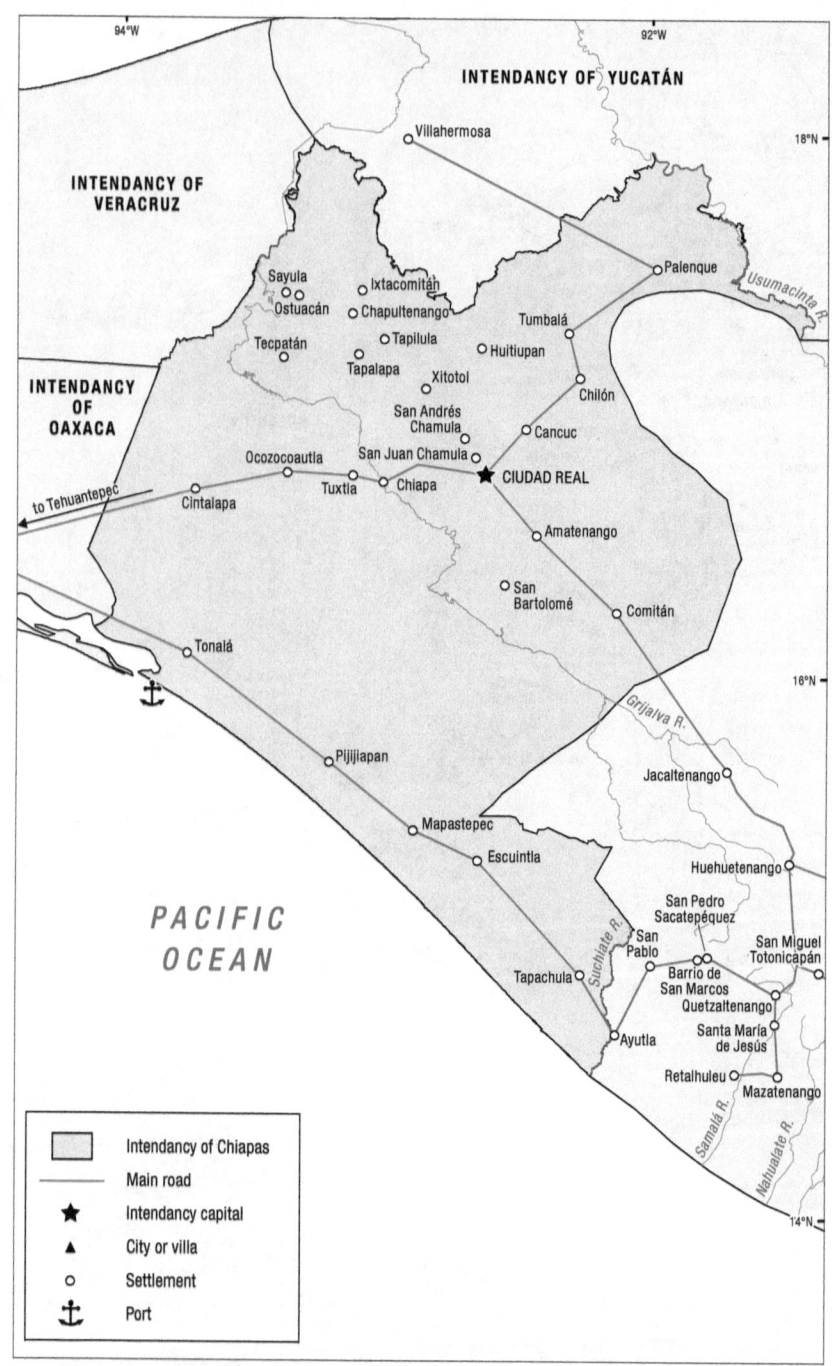

Intendancy of Chiapas, ca. 1810. Cartography by Erin Greb, based on map by Marel Hernández Quiñones.

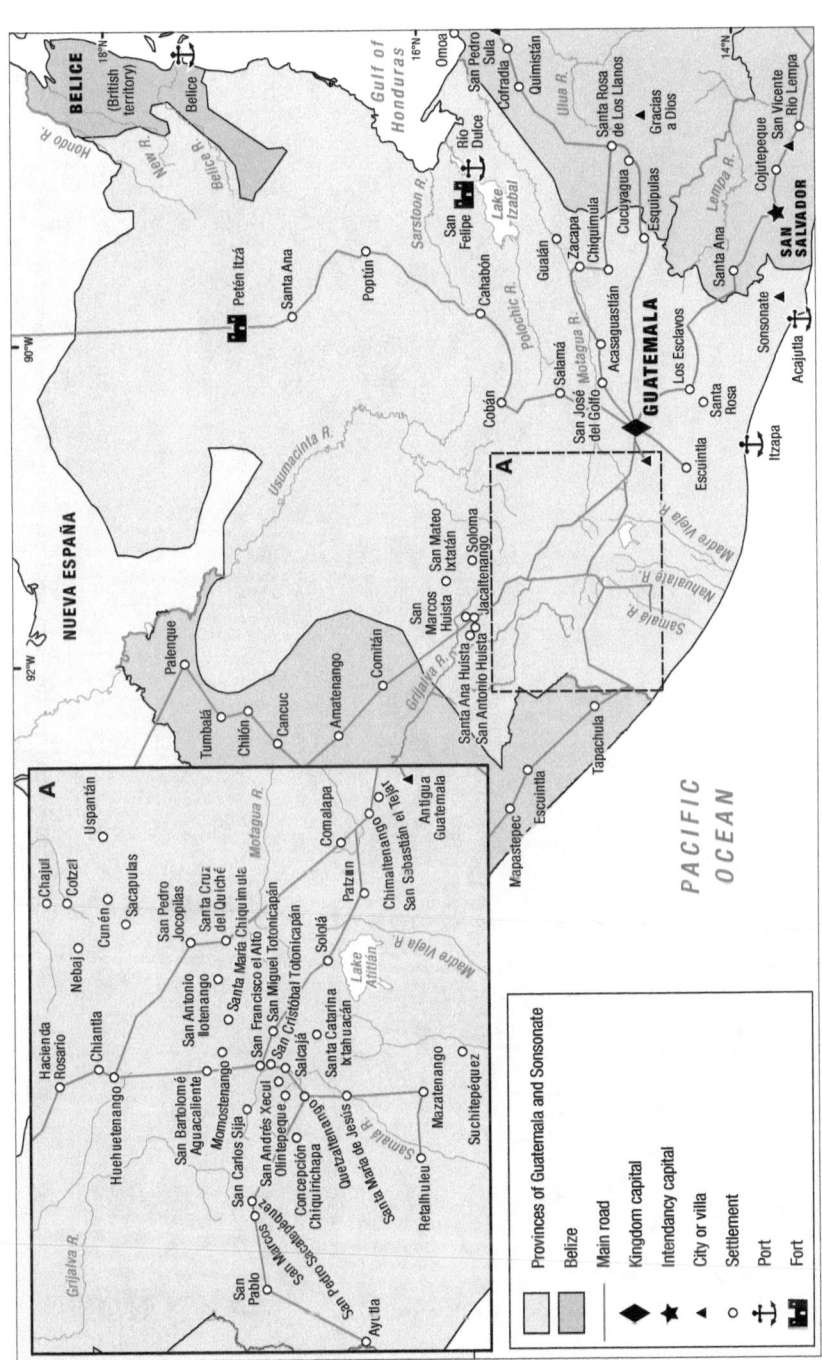

Guatemala and Sonsonate, ca. 1810. At this time, the territory of the future state and later country of Guatemala was administered by the alcaldías mayores of Chimaltenango, Escuintla, Sacatepéquez, Sololá, Sonsonate, Suchitepéquez, Totonicapán, and Verapaz and the corregimientos of Chiquimula and Quetzaltenango. Cartography by Erin Greb, based on map by Marel Hernández Quiñones.

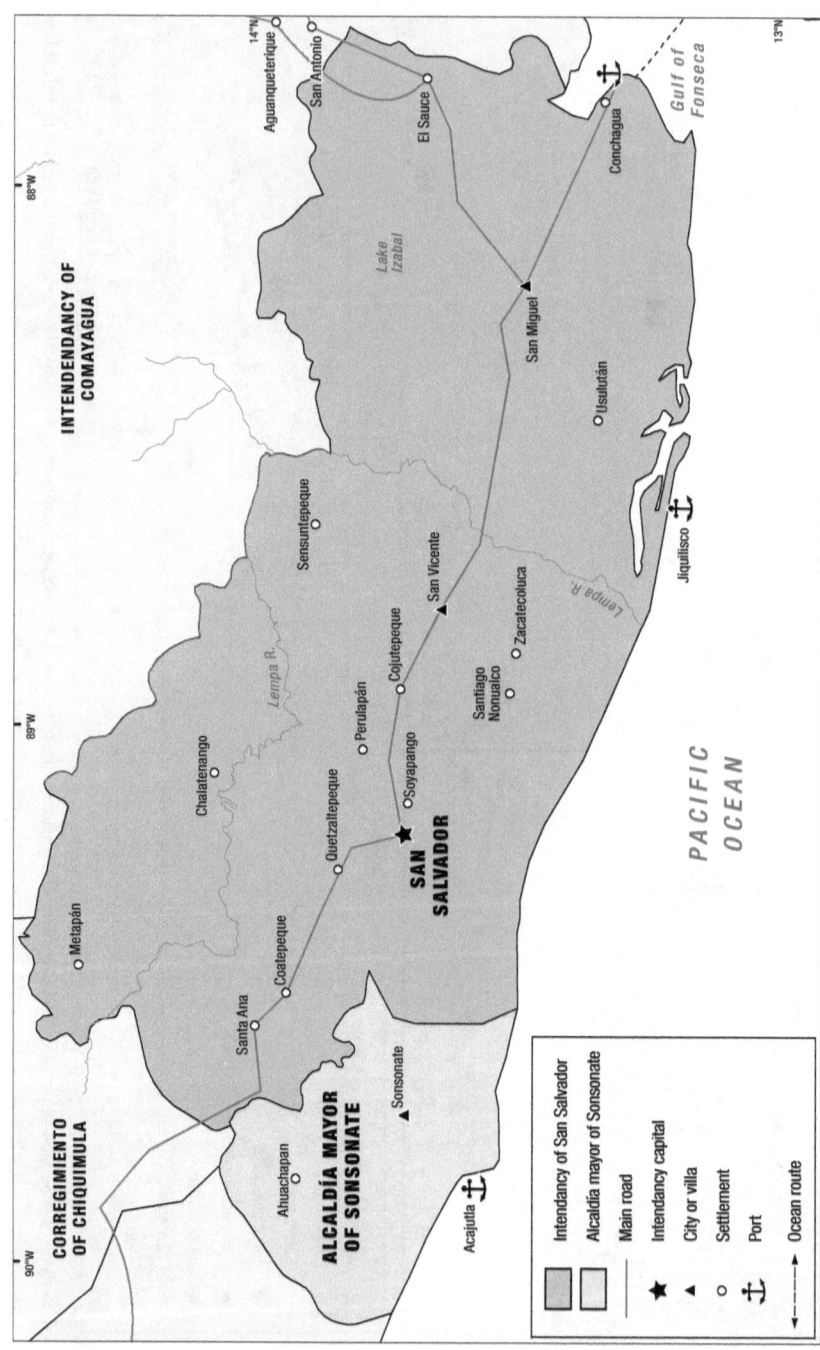

Intendancy of San Salvador, ca. 1810. Cartography by Erin Greb, based on map by Marel Hernández Quiñones.

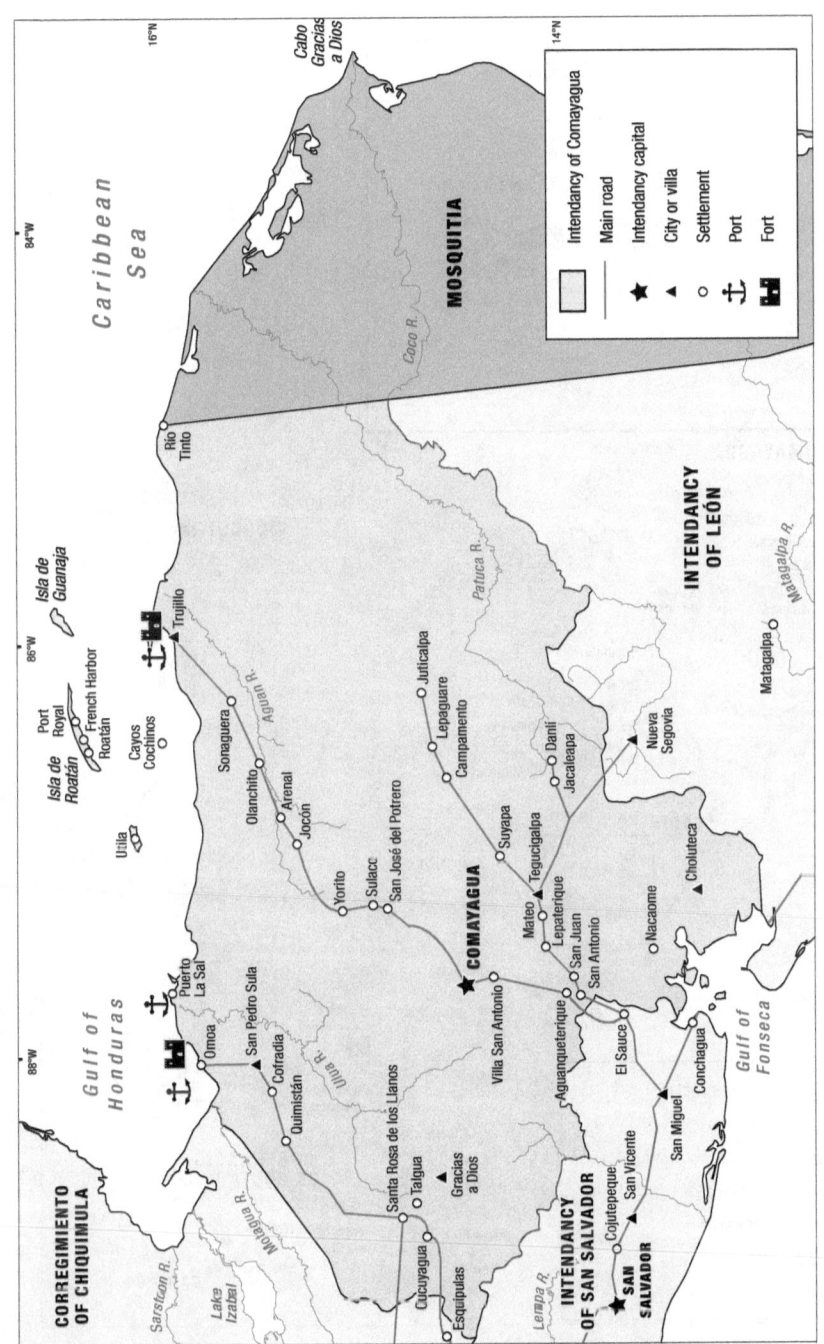

Intendancy of Comayagua, ca. 1810. Cartography by Erin Greb, based on map by Marel Hernández Quiñones.

Intendancy of León, ca. 1810. Cartography by Erin Greb, based on map by Marel Hernández Quiñones.

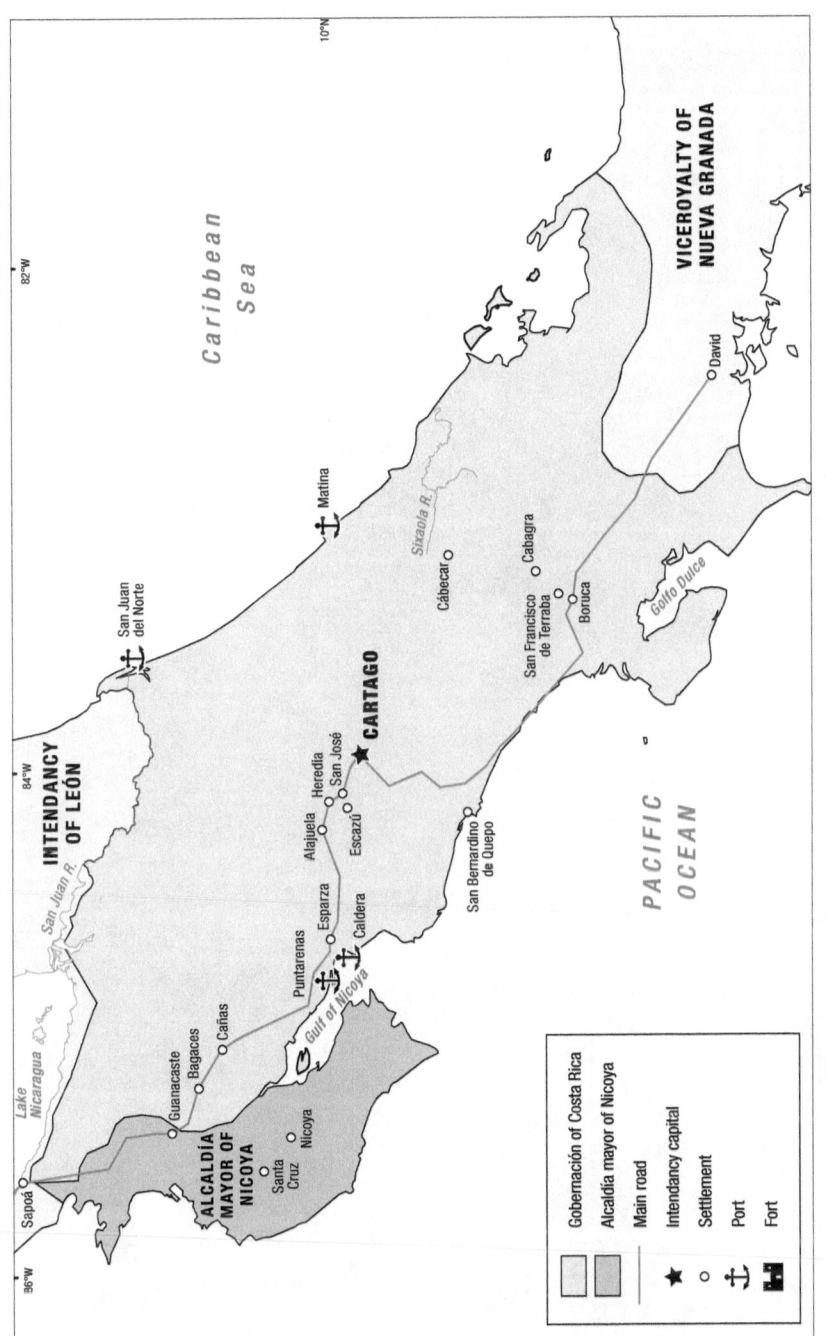

Gobernación of Costa Rica, ca. 1810. Cartography by Erin Greb, based on map by Marel Hernández Quiñones.

BY WAY OF INTRODUCTION TO CENTRAL AMERICAN INDEPENDENCE
A Historical and Historiographical Overview

AARON POLLACK

The essays collected in this volume offer the reader an introduction which, although inevitably incomplete, is representative of recent historiography of the independence period in Central America. Focusing on what the discipline has divided into political and social history, these works consider themes that include the analysis of concepts, symbols, ceremonies, social networks, rebellions, and repression. In temporal terms, the seven chapters cover a period that begins in the late eighteenth century and ends with independence from Spain and the debate that surrounded the decision to join the Mexican Empire; geographically, they cover nearly the whole Kingdom of Guatemala. Contributors discuss the intendancies (*intendencias*) of Ciudad Real and León as well as the gobernación of Costa Rica and the region that later formed the state and then the nation of Guatemala. There are no specific chapters on the intendancies of Comayagua (Honduras) or San Salvador.

The first part of this introductory chapter offers some general ideas to help locate the reader in the process—unique, like every process—of Central American independence from Spain and from the Mexican Empire. Divided into three sections, it begins with a general description of the Kingdom of Guatemala, then enters into a discussion of the reforms put in place during the latter part of the eighteenth century and the new ideas that spread in the kingdom during that same period, before offering an interpretation of how independence in the region related to similar processes in other parts of Hispanic America. The second part of the introduction offers a brief description of the different chapters and their pertinence to current debates surrounding the independence period in Central America.

THE WARP AND WEAVE OF CENTRAL AMERICAN INDEPENDENCE: NOTES FOR THE UNINITIATED

The Kingdom of Guatemala

The audiencia and captaincy general of Guatemala, the land in the "Center of America," as the new republic that occupied a good part of the territory after 1823 briefly called itself, shared a border to the north with the audiencia of Mexico and to the south with the New Kingdom of Granada, though the oceans provided the captaincy with its most extensive boundaries.[1] The region was endowed with an extremely varied physical geography, including fertile plains on the Pacific coast and in the highland valleys—the areas in which population has been concentrated since prehispanic times—and extensive jungle and forest areas with relatively little population in the regions nearer the Atlantic. The mountainous and marshy territory of the Kingdom of Guatemala, where rivers often flooded during the rainy season, made internal communication difficult and promoted the development of a social and economic organization with strong regional traits.

At the time of the Spanish invasions, a great number of political entities occupied the territory of the isthmus. Political division continued with the campaigns of at least four different conquistadors, often accompanied by native soldiers; the conquest zones were finally united as the Audiencia de los confines de Guatemala y Nicaragua, formed in 1542. With the establishment of the audiencia, which only in 1569 adopted the territorial form it would maintain until independence from Spain in 1821, the region was placed under a single judicial, political, administrative, and military jurisdiction. Included were the present-day Mexican state of Chiapas and the countries of Belize, Costa Rica, El Salvador, Guatemala, Honduras, and Nicaragua. But a good part of this territory was beyond Spanish control, even up until independence, especially in the Atlantic coastal region. There, the native peoples (called "Indians" by the Spaniards and others), joined by arrivals of Caribbean and African origin, took advantage of their commercial connections with the English to strengthen their political and economic positions (the English had established permanent ports during the seventeenth and eighteenth centuries). The territorial divisions created with the conquest remained visible in the four bishoprics of the audiencia (Ciudad Real, Guatemala, Comayagua, and León), which were suffragan to three different archbishoprics (the first two to Mexico, the third to Santo Domingo, and the fourth to Lima) from the middle of the sixteenth century until the establishment of the archbishopric of Guatemala in 1743.[2]

Until the establishment of the intendancy system in 1785–86, the number of judicial, administrative, and military territorial divisions—known as alcaldías mayores, corregimientos, and gobernaciones—changed, yet each one remained under the direct supervision of the captaincy general, government, and audiencia, whose seat was permanently fixed in Santiago de Guatemala in 1569, then transferred to Nueva Guatemala (Guatemala City) after an earthquake destroyed the old capital in 1773. With the implementation of the new system, an administrative and territorial expression of the Bourbon reforms, the four intendancies of Ciudad Real, San Salvador, Comayagua, and León came into existence, each with its respective subdelegations. The territories of what would become the Republic of Guatemala, along with Sonsonate, continued as alcaldías mayores and corregimientos, although organized under a single unified treasury authority, known as a superintendencia hacendaria, located in the capital.

Officially a part of the Viceroyalty of New Spain, the Kingdom of Guatemala was, with few exceptions, governed independently.[3] At the beginning of the nineteenth century, with two-thirds of its total population defined as Indian and almost all the remaining third classified as ladinos,[4] the captaincy general harbored only a small number of peninsular and American Spaniards (*criollos*, or "Creoles"). The common interests of the criollos and peninsular Spaniards promoted more alliances than conflicts between them, and they formed virtually the entire royal bureaucracy while dominating the economy of the kingdom. Toward the north, especially in parts of San Salvador and the highland areas of both Chiapas and Guatemala, the kingdom had a predominantly Indian population. In other parts of Chiapas, San Salvador, eastern Guatemala, and the provinces of Honduras, Nicaragua, and Costa Rica, the presence of a mestizo and mulatto population increased and became predominant in many towns and regions. Throughout its whole expanse, the kingdom had only a few Spanish cities and villas with ayuntamientos, located principally in the Pacific lowlands.[5] Prior to 1804, in the territories of present-day Guatemala and Chiapas, as an extreme example, there were only three: Ciudad Real, Antigua Guatemala, and Nueva Guatemala.[6] Economically subjugated by the commercial and financial elite of Guatemala City—or, in the case of Chiapas, abandoned by them—the more powerful groups that politically and economically dominated the other provinces sought the means to free themselves from this elite; in the last third of the eighteenth century their efforts received the support of the Bourbon reformers.

Enlightenment and Reform

Driven by competition between empires and imbued with some aspects of what has been called Enlightenment thinking (see Belaubre, this volume), the Bourbon reforms began to be implemented decisively in Spanish America, as opposed to the Iberian Peninsula where they had begun decades before, only after the successful English attacks on Havana and Manila in 1762. Somewhat successful,[7] the reforms sought primarily to finance Spanish defenses and assure that a large portion of their construction and maintenance costs would come from the colonies, which required an administrative and fiscal reorganization that was to have many long-term effects. With their standardizing and absolutist impetus, the new systems implied changes in the existing forms of organization that met with resistance from different groups, both on the peninsula and in America, which often forced modifications. In the end, the Bourbon authorities negotiated their new policies, much as their Hapsburg predecessors.

In the Kingdom of Guatemala,[8] as in other parts of Spanish America, the reforms had military, fiscal, economic, territorial, and administrative impacts: the reduction of the English presence on the Atlantic coast; the restructuring of the militia; the implementation of economic policies intended to promote growth and income for the Spanish treasury (how much growth they actually developed is another question); the creation of the Real Sociedad Económica de Amantes de la Patria de Guatemala (Royal Economic Society of Lovers of the Homeland of Guatemala); the centralization of fiscal control in the hands of royal authorities; and the drawing up of new territorial divisions with the creation of intendancies and subdelegations.[9] These reforms created a great deal of tension around fiscal issues, especially—though not only—among the urban poor and the Indians, as the near revolt in Guatemala City in 1766, the widespread and violent resistance to the implementation of a the liquor monopoly in Quetzaltenango in 1785, and the 1803 riots in Cobán in response to reform in Indian tribute clearly demonstrate.[10] In each of these cases, resistance to crown policies forced Bourbon bureaucrats to rescind or simply not apply new policies, potentially pointing toward changes in the political culture during the latter third of the eighteenth century.[11]

Certain events, such as participation by city elites in the events of 1766 in Guatemala City and the tensions between the intendant of Ciudad Real, José Mariano Valero (see Belaubre, this volume), and the Creoles who dominated the city of the same name (1805–9), support the notion that attempts by the crown to centralize power provoked Creole resistance. Yet in the Central American case the crown backed down in these confrontations, as Dym and Belaubre have observed.[12] Nonetheless, despite the tensions these changes engendered, prolonged opposition to the crown, such as that which provoked the Andean rebellions of 1780–81, did not develop, and, as Palma demonstrated decades ago,[13] a division between Creoles and peninsular Spaniards such as Brading has argued in the case of New Spain did not occur.[14] Many of the new policies, especially those related to stimulating production and commerce, were well received by the economically more powerful groups in the principal cities, who participated freely in the new spaces of the public sphere,[15] which the Spanish authorities themselves had promoted. Nonetheless, the resistance engendered by the reforms and the possible changes in the political culture they may have implied, especially in that of subaltern groups, could be considered as a precursor to the cycle of popular mobilizations and rebellions that became visible after 1811 and lasted until mid-century.[16]

In the Kingdom of Guatemala, the boom in indigo production and commerce during most of the final third of the eighteenth century marked a time of relative abundance, until the British blockade, begun in 1797 to weaken France and her allies, gave the first warning of what would later result in the end of the indigo period. These years of macroeconomic success probably reduced, but certainly did not eliminate, potential resistance to the reforms, especially among the wealthiest, who were also the greatest beneficiaries of the dye bonanza.[17] In like manner, it is easy to imagine that the wish to maintain this success would have been one of the reasons (in addition to the desire to legalize the flourishing contraband trade in English textiles) behind the interest certain Central American merchants expressed in promoting free trade—no longer only within the Spanish monarchy but rather with any friendly or neutral nation.[18]

After the coronation of Charles IV in 1788, the French Revolution the following year, with the fears that it awakened, and the Napoleonic wars that would follow shortly thereafter, the reformist spirit coexisted with political and fiscal emergencies that transformed it. With the passing of years and the weakening of the Spanish position—to a large extent a consequence of the aforementioned disruption in American commerce—measures such as the consolidation of the *vales reales* (royal bonds) resulted from the growing need for economic resources,[19] which can be better interpreted as acts of desperation than as plans for reform.[20] Born of an effort to support the Spanish position in interimperial competition, the reforms did not achieve their goals. Spain, effectively unable to maintain itself at the level of its principal rivals France and Great Britain, reduced its reformist focus when confronted by the necessity to survive.

Many of the great Central American thinkers distinguished themselves in the fields of medicine, archaeology, and political economy. They had been trained intellectually in debate—at the university, in the pages of the *Gazeta de Guatemala*,[21] and at the Real Sociedad Económica de Amantes de la Patria de Guatemala—regarding themes under discussion in the new European and American public spheres and their application to contemporary local problems.[22] Adopting leadership roles during the early decades of the nineteenth century, they occupied important political positions during the crisis of the monarchy, the creation and application of the Cádiz reforms, and—although with a partial generational renewal—the political ruptures with the Spanish monarchy and the Mexican Empire.

Important changes that had occurred during the final third of the eighteenth century, many resulting from or influenced by reforms imposed by "Enlightened" absolutism, affected the local response to the crisis of the Spanish monarchy. New ideas associated with the Enlightenment, clearly in constant interchange with older scholastic thinking, dominated intellectual and political debates in Central America.[23] The indigo boom—though not tightly linked with crown policy—once hopeful, faded only a few years before the crisis, partly because of the impact of interimperial rivalries. Of similar importance were the establishment of new territorial divisions, the resistance to crown edicts among different social strata, and the increasingly desperate fiscal policies of the monarchy, at least after 1800, particularly visible in the consolidation of royal vouchers and the attempts to standardize Indian tribute charges.

Central America in the Course of Latin American Independence

The territories that formed the Kingdom of Guatemala showed similarities and differences when compared to other Spanish American regions during the period that began with the crisis of the monarchy and ended with full independence in all of continental Spanish America (1808–25). Three fundamental particularities worthy of note for understanding the Central American case are the absence of an army of independence; the virtual absence of armed conflict; and, to a greater or lesser degree, the rarity of national heroes tied to independence. In other aspects, nevertheless, there are many similarities between the experience of the isthmus and that of other Hispanic American territories; these I work to tease out through comparisons that offer new interpretations.[24]

I emphasize not only that the calls for governing juntas in San Salvador and León were similar to those in South America during this period[25] but also that the rejection of these calls by ayuntamientos in their respective intendancies were too. Although slighted in much historiography, the fear inspired by the class and ethnic dimensions of the revolt by Hidalgo in Mexico worked against the creation of juntas in the territories that would later form Guatemala and in Chiapas. Additionally, in the case of Guatemala City, the de facto autonomy and power that the elite groups of Guatemala City wielded through the ayuntamiento, at least through 1812, made the risks involved in establishing a junta outweigh the benefits that such an endeavor might provide. The attitude of the Central American elites can be seen clearly in their declarations of loyalty to the Spanish regency council in 1810, at the moment when many South American territories did not recognize that body.

This introduction also works toward integrating subaltern groups—especially Indians—more forcefully into a history of the independence period, in part as a clear response to what I perceive to be the limited role that much recent historiography offers them. Many researchers identified with what can be called the "new Latin American political history" tend to give scant attention to popular participation in the events of the independence period.[26] Although this is an understandable antidote to many histories of Central American independence—especially those written in the wake of the revolutionary wars that marked the region—which saw class struggle as the motor of history, it nonetheless leaves too many spaces unconsidered and too many questions unanswered. The traditional disciplinary division between political and social history leaves the study of subaltern politics unattended as (new) political history takes center stage. As Gabriel Di Meglio and Raúl Fradkin put it, "The temptation often exists to confine the analysis of the popular to the fields of social and cultural history, leaving political history only for those approaches centered on the elites. . . . There is still a great deal to be learned about the popular means of understanding and intervening in political space." For that reason, in the introduction of a collective volume whose translated subtitle can be rendered as "Popular Participation in Nineteenth-Century River Plate," these authors clarify that their book does not deal with "social history, but with political history."[27]

With the abdications that Charles IV and Ferdinand VII presented to Napoleon in Bayonne, the Spanish territories on the peninsula and in America faced the anomalous situation of a leaderless monarchy or, in the minds of some, one that had fallen into the hands of Joseph Bonaparte, brother of the French emperor. Armed movements rose up in opposition to the French in several areas of the peninsula, and many spontaneously created juntas demanded their right to govern in the absence of the king and joined together as a Supreme Central Junta to act in his name. In America as well, during the "critical two years" of 1808–9, efforts were undertaken, often successfully, to establish juntas in Buenos Aires, Caracas, Chuquisaca, La Paz, Mexico City, and Quito, all of them, with the exception of La Paz, capitals of viceroyalties or captaincies general or audiencia seats.[28]

In the Kingdom of Guatemala, although there are references to members of the Guatemala City ayuntamiento who were interested in creating a junta, there is no indication that the proposal produced much resonance among the elite in the capital or elsewhere in the isthmus; effectively, beyond the aforementioned interest, there was no real intent to form one.[29] As in Havana, Santiago de Chile, Lima, and Santa Fe de Bogotá (capitals of captaincies general and viceroyalties) as well as Cuzco and Guadalajara (audiencia seats), the uneasiness of the Central American elites did not result in any effort to create provincial government juntas. Nonetheless, the beginning of the *vacatio regis* did generate protests on the capital streets and other actions that drove Captain General González y Saravia to take repressive measures.[30]

What did occur in Central America in response to the abdications in Bayonne was a foretaste of trends that would be present in the following years: the propensity within the political and economic elite of Guatemala City and within the dominant sectors in the provincial capitals to negotiate their own interests and zones of partial autonomy;[31] the desire among members of this elite in Guatemala City to act as a primary reference point among the different provinces and as representatives of the kingdom; public protest from subaltern sectors; and a government that sought to prevent and repress any and all actions it perceived to be potentially subversive. The attitudes and actions of these different actors showed the progressive weakening of the monarchy and of the power its representatives wielded in the Kingdom of Guatemala as the crisis continued, with no real resolution in sight. This situation expanded the spectrum of possibilities that groups and individuals in Central America could imagine for themselves and the actions they could carry out; these in turn provoked fear among the authorities. Aggravated by a critical economic situation and the crisis of the monarchy, conflicts between subaltern and dominant sectors combined with skirmishes among the more powerful groups in different territories, paralleling events in the rest of Latin America. All these reactions had historical antecedents that now manifested themselves in the context of a power struggle for control of the monarchy and an interimperial war (two conditions that had existed a century earlier and had caused something akin to a civil war in the Kingdom of Guatemala),[32] at a moment of great intellectual effervescence strongly influenced by ideas of liberalism and modern republicanism, both still in the process of development.

Many American ayuntamientos questioned the decision made by the Supreme Central Junta in January 1810 to dissolve itself and transfer the sovereignty of the monarch to the regency council, citing as part of their criticism the weakness of the council against French attacks, the risk that it might fall under the influence of the Cádiz junta, and the illegality of making a decision of such magnitude without consulting the entire nation. The ayuntamiento of Guatemala City divided over the recognition of the regency council, and although after two weeks of heated debate it decided favorably, a group of four city councilors (*regidores*) voted against recognition, considering among other things that the transfer of sovereignty had been carried out without their consent.[33] The ayuntamiento of Comayagua, despite expressing doubts about the legitimacy of the process, voted in favor of respecting the regency, as did the other ayuntamientos of the kingdom.[34]

In South America, with the dissolution of the central junta and the appearance of the regency council, local juntas were (re-)established in the capital cities of Buenos Aires, Caracas, Quito, Santa Fe, and Santiago as well as in some provincial capitals. From Cartagena, information was sent to the ayuntamiento of Granada, and forwarded to that of Guatemala, presumably regarding the junta that had been formed there. This caused the ayuntamiento of Guatemala to request that direct communication, previously cut off as a precautionary step by decision of the captain general, be reinstated between Cartagena and the captaincy general.[35] The creation of these juntas, with their rejection of the legitimacy of the regency council, more than any other event, marked the beginnings of the wars of independence in South America. Accordingly, the decision of the Central American ayuntamientos to maintain their loyalty to the regency council should stand out in an analysis of Central American singularity in the processes of independence in Latin America.

In the years that followed, in large measure as part of the efforts to assure a certain autonomy (in the case of Quito, even with the consent of some royal authorities) or independence, the South American territories lived through wars which, in addition to putting patriots in confrontation with royalist troops, often included battles between capitals—whether of viceroyalties, captaincies general, audiencias, or those of lesser importance—and other provincial cities.[36] Between the middle of 1810 and the return of Ferdinand VII in 1814,[37] all the Hispanic American regions of South America, with the exception of Peru and Upper Peru, enjoyed, whether or not they accepted the sovereignty of the regency council and the Courts of Cádiz, periods with a great amount of de facto autonomy. In this period, the old South American provinces were divided internally, but in any case, with the exception of Peru, Upper Peru, and those regions momentarily under royalist military control, autonomy was a reality. This was the case even in Quito, where at different times not only was Ferdinand VII recognized (as occurred in the rest of South America) but so were some of his representatives in America.[38] Analyzed in terms of the potential relations between the Spanish monarchy and its overseas provinces, South America showed a broad spectrum of possibilities. Though in the Kingdom of Guatemala no collective body declared itself ruler of the territory or denied the authority of the captain general, violence and negotiation were used to pursue, and even achieve, at certain moments and in specific places, the same autonomy sought, and often gained, in South America.

In September 1810, the Hidalgo rebellion, with the violent eruption of a rural peasant and Indian army, irrevocably pushed New Spain into a war with autonomist or pro-independence goals. Despite its beginnings as the product of an aborted conspiracy planned by upper-class Creoles, the movement was marked—and known throughout the Kingdom of Guatemala—by its initial violence and the ethnic overtones carried within it. This rebellion, nonetheless, did not have much in common with the South American experience of urban-based juntas and rivalries between capitals and other cities and towns.[39] Rather, in New Spain the cities (although there certainly was important support that came from urban areas) tended to remain as bastions of royal power and defended themselves against the possible arrival of rural armies often formed of poor Indians, mestizos, and mulattos.

The actions of Hidalgo and his army became known with relative speed in Guatemala City, not only among the elites but also on a more general level. At the beginning of 1811, the Guatemalan ayuntamiento volunteered to mediate the conflict in New Spain,[40] and in the following months three women—of something other than elite extraction—were accused before Inquisitional authorities in Guatemala City of showing support for the "heretic priest."[41] Two years later, the movement of insurgent troops under the command of Matamoros toward the border between New Spain and the Kingdom of Guatemala led to the mobilization of the royalist army and militias, which, after disobeying orders and making an incursion into Tehuantepec (in the intendancy of Oaxaca), were defeated in Chiapas, causing considerable anxiety among the wealthy and powerful in Guatemala City and terror in Ciudad Real.[42] With their victory on the border, Morelos's army caused two significant reactions on almost the same date, May 1, 1813. In Guatemala City the ayuntamiento adopted a position before Captain General Bustamante so demanding that councilman Beltranena proposed the formation of a governing junta with representatives from the provinces, under the command of Bustamante, to improve their collective defenses.[43] In San Salvador several leaders drew up a letter addressed to Morelos in which they declared an affinity for the ideas of the insurgent commandant and their support for his cause.[44]

Although the movements led by Hidalgo and Morelos clearly influenced Central American processes during these years, urban uprisings in the region were much more similar to what was happening in South America. Nonetheless, the response of the dominant sectors of Guatemala City in the face of this violence corresponded to that of their counterparts in Mexico City after the uprising of Hidalgo and his army: alliance with royal power to weaken the resistance movements. The powerful rebellions that rocked many parts of the Kingdom of Guatemala between the end of 1811 and the middle of 1812 (see Payne, this volume) were as much or more a consequence of popular unrest as of interests in autonomy or independence. In practice, these urban movements demonstrated both their greatest strength and their greatest weakness in the relationships between the popular sectors and local dominant groups.[45] These movements, which would result in attempts at forming provincial juntas in León and San Salvador, came into being much later than the successful establishment of similar South American juntas, formed in opposition to the regency council. The Central American juntas, it would seem, had developed from different origins.

As has been mentioned, the actions of the powerful, generally ayuntamiento-based sectors in the Kingdom of Guatemala faced with the decision to recognize or not recognize the regency council in 1810 turned out to be fundamental to the political process in ensuing years.⁴⁶ The creation of governing juntas like those established in several South American cities would have been feasible. Yet it is easy to imagine that an attempt to create a governing junta might have provoked battles between cities similar to those in South America during these same years. Some Central American cities responded violently to calls for the formation of regional juntas in 1811 and 1812. A few years later, the ayuntamentos of the kingdom adopted different postures in response to Iturbide's proposal regarding the annexation of the territory to the Mexican Empire.

Whether or not concerns about wars among the cities did actually influence its decision, the ayuntamiento of Guatemala City (and initially the other ayuntamientos) chose another way forward: to negotiate with the captain general and the audiencia regarding new limits to its power at the provincial level, supporting these efforts through active participation in the Courts of Cádiz and in the liberal experiment in Central America.⁴⁷ But the position of the ayuntamiento showed a notable ambivalence; scarcely six weeks after voting to recognize the regency council, this same body selected a committee to write the instructions for Antonio de Larrazábal, deputy-elect to the Courts of Cádiz—and that committee comprised three councilmen who had voted *against* that decision.⁴⁸ While maintaining a position of loyalty toward the regency council, the Courts, and also the captain general, even when in conflicts with the latter, the ayuntamiento of Guatemala City effectively expanded its power kingdom-wide, exacerbating the tensions already existing between it and the provincial capitals. In brief: Why rebel when loyalty will better serve your ends?

Between 1811 and 1814, a series of uprisings and protests weakened Spanish authority in the Kingdom of Guatemala, making the Central American situation, as already mentioned, more like the conflicts in South America in terms of form and content, although not in terms of virulence. When analyzed in depth, these movements are at times difficult to describe because of the overlapping interests of the actors involved, but it is clear that the urban uprisings in San Salvador and León at the end of 1811 repeated the calls issued by South American cities to form provincial juntas, and the negative replies of the main cities in their respective jurisdictions were also similar. Even more to the point, the importance of the subaltern actors in these two cases—as in Granada (1812), Tegucigalpa (1812), and Totonicapán (1813)—show similarities to the leading roles of subaltern groups in different parts of South America during this same period.⁴⁹ Existing research into these protests, my own included, could benefit from an attempt to understand these actions in terms of the history and evolution of subaltern political culture, and a more precise analysis of these actions, as proposed by Raúl Fradkin and Sergio Serulnikov.⁵⁰

The wave of protests and uprisings began at the end of October 1811 in Patzicía, an Indian town in the Guatemalan highlands, where uncertainty about the recently reduced tribute payment combined with other questions related to civil and religious administration to engender protests finally put down by ladino militiamen. A similar situation appeared farther west in the town of Momostenango a few weeks later.[51] On November 5, the uprising in the city of San Salvador, which involved broad sectors of the popular classes as well as Creole leaders, served as a spark, but not as a rallying point, for a series of revolts in several towns in the Salvadoran intendancy[52] and also for the taking of León by rebel groups in December of that year. In turn, the uprising in León, in the intendancy of the same name, contributed to another in Granada and similar actions in towns throughout that province (see Payne, this volume).

Linking an analysis of the rural and urban rebellions—which managed to become regional uprisings, even though they were never able to coordinate efforts at that level—to that of the complementary relationship that had developed between the ayuntamiento of Guatemala and the captains general makes clear another similarity to South American regions: the rejection by the provinces of efforts by the capital cities to consolidate their power during the moments of crisis. This appreciation is important for an understanding of the autonomous positions taken by the cities of San Salvador and León toward Guatemala as well as of the rejection by San Miguel and San Vicente of the aspirations of San Salvador to form a provincial governing junta, and the similar response from Granada and Cartago concerning an analogous effort undertaken by León. In the Central American case, unlike many of the South American capitals, there was never an effort on the part of the capital elites, or by any part of that group (with the exception of the Belén conspiracy, discussed in Hawkins, this volume), to overthrow Spanish authority. This despite the relative ease with which it could have been undertaken (as it was in South America), at least until the restructuring of the police that Bustamante began in 1812, which would have made any such attempt more difficult (see Hawkins, this volume).

After the rebellions in the intendancy of León, the ayuntamiento of Guatemala City distanced itself from Bustamante, but the Constitution of Cádiz, published there in September 1812, offered many new opportunities to the Guatemalan city councilmen that could strengthen their efforts to act as representatives of the whole Kingdom of Guatemala, especially when faced with the year-long delay in the creation of the new provincial councils (*diputaciones provinciales*) established by the constitution.[53] At least one member of the Guatemalan ayuntamiento, the young councilman José Francisco Barrundia, became involved with other Central Americans in the suspected conspiracy of Belén,[54] which would have involved the armed forces stationed in Guatemala City in a coup planned for the last days of 1813. Although the ayuntamiento had been pressing for the removal of Bustamante since the previous year, with the arrest of councilman Vicente López, apparently without reason (though he was accused of participating in the Belén affair), and the flight of the similarly accused Barrundia, the ayuntamiento of Guatemala and Bustamante definitively parted ways (see Hawkins, this volume).

Beyond the anxiety expressed in the context of the abdications of 1808, the debate within the ayuntamiento in 1810 about the dissolution of the central junta, and the proposal of Beltranena to create a local governing junta after the skirmish with the New Spanish insurgents, the conspiracy of Belén would have been the only effort to take power from the royal authorities in Guatemala City. The participation by personages who had important political trajectories in different parts of the kingdom meant that the Belén conspiracy enjoyed potentially significant geographic breadth: the cities of Granada, León, San Salvador (the principal centers of revolt up to that point), and Guatemala City, as well as Cobán and Mazatenango. The plot developed in meetings between October and December 1813, at the same time that an unusual dispute took shape in Totonicapán,[55] and a few months after the already-mentioned disastrous defeat suffered by the troops of the captaincy general at Tonalá and the responses to it. In this context, it seems reasonable that the conspirators may have considered that Belén would lead to uprisings in other cities, such as the one in San Salvador that took place in January 1814.

In March 1814, Ferdinand VII returned to the Spanish throne and abolished the Constitution of 1812 as well as the other legislation the Courts had implemented, thus effectively weakening the autonomist movements in America. With his reappearance in Madrid, Ferdinand eliminated the justification for the different juntas then operating in his name and, in those territories where autonomy was sought from within the Spanish institutional frameworks without denying Spanish authorities—such as the Kingdom of Guatemala—he drastically reduced the room for maneuver. Ferdinand abolished representative government in the ayuntamientos, the provincial councils, and the nationally elected courts and also abolished freedom of the press. By weakening this intermediate route, Ferdinand strengthened the movements that openly supported independence, which gained strength in the years that followed and managed to gain control of, through military action, both Santiago de Chile in February 1817 and Santa Fe de Bogotá in August 1819.

The years between 1814 and the reestablishment of the Cádiz Constitution in July 1820 have been largely neglected by Central American historiography, and as a consequence it would be made to appear that all sectors, despite high levels of activity in previous years, must have accepted without further protest the elimination of the rights they had acquired and demonstrated even less interest in struggling for autonomy or independence. Significantly for Central American scholarship, although for many years historians largely assumed that this had been a period of relative calm in neighboring New Spain, research undertaken in recent decades demonstrates not only the importance of continued insurgency[56] but also a richly nuanced moment.[57]

As soon as the Cádiz Constitution was reestablished in 1820, the American problem became more worrisome for the crown, and a point of division arose between liberals and absolutists on the peninsula. Several circulating proposals sought to establish a system that would permit the monarchy to remain unified while respecting American interests in autonomy, but the political chaos on the peninsula hindered the implementation of a feasible proposal.[58] And while in much of South America the return to constitutionalism did little to change the situation, since most of the territory had become independent of Spain and most of the rest was at war, in New Spain, Peru,[59] Central America, and Cuba the resurgence of the constitutional system awakened considerable interest. Although they did not go so far as to force an immediate declaration in favor of the constitution, as happened in Havana and several cities in New Spain—even in Mexico City the declaration was announced earlier than had been planned because of popular demand[60]—the reestablishment of the constitution produced a notable increase in the activities of intellectuals in Guatemala City, who immediately promoted public debate in weekly newspapers and, with the support of Captain General Urrutia, the rapid application of constitutional provisions.

A little more than one year after swearing obedience to the Cádiz Constitution, a meeting of the principal authorities present at that moment in Guatemala City declared independence from Spain on September 15, 1821 (see Avendaño, this volume) and left the decision on a possible union with the Mexican Empire for a general congress, set to meet six months later. Faced with the three possibilities discussed on September 15—an independent Central America, a Spanish Central America (which became less feasible with an independent Mexico), or a Central America that would form part of the new Mexican Empire—the Plan de Iguala showed certain advantages, even without the pressure from the Mexican leader Iturbide, which was not long in coming. Some individuals, ayuntamientos, and provincial councils expressed this sentiment between September and November 1821, *before* the threatening insinuations of the future emperor were disseminated.[61]

The September 15 declaration and the responses it provoked can best be analyzed by apportioning the proper weight to the Plan de Iguala and the relationship between Mariano Aycinena—representative of the most economically powerful families in Guatemala City—and Iturbide. In such an analysis, the continued presence of some of the trends identified above concerning this period can be appreciated: the propensity among the political and economic elite of Guatemala City and the dominant sectors in the provincial capitals to negotiate their own interests and areas of partial autonomy; the desire of these same sectors in Guatemala City to act as a link between the different provinces and to serve as representatives of the residents of the kingdom; and the participation of subaltern actors in the process. A fourth trend mentioned, government activities that sought to prevent and suppress any action it perceived to be potentially subversive, had been modified as of September 1821 since by then the principal provincial authority, Superior Political Chief Gabino Gaínza, shared a desire to declare independence from Spain, certain that he would remain in charge of the new government that would be formed. Nonetheless, Gaínza or others would repress initiatives that opposed union with the Mexican Empire, be they public protests in Guatemala City or a refusal to accept the annexation by the province of San Salvador.

The economic elite of Guatemala City, led by Mariano de Aycinena y Piñol and his nephew the Marquis Juan José, openly supported separation from Spain and annexation to Mexico, believing that this formula would allow them to face independence with few conflicts and, in the classic fashion of Di Lampedusa's *The Leopard*, change everything so that everything would remain the same (or potentially favor them even more).[62] In their efforts to achieve independence from Spain, the dominant families had become allies with the more radical liberals of the period, known as *liberales*, *fiebres*, or *cacos*, who had supported this position at least since the conspiracy of Belén in 1813.[63]

Many of the men called to the meeting on the fifteenth, led by Archbishop Casaús y Torres, absolutely opposed independence and abandoned the building when it became clear that the outcome of the session would be a declaration in its favor. Additionally, José Cecilio del Valle insisted that the individuals brought together for this meeting did not have the authority to make a decision in the name of the entire kingdom, but rather that such a decision should be made in an assembly with representatives of the whole territory.[64] A decision on whether or not to join with Mexico divided the fiebres and the oligarchy—the two groups that had joined together in support of independence from Spain—and the junta decided to postpone the discussion of this topic until representatives from all the Central American provinces could meet in the above-mentioned congress, originally scheduled for March 1822.

In the months that followed, reflections on independence from Spain and annexation to Mexico provoked constitutional ayuntamientos and provincial councils throughout the isthmus into a variety of positions.[65] In addition to discussions about a republican or monarchical form of government, concerns about defending Central America from foreign powers colored the debates: the possible interests of Iturbide, those of Colombia in the southern part of the territory, the lack of control over Caribbean ports—obvious from the attacks on Trujillo and Omoa undertaken by the corsair Louis Aury in April and May 1821 under the flag of the new South American nations—and about a perceived U.S. interest in the construction of an interoceanic canal.[66]

Decisions taken by the different bodies reflected the type of competition between capitals and provincial cities that had occurred in Central and South America during the *vacatio regis* (and the responses by ayuntamientos to calls for regional juntas in the intendancies of León and San Salvador during the same period). The provincial councils of Comayagua and León, cities that were both intendancy capitals and seats of bishoprics, declared their political adhesion to Mexico and their independence from Guatemala City. Tegucigalpa and Granada, the principal rivals of the respective capitals of Comayagua and León, declared their independence from Spain and political adhesion to Guatemala City. The authorities present in San Salvador at first swore "independence" and "loyalty to the American monarchy," although in the weeks that followed, after republicans ascended to power in San Salvador, they dropped their early adhesion to the Plan de Iguala.[67]

The gobernación of Costa Rica—until that time politically, administratively, and fiscally dependent on the intendancy of León and part of the provincial council and bishopric seated in the capital of the same province—declared itself, after months of argument, independent from Spain and free to choose its adhesion to another American power (see Rodríguez, this volume). The ayuntamiento of Quetzaltenango, at that time capital of the corregimiento of the same name, which since 1813 had been maneuvering to become the capital of a new intendancy, declared itself in favor of the Plan de Iguala and of adhesion to Mexico, with the expectation that the government of Iturbide would grant it dominion over a larger territory (while its rival, Totonicapán, opted to remain loyal to Guatemala City).[68] Other ayuntamientos made their decisions in terms of their specific realities and local rivalries, but in the absence of a representative assembly, general discussion about the collective future of the ex-kingdom would be postponed until July 1823, after the fall of Iturbide.

In the September 15 act, the term *pueblo* appeared to mean a variety of things.[69] In the document, "the people seen in the streets, square, courtyard, corridors and anterooms of this palace" raised the "clamor of 'Long Live Independence,'" which was repeated incessantly," but also "the general will of the people of Guatemala" was "Independence from the Spanish government," and, further, it was necessary to declare that independence "to prevent consequences that would be frightful in case the people themselves were in fact to declare it."[70] A wider inquiry on this subject is indicated, but the people described in the existing historiography seem drawn from the "prose of counterinsurgency," which seeks to understand the political action of subaltern groups as the result of manipulation or uncontrollable rage.[71]

Despite the decision to convene a congress, which would have met on March 1, 1822, to decide "the topic of Independence and to fix, if they agreed on it, the form of government,"[72] the mounting pressures of Iturbide on Central American authorities induced them to carry out a consultation with the constitutional ayuntamientos, each one of which should have held an open town meeting (*cabildo abierto*) in which a decision would be made regarding annexation to Mexico. So strong were the Mexican pressures that the documents requesting the vote of the ayuntamientos were sent accompanied by a copy of a letter Iturbide had written to Gaínza in which he threateningly mentioned an expedition of Mexican troops to the south, and also a document from Gaínza himself indicating his support for the annexation and mentioning the potentially negative impact the Mexican army could create.[73]

The Provisional Advisory Junta, which had been formed during the September 15 meeting, remained divided on the legitimacy of the consultation, and even at the moment of counting the votes emitted by the ayuntamientos there were internal disagreements over how to proceed. On January 2, 1822, the provisional junta closed voting and counted the 170 votes received from the 237 convoked ayuntamientos; there was a clear majority in favor of joining Mexico. Nonetheless, a third of the members, Cecilio del Valle among them, voted against annexation. In addition to alleging that votes from the ayuntamientos could not be substituted for those of the congress and that in any case the absent votes should be awaited, José Antonio Alvarado argued that the vote could not be considered valid, given the fact that the information sent to the ayuntamientos about the arrival of Mexican troops had been false. Despite the protests of the minority, the annexation to the Mexican Empire carried the same day.[74]

For a year and a half, until the fall of Iturbide in 1823, Central America formed a part of the Mexican Empire, and it was not until July of the same year, during the congress convened almost two years earlier, that what was initially called the United Provinces of the Center of America was established. In the decades that followed, the Central American Federation suffered the same dynamics that had begun to show themselves with the abdications of Bayonne: battles between dominant groups, divided by different political and economic purposes as well as by regional interests, increased the power of subaltern groups, giving them greater strength in their negotiations with other sectors. If the Kingdom of Guatemala was saved from the virulence of the conflicts South America lived through in the second decade of the nineteenth century, the Central American Federation suffered it during the Federal War (1826–29)[75] and the ensuing conflicts in the '30s. By 1838, tensions within the federation and the weakness of the State of Guatemala had led to the establishment of the State of Los Altos in western Guatemala, the sixth in the federation, while in eastern Guatemala, under the leadership of Rafael Carrera and with ample support from both popular sectors and certain hacienda owners (some of whom were of African descent), the uprising of La Montaña managed to overthrow the divided "liberal" government of the State of Guatemala and effectively ended an already moribund Central American Federation.[76]

CURRENT HISTORIOGRAPHY AND THE CONTRIBUTIONS MADE IN THIS VOLUME

Central American historiography has frequently returned to a discussion of the independence period through investigations that have taken it up with different perspectives, themes, geography, and periodizations; a helpful discussion of contemporary works on the topic has been published by Coralia Gutiérrez.[77] With the hope of contextualizing the contributions contained in this volume, I offer a few considerations of some of the themes that have dominated the debate on the period in recent years and on how the chapters in this collection are positioned within it.

Until the middle of the last century, Central American historiography regarding the independence period was largely defined by the parameters established by nineteenth-century historians and focused mainly on identifying and praising illustrious Central American individuals, especially those identified as *liberales*, whose actions were interpreted in terms of their ultimate intent to establish independence.[78] This would change around mid-century, initially with Costa Rican researchers who drew on a more economics-based analysis of the period and a look toward both external and internal factors as causes for independence.[79] Beginning in the 1950s, some Guatemalans and Salvadorans opened a new vein in nationalist history, making an effort to highlight the contributions of Indians and the popular sectors in the independence processes.[80] In the 1960s, a new Central American historiography appeared, clearly distinguishable from the nationalist histories, which attempted to understand longer-term processes and weigh the importance of economic and social aspects for explaining political phenomena like independence. More heavily influenced by the social sciences, this form of historical research followed intellectual currents of the period in Latin America, the Annales school, and English social history.[81] To a certain extent, many authors in this generation assumed *political* independence to be of little importance because it did not modify unjust social structures or existing relationships of international economic dependence.

In recent decades, in part following the "cultural turn," much historiography on the independence period in Latin America has distanced itself from the largely economic and social analyses that dominated the earlier period. Instead, it has moved its focus to a field of study centered on a form of political history that draws not only upon what was traditionally considered to be the political but also on intellectual and cultural histories. In line with the more socioeconomic historiography that preceded it, and in contrast to the earlier liberal, nationalist histories, some of the most recent contributions have mainly addressed medium-duration changes deemed to have occurred, loosely, between 1750 and 1850, though now the interest revolves around institutions, political cultures, and political languages, focusing less attention on the political *break* between the metropole and its colonies (as the Bourbon reformers would have had it). The meaning of political culture, however, remains somewhat unclear and, whereas Brian Connaughton understands it in terms of the "the filter through which pass tensions and conflict, crisis and transformation, of both the institutions of sociability and the government of society," many authors seem to reduce its sphere to that of the written or spoken word, and others shrink it further to include only the words habitually produced in what I have referred to above as the "public sphere."[82] The new Latin American political history has influenced many recent works on Central American independence and the majority of the texts included in this collection.

Among the most representative changes driving the new Latin American political history of the independence period is the emphasis attached to the explanatory importance of the crisis of the Spanish monarchy (1808–9) for independence,[83] comparable to that assigned in earlier years to the impact of the Bourbon reforms, the Enlightenment, competition between peninsular Spaniards and Creoles, or a growing Creole identity that erupted into protonationalism.[84] To summarize, between 1970 and 1990 the dominant historiographical paradigm affirmed that independence resulted from those trends already present in the latter part of the eighteenth century, if not before, and that the crisis of the monarchy served as a catalyst for an inevitable process. From 1990 to the present, however, a new generation of historians have maintained that pressures prior to the monarchic crisis influenced the process of independence much less than their predecessors had supposed, and that the *vacatio regis* not only served as a catalyst but was one of the main causes of the move to independence.

This group of authors, who have dominated much of the literature on the period, abandoned the belief in the inevitability of independence, firmly rooted in a romantic vision of the nation as a cultural unit, unsustainable in the face of the nation-states that were finally established. In some sense, the proposal of a multicultural state currently being considered in several Latin American countries is more closely aligned to the concept of the nation as a political association that dominated Latin American thought during the early decades of the nineteenth century; only later would the idea of the nation as culturally homogenous gain ground.[85] At the same time, these new approaches emphasize the importance of Cádiz liberalism in the development of Latin American political languages in the decades after independence.[86]

The above-mentioned "new Latin American political history" (which should not be confused with the "new political history" in the United States) focuses especially on the nineteenth century and, to its great credit, has begun to analyze Latin America on its own terms. The themes this generation of historians focus on—such as liberalism, republicanism, elections, the public sphere,[87] political languages, secularization, the passage from the ancien régime to "modernity,"[88] public opinion, sovereignty, and citizenship—are treated as they actually developed in Latin America and not in relation to how they should have developed according to the abstract proposals of political philosophers or how they did develop in Europe and the United States.

One of the important foci of these efforts in the new Latin American political history involves moving beyond a history of ideas to a history of the changes in political languages, which, according to Elias Palti, referring to one of the contributions made by François-Xavier Guerra,[89] requires understanding that "the 'context' is no longer an external stage for the performance/development (*desenvolvimiento*) of 'ideas' and constitutes an inherent part of discourses, determining from within the logic of their articulation."[90] The complexity of the political languages in Central America, which drew on pactism and absolutism as much as on liberalism and modern republicanism (as was common enough at the time),[91] can be seen in the contributions to this volume by Sajid Herrera Mena and Pablo Rodríguez Solano. Although the new political history has received criticism because "in the tension between conceptual models and an emphasis in historical detail, the authors . . . seem to be inclined toward the former,"[92] in these contributions the description, narrative, and attention to detail are not lost.

One interesting aspect of Central American historiography is the importance given to the crisis of the monarchy and particularly to liberalism early on—after the influential book published by U.S. historian Mario Rodríguez in English in 1978 and in Spanish in 1984, *The Cádiz Experiment in Central America, 1808 to 1826*, and the works of Jorge María García Laguardia, also published long before the present concern with these issues.[93] In recent years, the themes of the *vacatio regis* and of Cádiz liberalism have been taken up again by, among others, Xiomara Avendaño, Jordana Dym, and Sajid Herrera.[94]

In his contribution to this collection, Herrera analyzes several official ceremonies celebrated at the end of the eighteenth century and the beginning of the nineteenth, undertaking through that effort an in-depth study of semantic changes visible in the different mechanisms used by those in power to reaffirm and emphasize sovereignty, that is, how political languages change to legitimate the wielding of power under new circumstances. He describes the continuation of Hapsburg rituals in the absolutist period and equally how certain representations typical of the ancien régime maintained their importance in the oath-taking ceremonies used when the Constitution of 1812 was established.[95] Through this analysis, which concentrates on the symbols of power, Herrera indicates how ceremonies show the contemporary presence of different political doctrines and allow us a glimpse of ongoing social conflicts.

The ideas that drove the intellectuals, politicians, and others who participated in the public sphere, unlike the economic and social problems of the eighteenth and early nineteenth centuries, receive detailed analysis in the new political history, given its focus on the development of political languages and their importance as part of the intellectual baggage Hispanic Americans, among them Central Americans, used to enrich political debates of the period, in America as well as in Cádiz. Enlightenment thinking, as Herrera argues in this volume, carried within it the ideas of previous epochs; and, as Pablo Rodríguez Solano maintains, many of the political ideas discussed during the period of independence drew upon pactism and natural law.[96]

Several years ago Adolfo Bonilla argued that in Central America the Enlightenment influenced all political positions of the period and that clearly these were not fully represented by the categories "liberal" and "conservative."[97] According to Bonilla, in Central America these positions can be better understood in terms of three categories: "liberal," "republican," and "Enlightened absolutist." Bonilla's proposal is nuanced in the chapter by Rodríguez when he identifies not only Enlightenment thought in debates of the epoch but, as often occurred in this period, also the continued presence of pactism, both as a justification for the creation of governing juntas and in support of a number of political proposals that surfaced in the ensuing years.

Rodríguez carefully analyzes the origins in natural law of the Pacto de Concordia, signed in December 1821 and sometimes described as the first Costa Rican constitution. This allows for a clearer understanding of the ideas present among Costa Rican thinkers at this time that guided the authors of the Pacto. He argues that the impacts of liberalism in Central America during a large part of the nineteenth century carried less weight than many authors have argued, from Marure and Montúfar in the nineteenth century through the present, and sustains his position with a careful historiographical account. With these considerations, any effort to categorize intellectuals and politicians becomes a difficult task. And with that, other commonly held suppositions, remnants of liberal nineteenth-century histories, do not obtain, such as the notion that all of those who at any time opposed independence or the more radical liberalism of Gálvez y Morazán inevitably supported a return to the polices of the ancien régime.[98]

Studies of the ayuntamiento as an institution, following paths similar to those blazed by Antonio Annino, have been one of the principal veins of the new historiography regarding the independence period and the nineteenth century in general.[99] Historians have emphasized how the leading role the Spanish ayuntamientos had played since the conquest, which had allowed the political representation of this small but dominant stratum throughout the colonial period, was maintained in this period. At the same time, studies have been made of the new constitutional ayuntamientos established by the Courts of Cádiz in royalist-controlled regions (like Guatemala) in any town with the requisite number of residents. These studies often focus on the institution of the ayuntamiento, rather than on the people and groups who composed it. Some of these same studies underestimate the power Indian cabildos had developed and maintained during the colonial era.[100] In Central America, recent works that start from this premise have given special weight to the power of the ayuntamientos as a means to explain the exacerbation of regionalisms that influenced the decline of the Central American Federation.[101]

Regional histories have frequently analyzed the years of the Central American Federation in tandem with the independence period, a division that responds to a certain continuity in political debates and the important presence of liberal and republican thought throughout these years. Historians are correct to focus on these concerns in order to understand more fully not only the dynamics that transformed the federation into five Central American states but also why Guatemala and Río de la Plata were the only continental audiencias of Spanish America that did not maintain their territorial unity after independence.[102] More recent interpretations mentioned above, focused specifically on the ayuntamientos, build on earlier works that analyze the dissolution of the federation more in terms of the debates between liberals and conservatives (respectively identified with federalism and centralism), the governing structure of the federation, and economic interests and the relationships among classes in the different regions of the federation.[103]

In her contribution to this volume, Xiomara Avendaño Rojas again takes up the theme of the constitutional ayuntamientos in her analysis of the different forms in which independence from Spain was declared, sworn to, and celebrated in the territory of what would soon become the state of Guatemala. Beginning with activities in Guatemala City, she moves geographically to the oath-taking carried out in other population centers and thematically to the debates undertaken in different towns surrounding the decision to support either the Plan de Iguala or the new government in Guatemala City. Avendaño describes in detail the symbolism present in the objects used in the ceremonies and the different discourses developed to legitimize the new guises of power, but with a great deal of attention on what occurred in small towns, often underrepresented in studies of this kind. Although there are also differences to be found, the continuities between the ceremonies analyzed by Herrera and those considered by Avendaño are striking since authorities drew on their past experiences and a common symbolic language as they designed ceremonies to celebrate independence.

Christophe Belaubre, in his contribution to this volume, traces the diffusion of Enlightenment thought in the intendancy of Ciudad Real during the last third of the eighteenth century and first years of the nineteenth, describing how it passed initially from the high clergy and civil authorities before spreading into broader social networks. This Enlightenment, the author argues, despite having been largely limited to the promotion of economic development and to administrative improvements, had notable impacts that were expressed in political proposals developed in Chiapas during the independence period.

One of the myths of the period of independence questioned in recent decades is that of the Creoles as the only engines of the autonomist and independence movements of the epoch. This idea has been refuted through point-by-point analyses that allow the discovery of the roles taken on by popular sectors, sometimes as leaders, during the early decades of the nineteenth century, including the active participation of Indians, mestizos, and people of African descent.[104]

As has been mentioned, in the 1960s the proponents of the shift in Central American history argued for research with a broader social and economic focus. In their investigations into this era, they stressed the importance of social conflicts and class struggles, but the distinctive features and nuances of those conflicts were often lost in the macroanalyses they aspired to undertake. Nonetheless, it is without doubt the works of this time that have been the starting point for a new wave of interest in the behavior of the popular sectors, even though they are now freed, as Ranajit Guha proposed, from a preoccupation with analyzing the behavior of subaltern actors necessarily in terms of patriotism or class struggle.[105]

In line with a what would appear to be a new wave of thinking about the independence period,[106] the chapters by Elizet Payne Iglesias and my own turn their gazes to key moments in social organization and rebellion during the period of independence: Payne analyzes the uprisings in the intendancy of León during 1811 and 1812, and I discuss the rebellion of Totonicapán in 1820. Noting that events in the intendancy of León started from conflicts among local dominant sectors, Payne stresses the active participation of mulattos and Indians as well as the influence of Caribbean blacks. She also emphasizes that decisions made in the Courts of Cádiz influenced the behavior of these social sectors, especially the restriction of voting rights for citizens of African descent and the elimination of Indian tribute.

In my discussion of Totonicapán, I highlight the impact the decisions of the Courts of Cádiz concerning the elimination of religious taxes and Indian tribute produced in the Guatemalan highlands. I also emphasize the importance of analyzing this rebellion as part of a great wave of social movement throughout Central America, which lasted from the beginning of the crisis of the monarchy until the establishment of the government of Rafael Carrera.[107] I also point out the importance of ethnicity and of the rivalry between Totonicapán and the neighboring city of Quetzaltenango for understanding the rebellion.

Until recent years, studies of the independence period focused on the episodes of war and violence, or on the actions and thought of autonomist or independence-minded political and military leaders, with little attention to the actions of individuals and groups that remained loyal to the crown, whether leaders or subaltern groups, royal bureaucrats or specific individuals. New investigations have begun to better explain these actors and their importance to processes in the first part of the nineteenth century, such as the contribution to this volume by Timothy Hawkins in which he summarizes the argument regarding Captain General Bustamante that he developed nearly twenty years ago in his doctoral dissertation.[108]

In an original historiographical interpretation, Hawkins proposes that the widely recognized "Bustamantine terror," which would have rendered impossible any independence initiatives in the Kingdom of Guatemala, never existed; it was produced a posteriori to justify the limited mobilization of Central American Creoles in support of independence. Therefore, "the Kingdom of Guatemala was witness to the appearance of its first state of counterinsurgency during this period, but not to a reign of terror." Hawkins describes the conduct of Bustamante, captain general between 1811 and 1818, when faced with outbreaks of political violence during the Cádiz period (such as those described by Payne in this volume), in relation to his training as a military officer and bureaucrat in the Bourbon tradition, which demanded that he assure the integrity of the Spanish empire, first through negotiation and then through a counterinsurgency system carried out through the application of police tactics learned from the viceroys in neighboring New Spain.

The new political history of Latin America has led to more careful and serious considerations of the American processes within Atlantic history, the impacts of the crisis of the monarchy and of Cádiz liberalism, the important roles of institutions, the discourses of political leaders, and the contextualization of the political languages of the epoch. Succinctly put, this current has successfully introduced itself into the field and has noticeably pushed the debate in the direction of the themes already mentioned. However, moving to a discussion in which political matters are divorced from economic and social issues, and to some extent from those aspects of the material world beyond political discourse and institutional behavior, rejects themes vital to an understanding of the independence processes. Although its contributions are fundamental to a current understanding of the nineteenth century, a new synthesis must be achieved that better balances the contributions of this new approach with the interpretations of previous generation of historians, for whom matters of politics, economics, and social issues were inevitably intertwined.[109]

Nearly all of the contributions to this volume demonstrate the impact the turn toward the new political history has had in Central American historiography, but at the same time they show how this new current can become integrated into others, with investigations that offer a new synthesis between the previous generation of historians, who emphasized long-term social and economic considerations, and a new one, focused on a precise analysis of the independence period with special attention to institutions and political languages. Many of the proposals of the new political history find fertile ground in the audiencia of Guatemala because it was the only one in continental Spanish America in which no rebel army ever occupied territory, allowing the Cádiz reforms a better chance to be carried out. But even in the case of Central America, the process of independence cannot be understood without a comprehension of the development of Enlightenment thought that preceded it, which overlapped and mixed with scholasticism, of the resistance the Bourbon reforms provoked, or of the mobilization and social violence that faced a counterinsurgent state. Perhaps the pendulum has reached the end of its arc and is beginning to return, or perhaps Central American historiography is assuming a new course.

NOTES

I thank Mario Vázquez Olivera for conversations regarding several of the themes developed in the original Spanish version of this text and his suggestions and comments on a first draft of that text. I am also in debt to Brian Connaughton and Juan Carlos Sarazúa for their comments on the heavily revised English version of this introductory chapter.

1. The Spanish monarchy divided its territory into extensive audiencias with primarily judicial functions.
2. Hall and Pérez Brignoli, *Historical*, 110.
3. The Kingdom of Guatemala never housed a court of the Holy Inquisition, and between 1806 and 1810 it annually received funds in the form of *situados* (funds) from New Spain, the majority if not all of which were destined for the defense of the Mosquito Coast. In earlier years these situados were sent through Havana. TePaske, *Real*; Grafenstein, "Situado," 154, and tab. 7, 169.
4. The meaning of the term *ladino* has varied geographically and changed through the centuries. During the early part of the nineteenth century in Central America, *ladino* usually referred to people not considered to be Indians or Spaniards. It was a social, legal, and fiscal reference that included people who could also have been classified as *castas*, mestizos, mulattos, or *pardos*. In certain contexts it could also refer to anyone who was not an Indian.
5. American and peninsular Spaniards controlled the ayuntamientos, or city councils, that governed the *ciudades* (cities) and villas whose legal status differed from that of the Indian towns.
6. In Chiapas, the town of Comitán became a villa in 1804 and with clear counterinsurgent logic was classified as a city in 1813, the same year Tuxtla and Tapachula were distinguished with the title of villa. In the Guatemalan highlands, Quetzaltenango was given an ayuntamiento in 1805.
7. Researchers disagree. Gabriel Paquette offers a discussion of recent interpretations of the reforms and their impact in "Dissolution," 183–87.
8. The classic source on Bourbon reforms in Central America, published by Miles Wortman more than three decades ago, has recently been supplemented by the contributions in Dym and Belaubre, *Politics*, 2007. See also Wortman, *Government*; and Belaubre, this volume. For background on the period, see Solórzano, "Años"; Lindo Fuentes, "Economía"; and Hall and Pérez Brignoli, *Historical*, 2003.
9. Diego-Fernández et al., *Reinos*. The Colegio de Michoacán has established the Network of Studies of the Regime of Subdelegations in Bourbon America; for more information, see www.colmich.edu.mx/rersab. On subdelegations in the Kingdom of Guatemala, see Fernández Hernández, *Gobierno*, on Comayagua; Polushin, "Bureaucratic," and Gutiérrez, "De la intendencia," on Chiapas; and López, "Poderes," on San Salvador.
10. The changes proposed in the collection of the *alcabala* (internal customs duty, sometimes referred to as sales tax) and the implementation of *estancos* (state tobacco and liquor monopolies) caused a tense situation in Guatemala City in 1766, involving both retail tobacco sellers and members of the ayuntamiento, similar to conditions before the rebellion in Quito the previous year. Luján, "Establecimiento." On Quito, see Andrien,

"Economic." The attempt to implement a liquor monopoly in Quetzaltenango in 1785 failed. González, "State." See Martínez, *Motines*, 59, 94–95, 97, 149, 159, 162, 191, 215, 219, 232, 256; and Gutiérrez, "Racismo," on Cobán.
11. The changes Sergio Serulnikov observes in parts of Upper Peru can provide an important reference in this regard. Serulnikov, *Conflictos*, and "Nuevas," 15.
12. Dym and Belaubre, *Politics*, 1–15. Clearly, though the tensions in Ciudad Real became visible prior to 1808, it was in the midst of the crisis of the monarchy that the members of the ayuntamiento took it upon themselves to arrest the intendant. As Torres and Avila put it, "What the absence of the king consented, in order to resolve a pressing problem that was present day after day, was a discursive exit that would justify the actions to come: the putting in practice of the theory of the retroversion of sovereignty." Torres and Ávila, "Ayuntamiento," 130–31.
13. Palma, "Núcleos."
14. Drawing on Lynch's definition of the Bourbon reforms as a "second conquest," Brading has argued that in their efforts to centralize power the reformers alienated the *criollos* (American-born Spaniards), in some ways encouraging interest in independence. José María Portillo, writing in a notably different moment in terms of historiographical context, nuances the proposal put forth by Brading while reiterating that the loss of power by local elites, both on the peninsula and in America, inevitably created tensions that would influence attitudes during the crisis of the monarchy and the independence struggles. Brading, "España"; Lynch, *Revoluciones*; Portillo, *Crisis*, 51–52.
15. Habermas identified as one of the most important aspects of the Enlightenment not only the novelty of the ideas but also the fact that they were socialized in new spaces: cafés, newspapers, and scientific and literary academies, understood to create a public sphere of discussion regarding political decisions and leading to modern republicanism and liberalism. Furet describes these same spaces as "sociabilities," and François-Xavier Guerra draws his inspiration more from the later than the former. Piccato, "Public." See Herrera, "Escenarios," for a discussion of the public spheres in San Salvador in 1811; and Guerra and Lempérière, *Espacios*, on Latin America more generally.
16. Pollack, "Centroamérica." Compare to what Fradkin describes as a *ciclo tumultario* (cycle of riots/protests) for the province of Buenos Aires in 1806–29. Fradkin, *¿Y el pueblo?*, 28–43.
17. Several reforms were instituted in an effort to weaken the credit-granting power Guatemala City merchants held over the indigo producers—mainly from San Salvador and Sonsonate—and also over the miners of the region surrounding Tegucigalpa and the stockmen of Nicaragua and Honduras. These reforms, which began to take place in 1773 and reached their heights with the policies of Captain General Matías de Gálvez (1779–83), had little success against the steely resistance of the merchants, and by the first years of the nineteenth century there were no institutional traces of their existence. Smith, "Indigo"; Floyd, "Indigo"; Wortman, *Government*, 164–66.
18. Palma, "Es necesario."
19. Marichal, "Iglesia."
20. The consolidation of the *vales reales* (royal bonds) is the most resounding example. Cabat, "Consolidation"; Wobeser, "Gestación." It may well be asked whether the decision in

1801 to apply the standardizing of the amounts of native tribute to be paid, which had been ordered in the New Spanish *ordenanzas de intendentes* in 1786, did not originate in the same financial urgency. Fernández Molina, *Tributos*. The negative impact of the consolidation on the Kingdom of Guatemala can be measured if one considers that, on finding out about the abdications of Bayonne in 1808, the only noteworthy action taken by Captain General González was the suspension of the activities of the consolidation office, exactly what had occurred in New Spain. Fernández Hernández, *Reino*, 179.

21. See Hernández, *Gaceta*, for a recent discussion of the concerns brought to discussion in the *Gazeta*.
22. Lanning, *University*; Meléndez, *Ilustración*; Carvalho, *Ilustración*; Bonilla, *Ideas*; Sagastume, *Trabajo*; Belaubre, *Élus*; Belaubre, this volume.
23. See Dym and Herrera, *Centroamérica*. The presence of ideas and symbols coming from pactist, absolutist, and liberal imaginaries is one of the themes taken up in the works of Sajid Herrera and Pablo Rodríguez, including those in this volume.
24. Jordana Dym has made a similar study for the first years of the period considered here. Dym, "Soberanía."
25. Ibid.
26. Palacios uses the phrase "new Latin American political history," and though he questions its adequacy it does, in general terms, refer to an identifiable body of literature. At the same time, because of its close relationship with Atlantic history, the term inevitably refers to experiences beyond Latin America. Palacios, "Entre"; see also Breña, "Introducción," 14.
27. Fradkin and Di Meglio, *Hacer*, 10.
28. Rodríguez, *Independencia*; Breña, *En el umbral*.
29. There are three specific references: Simón Bergaño y Villegas, implicated as the driving force behind an artisan uprising in the San Sebastián barrio in Guatemala City, swore that city councilman José María Peinado had spoken in favor of the creation of a junta. Baumgartner, *José de Valle*, 58. Then-captain general González Saravia later commented that during the meeting with the authorities of the kingdom, which had been convened in August 1808 to discuss the abdications, some individuals mentioned ideas that he found "singular" and "metaphysical," which could have been interpreted as a reference to the possibility of forming some sort of governing junta. In September 1808, Antonio Juarros, the first mayor of the ayuntamiento of Guatemala City, proposed to that council that it share control, or take leadership, of the kingdom. Dym, "Soberanía," 110–12.
30. These measures overlapped with kingdom-wide efforts to prevent incursions by Napoleonic emissaries. Hawkins, "Fighting." On the government of González Saravia, see Fernández Hernández, *Reino*.
31. The example of Mariano Valero, mentioned earlier, is important. Carvalho, *Ilustración*, 212–17; Polushin, "Por la patria"; Torres and Ávila, "Ayuntamiento"; Belaubre, this volume.
32. León, *Levantamiento*.
33. Rodríguez, *Cádiz*, 45. See Herrera, this volume, regarding the pactist ideas that sustained this position.
34. Dym, *From Sovereign*, 81–82.

35. Fernández Hernández, *Reino*, 183. The correspondence between civil and religious authorities of Guatemala City, Quetzaltenango, and Ciudad Real in these years shows that knowledge of events in South America and New Spain was shared, at least at that level. Inda and Aubry, *Insurgentes*, 22.
36. For an excellent analysis of the war in Venezuela and Nueva Granada, see Thibaud, "Formas."
37. Only the provinces of Río de la Plata, excluding the Banda Oriental and Upper Peru, never returned to royalist control, although some other territories remained liberated.
38. Royalist troops marched or sailed from Peru and Upper Peru to confront initiatives for autonomy and independence in Chile, Quito, Upper Peru, and even Jujuy and Salta. Although the viceroy of Peru never recognized it, the Treaty of Lircay of May 3, 1814, in Chile showed how at least some royal authorities (in this case Brigadier General Gabino Gaínza, future captain general of the Kingdom of Guatemala and first chief of government of Central America after independence) were willing to permit the presence of an autonomous government as long as the king and the Courts were recognized. According to the terms of the treaty, Chile would have been permitted to maintain an "internal government with all its power and faculties, and free trade with allied and neutral nations, especially with Great Britain," while the Courts decided on the future of the territories. Article 1 of the "Agreement Celebrated between the Generals of the Armies Identified as National and of the Government of Chile," cited in Rubio, *Gabino Gaínza*, 24. See also Rodríguez, *Independencia*, 255–56.
39. In the South American juntas, the subaltern presence made itself felt through different means. Di Meglio, "Participación"; Granados, *En el espejo*, 31–137.
40. Salazar, *Historia*, 135.
41. Mérida, "Historia," 56–64.
42. Hawkins, *José de Bustamante*, 160–64; Inda and Aubry, *Insurgentes*.
43. Salazar, *Historia*, 170.
44. Gavidia, *Historia*. It is not known whether this letter was sent.
45. It has been argued that in the San Salvador uprising of 1811 the Creoles actively restrained the enthusiasm and organization of the popular sectors. Peccorini, *Voluntad*; López, "Noviembre." Di Meglio discusses the process of negotiation in similar contexts between popular sectors and local elites in other parts of Hispanic America. Di Meglio, "Participación."
46. The broadest discussion of the debate over the regency council within the ayuntamiento of Guatemala may be found in Rodríguez, *Cádiz*, 45–46.
47. In his analysis of American reactions in the face of the crisis of the monarchy, Adolfo Bonilla describes the position of the Kingdom of Guatemala in the following terms: "Loyalty to Spain, a rejection of the absolutist system and decided and active support of constitutional thought." Bonilla, *Ideas*, 156.
48. José María Peinado, Antonio Juarros, and Vicente de Aycinena.
49. The situation in Nicaragua is explored in Payne's work in this volume; for the situation in San Salvador, consult Peccorini, *Voluntad*; and López, "Noviembre." For Totonicapán, see Pollack, "Cortes." On South America, see Lasso, "Revisiting"; Di Meglio, "Participación"; Granados, *En el espejo*, 31–137.

50. Fradkin, *¿Y el pueblo?*, 26–27. Serulnikov argues that the crisis of the colonial political cultural in Spanish America took place over the short and medium terms. Serulninikov, "Nuevas," 47.
51. See Pollack, this volume. It would be possible to see the beginnings of a longer cycle of Indian protests beginning at the turn of the century, though the density of protests in the Western Highlands between 1811 and 1814, paralleling the time frames of the urban and rural uprisings in the intendancies of León and San Salvador, pushes me, at least for now, toward focusing on the years of the *vacatio regis* as a particularly significant period. See Carmack, *Rebels*, 118–22; Pollack, *Levantamiento*, 81–83, and "Protesta"; Martínez, *Motines*; and Gutiérrez, "Racismo."
52. Payne, "¡No hay rey!"; López, "Noviembre."
53. During 1813 and 1814 two provincial councils functioned in the Kingdom of Guatemala, in the cities of León and Guatemala City. There is little information on their operation, due in large part to the decision by Captain General Bustamante to destroy the documentation relative to the Cádiz period when Ferdinand VII returned to the throne in 1814.
54. Belaubre, "Al cruce."
55. Pollack, "Cortes."
56. Hamnett, "Royalist"; Archer, "En busca."
57. See the contributions in Serrano, *Sexenio*.
58. Proposals of this nature had been discussed since the times of Charles III, though often with the colonialist intent of strengthening the metropole, but by 1820 they had become more common and were developed within the discursive formation of the American territories as fundamental parts of the Spanish monarchy. Rodríguez, *Independencia*, 307–8, 352–54; Portillo, *Crisis*, 49.
59. Sala, "Trienio," "Justicia," and "Derecho."
60. Rodríguez, *Independencia*, 342.
61. Vázquez, *Imperio*, 39–85.
62. Palma Murga has noted that the same group had demonstrated this type of behavior regarding Spanish free trade policies. Palma, "Es necesario."
63. This faction was led by José Francisco Barrundia, Pedro Molina, and José Francisco Córdoba. See Cabezas, *Independencia*, regarding the "Pacific Plan" for independence written up by members of the Aycinena family and the *cacos* regarding how to stage what would eventually be the September 15 meeting, including participation by popular sectors.
64. Valle was the editor of the newspaper *El amigo de la patria* and one of the most important intellectuals and political figures of the epoch, as well as one of the principal leaders of the group known as *gasistas* or *bacos*. Members of this group were branded by their enemies as *serviles*. Valle maintained his position throughout the entire process of decision making on adhesion to the Mexican Empire. His opposition was based on the lack of representation characterized by those present at the meeting on September 15. See Avendaño, this volume.
65. The provincial councils of San Salvador and Ciudad Real, whose existence had earlier been decreed in Madrid, began to meet only after September 15.

66. Woodward, "Economic," 561; Meléndez, "Rasgos," 10; Vogel, "Rebel," 7; Vázquez, *Imperio*, 83. Gámez mentions the presence of independent South American ships in Realejo in April 1819. Gámez, *Historia de Nicaragua*, 317.
67. Vázquez, *Imperio*, 64; Cabezas, *Independencia*, 101–2.
68. Taracena, *Invención*, 79–81.
69. See Gutiérrez, "Pueblo/Pueblos," and the different entries under the heading "Pueblo/Pueblos" in Fernández Sebastián, *Diccionario*, 1115–250.
70. Article 1 of the "Act of Independence," in Cabezas, *Independencia*, 90.
71. Guha, "Prose." Several descriptions of the participation of the people on September 15, 1821, have been collected by Horacio Cabezas Carcache, and they contradict one another. Cabezas, *Independencia*, 92–93. In this case the people did in fact show their rage when they attacked the archbishop as he left the royal palace and destroyed a painting of the conquistador Pedro de Alvarado after the session. Pardo, "Independencia," 204. The same author mentions that the following year, on the anniversary of independence, September 15, 1822, the people destroyed a statue of Charles III. Fradkin notes, perhaps in reference to the Argentine or River Plate case, that, in addition to manipulation as an explanation for subaltern political action, some authors attribute it to their identification with leaders or with a romanticized version of the "immanent popular consciousness." Fradkin, *¿Y el pueblo?*, 10.
72. Article 2 of the "Act of Independence," cited in Vázquez, *Imperio*, 54–55.
73. Vázquez, *Imperio*, 102.
74. Ibid., 101–12; Cabezas, *Independencia*, 115–18.
75. Taracena, *Primera*.
76. Recent works on this subject have showed how mid-size landholders in the region facilitated its success and have made great advances in rethinking the uprising in terms of the defense of the agrarian sector in the face of pressures from the government in Guatemala City. Sarazúa, "Territorialidad"; Jefferson, "Nuestra."
77. Gutiérrez Álvarez, "Historiografía." The historiographical periodization presented here corresponds, with some modifications, to other overviews of Latin American independence historiography. Chust and Serrano, "Debate"; Adelman, "Independence," 157–62.
78. Some of the more common references from the period are Montúfar, *Memorias*; Molina, *República de Costa Rica*; Romero, *Bosquejo*; Montúfar, *Reseña*; García, *Memorias*; Salazar, *Historia*; Gámez, *Historia de Nicaragua*; Ayón, *Historia*; Marure, *Bosquejo*; and Gavidia, *Historia*. It should be noted that Ayón frequently mentions the importance of the different subaltern sectors and considers them to have formed a part of the pro-independence zeitgeist of the epoch and often pressured their supposed leaders. Ayón, *Historia*, 3.443–46, 453, and especially 475–77.
79. See Rodríguez, this volume, and Molina regarding the contributions of Carlos Monge Alfaro and Rodrigo Facio Brenes. Molina, *Revolucionar*, 17–19.
80. On this discussion, in reference to Guatemala, see Taracena et al., *Etnicidad*, 2.65–66; and the examples in Contreras, *Rebelión*, and Samayoa, "Proceso." For Salvadoran examples, see Domínguez, *Ensayo*, and Peccorini, *Voluntad*.
81. Marroquín, *Apreciación*; Martínez, *Centroamérica*; Zelaya, *Nicaragua*. This current also includes the works of Pinto, *Centroamérica*, and "Independencia." For more information

on the influence of Marroquín and Pinto, see Avendaño, "Independencia." Within this historiographical tendency, although not specifically related to independence but rather with longer periods, can be placed the works of Miles Wortman, Hector Lindo Fuentes, and David McCreery. Lindo, *Weak*; McCreery, *Rural*; Wortman, *Government*. Lorena Carrillo stresses the interest that Severo Martínez Peláez held in the works of historians associated with the Annales school. Carrillo, *Árbol*, 45n5. For a discussion of this period of historical studies on independence in Latin America, see Adelman, "Independence," 157–62. Interestingly, Molina Jiménez sees the earlier contributions of Costa Ricans Monge Alfaro and Facio Brenes as drawing from, among others, Henri Berr, considered a precursor to the Annales school. Molina, *Revolucionar*, 17–18. Although some of the authors mentioned, such as Marroquín, Martínez, and Pinto Soria, wrote from a clearly Marxist perspective, I find the economicist perspective that dominated nearly all of these authors to be of greater significance for understanding the historiography of independence during this period. See Chust and Serrano, "Debate," 21, on this theme in Latin American independence historiography.
82. Connaughton, "Introducción," 9.
83. This was one of the fundamental proposals of François-Xavier Guerra, *Modernidad*, 115–225. See also Breña, *En el umbral*.
84. Portillo shows that the different peninsular kingdoms were developing similar proto-nationalisms during the eighteenth century even as a Spanish nationalism, which clearly did not include America, also began to take shape. Portillo, *Crisis*, 32–53.
85. Chiaramonte, "En torno," 1999.
86. For recent discussion, see the contributions in Eastman and Sobrevilla Perea, *Rise*. Luis Fernando Granados offers a critical view of the growth of this perspective in which the celebration of nineteenth-century liberalism in Mexico is seen to dovetail well with the celebration of late twentieth- and early twenty-first-century neoliberalism. Granados, *En el espejo*, 139–70. See also Rodríguez, this volume.
87. Although research has shown that readers shared newspapers with the illiterate and the cafés could in fact be spaces for discussion in which even the poor had access, it would be safe to assume that the poor and illiterate probably did not initiate the discussions in those parts of the public sphere to which they did have access, and even less in the salons and academies. Further study should consider other spaces of the public sphere in which subaltern groups predominated (workplaces, town assemblies, public protests, etc.) in order to take stock of the variety of political cultures active at any given moment.
88. Elias Palti has argued that Guerra replaced the previously existing teleology of Spanish American independence with another of "modernity" in which "the final imposition of the modern liberal model is a sort of moral imperative." Palti, *Tiempo*, 48. Palti goes on to argue (50) that Guerra and others unfortunately reproduce the dichotomy present in earlier historiography: "modernity = individualism = democracy" and "tradition = organicity = authoritarianism."
89. The authors who can be located in what I refer to here as the new Latin American political history point consistently to the work of François-Xavier Guerra as the primary point of departure for the revitalized vision of the period, though many authors who predated him emphasized many of the same concerns, and over past decades many others have

contributed to the field. Guerra, *Modernidad*. Nonetheless, the importance of Guerra cannot be overemphasized. His work has been both lauded and criticized, often by the same people, yet many fundamental aspects of his work that have since been questioned and corrected by some authors continue to inform the new Latin American political histories. Roberto Breña, in particular, has questioned whether the Atlantic history that propounds a "discourse of the 'Age of Revolution' that goes from Philadelphia to Angostura via Paris and Cádiz . . . is able to give us new and different insights about the *revoluciones hispánicas* from an intellectual, ideological and political point of view." Breña, "Emancipation," 58.

90. Palti, *Tiempo*, 45. As might be surmised, Palti draws heavily on J. G. A Pocock and Quentin Skinner.
91. Fernández Sebastián, *Diccionario*, 38. On these political languages in Central America in the early nineteenth century, see Dym and Herrera, *Centroamérica*.
92. Crespo, "Sobre Guillermo Palacios," 528.
93. Rodríguez, *Cádiz*; García, *Orígenes*.
94. Herrera, "Herencia"; Dym, *From Sovereign*, and "Central America"; Avendaño, *Centroamérica*.
95. See Cañeque, "Imaging," and Osorio, "Courtly," regarding images, ceremonies, and representation under the Hapsburgs in America.
96. On this theme and on the Enlightenment in Latin America, see Cañizares, *Cómo*.
97. Decades ago, Charles Hale made this argument regarding nineteenth-century Mexico, though he refers to the influence of Bourbon policies rather than Enlightenment thought. Hale, "José María Luis Mora," 208–20.
98. Montúfar, *Memorias*; Marure, *Bosquejo*. Gálvez and Morazán were chief of state in Guatemala and president of the Federation, respectively, during the decade of the thirties when the State of Guatemala implemented radical liberal reforms.
99. Annino, "Prácticas," and "Voto."
100. Hensel, "¿Cambios?" The term *cabildo* could refer to any town or city council, or at times the governing bodies of other corporate entities.
101. Dym, *From Sovereign*; Avendaño, *Centroamérica*.
102. The situation of Río de la Plata is more obvious, at least in the case of the Bando Oriental of Uruguay that sought to assure its independence after the crisis of the monarchy and negotiated its position between the Portuguese territory and Buenos Aires during these years. The Paraguayan experience is less clear.
103. Rodríguez, *Cádiz*; Pinto, *Centroamérica*; Wortman, *Government*.
104. Van Young, *Other*; León-Portilla and Mayer, *Indígenas*; Lasso, "Revisiting"; Álvarez and Sánchez, *Visiones*; Serulnikov, "Nuevas"; Di Meglio, "Participación," and *¡Viva!*; Fradkin, *¿Y el pueblo?*; Granados, *En el espejo*, 31–137.
105. Guha, "Prose"; Payne, "¡No hay rey!"; Pollack, *Levantamiento*, and "Protesta"; López, "Noviembre."
106. In the past few years, the work of Raúl Fradkin, Sergio Serulnikov, Gabriel Di Meglio, and Daniel Santilli in Argentina and that of Luis Fernando Granados in Mexico have forcefully argued for an analysis, drawing inspiration from the work of social and economic historians who dominated the field prior to the appearance of the new political

history, of the ways in which popular (or subaltern) sectors participated in the independence processes. They also explicitly value the importance of the medium duration, and therefore that of the Bourbon reforms and of the popular memory of resistance to them. See, for example, Fradkin and Di Meglio, *Hacer*; Santilli et al., *Rebeldes*; Serulnikov, "Nuevas"; Di Meglio, *¡Viva!*; and Granados, *En el espejo.*

107. Granados argues that the independence struggles involved a tense and negotiated relationship between elites interested in autonomy or independence and popular or subaltern groups with different concerns. Granados, *En el espejo*. The Central American experience, it could be argued, confirms what Fradkin has proposed regarding the River Plate region: that the decades after Hispanic American independence involved a struggle by the elites to regain control over the popular or subaltern groups, and that this process would reach fruition, for the most part, only in the second half, or even last third, of the nineteenth century. Fradkin, "Paradigmas," 102. Quijada would add that "it is not just that it is hard to close Pandora's Box once it's open. It is also about the fact that the ideological and political context that brought about its opening did not remain unchanged over time." Quijada, "Caja," 634.

108. Hawkins, "To insure," and *José de Bustamante*.

109. Breña would seem to support this sort of suggestion. Breña, "Introduction," 15–16.

PART I
Concepts, Ceremonies, Symbols, and Networks
CONTINUITIES AND CHANGE

REPRESENTING SOVEREIGNTY IN OATH-TAKING CEREMONIES
The Kingdom of Guatemala, 1790–1812

SAJID ALFREDO HERRERA MENA

Political rituals have been and continue to be necessary for bringing meaning and legitimacy to power. As Juan Carlos Garavaglia has indicated, even today the "theater of power" needs civil-religious ceremonies to sustain its authority, necessarily dependent on the loyal attitudes of citizens, constructed through symbolic mechanisms.[1]

With independence from Spain, some of the newborn nation-states established rituals requiring that an oath of loyalty and obedience to the executive power, as well as to the laws created by the sovereign nation, be taken in the presence of the ruler. They copied, then, the ceremonies American populations had become accustomed to during the period of Spanish rule, though these had been performed absent the physical presence of the king. What had happened in those cases? How was the sovereign represented? Especially, to whom was fidelity sworn during the liberal Cádiz period when the Courts declared the nation to be sovereign?

In this essay I do not examine the continuation of colonial rituals in republican Central America. Suffice it to say that a large portion of the symbols, rhetoric, and dramaturgy used since the sixteenth century did not disappear with the start of the independent era, and for that very reason they should not be considered as superficial or tangential to the processes of state formation (see Avendaño, this volume). Rather, my intent is to show, through examples of several oath-taking ceremonies carried out in the Kingdom of Guatemala, how, notwithstanding the continuity in ritual practices, the semantic variants of sovereignty were represented ("made present" through the use of symbols).[2] Stated another way, I am interested not so much in the liturgies in and of themselves[3] as in the semantic changes with which the objects of political veneration were imbued during those ceremonies, as a means to observe the propagandistic and pedagogic intentions managed from the seats of power to ensure that both vassals and citizens could assimilate the reality of the absent sovereign.[4]

In the American territories, oath-taking ceremonies began to be used in the sixteenth century, when the Hapsburg dynasty established that the raising of pennants would be used to proclaim new monarchs.[5] According to the 1732 *Diccionario de la lengua castellana*, to take an oath (*jurar*) at that time meant not only "to appeal to God as a witness of what one affirms or denies," "to take a vow of something," or to have a "vice" (the vice of swearing) but also "to acclaim or publicly affirm the Prince as sovereign, with an oath of fidelity and those ceremonies that are meaningful thereto."[6] A ceremony of this nature had to be public, so multiple strategies were developed in each part of the Spanish monarchy to assure that each corporate group might participate according to the position it occupied in the social hierarchy, thereby reinforcing established order.

In the American case, the physical absence of the king was remedied by the use of various symbols, among them the funeral catafalques built during the ceremonies in memory of fallen monarchs or the portraits and royal pennants displayed during the proclamation of their successors.[7] What happened when the Courts meeting in Cádiz proclaimed the sovereignty of the nation in 1810? Some symbols and liturgies were maintained in the public readings and oath-taking ceremonies surrounding the implementation of the Constitution of 1812. The significance of sovereignty was no longer the same, however. At least in Guatemala, the portrait of the king and the royal pennant were placed in positions of lesser importance than that of the constitution, which represented the voice of the nation.

This chapter also stresses that in the Kingdom of Guatemala the shift in notions regarding sovereignty that took place around 1810, moving away from those that dominated during the Bourbon period, should not be interpreted in linear form, simply as a step from a notion of absolute power to one of a liberal-constitutional hue (see Rodríguez, this volume). Although political propaganda used during the funeral ceremony of Charles III and especially in the oath-taking ceremonies for Charles IV (1790) underscored the submissive relationship between subjects and the monarch, in the rituals themselves there was no shortage of expressions that appealed to the pactist imagination. At least two political traditions were therefore present when oath-takings for the Cádiz Constitution were organized.

Obviously, these political traditions, like Cádiz constitutionalism, were not homogenous doctrines, unbendingly unified in their principles. On the contrary, they were understandings of the world which, though they shared a common denominator, showed many nuances; their categorical architectures had changed over time, their meanings modified through appropriation and reappropriation on both sides of the Atlantic.

For ceremonies of oath-taking to King Charles IV in the Bourbon period, I analyze the report penned by the priest of the Nicaraguan city of Granada, Pedro Ximena.[8] That report was written in 1790 and published in the capital of the kingdom in 1793 in a press owned by Ignacio Beteta. The object of the report was, as mentioned by its author at the end of the text, to promote respect, submission, and loyalty toward the Spanish monarchs. To understand the ceremonial process better, I allude first to the funeral services of Charles III also celebrated in Granada. The example of the oath-taking ritual I use turns out to be extremely interesting, because it quashes any expectation that the festivities would be a demonstration of unanimity regarding the absolutist principles of power. In the case of ceremonies during the captivity of Ferdinand VII (1808–9) and for the Cádiz Constitution, I depend fundamentally on news published in the *Gazeta de Guatemala*. Like the report written by Pedro Ximena, the *Gazeta* intended to create consensus among vassals around obedience and loyalty toward the authorities. As the only newspaper in the Kingdom of Guatemala at that time, the *Gazeta* did not limit itself to sharing illustrated eighteenth-century paradigms with its readers or to providing news about the "heroic" Spanish resistance to the French invaders. The *Gazeta* also attempted to inform vassals about the new political structure of the Spanish monarchy that was then under construction in Cádiz, exciting their adherence to it.

THE SOVEREIGN KING: FUNERAL RITES AND SWEARING LOYALTY TO THE BOURBON MONARCHS

On May 22, 1789, the Granadan priest Pedro Ximena received a circular from the bishop of León, Nicaragua, Juan Félix Villegas, which was accompanied by a royal dispatch of December 14, 1788, in which all parish priests and ayuntamientos were instructed to celebrate a royal funeral in memory of King Charles III. In response, the ayuntamiento declared mourning,[9] which required the population to adopt an appropriate form of dress beginning on May 28, and ordered that funeral services be held on the following day.[10] Beginning at 3:00 on the afternoon of the twenty-eighth, the bells in the parish church and the other churches of the city rang sixty times. News regarding the death of the monarch thus circulated, and all public performances were prohibited.

In the parish church a funeral catafalque was prepared, "which although bare of symbols, hieroglyphics, emblems, epigrams, elegies and other elegant decorations of ingenuity and art, nonetheless showed in the simplicity of its pomp the noble affection of the patricians" of Granada who had financed it. The Granadans adorned the catafalque with black linens and designed its center to include two sections: one, on the bottom, displayed "a crimson pillow bordered with gold braid" containing a crown "as the sorrowful remains and pitiable relics of inexorable death." Above it, a hat decorated with gold and a baton with a handle of the same metal, "unmistakable signs of royal power," rested on another pillow.[11]

At 5:00 on the morning of the twenty-ninth, an artillery company began to fire cannon salvos that would be repeated every half hour, throughout the day and the following night. At 8:00 in the morning, the leaders of the religious orders of the city, together with the parish priest, received some of the Granadan corporative bodies at the doors of the church: representatives of the ayuntamiento, the town elite, and members of the militia. Cannons fired volleys and soldiers presented military honors in the plaza. After mass, the priest delivered a memorial speech and then "reminded the people of the sublime virtues of the dead man, inspiring in all most tender feelings of submission and respect for the sacred personages of the kings."[12]

The ceremony ended with a funeral oration, during which those present lit candles. According to Ximena, all of this sorrowful setting, full of the sights and sounds of bells and cannons, canticles, religious ceremony, military honors, and of course the catafalque, generated an atmosphere of sadness and mourning. In any event, those were the sensations the Granadan authorities intended to engender among those present.

With the king before his vassals, made present through the elaborate funeral bier, fragile and impotent in the face of death like any other worldly being, the organizers made an effort to compensate for his condition by extolling his virtues, his defense of the faith, or the grace he had achieved during his life.[13] In this way, rituals of power were converted into means of diffusing such values through the community. Pedro Ximena himself stressed it: "The panegyric for the dead is a call to the living to see among the sad remains of death the final end of human greatness."[14]

But the continuity of the monarchy had to be celebrated with a ritual that would emulate on a political level what occurred every year in the religious realm: the resurrection of Christ. The Granadan ayuntamiento, in coordination with militia officers, organized the oath-taking act, or "royal homage," to the new monarch, Charles IV, as well as the festivities that would accompany it, beginning on April 11, 1790. It is unclear why the city of Granada celebrated the oath-taking ceremony nearly a full year after the royal funeral; the decision probably depended on coordination among the different corporate bodies but especially on their budgets.[15]

By edict, the organizers invited everyone in Granada, along with the Indians and ladinos of nearby towns,[16] to prepare for the occasion. The royal standard-bearer ordered the construction of a kiosk near the town hall, which would sustain the portraits of Charles IV and his queen, especially painted by José Palavicini, a native of Lima and a Granadan resident. They were two full-length portraits, resembling, according to Ximena, "live images, if moving the eye closer to them did not distinguish reality from appearance." Both figures appeared seated "under a magnificent canopy, rugs and pillows at their feet." The king was painted with a scepter and crown of gold.[17] The portraits and the pennant became the central images in the festivities (described below).

Once blessed in the parish church, the standard-bearer carried the royal pennant to a platform that had been constructed in the middle of the central plaza.

Members of the ayuntamiento, royal officials, and Indian mayors formed the retinue that followed to the plaza, where they swore fealty to the new monarch, as the standard-bearer pronounced his name, fluttering the pennant at the sound of rounds fired by the artillerymen. According to custom, members of the ayuntamiento threw coins to the crowd as a sign of the generosity of the new monarch. Members of the militia then formed an honor guard around the portraits, and the standard-bearer placed the pennant in their midst. The celebration began immediately afterward and lasted for five days: parades, concerts, free beverages, dances, and nocturnal illumination turned the tranquility of Granada upside down. The most impressive religious ceremonies, the mass and the Te Deum, took place on April 12. Existing social hierarchies were reproduced inside the church itself during these ceremonies, as the most distinguished elements of the city positioned themselves in their respective seats. Militiamen and artillerymen fired volleys in honor of the new king.

Amid the uproar, the portraits were constantly honored. At a dramatization performed on the thirteenth, representing the subordination of Aztec and Inca power to the Hispanic monarchy, the men who played the roles of Moctezuma and an Inca king kissed the hands of the monarchs and knelt, depositing scepters and crowns at their feet. Militiamen dressed as battle-hardened Amazons did the same, kissing the hands of the royal portraits. Further, on the last day of the festivities the images, placed in a carriage, joined a procession, and thus their subjects brought them to life.

This media culture, typically baroque in the midst of a Bourbon era, deserves further analysis. Differentiating each of the corporate entities (ayuntamiento, militias, distinguished residents, Indian justices representing their towns, and religious orders) during the oath-taking ceremony demonstrated the social hierarchies and the "state," that is, the place of each and everyone in the social order. The oath-taking ceremony took place in the principal Granadan plaza, which symbolized the center of political and religious power as well as that of the Creole elite, whose homes were in fact concentrated around it.[18]

A very Bourbon embellishment—the constant use of the militias, with their firearms and artillery—can be noted in both the funeral services and the oath-taking ceremony described by Ximena. It is what some have called, in terms of both symbolism and the media, the beginning of a "military hegemony" or the "militarization of society" brought to bear by the Bourbons. If the chiming of bells had previously marked political, religious, and daily life for American residents, in the eighteenth century the authorities began to regulate their use and, in part, to replace them with cannon thunder.[19]

The multiple symbols seen in the oath-taking ceremony reveal a very syncretic culture, something not unique to Granada but typical of ceremonies celebrated throughout Hispanic America. The king, in addition to being identified with the sun ("You are the sun," "The sun will come out for you," read some of the notes tucked into the columns that held up the ephemeral architecture honoring the royal portraits), was also associated with the pantheon of Greek gods. He was Apollo, and the queen, María Luisa de Borbón, was identified with Diana. Still, as Thomas Calvo has observed about eighteenth-century Guadalajara, this connection was not innocuous; rather, it added the Bourbon seal to the rendering of tribute to the monarchs. If in the Hapsburg period the sovereigns were identified as Christ-like sun kings, in the eighteenth century they evoked the "Apollo of Versailles." "This mythological reference," added Calvo, "erased the providential aspect that until then was at the center of the contract between the Divinity and the Catholic monarchy."[20]

Other symbols included the ship, representing the Hispanic monarchy, and the Aztec and Inca "nations," who in dramatized form submissively recognized the new monarchs "as their legitimate kings and natural lords."[21] But none of those symbols was as important as the portrait and the pennant in representing the monarch, his power, and his relationship with his subjects. The portrait was a simulacrum of the king, that is, a reproduction, a copy of a copy of his person, since he himself never visited the Kingdom of Guatemala.[22] All in all, that simulacrum embodied the royal monarch to the residents of Granada, to such a degree that his image was the object of constant veneration. Political propaganda focused on the image sought to make the subjects aware of who their sovereign was, and speeches and poems written for the occasion strengthened these strategies. One might suppose that these spoken and written complements to the mentioned imagery would have availed themselves of an absolutist style, given a reigning Bourbon dynasty that did not hesitate to legitimize monarchical authority over the "dominions of its colonies" in America through absolutist and regalist theories: kings, considered demigods, derived their power not from an agreement with the political community but directly from God, who also had entrusted them with the protection of the temporal and spiritual power of the Indies, without any intervention from Rome. Notwithstanding the inclusion of some ideas that could be considered absolutist, the oath-taking ceremony contained other elements identified with the pactist vision of power (see Rodríguez, this volume).

Pedro Ximena came to maintain that God installed the kings "for the perfect harmony of the universe, clothing them in His power, majesty, and glory. . . . When God perpetuates on the thrones the legitimate succession of His sovereigns, His mercy spreads over the people." In like manner, he recalled the beginning of the relationship between altar and throne: "Religion authorized and ratified the oath of homage that we make to our kings and natural lords, a tie so sacred that we cannot dissolve it without earning the anathema of heaven." Further on, the priest declared that the Spanish monarchs were "kings and natural lords chosen by God to cooperate in His eternal designs for the conversion and sanctification of numberless souls."[23]

Such expressions leave aside the role of the political community or "republic" and underscore the notion that the sovereignty of the monarch was not shared. According to pactist tradition, it was the community that entrusted the king with his power. The sovereign was the legislator, although always subject to the laws that governed the republic.[24] If power did not derive from the latter, but rather from God, it was always present within the republic, where it could potentially become active.

The very presence of royal portraits at the Granadan festivities demonstrated the continued presence of a "personal" relationship between the king and his subjects that had begun under the Hapsburgs. Referring principally to the end of the eighteenth century, Alejandra Osorio has shown that in Bourbon Peru the portrait of the king was replaced during oath-taking ceremonies by the royal pennant, which indicated a move from the "more personal" relationship of the Hapsburgs with their kingdoms toward a "more abstract representation of the figure of the monarch and of his political powers," which Bourbon viceregal authorities wished to strengthen.[25] What occurred in the province of Nicaragua also took place in other regions of Spanish America, where the portrait continued to preside over the oath-taking ceremonies.[26] The portrait reminded subjects of the ties and pacts established with the monarch, their "father" or "master," who helped them in exchange for their loyal service in a relationship profoundly colored by patron-client bonds. The king, then, was obligated to show his subjects the virtues of liberality and generosity.[27] Paradoxically, the Bourbon celebrations themselves contributed to weakening the aura of sacredness that surrounded the sovereign—Granada is a case in point—by placing him beside his queen in portraits and by removing the veil, which had surrounded them with a certain sacred mystery.[28]

The dramatizations presenting the prehispanic "nations" in the Granadan royal celebrations showed again the pactist vision of the monarchy, expressing what Eugenia Bridikhina has called "the tacit pact between the crown and the Indian elite . . . the product of constant negotiation which legitimized both powers."[29] Effectively, memory was renewed, in part, through these devices, as can be appreciated in the report made by Ximena. Through the dramatizations, the Granadan authorities intended to demonstrate how the Indians transited from paganism to the knowledge of the Gospel thanks to their "loving surrender" to the Catholic monarchs, their legitimate natural lords. But a text associated with this dramatization shows another component of the reconstructed memory the authorities sought to disseminate. It glorified the "conquest of the Indian empires," whose "luminous history, despite the blind and perfidious envy of European nations, will forever perpetuate the greatness and magnificence of our august monarchs, and the intrepidity and bravery of the Spaniards." It was not only Indians who renewed their pact with the king. The Creoles as well, since they were descendants of those "intrepid and valiant Spaniards" and organizers of the royal festivities, took advantage of the past to remind the new sovereign to fulfill his promises.[30] The militia battalion prepared the spectacle, dressing one hundred young Indians in the traditional attire of the ancient Indian empires.

A poem, reproduced on canvas, accompanied by the figures of a pomegranate and a city, alluding to the locality that swore loyalty to the new king, provides another example of the pactist tradition present in the royal festivities of 1790:[31]

> The beautiful nature
> of the one whom by grace I was fortunately raised
> wished to have me crowned
> by the splendor of her greatness.
> Unequaled is the kindness
> that I recognize in her giving birth,
> because it was so very great
> the honor that she gave to my life
> I have prepared it
> for my king CHARLES IV.
> From the noble city
> Granada my home
> I want to show my happiness
> and loyal generosity:
> removing briefly
> the crown that I possess,
> I give it with the wish
> to my generous CHARLES,
> that rather than on mine, my joy will grow
> when on his brow I see it.

The poem indicates in metaphorical, even secular, language that power ("the crown") is held by the political community (the city of Granada), which transfers it to the new monarch. Since, according to the poem, sovereignty was first given to the "republic," it therefore maintains a position of ontological supremacy relative to the kings. And although there is no explicit reference to the *pactum translationis* in the poem, its presence can be surmised since, just as the citizens of Granada granted sovereignty to Charles IV, their ancestors must have done the same during previous oath-taking ceremonies. Further, with the death of Charles III they probably understood that sovereignty "momentarily" reverted to them on an interim basis.

As I mentioned at the beginning of the chapter, pactism and Hispanic constitutionalism were not solidly homogeneous doctrines in terms of how their principles were formulated. Pactism had incorporated traditions used by the Castilian *comuneros* and neoscholasticism, as well as the experiences generated by the conquest and colonization of America. It was not a form of contractualism, as modern philosophers would have it, because it was an agreement not among equals but rather among men who held different positions in a social hierarchy and were members of corporate bodies. The "people," the community or "republic," was the body that gave its consent to the authority of the king through the pact. The Navarrese philosopher Martin de Azpilcueta, for example, would maintain that although the king held power it was also to be found in the community, but in a potential state that could become effective in cases of vacancy or injustice.[32]

All in all, sovereignty was expressly awarded to the Catholic monarch, so we must wait for the crisis of the Hispanic monarchy, initiated in 1808, to see a surprising political transformation on both sides of the Atlantic. Propaganda surrounding the ceremonies was one of the vehicles deploying the new ideas.

THE SOVEREIGN NATION:
THE CONSTITUTIONAL OATH-TAKING CEREMONY

Once word got out regarding the abdication of Charles IV, the conspiracies undertaken by his son Ferdinand, and the imprisonment of the royal family by Napoleon (whose brother Joseph ascended to the throne as the new king of Spain and the Indies), the Kingdom of Guatemala prepared, like other regions of Spanish America, to swear loyalty to the man they considered their new and legitimate sovereign: Ferdinand VII. The year was 1808. Curiously, the disloyalty Ferdinand VII had shown toward his father was rapidly forgotten by his subjects because of the propaganda emitted in newspapers, sermons, and oath-taking ceremonies, where he was depicted as a victim of the French. Subjects were commanded to cooperate, not only with prayers but also with funds, to face the invaders then present on the peninsula.[33] Quickly, the image of Ferdinand changed to that of a captive hero, the king "desired" by a nation that found itself without a father. In certain towns in America, in a kind of collective hysteria, it was even said that he had been seen fighting beside the insurgents. Nonetheless, in some places people questioned this propaganda, pointing out that "the desired one" was no more than a rhetorical figure.[34]

In the Kingdom of Guatemala, pactism resurged with the crisis of the Spanish monarchy. As Jordana Dym has pointed out, not only in the urban world but also in the interior of the provinces there were those who argued that the power of the kings had been granted by the people. Such was the case in Metapán when, in the 1811 revolt, the leader of the uprising, Juan de Dios Mayorga, confronted the affirmations of the town priest, who defended the power of the kings as a direct emanation from God. In cities the ayuntamientos used pactism to show either their loyalty or their insubordination to superior authorities. They accepted, for example, the fact that the Supreme Central Junta was the "depository" of the sovereignty of the king. Likewise, some city leaders in Guatemala opposed the transfer of sovereignty from the Supreme Central Junta to the regency council because they believed that the nation as a whole had not been a party to that decision. The argument was the same: the original sovereignty of the people reverted to them in the absence of the monarch.[35]

On July 21, 1810, the minutes of the first general meeting of the recently founded College of Attorneys of Guatemala, signed on June 29, maintained that it was proper to recognize the Supreme Central Junta of Spain and the Indies and the regency council as long as they represented the authority of the captive monarch. For members of the College, the laws of the body politic indicated the procedures surrounding a "sacred and inviolable right" such as that regarding who should occupy the throne of the monarchy, before whom "the nation" is subject without restraint, recognizing him as "a person anointed by God, since from Him comes all power, according to the Holy Apostle [Saint Peter] and fundamental Law." This acknowledgment they called a "very solemn pact" between the sovereign and the nation. In moments of crisis, recognizing and obeying interim authorities was required, not only to protect the body politic but also to work according to the designs of God. Thus, according to this association of attorneys, men must always be subject to a legitimate power that will defend them and curb their passions. Resisting this power meant resisting "the order of God." The attorneys ended by declaring their submission to the sovereign and legitimate authority of Fernando VII, to whom, as faithful subjects, they owed allegiance.[36]

Sovereign monarch, theological legitimization of the throne, submission of the subjects: it was the same language used more than twenty years before at the oath-taking ceremony organized under the reign of Charles IV. Nonetheless, the use of the term "nation," as we see below, undergoes an important semantic shift in the Courts of Cádiz. But, returning to demonstrations of loyalty, all the cities, villas, and towns of the kingdom publicly showed their support of Fernando VII, just like the College of Attorneys. In the province of Costa Rica, the oath-taking ceremony and the royal festivities were quite elaborate. In the capital, Cartago, on January 15, 1809, the oath was taken before the pennant, the principal corporative groups paraded through the streets, coins were thrown to the attending public, drinks were distributed, fireworks were set off, and a short play was presented.[37]

Two years later, the *Gazeta de Guatemala* reported that Indians of the towns of Laiguala and Talgua in the district of Gracias, intendencia of Comayagua (Honduras), had shown their fervent loyalty to the monarch in a variety of ways, encouraged by their priest, José María Jalón. They gave extra donations, carried out public celebrations, and financed a portrait of the king. Indian representatives from these towns called Ferdinand VII "our captive father" to whom they owed, as had their ancestors, "the felicity of having taken us out of our paganism."[38]

Despite the above-mentioned sentiments and the media strategies that strengthened them, in these same years the constitutional and liberal "revolution" unleashed in the city of Cádiz was taking its first steps. On September 24, 1810, the Courts, meeting on the island of León, proclaimed the sovereignty of the nation. A daring change, treachery toward the king, or hope for those wanting a regime free from despotism? Whatever reading was given to this first principle of the liberal revolution sparked that day, it is clear that the subject to whom supreme power was assigned would confer executive power on the monarch through the constitution. The king would thus be converted into a "chief of government," the "first magistrate of the nation," with powers clearly limited by the Courts. These last, of course, would claim for themselves full legislative power, dismantling the absolutist argument of the monarchy and even making possible the creation of substitute matriarchal images or allegories (e.g., the allegory of the nation seated on her throne).[39]

On March 19, 1812, the Spanish constitution was promulgated in Cádiz by peninsular and American representatives. Despite the fact that the representatives had insistently stressed that it was a hereditary code of the basic laws or ancient jurisprudence bequeathed by "the elders," that is, their ancestors, it really was a modern charter, "a liberal constitution," as they themselves called it. It had decreed national representation based not on estates but on population, liberty of the press concerning political themes, the individual dimension of rights and obligations, equality before the law, and making public the financial condition of the nation.[40]

At that time the people living in the territory of the Spanish monarchy were clearly aware of an equally liberal statute or "constitution" which, in principle, ruled on both sides of the Atlantic during the reign of Joseph I. It was debated by American representatives living on the peninsula (the *afrancesados*, or Francophiles), who had voice but no vote in the assembly of Bayonne. Even so, in practical terms the Bayonne constitution was a dead letter in America.[41] At that time, several insurgent American constitutions were also known, more radical in their political principles than the one from Cádiz. None of them, however, had any application whatsoever in the Kingdom of Guatemala.

On September 24, 1812, the Spanish constitution was publicly presented in Guatemala City with "pomp and majesty," as mentioned in the *Gazeta de Guatemala*. Beginning at four in the morning, the artillery fired volleys every ten minutes. Four hours later the audiencia, the ayuntamiento, militia officers, and distinguished residents met at the royal palace, starting the promenade along "the usual path, richly hung with damask draperies." When audiencia president

Bustamante exited the palace, he presented the constitution to the public, "and the troops presented arms and loosed a general volley, which was answered by a salvo from the artillery," located in the old plaza. The procession accompanying the constitution took the following order: the artillery detachment marched first; then, the authorities of the Indian towns; next, the clergy, including parish priests, prelates, religious orders, and cathedral canons. They were followed by the city ayuntamiento and the audiencia, led by Bustamante, who carried the constitution in his hands. The parade ended with military battalions, including the militia. According to the report, a stage had been built in the plaza to hold the portrait of Ferdinand VII. Three scribes read the entire constitution. At the end, they invoked the Trinity and the troops fired a volley. After the reading of the constitution, specially minted coins were thrown from the stage. On one face of the coins an open book (the constitution) emanated rays of light, and on its pages could be read the words "Justice; Equity." Around this symbol was the expression "For the political constitution of the Spains." The other face of the coins showed the shield of the city with the commemorative date, September 24.[42]

Oath-taking to the new charter occupied the following days (compare to Avendaño, this volume). José Bustamante and the oidores of the audiencia took their oaths and went to the cathedral for the Te Deum led by the archbishop of Guatemala, Ramón Casaús y Torres. Oaths were then taken by university personnel, religious orders, employees of the revenue, mail, and mint divisions, as well as officers with their battalions. The report in the *Gazeta* concluded by saying that in that manner "the great work of our Congress" had been "settled in the souls of these very loyal residents . . . and so this sweet monument to liberality and justice has been celebrated."

But had the semantics of the new object of political veneration truly been "settled in the souls" of those in attendance? Probably not, because it was very early for these semantics to settle in deeply. Even so, the impact may well have been longer lasting, to the degree that an important portion of the residents were aware of, or active in, the political culture promoted by the Courts and the constitution through information disseminated in the *Gazeta*;[43] the electoral processes; the training of local, regional, and national authorities; the dissemination of information about their rights, and the like.[44] The publicity impact of the ceremony may have been as ephemeral as the very art created for the occasion, yet the semantics of the symbols and dramatizations continued to be important because they reveal what the political speeches sought to affirm through other means.[45]

In the oath-taking ceremony for the Constitution of 1812 in Guatemala we find a continuity of rituals with respect to the one celebrated in Granada twenty years earlier: the presence of a portrait of the monarch, parades, participation by corporative groups, religious ceremonies, the use of artillery, and the printing of commemorative coins later thrown to the public.⁴⁶ The novelty consisted in the fact that the importance of the portrait of the king was, to some degree, diminished in the face of a copy of the constitution that was accorded visual, symbolic, and ceremonial preeminence. There is no doubt that the new liberal regime used aspects of the old ritual. It legitimized the new system from the altar (actually, Article 12 of the constitution pointed out that the nation would forever maintain the Catholic, apostolic, and Roman confession) and from the throne. Although the monarch was no longer sovereign, his symbolic presence continued to have a place in the ceremony; also, the government, according to Article 2, would be characterized as a "moderate hereditary monarchy."

Notwithstanding this continuity, the rituals certainly suffered significant changes.⁴⁷ In fact, the continuity that had existed in terms of the rituals or the realm of the symbolic in the oath-taking ceremonies carried out during the Hapsburg and Bourbon periods had also shown significant modifications, as discussed in the previous section. Appealing to the altar, then, did not imply that the celebrations of Cádiz liberalism were identical to those of the Bourbon regime, assuming that neither would represent a modern secularizing policy. Was there no secularizing policy surrounding the image of the new monarch in the oath-taking ceremony in Granada in 1790 when he was painted with his queen, and when their portraits were uncovered throughout the celebrations? Did the Courts not adopt a secularizing policy when they stripped the king of a power previously understood to have been directly derived from God? In any form, and as Garavaglia reminds us, it is very difficult for modern politics to divorce itself from religious rituals, no matter how secularized politicians consider themselves to be.⁴⁸

Accordingly, it is impossible to distinguish those liberal ceremonies from the rituals and symbols of the ancien régime, which were effectively everywhere. The formula the towns used to swear their loyalty to the constitution read as follows: "Do you swear by God and by the Holy Gospels to protect the political constitution of the Spanish monarchy, sanctioned by the general and extraordinary courts of the nation, and to be faithful to the king?" In cities like San Salvador, street processions were undertaken not only with a copy of the constitution but also with the royal pennant, recalling the power—although now limited—of the monarchs.⁴⁹ Further, the participation of the corporations, indicating their position and hierarchical order in the parade, and thereby reflecting societal composition under the ancien régime, went against the individual and abstract ideal of the constitution itself, for which "the Spanish nation was a coming together of all the Spaniards in both hemispheres" (Article 1). Faced with these "aporias," Ivana Frasquet has maintained that they do not represent simply continuity with the past but rather the strategy of Cádiz liberalism "to maintain the symbolic parameters of a society which must accept revolutionary changes."⁵⁰

To my way of thinking, the new object of public veneration, the Cádiz Constitution, was what made possible the real encounter of the people (*los pueblos*) with the nation, with itself, through their written voice, emitted by their representatives. In contrast to the swearing of allegiance to the kings, where a portrait was used, when pledging fidelity to the constitution it was a code, a book, that evoked the presence of the nation. That was probably too abstract for most people, especially for those accustomed to anthropomorphic images. At any rate, liberal propaganda tried to accentuate the importance of the constitution with a public reading (to familiarize the populace with its content) and with the multiplication of its image on coins thrown to the crowds, as well as by explaining how magnanimous the new system would be. It is interesting to note that bright rays, previously used as an effect forming part of the representations of kings as "suns," were now placed on the images of the constitution incised on coins.

The constitutional oath-taking ceremonies sought to propagate the idea of a sovereignty that essentially belonged to the nation. This was exactly what Article 3 of the new code affirmed. Said statement, apparently unimportant, opposed the traditional pactism observed in oath-taking ceremonies in Granada in 1790. If pactism in the Bourbon era represented an excellent anti-absolutist principle and legitimized the need for the consent of the political community, in the Cádiz era this gave way in the face of a liberal perspective that understood sovereignty as an attribute that previously coexisted, coexists now, and forever shall coexist with the nation. In that manner Cádiz liberalism surpassed and abbreviated that triangular movement of power, emanating from God and granted to the king through the "republic." If pactism considered a real sovereignty (that of the monarch) and a virtual one (that of the "republic"), the liberals of the Courts believed that there was only one sovereignty, that of the nation, which was inalienable since only its exercise was delegated to the authorities.[51] This modern principle was not the result of homogeneous feelings among the representatives in Cádiz. Instead, it was attributable to the games, strategies, and alliances undertaken by the liberal representatives and their opponents in the trans-Atlantic congress.[52] However, the informative mechanisms of Cádiz liberalism probably had no decisive and immediate impact on the population in terms of providing a detailed decoding of the principle of national sovereignty. The single public reading of the Cádiz code was not enough. Therefore, it was here where political practices unleashed by constitutionalism itself turned into a pedagogical mechanism within the towns whereby peninsular Spaniards, Creoles, Indians, mestizos, ladinos, and other sectors came to understand the new system much better.

Who would have assimilated with greater ease the significance of the new symbols presented during the rituals of power in the liberal Cádiz era? Without doubt, it was the elites and intellectuals who, even before the crisis of the monarchy, were "imagining" a community with its own fundamental code. Since at least the end of the eighteenth century some "Enlightened" Spaniards, by demanding monarchical reform in their writings and letters, had seen the need to form a constitution for the nation, not for individuals—that is, a code for the integrity of the people who made up the monarchy.[53]

In their 1810 instructions to Antonio Larrazábal, their representative to the Courts, members of the Guatemala City ayuntamiento appealed enthusiastically to the nation for a constitutional monarchy. One of the two groups of councilmen that together formed the ayuntamiento argued, among other things, that the Spanish nation was one and indivisible, that its religion was Catholic, and that it would hold legislative faculties. In the face of obscure and arbitrary administrations that made their subjects "a troop of slaves," they proposed a constitution that would preclude despotism and place limits on power. The other group in the ayuntamiento charged representative Larrazábal with, among other proposals, negotiating a liberal constitution for the monarchy, one that would recognize equality on both sides of the Atlantic, giving the king all power and majesty while still preventing despotism.[54] They were all men who could most immediately understand liberal propaganda and the new political fetish.

One might think that the rest of the population did not develop familiarity with these kinds of rituals and symbols, based as much on what is expressed above as on the ephemeral nature of the two constitutional periods. Also, it would be easy to believe that the post-independence regimes would have abandoned this form of political propaganda in their media strategies.[55] Nonetheless, the Central American governing elites of the republican era used the portraits and the constitutional oath-taking for the same ends to which they were applied in the Hispanic era. For example, Héctor Lindo has highlighted the stupendous entrances, the parades, and the enthronement of the portrait of President Gerardo Barrios organized by the people of El Salvador in the first half of the nineteenth century.[56] In 1861 this same president had decreed that in order to accept, whether in full or on a temporary basis, any ecclesiastical benefice, every priest must render his oath before the president to submit without restriction to the constitution and to his government. In the judgment of Barrios and his regime, the church was not complying with the law of the republic and was disobeying the executive, using the pulpit for political purposes.

The formula for the oath: "Do you swear by God and the Holy Gospels to be faithful to the government; to obey and comply, where they concern you, with the Constitution and secondary laws of the Republic, dictated by the sovereign of the nation for the well-being of Salvadorans, and for the protection of the faith of Jesus Christ, the Catholic religion, and its worthy ministers?" The appropriate response:

"Yes, I swear it." To the Barrios regime, the stubborn attitude of the clergy about the oath showed both recklessness and boorishness: it could be argued that since the Constitution of 1812 all clerics had been taking an oath to the principal laws of the land.[57]

CONCLUSION

Symbols, rituals, rhetoric, and images were indispensable instruments in the creation and re-creation of political culture in Hispanic America. What was seen in the Kingdom of Guatemala between 1790 and 1812 cannot be understood outside of the "politics of images" put in motion by the Spanish crown. According to Gruzinski, from the seventeenth century onward the crown did not simply impose a form of the sacred on the territory, beginning with the destruction of native idols or the re-creation of a new landscape full of constant miracles and marvels. Its ambitious program based on religious imagery also made it possible to integrate spaces, as well as to create economic, political, symbolic, and commercial exchanges. In this program, political images also played an important role, although perhaps they did not permanently inundate everyday colonial life or have the iconographic simplicity of the religious images. Even though some of their expressions, given the erudition displayed in allegories and symbols such as the triumphal arches erected to receive the viceroys or the oath-taking ceremonies for a new monarch, could be understood only by the educated circles, the mechanisms sought out by the crown to make the political images accessible to the population at large were highly varied.[58]

The oath-taking ceremonies for Charles IV and Ferdinand VII as well as those for the Cádiz Constitution sought, through media strategies designed by local authorities, to generate an unconditional adhesion to power among residents of the Kingdom of Guatemala. Did they achieve it completely? It is difficult to answer in the affirmative. In the case of the Constitution of 1812, we must make allowances for the propaganda problems the liberal Cádiz regime faced, given the newness of this object of political veneration. Clearly, the association with the sacred made by the portrait, the pennant, and the constitutional text during the ceremonies gave tremendous aid to this media strategy. Nonetheless, a careful reading of the reports and news on these rituals has led me to consider, on one hand, that it would be simplistic to claim a straightforward continuity from Bourbon celebrations through those for the constitution based on the appeal to the altar, when we can see basic changes in the images used and in their semantics. Further, in all cases, some of the celebrations included certain dramatizations and rhetoric of a secularizing nature.

At the same time, there was also no transition from absolutism to liberalism. The ceremonies showed both continuities and breaks with tradition, so there is no linear reading of the reception and utilization of political doctrines in the Kingdom of Guatemala. Despite the fact that the oath-taking for Charles IV was carried out in a period characterized by absolutism and regalism, some demonstrations of loyalty to the new monarch were derived from pactist political principles. The same could be said of the oath-taking of 1812, when liberal elements coexisted with corporatist practices held over from the ancien régime.

Understanding the semantic changes in the concept of sovereignty through an analysis of the Bourbon- and Cádiz-era oath-taking ceremonies can certainly contribute to improving an understanding of independence processes in the Kingdom of Guatemala. Separation from the Spanish crown demanded not only the continuity of certain rituals to legitimate the new authorities but also an urgent discussion about who retained sovereignty. Logic would indicate that the Central Americans assumed that sovereignty resided in the "people" or the "nation," but circumstances surrounding independence demonstrated a lack of clarity in this regard or, more simply, a power struggle, even during the federal era when it would have seemed that the rules of the republican game were clear.

To sum up, the media function of the symbols and images in the period under study should no longer be considered solely as an attempt by local powers or the monarchy to manipulate the manner in which people thought. This is true notwithstanding the fact that the architecture of propaganda in this period was similar to that of the Baroque era and that the general perception of that era as a world of political and social spectacles carries a great deal of weight in contemporary analyses. Effectively, it is thought of as a world of masquerades and illusion, where the visual senses predominated as means to decode the various representations of reality (emblems, symbols, theater, processions, triumphal arches, etc.) and where everyone was seen as an actor who should play his role in the comedy of life. Despite, then, the unidimensional reading of the effects and uses of rituals and symbols that we might have, there is no doubt that metaphors, emblems, and images were and are important for human survival.[59]

In that sense, propaganda deployed in Hispanic America through spectacles, symbols, and discourse fulfilled the purpose of transmitting values that facilitated the normal functioning of government,[60] but above all it was an instrument through which the political community reminded the power structure of its acquired obligations and responsibilities. Religious and political rituals should therefore not be understood as events that maintain social balance through the media resources used, when on many occasions they express dysfunctionalities, ruptures, or renegotiations, as can be appreciated in late eighteenth-century pactism.

NOTES

To the memory of Ana Margarita Gómez

1. Garavaglia, *"Teatro."* Garavaglia argues that the May 25 celebrations and the presidential inaugurations in Argentina, as well as the funeral services for French president Francois Mitterand in 1995, illustrate the importance of civil-religious ceremonies in the spheres of power.
2. A reflection along these lines may be found in Frasquet, "Alteza."
3. There are many studies of "ephemeral art" during the period of Spanish rule in America. See Fajardo, "Jura."
4. Leal demonstrates how vassals understood the sense of political thought, order, and hierarchy through ceremonies. Leal, *Discurso*, 22.
5. Mínguez, "Ceremonia," 275.
6. *Diccionario de la lengua castellana* (1976).
7. Other important symbols included royal seals, which were ceremonially received in American cities since they represented the authority of the king. See Bridikhina, *Theatrum*, 180–81.
8. *Reales exequias, por el señor don Carlos III*.
9. The two members of the ayuntamiento commissioned to organize the celebrations were regidor Ubaldo Pasos and royal standard-bearer Joaquín Solórzano.
10. On the importance of wardrobe in a society divided into estates, see O'Phelan, "Vestido."
11. *Reales exequias, por el señor don Carlos III*, 86.
12. Ibid., 87.
13. Valenzuela, *Liturgias*, 190.
14. *Reales exequias, por el señor don Carlos III*, 82.
15. In any event, the oath-taking ceremonies in Granada took place on dates that were generally speaking similar to those of other cities. In Cali and Panama, in the Viceroyalty of New Granada, for instance, ceremonies were held at the beginning of 1790. Rodríguez and Mínguez, "Cultura simbólica," 123–25.
16. These were Xalteva, Nandayme, Diriá, Niquinohomo, San Juan, Santa Catalina, Namotiva, Masatepe, Nandasmo, Xalapa, Ginotepet, Diriamba, Masaya, Nindirí, Managua, Matiare, Acoyapa, and Tipitapa.
17. *Reales exequias, por el señor don Carlos III*, 121.
18. Nonetheless, some argue that by the end of the eighteenth century this space was less attractive to the Creole elite and had lost something of its symbolic importance for them, because of a larger presence of peninsular Spaniards and the progressive encroachment of artisanal activities, among other "problems." Vives, "Ámbito." On the representation of social order in ceremonies, see Leal, *Discurso*.
19. Valenzuela, "Entre campanas"; Calvo, "Jura," 79–80. On the militarization of society in Guatemala in coercive terms, see Gómez, "Máquina."
20. Calvo, "Jura," 77. In Puebla, King Louis I, son of Philip V, was identified with Hercules. Ramos, "Arte."
21. *Reales exequias, por el señor don Carlos III*, 137. In the Andean regions of Peru and Charcas (present-day Bolivia), presenting dramatizations and iconography of governing Incas

prior to the Spanish monarchs was part of a political program that sought to legitimize the Peruvian viceregency as a fragment of the Hispanic monarchy. It attempted to represent the continuity between one empire and the other, but with the uprisings of 1780–81 the crown ordered the confiscation of all portraits from the Inca dynasty. Bridikhina, *Theatrum*, 217–18. In the Kingdom of Guatemala, this kind of representation continued until the beginning of the nineteenth century. In 1809, during the oath-taking to Ferdinand VII carried out in the capital, the four kingdoms of Guatemala were represented in allegorical form: Kiché, Kakchiquel, Hapsburg, and Bourbon. See Chinchilla, "Nacionalismo," 6.
22. See Osorio, "Rey," 87.
23. *Reales exequias, por el señor don Carlos III*, 130, 137–38; also, a defense of the "enlightened" monarch can be found on 34–66.
24. In his report, Ximena himself had in fact proposed the need for a renewal of the legal corpus, based on ancient laws, which would engage with the dispersed Enlightenment legislation that had been put into effect by Carlos III. See Herrera, "Constitución," 78.
25. Osorio, "Rey," 111–12.
26. For example, in Cali. Henao, "Ceremonias," 12.
27. Feros, "Clientelismo."
28. In some places in Spanish America during the Hapsburg era, the portraits of the kings were covered during the oath-taking ceremonies. Calvo, "Jura," 80.
29. Bridikhina, *Theatrum*, 214–19.
30. *Reales exequias, por el señor don Carlos III*, 137.
31. *Granada* means pomegranate in Spanish [Editor's note].
32. Stoetzer, *Raíces*, 47–50; Quijada, "'Dos tradiciones'"; Ávila, *En nombre*, 41.
33. Lévano, "Por la salud," 126.
34. Van Young, *Crisis*, 388; Guzmán, "Imaginario."
35. Dym, "Soberanía."
36. *Gazeta de Guatemala*, no. 161, July 21, 1810, fols. 127–30. Víctor Gayol has affirmed that "taking an oath to an abdicated king . . . was like reinventing or newly founding his legitimacy." Gayol, "Retrato," 179. This group was composed of Manuel Talavera (dean); Antonio Isidro Palomo (first representative); José Aycinena (second representative); Bernardo Martínez (third representative); Pantaleón Isidro del Águila (fourth representative); Juan de la Cruz Moreno (president); José Antonio López (vice president); Antonio Robles (legal accountant); Alejandro Díaz Cabeza de Vaca (secretary); José Antonio Larrave (assistant secretary); Mariano Méndez (treasurer); and Miguel Aragón (collector).
37. Brenes, "Fidelidad," and "¡Viva!"
38. *Gazeta de Guatemala*, no. 245, November 21, 1811, fols. 39–40.
39. Cuadriello, "Trono."
40. *Discurso preliminar leído*, 1–120.
41. Domínguez, "América española."
42. *Gazeta de Guatemala*, no. 280, October 2, 1812, fols. 297–99. The event was organized by the city ayuntamiento, which was already beginning to distance itself somewhat from the counterinsurgency policies implemented by José Bustamante, president of the

Guatemalan audiencia, as well as having serious complaints regarding certain rebuffs he had directed toward it. In short, Bustamante came to be seen in the constitutional context as a hypocrite and a tyrant. See Hawkins, *José de Bustamante*, 141, and Hawkins, this volume. As is seen later, the fact that the capital ayuntamiento organized the oath-taking ceremony shows that it was one of the few privileged sectors that clearly understood the new constitutional idiom. On the creation of allegories by Hispanic constitutionalism, see Reyero, *Alegoría*.

43. The *Gazeta* published the constitutional oath-taking ceremony undertaken by the congressional representatives and other authorities present in Cádiz. *Gazeta de Guatemala*, no. 270, June 20, 1812, fols. 209–16; it also published continuing notices about the war against the French and the work of the representatives in the Courts.
44. See Pollack, *Levantamiento*; and Herrera, *Ejercicio*.
45. Compare with similar experiences in the Hispanic world. Ortemberg, "Cádiz"; López, "Hablar."
46. The same things occurred in other cities. Velasco, "Fiesta."
47. Conde and Monsalvo, "Construcción."
48. Garavaglia, "Teatro."
49. "La promulgación de la Constitución de 1812."
50. Frasquet, "Alteza," 264.
51. Some historians have noted that after the Cádiz Constitution was promulgated, nineteenth-century Latin American constitutionalism saw a renewal of pactism in which the sacred, the mystic, the transitory, the multiplicity of actors who formed the pacts, and so forth all came into play. Demélas, "Pactismo."
52. Piqueras, "Ilustración"; Varela, *Teoría*.
53. Portillo, "Constitucionalismo."
54. "Instrucciones para la constitución fundamental," 111–22; "Apuntes instructivos que el señor don Antonio Larrazábal," 205.
55. An example of their use can be found in Díaz, "Jura."
56. Lindo, "Límites."
57. "El ministro de Relaciones y Gobernación. Manuel Irungaray (Gaceta Oficial, 13 de noviembre de 1861)," in García, *Diccionario*, 4.7–8.
58. Gruzinski, *Guerra*.
59. González, *Metáforas*, 11–22, 45–73.
60. Cárdenas, "Razón."

THE COSTA RICAN CONCORDIA COMPACT, 1821–1823
A Constitutionalist Perspective on Independence

Pablo Augusto Rodríguez Solano

> Natural law and all others dictate the need for finding a means to conserve and defend [independence]; and to build in the very bosom of these nations a system of government which will ameliorate their obvious defects, exercising those rights of sovereignty that thereby have fallen to the people, in conformity with the principles of the wise ancient Spanish Constitution, and the maxims taught and published in innumerable papers authored by the now defunct supreme junta.
>
> —Caracas cabildo, April 19, 1810

On October 29, 1821, a meeting of men representing "the peoples" of the province of Costa Rica decided to support the terms of the Independence Act signed in Guatemala City on September 15, 1821. Additionally, they chose to support the clauses attached in the Acta de los nublados signed in Nicaragua on September 29.[1] With that began the process of defining a political society under new terms, though the significance and consequences of these decisions had not been fathomed by those present.

The present essay analyzes the historiographical interpretations of the independence processes in Costa Rica. I hope to give new meaning to this moment through a critique of the absolutism/liberalism argument used to explain the events of 1821–23 and commonly referred to in historiographical discussions on the subject. I also suggest that the review undertaken here allows an analysis of the forms in which independence has been understood in Costa Rica and thereby demonstrates the specificities of the new interpretation presented here. The intention is to allow comparisons with other research undertaken regarding this period, including the other chapters in this volume.

I start with the generally accepted premise that Costa Rican independence resulted from pressure the Mexican revolution caused in the region and from new currents in Hispanic American political thinking that reinterpreted the Spanish legal tradition in the context of the disintegrating social pact that existed under the monarchy. This vision implies considering that the leaders in this period fell back on natural law, and specifically on the scholastic tradition,[2] as a compass that would allow them to find their way through the turbulent times the continent was experiencing.

In terms of method, I focus on an ample historical bibliography dedicated to Costa Rican independence. I work specifically on the first constitution of the Costa Rican state, called the Interim Fundamental Social Pact of the Province of Costa Rica, known as the Concordia Compact (Pacto de Concordia), promulgated on December 1, 1821. It is precisely on a comparative analysis of the historiographical framework and the constitutional text that I base my argument: the absolutism/liberalism formula used to explain independence and to understand the first steps of the new political entities is insufficient but can be complemented by an analysis of the broader legal and ideological setting that natural rights and Hispanic scholasticism provide.

The chapter is divided into three sections. The first is a brief reconstruction of political events, which serves as a context for Costa Rican independence between 1821 and 1823. In the second, I analyze the text of the 1821 constitution and propose certain points for a discussion about the basis of independence and of the state in Costa Rica. In the final section, I undertake an analysis of historiographical positions adopted by Costa Rican scholars regarding these themes. These positions serve as points of comparison and permit a critique that suggests the need for new perspectives if our understanding of the independence processes is to advance.

COSTA RICA AT THE MOMENT OF INDEPENDENCE

When we speak of Costa Rican independence, we refer to the political process that took place in what is called the Central Valley between 1821 and 1823. This area is a tectonic depression in the center of current Costa Rican territory that historically has been the most densely populated region of the country. Given its reduced population and the absence of mineral resources, Costa Rica remained administratively tied to the government of Nicaragua during the entire colonial period. The absence of a stable bureaucratic presence, except for the governor and the administrators in charge of the tobacco monopoly (Factoría de Tabaco), allowed provincial notables to develop a certain degree of autonomy.

At the time of independence in 1821, the provincial territory included some 63,000 residents.[3] About 80 percent of the total population were mestizos or mulattos, and small Indian and Creole populations made up the remainder, an ethnic breakdown that resembled that of El Salvador. Nevertheless, one particular phenomenon allowed for the growth of the unique characteristics of the sociopolitical system of the province: colonization.

Starting in the mid-eighteenth century, demographic pressures pushed some people from the capital of the province, Cartago, toward the west. The first result of this movement was the creation of new population centers, of particular importance San José, Heredia, and Alajuela. Additionally, a rural mestizo population developed, gaining access to royal lands (*tierra realenga*) and eventually managing collectively to consolidate their possessions, which in the long term meant that part of the rural population would own land privately.[4] Third, new commercial cycles took advantage of agricultural production for trade with Nicaragua and Panama, the latter being the principal commercial destination for Costa Rican trade.[5]

Four economic cycles moved the economy of Costa Rica during the eighteenth century and first half of the nineteenth. The first, based on cacao, started on the Caribbean coast in 1690 in the port of Matina and led to monetary accumulation and the development of commercial links between the provincial notables and ports to the south—Cartagena and Portobelo.[6] It is believed that toward the middle of the eighteenth century cacao production began to decline due to competition from Guayaquil and high production costs in Costa Rica. But the commercial crisis of the first half of the eighteenth century transformed the port of Matina and cacao production into a direct link with the English in Jamaica, Belize, and the Mosquito Coast. This transformation was fundamental in shaping the internal and external markets of the province. A flow of capital and products was created, starting with the bartering of cacao for European manufactured goods, which were then exchanged for the peasant surpluses of the Central Valley and marketed in Nicaragua or Panama for cash.[7]

The second cycle developed from tobacco, which since 1766 had been considered a crown monopoly and in 1782 was established as such in Costa Rica. Tobacco allowed farmers to accumulate capital and consolidated San José as the most economically powerful population center, attracting a large number of merchants and a great deal of capital at the beginning of the nineteenth century.[8]

The third cycle included sugar cane (sugar loaf, *chancaca*), brazilwood, and mining. These developed from the beginning of the nineteenth century until 1830. Capital provided by these activities was, according to Iván Molina, a start-up factor in the credit market that permitted coffee cultivation, which made up the fourth cycle, beginning in 1840.[9]

These factors, plus the opening of the port of Puntarenas in 1814, facilitated the development of an export economy that was nonetheless still separate from the main colonial commercial cycles. The distance from Guatemala and the limited interest of the crown in the province allowed for relative autonomy, reinforced by the reduced impact of Guatemalan capital, which only indirectly affected Central Valley businessmen through their activities in Nicaragua.

The period 1800–1821 shows none of the great political or military conflicts that would lead one to think of an explosion of pro-independence sentiment. In 1811, because of the protests and uprisings in Nicaragua and measures seeking to limit commerce with Panama and regulate tobacco, there were protests in Costa Rica. These were quickly controlled and showed no independence-seeking tendencies. Nor did the Napoleonic invasion and the abdication of Ferdinand VII represent motives for conflict or calls for emancipation. On the contrary, they were a reason for public ceremonies seeking to strengthen bonds with the king and to show, through cheers of "Long Live Ferdinand VII," the loyalty of the cabildo and the people.[10] The convocation to the Courts of Cádiz marks the fracturing of the empire, not as an anticolonial uprising but rather as "a political revolution in the Hispanic world and the dissolution of the Spanish monarchy,"[11] in which a reformulation of peninsular legal thinking would be of the utmost importance.[12] The heavily pactist component of the language used in this period should not then be surprising: although in the Southern Hemisphere it justified autonomist thinking and actions—questioning the legitimacy of political actions on the peninsula—more than independence movements, in Central America it signified union with the Courts.

The Courts of Cádiz influenced Central American thoughts and institutions quite significantly, and Central American participation in them should be considered an important moment. For Costa Rica, the Courts meant important internal changes, among them the recognition of San José, Heredia, and Alajuela as cities with the right to elect ayuntamientos, a key factor in later political events. A second important aspect related to the Courts was the presence of the priest Florencio del Castillo, who functioned for a time as their president and would later serve as a conduit for the transmission of new ideas expressed in the first constitutions.[13]

On an institutional scale, the formation of the Provincial Council of Nicaragua and Costa Rica (1812–14 and 1820–21), with its capital in León, allowed for the development of a certain degree of autonomy with respect to Guatemala. The council, composed of seven popularly elected members (four from Nicaragua, two from Costa Rica, and one from Nicoya), was presided over by the intendant of Nicaragua.[14] The same laws that established the provincial council limited the powers of the intendant and gave broad influence to local and regional interests.[15]

The provincial council played a key, albeit short-lived, role after the reinstatement of the Constitution of Cádiz in 1820. It began to function again on August 3, 1820, and continued to be active until the declaration of independence at the end of 1821. Taking this experience into account, independence had several layers of meaning for Costa Rica: first, it was a separation from Spain; second, a separation from Guatemala; and, on a third level, a separation from Nicaragua, to which it had been united throughout the colonial period. Border disputes and tax problems between Costa Rica and Nicaragua during the nineteenth century also developed from this logic and from their historic union.[16]

The context for independence was fully developed in 1821 with events that took place in Mexico. Since the middle of that year the Plan de Iguala had made Mexico an important actor in Central America. Mexico had not yet been considered a threat in terms of armed force, but it was clear that the advance of the plan of the three guarantees—based on the principles of independence from Spain, support of the Catholic religion, and an empire under a Bourbon prince—was important in the Kingdom of Guatemala.[17] The August signing of the Córdoba treaties accelerated the processes and forced important decisions.

Independence was declared on September 15, 1821, in Guatemala City, and this news circulated throughout the region, along with a call for the establishment of a congress to decide on the possibility of annexation to Mexico. The sentiment behind the pronouncement was clear: it stated in the first article that the declaration was carried out to "prevent the terrible consequences which would ensue if the people themselves were to make the same proclamation."[18]

The independence declaration traveled the isthmus and reached Nicaragua on September 28, where the Acta de los nublados was added, which declared independence from Guatemala and only provisionally from Spain "until the clouds lift."[19] Both documents reached Costa Rica on October 13, where the reaction of the ayuntamientos and existing uncertainty led the Cartago cabildo and the governor of the province, Juan Manuel de Cañas, to convoke a meeting with representatives from important towns, including all of those with ayuntamientos.

As a result of this meeting, on October 29 Costa Rican independence was declared, refusing union with Guatemala or Nicaragua. Nonetheless, discussion continued on three possible positions: union with Mexico, Guatemala, or Colombia. This lack of definition was formalized in the first constitution of the province, promulgated on December 1, known as the Concordia Compact. The Compact declared that Costa Rica had the right to organize itself using the form of government it considered best and recognized the civil rights of its residents, but it postponed a decision on which state or federated system it would join.[20]

According to the Compact, the capital of Costa Rica was to alternate every three months among the four principal cities. The first provincial elections were undertaken almost immediately, and the members of the first superior governmental junta (*junta superior gobernativa*) were elected. Members took office on January 13,

1822, and adopted a commission system to address the most pressing problems. Given the attitude of Heredia, which separated itself from the province after questioning the legitimacy of the Compact and joined León, the first urgent problem posed was the question of annexation to Mexico. León had a strong interest in maintaining the territory that had been ruled by the provincial council under its control, and it had already voted for annexation to the empire.[21]

On January 5, 1822, under the threat of Mexican troops, Guatemala declared union with the Mexican Empire. When that news reached Costa Rica, the first junta superior modified the Concordia Compact, and in the latter half of the year the province officially joined the empire.[22] The first election of representatives to the Mexican courts was held on March 10, 1822, and José Francisco Peralta was elected; he was not able to serve and was replaced by Presbitero Florencio del Castillo, who lived in Oaxaca.[23]

The decision on March 21 by Agustín de Iturbide to close the courts prevented the promulgation of a constitution and caused a feeling of instability among the ayuntamientos in the Costa Rican province.[24] Another election at the end of 1822, for the members of the second junta superior, changed the balance of power and allowed the promulgation of a new constitutional document, known as the First Political Statute of the Province of Costa Rica, approved on March 19, 1823. The capital would be returned to Cartago and the government would fall back to a group of three individuals known as "the triumvirate." But the first article implied the greatest change, declaring the province free and independent, thereby returning uncertainty about any future union "with an American power that it would be convenient to join."[25]

A short time later, on March 29, a group of men seeking annexation to Mexico and led by Joaquín Oreamuno captured the Cartago arsenal. This led to the first armed conflict after independence, called the battle of Ochomogo, named after the mountain where the fighting took place. The forces of San José and Alajuela defeated those from Cartago, a loss for those who supported annexation to Mexico. After this, a new assembly was convened, elected members of the third junta superior gobernativa, and approved the Second Political Statute of the Province of Costa Rica, on May 16, 1823.[26] The capital was transferred from Cartago to San José. Heredia rejoined the provincial compact after a military occupation and was later invited to join the provincial assembly.[27]

Thanks to the departure of Mexican troops from Central America, the National Constituent Assembly was convened and on July 1, 1823, declared the provinces of what had been the audiencia of Guatemala to be absolutely independent. Costa Rican representatives were elected in September of that year, and on October 8 the provincial assembly declared itself in favor of the union, thereby dissolving itself.

The third junta superior continued to function until the end of 1824, and the first constitution of the state of Costa Rica as part of the federation was written and approved, then promulgated, on January 25, 1825.

NATURAL LAW, INDEPENDENCE, AND NEW POLITICAL ENTITIES

The interpretive transformations regarding Central American political evolution have permitted the continued existence of a very simplified vision of the sociopolitical and ideological process of independence. A supposed division between liberals and conservatives has dominated the analysis of the entire nineteenth century, reducing the political options to just a fragment of the spectrum of their possible relationships, thoughts, and goals. That criticism was put forth by Adolfo Bonilla several years ago, although, as Víctor Hugo Acuña points out, his typology of political thinking can be criticized for its rigidity.[28]

It is impossible to deny the importance of the Cádiz Constitution and its role in the spread of an early Hispanic liberalism, heir to a process of "hispanization" of Enlightenment thought.[29] Nor can we overlook the weight of Mexican independence, the Plan de Iguala, and the treaties of Córdoba in the decision the ayuntamientos of Central America made to become independent, as Mario Vázquez Olivera points out. The work of Dym and Avendaño regarding the intensity and role of the ayuntamientos in the process has helped to clarify a previously understudied aspect of Central American political and social dynamics in this period.

Nonetheless, these interpretations have not delved into the apparent contradiction between the spirit and reality of the purportedly liberal policies of the Central American isthmus, which, additionally, in most cases were applied by governments considered to be openly conservative. Although it would appear that liberalism was not dominant in the declarations of independence, it nonetheless seems to maintain a central role in explanations of the independence process.[30] The tendency to give liberalism such an important place began with the absolutism/liberalism binary initially discussed in the classic work of Miguel Artola that analyzed the impact of the revolutionary aspects of Cádiz thought.[31] It would later be adapted to studies of independence and political thought in Central America through research undertaken into the works of Marure and Montufar.

It is clear that with the passage of time, and with the presence of liberal political systems and liberal economic policies in a context of integration with international commercial cycles, liberalism became consolidated as an ideological position. But this did not occur until the second half of the nineteenth century, and in some cases, such as in Nicaragua, until the start of the twentieth—yet liberalism was nonetheless considered to be a viable explanation for the independence process.

The absolutism versus liberalism (or conservatism versus liberalism) formula is insufficient as a model for explaining independence and later political plans and proposals.[32] As Rabinovich put it, "Political reality was not marked by the linear installation of a designated state order, but rather by the confrontation . . . of a multiplicity of diverging plans, some of which prospered while the majority succumbed."[33]

From Texas to Buenos Aires and Santiago a series of juntas, towns, and congresses and a great number of political and military leaders declared independence in a thousand different ways, both written and oral. Out of hundreds of plans—republican, monarchical, federal, and so on—only a handful developed into stable political entities. Their foundational document, the constitution, was transformed into a code, necessary for understanding the different languages, ideas, and sociopolitical plans that informed each polity. Cases like the Republic of Texas, the Republic of Franklin (now Tennessee), the Republic of Río Grande do Sul, and the State of Los Altos in Guatemala are clear examples of failed plans that demonstrate the broad range of the ideas appearing during the period of independence and of the constitutions that began to appear in the last twenty-five years of the eighteenth century.[34]

Independence did not immediately give birth to solidified nation-states. Comparative studies have concluded that the colonial rupture that began in 1808 produced, only fortuitously and via a thoroughly tortuous road, independence.[35] That being the case, it is worth asking what elements kept the ayuntamientos of the Central Valley of Costa Rica together. Also, was liberalism truly what drove and molded society after independence? A quick glance at constitutional texts suggests that there is a much broader framework in which political thought of the epoch was moving, which is precisely the framework of natural law from which liberalism derives. The Hispanic scholastic thought of Suárez and Mariana was important not only for the *translatio imperii* formulation[36] but also for reinterpreting the idea of the state through the Thomist principle of distributive justice as it applied to the formation of the first public treasuries, laws, and the political community in general.[37]

The first constitution of the State of Costa Rica, the so-called Concordia Compact of December 1, 1821, provides an important clue in this respect. The text that introduces the document declares "In the name of the All-powerful God the Father, Son and Holy Spirit, Author and Supreme Legislator of Society," whereby, as people find themselves free to constitute themselves into the form of government which seems best to them, the province desires to "remain free, united, secure and tranquil through a pact of union and concord." Even clearer is the second article of the constitution, which declares that "the Province recognizes and respects civil liberty, property and other natural rights, legitimate for all persons and for any People or Nation.[38]

The term "concord" is repeated in the text and in other sources where the reference is made not only as concerns the constitution but also as an action—in the sense of "we shall arrive at concord"—and more commonly in relation to its synonyms "peace," "agreement," and "conciliation." The most common definition in the 1817 Real Academia Española dictionary of the term *concordia* (*aptare, acommodare*) is "conciliate and adjust that which is unequal, discordant or contrary." It implies "coordination, combination, or conciliation of different things (*combinatio, conciliato, conformatio*).[39]

But the term has an even deeper meaning when we delve into Spanish scholastic, Thomist, and even Aristotelian thought. At the start of the discussion lies this question: What is the *effective cause* of the existence of a political community at the beginning of 1821, that is, a cause as a principle of existence, of reality, of the subsequent state?[40] It is clear that the material cause of the existence of a political community in Costa Rica has been demonstrated to be a result of historical experience, either of social ties studied by Stone and Madrigal or of internal markets, economy, and communities studied by Molina, Gudmundson, Solórzano, Acuña, Fonseca, Alvarenga, and others. But I would argue, based on this reading, that the articulation of historical reality into an effective cause of the state was possible only through a specific ideological articulation, a plan of concord in the terms understood by Hispanic scholasticism. Historical reality does not exist independently of an ideological framework that is imprinted on customs and thought.

A reinterpretation of society and of the formation of the state in Costa Rica that begins from the knowledge and understandings held by the people who formed part of that society and who lived through the processes associated with state formation would be one possible result of the above discussion and of the answers to the question posed. To Aristotle, and therefore to the Schoolmen, concord can be translated as "political community." Concord, according to Aristotle, is very similar to "civil friendship," since it is in essence like being among friends.[41] "Friends respect each other, and because of that respect tolerate errors and excesses inherent in any mistakes, and friends above all share in projects, which is the cause of that friendship: a project that comes to be the very reason for its existence and well-being."[42]

Concord is wanting something in common, as St. Thomas said of the *societas*, as in "doing something in common," in the powerful sense of living in common.[43] The community—the state—is then natural to the individual, and natural or "distributive" rights assure the common good, which is the happiness of each person according to his merit.[44] Concord can be understood in general terms as peace, which assures the common good, prosperity, and conservation of the community.[45] It can also be understood as an effective operative cause of the state in the sense of the need to enforce common rules to promote and protect social cooperation and effective distribution of commonly held goods.

Scholastics such as Vitoria and Mariana understood the state based on the logic that social cooperation generates the appearance of common goods (common property goods such as land) which, if they exist, must be distributed following general criteria derived from distributive justice—not equitable distribution but rather distribution according to merit, "whereby he who contributes the most shall receive the most."[46] There are naturally existing rules to promote and protect social cooperation. These social rules require institutions run by men who will concern themselves with the collection of economic resources that should be taken from those who participate in the concord, also with a distributive justice criterion, so that he who has the most shall pay the most.[47]

To understand the state in the sense understood by the men who were confronted with the need to make decisions in 1821, we must explain more clearly and convincingly the historical reality of the independence moment and of ensuing events. Rethinking scholasticism as an ideological and political basis for states also permits the development of more flexible analytical frameworks and the possibility of sorting out the eternal analytical contradictions. What I propose so far is merely a call to discuss and analyze conditions that are much more complex than have so far been observed, in a fundamental period of American and peninsular history. It is the period of independence, of the definition of the paths to be taken, and of the formation of political entities, which in Central America covers the years between 1808 and 1849.

HISTORIOGRAPHICAL POSITIONS ON THE MEANING OF INDEPENDENCE IN COSTA RICA

An important part of my proposed exercise requires understanding the form in which Costa Rican independence has been defined. A deeper understanding of the discussions surrounding independence will allow a closer look at the particularities of the process, and also at the problems present at the heart of Central American historiography of this period. A historiographical discussion becomes important for what I argue in this chapter, that an integral understanding of the independence processes entails reconciling their local and regional dimensions, which in turn requires understanding the intractable problems inherited from the ways in which national historiographies have defined independence itself.

Liberal historiography in Costa Rica began with the work of Guatemalan Felipe Molina, who in the 1850s was a state diplomat. His ideas owed a great deal to positions taken by Rafael Francisco de Osejo, a Nicaraguan actively involved in the events of 1821–23 and a professor at the Casa de Enseñanza de Santo Tomás in San José.[48] Following Osejo, Molina stressed the importance of the federal republic for the subsequent formation of the state, a topic that remains open for discussion in the twenty-first century since national historiographies still dominate all Central American countries. For both intellectuals, effective independence began with the promulgation of the first federal constitution of the State of Costa Rica in 1825.[49]

Molina's work coherently articulated the thinking that had developed in Costa Rican political discourse since independence. According to this interpretation, the isolation Costa Rica suffered in colonial times had produced a hard-working, peaceful people, respectful of law and ethnically homogeneous—an argument that articulates the discourse of nation in the second half of the nineteenth century. The complete expression of Molina's arguments had a teleological and liberal tone, that independence was the "destiny of the people."

At the end of the nineteenth century, Francisco Montero Barrantes and Joaquín Bernardo Calvo reintroduced Molina's ideas with certain important changes. The work undertaken by Calvo was the first in Costa Rica to recognize independence in an American context, proposing the influence of French Enlightenment thinkers and North American independence supporters on Hispanic American movements while completely erasing all reference to natural law or the Schoolmen. Independence ceased to be "the destiny" of the people and became a "natural tendency" derived from political thought of the epoch—especially French, British, or American thought.[50]

One difference between the works of Molina and Calvo is in the weight of the "people" in independence movements. Molina stated that Central America had "the singular fortune of accomplishing such an important change on the pure strength of events, without the slightest of battles." Calvo, however, recalled the antitax movements of 1811 and 1812 in El Salvador and Nicaragua as preambles to independence. These movements demonstrated the interests of those who "with patriotism and unbreakable faith proposed to lead [the independence process] in the conquest of their rights and liberties."[51]

This conquest had not been gained by the people through wars or rebellion, as had been the case in Río de la Plata or Mexico, but rather promulgated at the initiative of government officials and cabildo notables as a consequence of the Plan de Iguala and Mexican independence. Costa Rica, like the rest of the region, had been a passive receptor of independence, which left a contradiction in the explanation proposed by Calvo. How could independence be explained as a struggle by the people if there had been no real armed conflict? The solution was to be found in the political actions undertaken by Costa Rican society.

Such authors as Ricardo Fernández Guardia, Manuel de Jesús Jiménez, Pedro Pérez Zeledón, and Francisco María Iglesias broadened and improved the chronology of events of the independence movement.[52] Based on their explanation, society could be divided between a tendency toward "imperialism" or "conservatism," identified with Cartago, and another, "republican" or "liberal," associated with San José. The events of the independence movement and later struggles were not just a "natural tendency" and consequences of outside influences but also—and this corrected the contradiction in Calvo—reflected an internal confrontation between the two political tendencies. Costa Rican independence grew from the conflict between the new order and the old, between progress and backwardness, which would end in the triumph of liberalism, a position late nineteenth-century nationalist rhetoric would support—and one that reinforced the explanatory force of the conservatism/liberalism (absolutism/liberalism) binary mentioned above.

In the 1940s and 1950s, Carlos Monge, Rodrigo Facio, and Hernán Peralta revised liberal arguments.[53] Monge, along with his student Rodrigo Facio, established the bases of social democratic thought. What resulted was a break with the past and a new form of doing history that accompanied the formation of the University of Costa Rica in 1940.[54]

According to these new arguments, during the colonial period a system of property ownership allowed "rural democracy" to be shaped. This was possible because of the poverty in which the "Costa Rican settler subsisted, resources dwindling daily, descending every day to the deepest levels of misery."[55] Poverty weakened the control of the government over the land colonization process west of the Central Valley, resulting in the formation of small property-holding systems.

According to this explanation, rural democracy promoted an ethnically homogeneous population, which Facio argued would be a secondary but important factor for Costa Rican stability.[56] This argument assumed that to the main tenets of the liberal position—industriousness, pacifism, and population homogeneity—should be added poverty and small landholdings as the basis for a feeling of "brotherhood," which could bind an existing nation to the independence movement.

According to Monge and Facio, after independence liberal capitalism led a process that began to dismantle small landholdings, striking at the roots of Costa Rican society. The criticism developed by Facio was not directed against political liberalism, which to him was a synonym for "democratic institutions," but rather against economic liberalism that with the establishment of a laissez-faire policy reduced interest in collective action.[57]

Independence, according to Facio, was caused by both external and internal factors. Reviving the dichotomy between San José and Cartago established at the beginning of the century, Facio put forward an economic explanation of the process, complementary to the political/ideological one. The existence of conservatives in Cartago was also an indication of economic backwardness and of the "dictatorship" of the old regime. The emancipation movement began when San José decided to take the reins in choosing the path the country would follow, taking advantage of the spaces opened by American emancipation movements.

October 29, 1821, is recognized as the official date of independence in Costa Rica, whereby it distinguishes itself from Central American independence. That separation from the region is what gives Costa Rican society unique attributes. From there, it is a short step to the denial of Central American nationality: the nation proceeded from the colonial period as a fragment of Spanish nationality. And these are the two axes that articulated the republican separatism that explains most of Costa Rican political behavior from the nineteenth century onward.[58]

According to Hernán Peralta, the Concordia Compact is considered the first constitution, and this idea established a new independence chronology. Independence thus began with the signing of the 1821 act and lasted until the conflicts among the cities of the Central Valley came to an end with the battle of Ochomogo in 1823. Peralta argued, and was seconded by Eugenio Rodríguez, Samuel Stone, and José Luis Vega Carballo, that with the victory of San José over Cartago a new stage of republicanism began that would affirm independence, and with it liberalism, as the basis of the constitution of the state.[59]

In the 1970s and 1980s, Francisco Gamboa and Rodolfo Cerdas introduced some modifications to this scenario, but with the same intention.[60] The first described Cartago and Heredia as bastions of a "feudal mode" that would clash with the positions of Alajuela and San José, whose more dynamic economies made them better "friends of liberty."[61] The latter author, more influential, would more clearly articulate previous arguments contrasting the closed feudal economies of Cartago and Heredia with the open capitalistic ones of San José and Alajuela. According to Cerdas, independence and the rise of the Costa Rican state could be explained by the triumph of the liberal economy in San José and Alajuela, in need of links with foreign markets, over the closed, aristocratic-type market deeply rooted in the old dominant provincial class of Cartago and Heredia.[62]

To sum up, this was the result of a class struggle and a struggle between economic systems. The influence of the Cerdas thesis is recognizable in the works of Rafael Obregón Loría, Rose Marie Karpinsky, Mario Samper, Manuel Calderón, Yamileth González, and Matilde Cerdas.[63] The main criticism of this position was made by José Luis Vega Carballo, who pointed out that the conflicts of the first twenty years of life under independence do not seem to be class struggles but rather conflicts within one social grouping, one single class.[64] During the 1980s and 1990s, historical works focused on reviewing these positions in depth to demystify the period and give it new meaning, a task undertaken from any number of economic and political angles. The works of Víctor Hugo Acuña, Juan Carlos Solórzano, Iván Molina, Mario Samper, Lowell Gudmundson, and Rico Aldave, among others, clarified key aspects of the indicated arguments.[65] These works allowed the development of a new position in the face of independence as "the unraveling of the colonial pact," in a society that did not fit the models of an egalitarian rural democracy suggested by Monge and Facio. For these authors, independence was the product of a combination of internal and external conditions, not simply a struggle between liberals and conservatives, although they still considered liberalism to be the main precursor to and actor in the historical moment.

By the end of the 1980s, for Iván Molina "the independence movement was the fruit of the re-conquest of Spanish America undertaken after 1765 through the Bourbon reforms," a movement with a continental character.[66] According to Juan Rafael Quesada, this began with the desires of the Creoles to separate themselves from the metropolis that oppressed them.[67] Old arguments and the San José-Cartago dichotomy were readjusted to the new position so that, now, localism inherited from the colonial order would intrude on the formation of a centralized state, the main intention of liberal intellectuals of the time. The installation of San José as capital would be decisive in the consolidation of state power.

The historiography of the 1990s analyzed the shaping of state and society to the degree that it accompanied the consolidation of agrarian capitalism, which was transforming old "colonial inheritances" into new liberal institutions, thanks to coffee.[68] As a result, a more carefully considered position regarding the causes and consequences of independence was coming to be defined. Viewed within a much larger framework, independence was the result of the complex development of European politics and economics that led to the crisis of the Spanish monarchy and to the questioning of the colonial pact beginning in 1808, within a context of a rural transformation pushed forward by agrarian capitalism.

By the end of the 1990s, Héctor Pérez Brignoli stated that "unlike the rest of Hispanic America, in Central America the process of independence was bloodless and actually precipitated by events in Mexico."[69] So "independence was the unexpected fruit of the social wildfire devouring South America and Mexico," and the result for Costa Rica was the posing of "a difficult dilemma: What place—Cartago, Heredia, San José or Alajuela—was to be the seat of future power?"[70] Localism was the immediate result of the process of independence and molded the sociopolitical structures of the state, causing conflicts in the first half of the nineteenth century—1823, 1826, 1835, and 1847–48.

A parallel tendency, also begun in the 1990s and deeply imbued with the ideas of Benedict Anderson, complemented the positions of Molina and Pérez Brignoli in a discussion of the origins of the nation in Costa Rica.[71] Without entering into specific arguments, some new elements in this discussion can be identified. First, the situation in 1808–12 showed that, far from holding a discussion about emancipation, the region stayed faithful to the crown; the discourse of independence and "liberalism" came up only after the signing of the Independence Act in 1821.[72] Second, by the 1840s a national discourse was beginning to consolidate itself, at least in the minds of Central Valley notables.[73] This adds coherence to the position, already defended in the 1970s by José Luis Vega Carballo, that armed conflicts in the province pitted members of a single group, rather than of differentiated and antagonistic factions, against one another. Developing its liberal thinking at the beginning of the nineteenth century, this group molded itself into a cohesive social unit.[74]

The weight of liberal thought in works after the 1980s owes a great deal to the interpretations of Mario Rodríguez and Adolfo Bonilla.[75] Rodriguez made the argument, recently taken up by Víctor Hugo Acuña, that Central American liberalism was a direct outgrowth of the thinking developed in Cádiz, and hence a specific Hispanic adaptation of Enlightenment thought, with notably less radical positions. According to Bonilla, the commonly cited division between conservatives and liberals never existed in reality, since both shared a set of ideas that drew heavily from Enlightenment thinking. In his classification of political thought and proposals, Bonilla included everything from reformed absolutism to republicanism.

Víctor Hugo Acuña synthesizes some of the most important interpretations regarding Central American independence and proposes that "independence in Central America was not the result of a war for independence, nor of important demands or mobilizations for independence." Movements from 1811 to 1814 in El Salvador and Guatemala cannot be considered as supporting emancipation. "Therefore, without real political or military mobilizations in its favor, independence became possible in Central America only when the process in Mexico became irreversible," so it was a direct consequence of the Plan de Iguala and the treaties of Córdoba.[76]

According to Jordana Dym, "The process or processes of independence in Central America did not develop within the margins of the narrative of struggles against imperial forces."[77] It was a "war of words" that showed up in accords, acts, decrees, and endless other manifestations. Together, these show the dynamics of a region that achieved independence as part of the dissolution of the colonial pact and the later reconstruction of pacts by "the people."

Four factors explain the process of independence in Central America, according to Dym:

First and foremost, there was not a revolution in opposition to a Spanish or Mexican army. Second, the process did not begin in the center or in the capital and then spread throughout the colony; on the contrary, it was a process which began on the peripheries, then spread simultaneously throughout the territory. Third, the main actors favoring Central American independence were not only Creoles and social elites but also royal officials. Fourth and final, Central American independence processes achieved their goals not by declarations from new authorities but through accords and acts approved by legitimate imperial institutions and authorities.

These last documents were approved between August and November 1821.[78]

Such factors, according to Xiomara Avendaño, allowed for the maintenance of an estate-based society that continued forward from the colonial period with its institutions intact. These positions favor the idea that the period 1821–23 can be conceived of as a moment in which power was politically redefined, culminating with the consolidation of the principal regional centers and of liberal leaders as well as the confirmation of independence in 1823.[79]

The works of Mario Vázquez show the sympathy felt for the plan of the Three Guarantees (Tres garantías, another name for the Plan de Iguala) and the interest generated in Guatemala over forming a union with the Mexican Empire, although conflicts also intensified between the capital city and some groups of regional notables who did not want to remain under its control. After 1821, two important positions were in competition: one based on the Plan de Iguala managed to influence several provinces that seceded and joined the empire; the other brought together those who favored the September 15 act. Defenders of the latter position argued that Guatemala owed nothing to Mexico and that it was urgent to declare absolute independence, united as an autonomous political entity. Finally, Vázquez concludes that the participation of Mexico as it tried to expand its actions and influence in what had been the Kingdom of Guatemala contributed to the "fragmenting actions of regional separatism, completely transforming the political order . . . and leading to its dismemberment . . . bringing it to the brink of civil war."[80]

In another study, Pablo A. Rodríguez analyzes the redrawing of the governing pact in Costa Rica as an internally negotiated process, heavily influenced by pressure that originated in regional dynamics and by the conviction that Costa Rica could not be a viable political body.[81] This condition, along with the marginal position of the province, allowed its first popular assembly (Asamblea de Pueblos) to devise its own pact, which proved to be important in the thinking of provincial leaders when faced with the possibility of adherence to the Mexican Empire of

Agustín Iturbide. According to José Santos Lombardo, "Costa Rica should not be counted among the provinces that adhered following the Plan de Iguala and the Córdoba Treaties [in 1821], since it did so under the Pact constituted in its condition of absolute liberty and independence."[82] Taking into account these discussions and works, it becomes evident that independence is a much more complex process than that often presented, and that historians are only beginning to rethink its meanings.

CONCLUSION

The historiographical perspectives discussed in this chapter allow an understanding that goes beyond the political facts behind independence; they open up space for questioning the basis upon which the concept of independence has been defined and for considering its ideological importance. Understanding independence in Central America requires a broad and complex research process that must include reinterpreting the particularities of the period from a perspective that gives weight to the ideological framework in which political actors, the authors of the documents that would give birth to each new state, were enmeshed. The discussion of how Costa Rican historiography has understood independence demonstrates a situation, common to the rest of the Central American cases, in which the tension among explanatory models has nearly completely erased references to the political and economic ideas of the time, and to the cultural ambience of the 1820s. The result has been a series of national historiographies, with little or no communication among themselves.

Broader explanations have corrected some of the most evident problems and facilitated a more general understanding of the independence period. Nonetheless, many of the explanatory problems mentioned above persist, principally the tendency to consider Central American independence as a phenomenon eminently produced by external causes. Although the Mexican process played a role in Central America, independence in the region cannot be understood without also taking into account complex internal dynamics that took place in spaces within each of the major territorial divisions, in the frontier spaces these territories shared, and in the different regions within these territories. The economic, social, and cultural cycles that profoundly modified all of the societies of the isthmus must also be considered.

An analytical review of the historiographical discussion surrounding independence in Costa Rica allows for a clearer observation of the processes which, throughout history, defined that moment as a phenomenon, given that the definition has been deeply influenced by changes and by the thinking of each epoch. One conclusion that can be drawn is that independence has played an ideological role throughout Costa Rican history, helping to justify or criticize economic, political, or cultural models. This ideological use of history has also impeded analyses of the independence period that go beyond discussions of the political. For the liberals, for example, independence meant a break with the colony, understood as a period of backwardness, thus explaining why scholastic thought disappeared as a significant element in historical depictions of the period. But this absence also makes evident the role the colonial powers of the time held in the imposition of visions of how the "Atlantic revolutions" developed and the theoretical references that inspired them.

This reflection should not lead researchers to forget another important conclusion: there is still much territory to be covered to explain independence in Central America fully. If the more general phenomena are very clear, such as those structural factors related to the imperial crisis or the role of Mexico in relation to the decision to declare independence, other aspect are less evident, such as the influence of scholasticism in the thinking that inspired the constitutions written in this period, the institutional conformation of states, or the deeply set regional relationships that ended up assuring that one decision be taken rather than others. These are not minor issues but rather of significant import for analysis since they could force a reinterpretation of some of the explanations more commonly accepted in the region and of the manner in which the subsequent processes of state formation are understood. In the end, this chapter offers more questions than answers, hoping to incite a change in the analytical perspective used to study independence in Central America, beginning with the demonstration that many of the ideas regarding this period should be rethought and that efforts must be made to reconcile local and regional spaces. Any researcher who desires to understand these phenomena must take these two scales into account in order to obtain more general and more complete explanations of Central American independence.

NOTES

Epigraph. Morón, *Historia*, 5.126–29.

1. The Acta de los nublados, literally the "Clouds Act," was the declaration made by the provincial council of León in response to the September 15 Independence Act signed in Guatemala City. In it, the council declared independence from Spain, "until the clouds are lifted." Further discussion follows. [Editor's note]
2. On this theme, see Giménez, "Doctrinas"; García, "Raíces"; Chiaramonte, "Principle," and *Fundamentos*; Portillo, *Crisis*; Molina, "Cabildos," and "Pactismo"; Paquette, "Dissolution"; and Armitage, "Declaraciones."
3. This is an estimated figure based on data from Pérez Brignoli, who indicates that in 1824 there were 65,000 residents in Costa Rica. Pérez Brignoli, *Población*, 180.
4. Fonseca, *Costa Rica*, 72–98, 285–312; Solórzano et al., *Costa Rica*; Rodríguez, "Estado, colonización."
5. Solórzano et al., *Costa Rica*, 241–58.
6. Ibid., 249–79.
7. Solórzano, "Comercio"; Chacón, "Cacao."
8. Rico, "Renta." According to Rico Aldave, the control of production by the royal monopoly avoided the development of a sector of large merchants and producers, helping to assure that income was better distributed among medium-size and small growers, facilitating improvements in their social positions, and shoring up a peasant sector with economic resources that would later invest in sugar cane.
9. Molina, *Costa Rica*, 181–281. The importance of silver contraband should not, however, be underestimated. Discovered in the 1820s, silver mines were, according to Frederick Chatfield, English consul in 1830, the reason for a strong contraband business, valued at up to 300,000 pesos, which passed through Matina. Public Record Office, Foreign Office, The National Archives, London, 21, vol. 12, fol. 43.
10. In 1809 the Cartago cabildo presented a theatrical performance honoring and showing its loyalty to the deposed king. This work, undertaken "with our greatest pleasure in ceremonies so deserved by the sovereign, our principal object," shows that thinking of independence as a time to be "longed for" is a very simple reading, and ultimately a mistaken one, of a much more complex process. See Díaz, "Comunidad," 5.
11. Rodríguez, *Independencia*, 25.
12. Guerra, *Modernidad*.
13. Some of these new ideas are cash consolidation, annual budgeting, fiscal and administrative centralization, and the delegation of power through representation (involving the division of powers). In this sense, one of the greatest impacts of Cádiz is felt through the new fiscal ideas that transformed the relationship between government and the people. Rodríguez, *Cuestión*.
14. The area known as Nicoya, located in the northwestern part of present-day Costa Rica, only officially became part of its territory in 1824 and would continue to be a cause of conflicts and disagreements between Costa Rica and Nicaragua throughout the nineteenth century.
15. Rodríguez, "Estado, fiscalidad," 58–61.

16. On border problems in both states, see Obregón, *Río San Juan*; and Sibaja, *Del Cañas-Jerez*.
17. Vázquez, "Plan de Iguala . . . de Guatemala," 398.
18. Acta de independencia de Guatemala 1821, Costa Rica National Archive, www.archivonacional.go.cr/index.php?option=com_content&view=article&id=86:acta-de-independencia&catid=40:rincon-pedagogico&Itemid=56.
19. Nicaraguans had been interested, from the moment that the intendencias were created, to achieve autonomy with respect to Guatemala. Plans from León were to form a single political unit along with Nicoya and Costa Rica, possibly including Comayagua, which maintained historical ties to Nicaragua. Even at this early date, then, independence from Guatemala was more important than from Spain, which was "conditioned" by circumstances. To read the contemporary texts and discussions, see Gámez, *Historia moderna*, 41–61.
20. Although the Costa Rican independence act declared separation from Spain and union with Mexico, the first constitution of the state, signed on December 1, 1821, annulled this decision, leaving clear the possibility of union with any *American* power thought to be appropriate. Costa Rican leaders principally considered joining Mexico, but Colombia was always on the horizon, and in 1823 they attempted to declare union with their southern neighbor, though this initiative would never come to fruition. Soto, "Costa Rica," 29n12; "Pacto Social Fundamental Interino de la Provincia de Costa Rica," in Obregón, *Constituciones*, 1.92.
21. The news that elections for imperial court representatives had been convened, published on November 27, 1821, in *La Gaceta Imperial Extraordinaria de México*, was given to the junta superior by the political chief of Nicaragua, then sent to the provincial ayuntamientos. Archivo Nacional de Costa Rica (hereafter ANCR), Provincial Independiente, exp. 363.
22. "Pacto Social Fundamental Interino de la Provincia de Costa Rica (reformado)," in Obregón, *Constituciones*, 1.108.
23. Obregón, *Proceso*, 50.
24. Ibid.
25. "Primer Estatuto Político de la Provincia de Costa Rica," in Obregón, *Constituciones*, 1.124.
26. "Segundo Estatuto Político de la Provincia de Costa Rica," in ibid., 1.135.
27. ANCR, Provincial Independiente, exp. 618, fol. 7, and exp. 1224, fol. 1.
28. Acuña, "Liberalismo," 121.
29. Breña, *Primer*, 28–34.
30. An analysis of land and property policies in Costa Rica and El Salvador suggests that liberal measures for land privatization were not applied until mid-century. In Costa Rica, the first laws on land privatization came into effect in the 1840s, and evidence shows that the purchase and existence of communal lands was still allowed into the 1850s. In 1851 the town of Palmares bought a large amount of land as a collective, following the eighteenth-century pattern. In El Salvador the law of "extinction of communities" (1881) and the "law of extinction of common lands [*ejidos*]" (1882) began the process of land privatization. See ANCR, Hacienda 16840, fols. 25, 25v, 32; Portillo, "Revisión," 4–6, 18; Rodríguez, "Estado, colonización."

31. Artola, *Orígenes*, vol. 1. Artola does not address the subject of America in this book.
32. As Arturo Taracena points out, the term "conservative," in reference to the political factions in Central America, appeared only with the publication of the *Toro Amarillo* by Juan José de Aycinena in the 1830s. Taracena, *Primera*, xi–xii.
33. Rabinovich, "Máquina," 4.
34. Taracena, *Estado*, and *Invención*; Barcellos, "Textos"; Guedea, *Textos*, 60–65; Armitage, "Declaraciones," 24–25.
35. Guerra, *Modernidad*; Rodríguez, *Independencia*; Portillo, *Crisis*; Ávila and Pérez, *Experiencias*; Paquette, "Dissolution"; Lucena, *Naciones*; Pérez, *Elegía*.
36. For scholasticism the pact is carried out between the prince and the community, a duality sealed by the very act of subjection (*pactum subjectionis*; *pactum societatis* would make no sense). This implied the fulfillment of obligations related to the common good that are to be found in principles of natural law. It opens a deep discussion of scholastic political theory developed from the idea of obedience and resistance, and in the end tyrannicide, based on the intensity of the transfer of sovereignty or power from the community to the prince. According to Vitoria or Suárez, once the *translatio imperii* was completed, power rested solely with the prince; for Mariana, power continued to reside in both parties, ensuring the foundations of the *pactum translationis* (compare to Herrera, this volume). The Costa Rican Concordia Compact assured the transfer of sovereignty from the people, by means of a system of elections, to "their parish electors, and from them to those of the district . . . to sanction this pact." And if the members of the junta exceeded the rights given to them in the pact, "they would commit a crime as charged by the people [*de acusación popular*]." "Pacto Social Fundamental Interino de la Provincia de Costa Rica," in Obregón, *Constituciones*, 1.94–102; Varela, *Teoría*, 67; Chiaramonte, *Nación*, 151; Tanzi, "Fuentes."
37. Roover, "Economía"; Chafuen, "Justicia"; Molina, "Cabildos."
38. "Pacto Social Fundamental Interino de la Provincia de Costa Rica," in Obregón, *Constituciones*, 1.91–92. Note that this article recognizes private property as a natural right, in contrast to liberal principles that hold that property is not subject to natural (distributive) rights but rather to civil (commutative) rights (see Chafuen, "Justicia," 5–6), since it is in the marketplace that its sale should be regulated, and not as part of a principle of redistributive justice. Moreover, it recognizes natural rights among persons and among peoples or nations, making way for the application of the law of nations (*ius gentium*) in relationships among political entities. This element is also present in the constitutions of 1822 and 1823.
39. *Diccionario de la lengua Castellana* (1817), 1.221.
40. This analysis considers the Aristotelian use of *causa* as the principle of the reality or existence of something and at the same time reviews the same principle of cause in St. Thomas. But since that discussion falls beyond the parameters of this chapter, the philosophical analysis of these categories cannot be particularly rigorous. Additionally, the term *causa* is used as analogous to "state," since in Aristotelian and Thomist thought only that which has substance exists.
41. Aristóteles, *Ética*, 245.
42. Cadavid, "Concordia," 65.

43. For St. Thomas, man is an animal that cannot survive without living in a group. Society can be described as the coming together of human beings to carry out work in community. Aquino, *Comentario*, 514–16.
44. Chafuen, "Justicia," 10; García, "Raíces," 70.
45. Cadavid, "Concordia," 65–66. All of these are recurring elements in Costa Rican political discourse during the first half of the century and constituted the basis on which nationalistic discourse would later be constructed. See Acuña, "Historia."
46. This principle may help us comprehend an articulation of an idea of citizenship that permits distributing merit according to the political or economic participation undertaken by people in society, which in turn may be useful for a discussion of the definitions of "citizenship" and of electoral systems in Central America.
47. Chafuen, "Justicia."
48. This was the first educational institution in the province. See Osejo, *Lecciones*; and Dachner, "De la individualidad," 109–12.
49. According to Molina, this was the "day when Costa Rica should be seen as a free society, led by a regular government." Molina, *República de Costa Rica*, 18. The first version of the text, published in the United States, was called *República de Costa Rica. Apuntamientos para su historia*; the version published in Spain was titled *Bosquejo histórico de la República de Costa Rica*.
50. Calvo, *Apuntamientos*, 233–34; Montero, *Elementos*, vol. 1.
51. Molina, *República de Costa Rica*, 17; Calvo, *Apuntamientos*, 235.
52. Fernández Guardia, *Independencia*; Jiménez, "Año"; Pérez, "Gregorio José Ramírez"; Iglesias, *Documentos*.
53. Monge, *Historia*; Facio, "Esquema"; Peralta, *Pacto*, and *Constituciones*.
54. Quesada, *Historia*, 408–10. This new thinking and the changes Monge proposed can be found in his "Conceptos sobre la evolución de Costa Rica en el siglo XVIII," originally published in 1937. It can also be found in a newer edition, Monge, *Conceptos*.
55. Monge, *Conceptos*, 15.
56. Facio, "Esquema."
57. Rodríguez, *Rodrigo*, 4–6.
58. Dachner, "De la individualidad," 120–21.
59. Rodríguez, *Biografía*; Stone, *Dinastía*; Vega, "Etapas," and *Orden*.
60. Molina, "Valle Central," 88.
61. Gamboa, *Costa Rica*, 24.
62. Cerdas, *Formación*, 65–69.
63. Obregón, *Costa Rica*; Karpinsky, "Dimensión"; Samper, "Productores"; Calderón, "Fuerzas"; González, "Continuidad"; Cerdas and González, "Actitud."
64. Vega, "Etapas," 48.
65. Acuña, "Historia"; Solórzano et al., *Costa Rica*; Molina, "Habilitadores," and *Costa Rica*; Samper, "Especialización," and *Producción*; Gudmundson, *Hacendados*, and "Campesino"; Rico, "Renta."
66. Molina, "Valle Central," 102. Molina's position derives largely from the work of John Lynch, John TePaske, and Herbert Klein and is probably what in large part laid the foundation for positions concerning the explanation and meaning of independence

in the following decades. See TePaske and Klein, "Seventeenth-Century"; and Lynch, *Revoluciones*.
67. Quesada, "Independencia," 90.
68. Molina, *Costa Rica*, 181–281.
69. Pérez Brignoli, *Breve*. The position arguing the passive reception of independence from Mexico, which also focuses on the economic and fiscal crisis of the crown in Spain and in America, had already been sustained by Héctor Pérez Brignoli and Ciro Cardoso in their important 1977 work on Central America and the western economy. In the same period, Miles Wortman also argued in favor of an economic and fiscal crisis as the cause of independence. See Wortman, "Government"; and Pérez Brignoli and Cardoso, *Centroamérica*. One more recent work that points in the same direction is Acuña, "Liberalismo."
70. Molina, *Costa Rica*, 310.
71. Palmer, "Sociedad"; Acuña, "Historia," and "Invención"; Díaz, *Construcción*, and *Fiesta*.
72. On this subject, the previously cited works of David Díaz are interesting. See also the work of Juan Rafael Quesada on education and citizenship during this period, in Quesada, *Educación*. Xiomara Avendaño has recently developed a clear position on this issue in Central America. Avendaño, *Centroamérica*, 19–74.
73. Acuña, "Invención," 195.
74. This argument has come to fruition with the works on social networks in Costa Rica, first by Samuel Stone in 1975, then revised and amplified by Eduardo Madrigal. See Stone, *Dinastía*; and Madrigal, "Cartago," and "Poderes." Madrigal is currently completing a study of social networks at the moment of independence.
75. Rodríguez, *Cádiz*; Bonilla, *Ideas*.
76. Acuña, "Liberalismo," 118. He does not deny the existence of resentment toward the Spanish regime, but rather that it became a stimulus for conflicts between provincial elites and those in the capital *before* it generated a discussion of independence. Accordingly, independence was first and foremost a reaction to outside influence, and second a separatist movement with respect to Guatemala—ideas that had also been suggested earlier by Pinto Soria.

At the beginning of the 1990s, Julio César Pinto Soria characterized the independence movement as a point of inflection between the outside context—which ended up deciding the independence issue—and interior social pressures in the territories of the region. The Mexican revolution would be the decisive factor in making a decision for independence, a decision that had as its object the maintenance of order and the control of the territory as well as the avoidance of revolution. To Pinto Soria, the antitax uprisings between 1811 and 1814 showed the urban articulation of the struggle against Spanish domination and were proof that the Enlightenment influence was behind these uprisings, since only in cities were there people capable of understanding the new ideas. Pinto Soria, "Independencia." This argument is also derived from Mario Rodríguez, who affirmed the conditional nature of Central American independence. Guatemalan notables "had in mind the reunification of the entire region under the authorities of the old capital." Rodríguez, *Cádiz*, 152.
77. Dym, "Actas," 3.

78. Ibid., 5–6.
79. Avendaño, "Centroamérica."
80. Vázquez, "Plan de Iguala... de Guatemala," 427. The region, according to Vázquez, was deeply divided over independence, which is usually understood to be associated with a homogeneous front in the face of the ambitions of Guatemala and the influence of the Plan de Iguala. Nonetheless, despite being allied in an aversion to the capital,

> separatists did not form a common block. Comayagua, for example, tried to take control of Caribbean ports and keep Honduran silver out of Guatemala. León sought to head a new *capitanía*. Quetzaltenango tried to strengthen its own project to dominate the Los Altos region, while Chiapas looked to tighten its mercantile ties with Oaxaca and Tabasco. Only in the case of San Salvador was the break with Guatemala associated with an alternative proposal for organizing the nation and a rejection of the Plan de Iguala (ibid., 408).

81. Rodríguez, "Derecho."
82. "Carta de José Santos Lombardo."

THEATERS OF POWER IN 1821
Swearing Loyalty to Independence in the Province of Guatemala

Xiomara Avendaño Rojas

For almost two centuries, the Independence Act of the Kingdom of Guatemala, signed on September 15, 1821, has been the object of a constant "reading," but rarely has there been an in-depth study of its meaning. The document expresses a political opinion, making clear the break with Spain while enunciating the legal and institutional framework in which a new political entity will be born, and indicating who should be responsible for assuring order and peace. The act also requires that adherence to independence be recognized through rituals, to be carried out in the same manner that had been used to honor the Spanish monarchs and even the 1812 Cádiz Constitution (see Herrera, this volume). These rituals or ceremonies were institutional in nature, solemn, and continually evoked the sacred. Those wielding power planned these activities with clear objectives in mind and with the certainty that authorities would be present. They were the celebration of order par excellence.

These ceremonies also had other purposes, among them to act as propaganda rituals designed to organize perceptions in a certain manner, in part by appealing to emotions. These public actions encouraged simplified thinking, even as they stimulated the senses. The men who organized the rituals prepared them to be seen and heard by a colonial society familiar with the mythical Christian universe, using a language of imagery, rich in analogies and allegories, which facilitated the creation of memories. Additionally, the ceremonies not only promoted love, veneration, and loyalty toward the person of the king but functioned as means to periodically rekindle a feeling of belonging to the empire.[1]

Royal ceremonies included those celebrated by the family of the reigning house on occasions such as births, weddings, baptisms, birthdays, funerals, and coronations. Motives for ceremonies also included praising the patron saints of the monarchy, commemorating military victories, praying after defeats, and taking oaths to new monarchs. These performances were seen as the incarnation, or part of the political embodiment, of the kingdom itself.[2]

In America, responsibility for royal ceremonies fell to the cabildo, which, as Jaime Valenzuela Márquez puts it, "would be thought of as an institutional pillar of the monarchy at the same time it served as a window of opportunity for political positioning among the elites."[3] Cabildo members took part in planning and organizing the ceremonies, which included not only the collection and disbursement of funds and materials but also the creation of means to spread propaganda. Through the inclusion of different social groups, the Hispanic ceremony facilitated their integration into a single body. As evidence of compliance with royal commands and to demonstrate loyalty, well-respected individuals were designated to prepare written texts with illustrations that described the ceremonies; copies were sent to the appropriate offices in the kingdom and in Madrid.

Since medieval times, a series of religious elements had been brought together in the procedures for coronating kings. During the Renaissance, especially in Florence, theater, Roman victory carriages, triumphal arches, and Latin allegories, among others, began to adorn public ceremonies. As of the seventeenth century, additions from Roman mythology included the presence of globes, pagan gods, and heroes, along with metaphors of subjected peoples and allegories that expressed virtues and vices. These "played with elements of power which were not understood by all, but definitely admired. . . . humanists, architects and artists transmitted new ideological concepts through a naturalistic/artificial combination of public spaces."[4] These expressions were intended to influence participants by demonstrating existing social hierarchies while ratifying the legitimacy of the political system.

In this chapter I work to discover the different ways in which the ceremonies of adhesion to the Independence Act were carried out in the province of Guatemala.[5] Who organized them? How was the act announced, sworn to, and proclaimed? Was it accepted? Did it generate conflicts? Did towns and cities accept the act only under certain conditions of their own manufacture? What roles did the church and the cabildo play? Were symbols reformulated?

OATH-TAKING DOCUMENTS: "BE SO KIND AS TO ACT IN ACCORDANCE WITH THE INSTRUCTIONS HEREIN"

In the Kingdom of Guatemala, independence was a process that originated elsewhere, beginning with the proclamation of the Plan de Iguala in New Spain in 1821. Constitutional monarchy was considered to be the ideal form of government in the isthmus, since it agreed with Creole interests, prompting adhesion to the Mexican Empire (1821–23). The ayuntamientos of the province of Chiapas were the first in the Kingdom of Guatemala to assert their independence from Spain, declaring themselves also independent of Guatemala City and in favor of the Plan de Iguala.[6]

In the province of Guatemala, the cabildos in the interior and urban residents alike brought pressure to bear for a declaration of independence. The pressures worried the highest authorities of the captaincy general, provoking a meeting that brought together the provincial council, the ecclesiastical cabildo, the audiencia, the university senate, the commercial consulate, the College of Attorneys, and the ayuntamiento of the capital of the kingdom. After discussion, the representatives of these bodies agreed that an independence act should be written, but the document was signed only by the members of the provincial council and of the Guatemala City ayuntamiento.[7]

First and foremost, the Independence Act declared a break with the Spanish government, since this was a concern shared by the provincial and capital elite.[8] Those who signed the act of September 15, 1821, were public officials whose names have endured in history by chance, only because at that particular moment their investiture as functionaries permitted their actions. Declaring independence was a political measure taken with the hope of maintaining control over the captaincy, but the provinces understood it as a means to free themselves, not only from the Spanish crown but also from Guatemalan domination.

But the Independence Act changed the government. The bodies that signed the document, the ayuntamiento and the provincial council, gave Gabino Gaínza a vote of confidence, allowing him to "continue with the supreme political military government."[9] Their next step would be the creation of a new governing body: "And so that the government may have a character appropriate to current circumstances, a Provisional Advisory Junta shall be formed."[10] The document named the most notable representatives of the above-mentioned bodies as the members of the new junta and included delegates from the different provinces of the captaincy.

With what politico-judicial backing was the above step taken? "In the meantime, there being no new changes in the established authorities, they shall continue to exercise their respective responsibilities with reference to the 1812 Cádiz Constitution, its decrees and laws, until that moment in which the indicated Congress should determine what might be most just and beneficial."[11] Indirectly expressed, a constitutional monarchy was adopted, but the future representatives were left to decide between accepting that system or seeking another. This differs from some Spanish American statements of independence that clearly declare the creation of a political system developed from republican ideals.

It should come as no surprise that at the moment they organized their oath-taking ceremonies the ayuntamientos from the interior of the province of Guatemala discussed whether they should declare loyalty to the Guatemalan Independence Act or to the Plan de Iguala. Both political bodies, New Spain and the captaincy general of Guatemala, clearly supported constitutional monarchy. Two aspects of this process deserve to be emphasized. First, a republic was not declared, though in Guatemala City and San Salvador voices were raised in its favor. It may be that such an alternative had been minimized by the Central American representatives to the Courts of Cádiz of 1820–21, who joined the Mexican representatives in signing a proposal to create the Monarchy of the North (*Septentrión*), which would have included the Philippines and the Greater Antilles. Second, the Provisional Advisory Junta, by maintaining legislation that had its origins in the Cádiz Constitution, would organize itself and act in accordance with the junta experience of the 1810s.[12]

Was the break with the Spanish crown also a break with the Vatican? In the last decade of the fifteenth century and the first of the sixteenth, the Spanish monarchy expressed its dominion over religious power and assured it through arrangements with the upper echelons of the Catholic Church expressed in two papal bulls from Pope Alexander VI, in 1493 and 1501, and one from Pope Julius II in 1508. In this manner the crown controlled ecclesiastical taxes and named higher church authorities and clerics in general. In every territory, viceroys, captains general, and governors, in their capacity as vice-patrons, named parish priests from a list prepared by the church. The crown used bishops as interim governors as needed (e.g., see Belaubre, this volume), at times even sending them to America without papal bulls that legitimated its decision.

The church was another branch of the royal government, another form of political control over the colonies, which fell under the guidance of the Council of the Indies and was united with Rome by tenuous bonds. The American episcopate was very royalist, and the church exercised a moral and spiritual influence that made it into the most powerful instrument used in the preservation of the dominion of the Catholic kings, thousands of kilometers away.[13]

In the 1810s, along with the adoption of constitutionalism, the trust sealed between the Hispanic crown and the Vatican in the *patronato real* was kept in force.[14] Instructions issued in 1811 by the cabildo of Guatemala City to its representative to the Courts, in the section regarding the constitution, recognized the Catholic, apostolic, and Roman religion in its first six articles. Cabildo members restated the position adopted more than a century before by Charles II, who stipulated in his will that his successors should keep the Catholic faith, seek the patronage of the Holy Mother Mary of God, and continue devotion to the Immaculate Conception. The authors of the Instructions also asked that Saint Teresa of Jesus be named as patron of the new constitution, leaving in place the existing celebrations of Saint James the Apostle, holy patron of the Spanish realms. They likewise requested that regional church councils be celebrated both in North America (including Mexico, the Caribbean, and Central America) and in South America.[15]

The Cádiz Constitution indicated that the religion of the Spanish monarchy "is and shall always be Catholic, apostolic, Roman, and the only true one. The nation is protected by wise and just laws, and prohibits the exercise of any other."[16] In 1821 there was no disagreement on the theme of religion, and the Independence Act stated "that the Catholic religion, which we have professed in earlier centuries and shall profess in those to come, remains pure and unalterable, keeping alive the spirit of faithfulness which has always distinguished Guatemala, respecting ecclesiastical ministers, both secular and regular, and protecting their persons and their properties."[17] The independence declaration made it very clear that the *patronato real* agreed to by the Catholic kings and the pope at the beginning of the sixteenth century would be preserved. The political rupture with the crown did not mean a break with the Catholic Church.

Changes or modifications in government cause uncertainty, so to reduce any problems the Independence Act might provoke the document called on clergy to support the "peace and calm" of residents and to exhort the people to act in brotherhood and unity so as to avoid divisions and what were considered to be potentially disastrous consequences. The act tasked the ayuntamiento with maintaining order and keeping the peace, and the captain general with the responsibility of emitting an edict or manifesto that would justify the signing of the act of September 15, 1821, and, of course, make clear that those who signed would maintain their loyalty to the future government.[18]

Gabino Gaínza did in fact write the text requested by the junta, a document that before independence could only have been written on royal orders. The text began by notifying the residents of "this honorable and virtuous place, [about] this glorious and important occurrence, so that when they all receive notice of it they can then organize their behavior accordingly and cooperate in the consolidation and strengthening of a *system so just and necessary* at all times, and especially at present."[19] It went on to indicate that any show of unrest and division would display a lack of respect toward the rights and Christian charity of the people, for which reason Gaínza deemed it necessary to establish the following:[20]

I. The independence proclaimed on the 15th is only so as not to depend on the government of the peninsula, and so as to do on our own soil all that formerly could only be done there.
II. Consequently, all the laws, ordinances and orders which formerly applied shall still remain in force, and if any should be inappropriate they shall be revised or repealed by the next national constituent Congress.
III. All tribunals, courts, and other public, military, civil, and ecclesiastical functions shall remain in force and in full exercise of their jurisdiction.

It is interesting to note how, in just a few lines, the captain general explained to the people the significant essentials of the act of September 15: assuming sovereignty, in his words, "to do what formerly could only be done on the peninsula," but taking on the Spanish legal and institutional framework. The rest of the edict establishes regulations to guarantee peace and tranquility for the people:

IV. Although it is not to be expected that anyone will oppose the expressed general will nor propose any disruption of the peace with which these honored people have entered into the enjoyment of their rights, if there should be anyone of any class, grade or condition who directly or indirectly, through speech or actions, should try to upset or discredit the adopted system of independence and reestablish the Spanish government, that person shall be dealt with, tried and punished as a conspirator, imposing the penalty of death in the form prescribed by law.

V. Any person aware that another, or others, plan to conspire against the independent and sworn government is obligated to denounce him to the legitimate authorities, and if he does not do so, he will be dealt with and prosecuted as an accomplice to conspiracy in the form prescribed by law.

VI. If any person, by word or deed, should promote division among honorable citizens of this city, who all together form one single family, he shall be treated as a disturber of the public peace, in the form prescribed by law.

VII. It is prohibited that any citizen abuse the transports of public rejoicing by ringing bells, bearing illegal arms, mistreating the windows, doors and residences of other citizens. . . . he shall be tried and punished. Anyone who plays music does so under his own responsibility and should advise one of the mayors beforehand.

VIII. Public order requires that there be neither gatherings nor crowds of people upsetting or disturbing residents, and those who are found to be disorderly after eleven o'clock at night will be detained and tried according to previous edicts and ordinances.

IX. Tavern owners and liquor merchants must comply exactly with regulations regarding their proper behavior, or face their respective penalties, which will be irremediably executed.

X. And, given that the respect and compliance owed to the constitutional mayors and other authorities is clear, this same treatment should be accorded to the councilmen, who support the former on their rounds to assure public tranquility; if anyone should question their rulings and preeminence, he shall be punished with all the severity that the laws allow.[21]

A decision of such magnitude as declaring independence could cause diverse reactions, from celebration to protest, and the edict made clear that protest would not be taken lightly. Conspiracy would therefore be punishable by death; disruption, disorder, and alarm punished according to existing laws. To avoid disturbances, liquor sellers would be required to comply with regulations, councilmen would serve as watchmen in their respective areas, and anyone who dared question these decisions would be processed using the full weight of the law.

These measures might seem extreme, but there had been a series of uprisings and antitax protests in the alcaldías and corregimientos of Guatemala province after the Bourbon reforms. Later, in the Cádiz period, expectations rose when tribute was abolished (see Payne and Pollack, this volume).[22]

One of the fundamental points of the act was to require oath-taking. For that purpose, the September 15 act and the edict issued by Gaínza were sent to authorities in Guatemala City: the Provisional Advisory Junta, the ayuntamiento of Guatemala City, the archbishop, the different courts, political and military chiefs, regular clergy and religious orders, as well as the bureaucracy, captaincy authorities, corporate bodies, and troops. In the rest of the province, ayuntamientos and military and ecclesiastical authorities were required to participate in the oath-taking ceremonies. All of these entities were obliged to attend a thanksgiving mass that would honor independence.[23]

RITUALS AND THE REELABORATION OF SYMBOLS

When it received the Independence Act and the edict from the captain general, the ayuntamiento of Guatemala City began assigning responsibilities to its members and making available the resources necessary for carrying out the oath-taking ceremony. Those charged with preparing the stage began moving vendors from the main plaza to the old plaza, thus guaranteeing ample space for the crowd. The authorities ordered that the stage be placed near the cabildo, adorned and painted "with an effort to achieve the greatest dignity and decorated with poetry which *would fill the citizens with enthusiasm and love* toward our felicitous independence."[24]

In this new ceremonial context, the façade of the stage was simple, the political rupture having made the symbols of the Spanish monarchy, their allegories, and poems in homage to new monarchs disappear. In their place, the stage bore the inscription "Independent Guatemala. September fifteenth, eighteen twenty-one. First year of its freedom." In like manner, on the back of the stage, visible from any spot in the plaza, was another phrase with letters made of gold or a good imitation: "Plaza of an independent Guatemala. September fifteenth, eighteen twenty-one. First year of freedom."

The decorations that adorned Nueva Guatemala de la Asunción (Guatemala City) can be seen as a demonstration of jubilation and joy. Through printed papers, residents were invited to place draperies and lights on their homes, and council members also brightened the portals of the ayuntamiento building and the stage with lights and decorations and assured that church fronts were similarly lighted. An orchestra played several melodies that were repeated at set intervals until 10:00 P.M., at which time the fireworks also came to an end, allowing ample time for the public to return home at a decent hour.

The capital city cabildo regretted not being able to produce a commemorative medal for the planned celebration, noting that any such effort would have to be postponed (discussed below), and instead the organizers ordered that some three hundred pesos in common currency be minted. The coins were to be put in four silver trays and placed on the stage when independence was proclaimed.

The ayuntamiento issued an edict that established rules assuring order and safeguarding the security of participants at such a large and momentous event. Any lack of restraint or commotion would be punished in accordance with established ordinances, watchmen and night patrols would be put into service, and outsiders, when they entered the city, were to leave their arms at the sentry box and retrieve them only on departure.

Invitations were prepared for the corporative bodies in general, particularly the archbishop, regular priests, military and revenue officers, principal residents, and all honorable citizens, especially those who had shown clear support for independence. The cabildo also invited the Indian towns surrounding the capital and asked them to bring banners and musical instruments.

The municipal government sent correspondence to the ayuntamientos in the different provinces of the kingdom calling for union and informed their counterparts in Ciudad Real and Tuxtla, in the province of Chiapas, that they respected the decision made to join Mexico. The final note regarding the ceremony indicated that the organization, preparation, and execution of the oath-taking ceremony was to be recorded in a written report, a task assigned to the municipal secretary.

Procession

September 23 was the day designated for the ceremony. As had usually occurred in similar sorts of events, council members and special guests met at the ayuntamiento building at 8:00 A.M. From there they walked to the government palace at the other end of the plaza, where they awaited Captain General Gabino Gaínza and the members of the Provisional Advisory Junta, the corporative bodies, and other guests. At 9:00 the traditional procession began, but this time one thing that for some three hundred years had distinguished this parade of authorities was missing. I refer, of course, to the royal pennant or standard, which traditionally had been carried by the royal standard-bearer who led the parade. A tricolor flag—symbol of liberty, equality, and justice, carried by the first mayor of the capital—replaced the pennant, and after the procession it would remain on stage all day, under a canopy and accompanied by an honor guard, until the moment that independence was proclaimed.

The distinguished retinue walked straight down the street to the church of San Francisco, crossed where the alcabala offices were located, passed the Santo Domingo and La Merced convents, then came to an end at the stage prepared in the main plaza.

Public Reading, Oath-Taking, and Proclamation of the Independence Act

On the stage, seats were assigned in hierarchical order. In the center front was the Provisional Advisory Junta, to its right the audiencia and newly titled Superior Political Chief Gabino Gaínza, and to the left the dean and the ecclesiastical cabildo. Behind them were the ayuntamiento, the faculty senate, the Tribunal del consulado, the College of Attorneys, the protomedicato, the prelates of the religious orders, the heads of the revenue office, and other individuals of standing.[25]

After all present were seated, three different ceremonies were carried out. First, the secretary of the cabildo read the September 15 act and the edict from Gaínza in a formal pronouncement. Afterward the first mayor, Mariano Larrave, took responsibility for the rest of the program and after a brief speech took the oath of loyalty from the large group that had assembled for the event. He asked, "Do you swear by our Lord God to safeguard the independence of your homeland? Do you swear to spill the last drop of your blood to uphold it? Do you swear to defend the Catholic religion and the persons and properties of all citizens, without consideration of origin or class, while respecting constituted authorities?" According to the report, the entire crowd, "full of enthusiasm and joy, shouted loudly: 'YES, I SWEAR.'"[26]

The public reading and oath-taking were solemn moments, but next came the proclamation, which was tremendous. It consisted in Mayor Larrave waving the flag, which had been specially made for the occasion, and shouting loudly three times, "Long live Guatemala! Long live its independence!" At that moment, the secretary, scribes, and councilmen of Guatemala City, located at the four corners of the stage, threw the newly minted coins to those present, the orchestra began to play, and church bells rang out. From the old plaza, artillery salvos along with rifle fire by the troops could be heard on the edges of the main plaza. After this moment of exaltation, the ensemble followed the superior political chief to his home, where he had prepared a meal for the authorities present. That ended the central aspects of the ritual: the pronouncement, oath-taking, and proclamation of the independence act.

PUBLICATION AND INDIVIDUAL OATH-TAKING: ASSURING POLITICAL LEGITIMACY

Beginning in the Cádiz period, the general population and corporative groups began to take oaths individually, though proclamations continued to be public, collective events, held only once in the main plaza, in the presence of the highest authorities and dignitaries, as described above.

The clerics began the process of oath-taking to the Independence Act with Archbishop Ramón Francisco Casaús y Torres, who swore loyalty before the superior political chief at the government palace. Next, the members of the ecclesiastical cabildo took their oaths before Casaús y Torres. The religious orders—the community of San Agustín and the college of Cristo Crucificado, the congregations of San Felipe Neri, San Francisco, Belén, and La Merced—carried out ceremonies in their own installations. The precepts of each order convoked its members and then read the act and the edict, after which the clerics swore on the Bible to uphold the content of the documents. They then attended mass, where a sermon alluding to the topic was read and a Te Deum sung. The sermons and prayers spoke of asking for peace, unity, and respect for constituted authorities and achieving a government that would seek the happiness of parishioners and respect the Catholic, apostolic, and Roman religion. Bell ringing and fireworks accompanied the celebrations, and at their end one of the monks wrote up a report that was signed and sent to higher authorities.[27]

The clerics were also responsible for assuring that the documents were made public in the capital for oath-taking among its citizens, undertaken first during mass and afterward in the atrium of the church. According to the reports recording the different events, parishioners of all ages and classes in the Guatemala City parishes of Sagrario, Candelaria, Remedios, San Sebastián, and Villa de Guadalupe listened carefully to the priests as they read the documents and then placed their hands on the Bible and swore their loyalty. The reports indicate that participants showed themselves to be in favor of maintaining order, tranquility, and unity, declaring themselves pleased that the new government would be in the hands of patriots worthy of esteem and high public opinion, and who had shown themselves to be interested in the happiness of the nation.[28] The same documentation notes that parishioners felt gratitude, respect, and a firm disposition to sacrifice themselves for the good of the homeland as well as for the strengthening of their independence. Those present declared themselves in favor of maintaining the current government unchanged until such time as the united provinces of Guatemala might have their own center of power and law, after the constituent congress scheduled to meet in 1822. When the ceremonies ended, all took part in Te Deums in thanksgiving, after which church bells rang and salvos of fireworks exploded.

Other prestigious and socially recognized corporate bodies gave proof of their loyalty in the face of political change. The full faculty senate from the University of San Carlos, called by Gaínza, appeared before the rector, Antonio Larrazábal. After reading the memorandum, the Independence Act, and the edict, the rector, hands on the Bible, took the oath and the professors then followed suit. They then signed a report and a copy was taken to Gaínza.

On September 21, the same day of the oath-taking by the university senate, the consulado del comercio called an extraordinary meeting in which members knelt before the image of Christ crucified and, after the secretary read the oath, affirmed their loyalty. Days later, the secretary and caretakers held the same service, and in the first week of August the officials and appeal judges did the same, since, due to work-related responsibilities, they had been absent during the first ceremony.

The report from the dragoon squadron describing how Col. Xavier Barrutia read the manifesto and the act, prior to taking the oath before his troops, provides some idea about how members of the military managed oath-taking. On the afternoon of September 20, he lectured the troops regarding the new political situation they would have to accept. Those who had not been able to participate in the oath-taking because they were in service elsewhere would swear their loyalty where they were stationed.[29] All workers in the offices of the new government needed to demonstrate their loyalty to independence by taking oaths, so in the different offices the department head would swear loyalty to the Independence Act and then take oaths from his subordinates.[30]

THE PROVINCE OF GUATEMALA:
ACCEPTANCE, TENSIONS, AND CONDITIONS

In the rest of the province, the constitutional ayuntamientos hurried to swear their loyalty, and the details provided in the reports describing the ceremonies show different responses to the Independence Act present in the discussions surrounding the celebrations, some in which the towns organized events without conflict or debate, and others in which the process provoked political confrontations. The city of Antigua Guatemala de Santiago de los Caballeros, just west of the capital, swore loyalty to the Independence Act in an extraordinary meeting of the cabildo in which, hands on the Bible, the first mayor took the oath from the senior member of the town council and then councilmen swore their loyalty before the first mayor. The commandant of the armed forces followed, and then the general population, before the townspeople moved to the church, where a Te Deum was sung. Once these events had come to a close, participants signed a report that had been written up to describe them.[31]

In the town of Salamá, the corregidor of Verapaz Pedro José de Arrivillaga and the ayuntamiento called for an open town meeting in the plaza, where the commandant of arms, the parish priest Fray José María López, and the priests from San Cristóbal and San Miguel joined them. The corregidor spoke a few words, and then his son, 2nd Lt. Manuel Arrivillaga, read the document sent from the capital. The corregidor swore loyalty before the first mayor, Pedro Berríos, and in turn the councilmen took their oaths before him. Next, according to the report describing the ceremony, the people congregated in the plaza declared loudly, "Yes, we swear." After the publication and oath-taking, those present moved to the church to share a Te Deum, which ended the ritual.[32]

After receiving the documents the town of Cahabón, also in Verapaz, decided to postpone the public ceremony because the priest was ill. Only after the priest recovered did the cabildo fix a date for the public reading and oath-taking of the Independence Act. The townspeople considered the presence of the priest necessary for two reasons: they needed his leadership in what was clearly a complicated situation, and they needed him to give the thanksgiving mass as well as the Te Deum. The ceremony in the provincial capital of Cobán clearly mentioned the expectation that the superior political chief would protect the general well-being through just principles of equality. According to the act describing the ceremony, the town carried out the oath-taking to celebrate liberty and the Catholic religion, and also to commit itself to obey the provisions of the authorities.[33]

In the east, the provincial capital of Chiquimula acknowledged receipt of the papers sent from the capital and then sent the respective copies to the district ayuntamientos. The documents were publicly presented in the cabildo, in the presence of the corregidor Crisóstomo Solís, Col. Simión Gutiérrez, the priest Julián Alfaro, other distinguished persons, and a great number of townspeople. The publication and oath-taking were solemnly celebrated in the plaza on Sunday, September 29.[34]

In Zacapa, also in the eastern portion of the province of Guatemala, the report that describes the ceremony indicates that the Independence Act and edict were received from the capital with rejoicing, and that independence was considered a triumph of freedom, a praiseworthy action undertaken by the people, on a day that deserved to be immortalized. Independence was understood to be the means to shake off the yoke of oppression, and in their ceremony the townspeople vowed to achieve happiness for all. Oath-taking was not held until October, since important community figures could not attend due to their labors with their livestock and ranches.[35]

In San Sebastián Tejar, a town in Chimaltenango west of the capital, the priest and the ayuntamiento managed everything related to the oath-taking ceremony. In its response to the event organizers, the Provisional Advisory Junta urged them to be vigilant in assuring peace and order, which it considered to be the main functions of the government to which they had sworn their loyalty.[36]

In some towns, the different opinions regarding adhesion to the Mexican Plan de Iguala or to the Independence Act signed in Guatemala provoked arguments, particularly in the west, where the ayuntamientos were located near, or bordering on, the province of Chiapas, which had pronounced in favor of the Plan de Iguala. These disagreements reflected a broader discussion that began to appear in the entire Kingdom of Guatemala. The western part of the province had a history of conflict whose roots were in the Cádiz era, when the Courts abolished tribute and Indian towns took to the measure immediately, much to the chagrin of the corregidores (see Pollack, this volume). The cruelty, mistreatment, and use of force by Spanish troops at the time of those protests also influenced thinking in the region.[37]

The town of Jacaltenango, in Huehuetenango district, seemed inclined to favor the Plan de Iguala, a position supported by the local authorities and people of the area, mostly Indians. The priest Eusebio Arzate, however, took advantage of the esteem and respect in which the town held him and managed to create a consensus that permitted the organization of a ceremony to celebrate the September 15 Independence Act with a public reading of the document followed by the oath-taking of the townspeople.[38] Those assembled at the town hall later attended church where a Te Deum was sung, and on the following day, September 28, the same cleric celebrated a thanksgiving mass. In his sermon, the priest presented a picture of the unhappiness the people had suffered under Spanish rule and exhorted his parishioners to live up to the oath they had taken. The secretary prepared a document that validated the ceremony and indicated that people reacted with cheers and exclamations of joy. Towns near Jacaltenango, like San Andrés Huista, San Marcos Huista, San Antonio Huista, Concepción Huista, and Santa Ana Huista, followed in the footsteps of Jacaltenango.[39] After giving up its pro-Mexico stand and recognizing Guatemalan authorities, Jacaltenango decided that the "glorious" day should be remembered and erected a column facing the town hall with the inscription "Long live September 27, 1821. The first day of Independence in Jacaltenango. Long live freedom." The surrounding towns followed the initiative of Jacaltenango and ordered the construction of similar monuments.

In contrast, tensions were high in the town of Quetzaltenango, and the ayuntamiento forcibly removed the corregidor, unleashing a flurry of letters to and from the capital. With the corregidor no longer in the picture, the ayuntamiento organized a ceremony demonstrating loyalty to the Independence Act, with portals decorated for the occasion. The first mayor took charge of receiving the oaths of the councilmen, employees, and troops posted there.[40]

In other towns, the reports sent to the capital to verify the oath-taking ceremonies expressed that loyalty was conditional or took advantage of the opportunity to express particular concerns. In Sololá, for example, the ceremony was held in the municipal building, with the presence of the priest and an Indian interpreter. The residents, according to the information sent to the capital, demanded specific conditions in the political, judicial, fiscal, and military spheres as conditions for their acceptance of the Independence Act. The Sololatecos demanded that Domingo Garcia be named governor until the constitutive junta opened its sessions, that Dr. José Valdés be recognized as the district representative to the Provisional Advisory Junta, and that new mayoral elections be undertaken. They also insisted that recognition of the Provisional Advisory Junta depended on maintaining the members of the town government of Sololá in their positions and on the assurance that new taxes not be levied. Interestingly, the signatories of the document demanded, as a means to assure greater respect for their rights, that the territorial audiencia not assume the functions of a supreme court, but instead that its decisions be subject to appeal to the Provisional Advisory Junta. Concerned about instability that independence could cause, the authorities in Sololá mentioned the need for a military presence there.[41] At the end of the meeting, those present cheered independence and chose September 30 as the date for the ceremonies, before signing the report that described these conditions and the celebrations and would later be sent to Superior Political Chief Gaínza.

In Patzúm, west of Guatemala City in the alcaldía mayor de Chimaltenango, organization and preparation for the oath-taking began once documents arrived from the capital, and the report sent to the central authorities mentions the presence of both Indians and ladinos in the ceremonies. On the eve of the celebration volleys were fired, the cabildo building decorated with hangings, and lights hung that would remain in place for three days. The following morning began with a thanksgiving mass at 7:00 and shortly thereafter, in the town plaza, ayuntamiento members, and later the rest of the townsfolk, swore their loyalty oaths on the Bible, prior to breaking into celebrations that included music, Indian drums, gunpowder explosions, and fireworks. The report mentions that the people were happy to be free of the yoke under which they had suffered for so many centuries, but the Indians stated that their happiness would have been even greater if their tribute obligations had been eliminated. The festivities ended with a Te Deum the next day.

San Marcos, west of the town of Quetzaltenango in the corregimiento of the same name, responded to the news that independence had been declared with a three-day celebration that included swearing loyalty to the Independence Act, illumination at night, a mass, a Te Deum, fireworks, and cheers in favor of independence. In the report sent along to the Provisional Advisory Junta, the ayuntamiento of San Marcos requested that the state liquor monopoly (*estanco*) office in their town be removed.[42]

Entertainment

For the most part, the reports sent in from the different towns make little mention of activities dedicated to entertainment during the oath-taking festivities, unlike other areas of Hispanic America. In Gualán, after the oath-taking in the plaza, bells rang, the artillery fired volleys, and the people danced the *zarao* that night at a party, accompanied by shouts of "Long live Independence!" In Santa Rosa, a town near the border with San Salvador and Comayagua (Honduras), singing and music in the streets marked the eve of the ceremony. After a thanksgiving mass the next day, the townspeople walked to the town hall where the priest urged the crowd to work for the well-being of the church, union, liberty, peace, and tranquility and to maintain their obedience to authorities. The mayor then climbed on stage and took the oaths of councilmen and citizens, after which, in lieu of artillery, fireworks, bell-ringing, music, and drums marked the celebration. Later, a theatrical production was presented in the plaza, meant to represent the liberty and union acquired with independence. A young Indian woman in chains was brought out, then two young women, one white and the other black, came on stage, removed her shackles, and threw them into the audience. The Indians then smashed the chains of the captive where they fell. Those in attendance walked to the church, where they sang a Te Deum, then returned to the cabildo for more music and cheers in favor of independence.

The townspeople of Mazatenango, on the Pacific coastal plain, celebrated the arrival of the independence documentation with music, rifle volleys, and cheers for independence and the Catholic religion. The next day, the Mazatecos took part in a thanksgiving mass and ayuntamiento members took their oaths. That same day the two militia companies paraded, while drums sounded through the streets and plazas in a call for obedience, veneration, and respect for the goddess of peace. The next day, the people, led by the first mayor, offered their oaths of allegiance to the Independence Act.[43]

An Exception?

In the documents consulted from the towns in the province of Guatemala, there are practically no references to the use of a standard or flag, which would indicate that the proclamation was not made. The use of a flag is mentioned only in the Chimaltenango celebration, where the cabildo organized the festivities, handing out instructions to build a stage and publish the edict; citizens were to decorate and illuminate their houses and the streets for three days and nights to make the best impression possible. On the day designated for the oath-taking ceremony, the secretary read the documents in a decorated plaza where the mayor received the oaths of the townspeople, then waved a flag for the American nation. The report indicates that the ceremony ended with joy, acclamation, and cheers for independence, and afterward the mayors ordered that a document certifying the event be drawn up and signed.[44]

THANKSGIVING AND A SERMON

As mentioned, the authorities of the Guatemala City ayuntamiento and the members of the provincial council signed the Independence Act, assumed to have been written by the well-known intellectual José Cecilio del Valle. The process of assuring declarations of loyalty to the document was guaranteed by the clergy of the capital and towns, and priests played a vitally important political role in convincing dissidents to remain with what had been the Kingdom of Guatemala. The sermons given during the religious rites formed a part of the rituals of political legitimacy that accompanied the process of emancipation.

On September 24, the cabildo in Guatemala City requested that a high mass be celebrated, and the sermon, which traditionally had been given for the coronation of monarchs, was entrusted to the canon José María Castilla.[45] Invitations to the event were sent to the religious orders, corporative bodies, public employees, and other individuals. The sermon read from the pulpit of the metropolitan cathedral contained a true politico-religious defense of the signing of the Independence Act.

In preparing for his sermon, Castilla faced the initial challenge of justifying the arrival of the Spaniards and their continued presence. The religious leader addressed the issue by comparing the American continent to the growth process of a person, describing three stages: infancy, youth, and adulthood. In his words, when America was conquered "it was an infant," so it could not care for itself and needed the Catholic religion and Spanish civilization to care for its liberty; it had not taken advantage of its riches to become a power capable of earning the admiration of the world.

As time passed, Castilla argued, "young America," enriched by knowledge, was able to see the monstrous nature of being ruled by another part of the world and finally broke its silence. This situation had resulted in America postponing its happiness, neglecting the education of its children, and not paying sufficient attention to their talents, merits, and virtues. America, continued the priest, saw the great distances that separated it from the colonial center, how its commerce had been taken over by the interests of that center, and how its work was seen as practically insignificant.

By the time it reached "adulthood," according to Castilla, America had come to know its best interests and wished to be free. The time had come to build a different family, in some sense imitating Spain, which had broken the Roman yoke after assuming its laws and customs. But freedom had not been achieved through the same means.

> Caracas announced liberty, Mexico repeated liberty, and the echo of liberty sounded in Guatemala. . . . God granted it to us at last, in an ecstasy of love: He has given it to us without the high price so many other nations have had to pay. North America sacrificed a large part of its population to independence. Mexico has sustained a destructive war for many years. And Venezuela has seen its temples washed with the blood of its sons to be free.

According to the canon, the mercy of the Creator had permitted war to be avoided in the Kingdom of Guatemala, and the children of that kingdom should demonstrate their gratitude and carefully preserve "the gift of independence which the Lord has put in our hands." Castilla continued: "I seem to hear at this moment the soft human voice of God who rests in that sacred altar: Be faithful to my religion and you will not become prisoners of your enemies." With these words, the canon promoted the idea that independence had been granted by heavenly providence and that, notwithstanding the absence of the king, power maintained its divine origin (compare to Herrera, this volume).

Castilla also mentioned the dangers caused by ambition, injustice, mistrust, impatience, and haste, arguing that citizens should never distance themselves from virtue, the basis for all government. Without it, anarchy, considered to be the worst of all social ills, would ensue, promoting strife among the provinces. A union based on Christianity, the canon considered, could cement together a stable and wise government, and, he argued, the citizens of the capital were united, without distinctions between "Indian and ladino, between black and white, between European and American." The priest proclaimed that under these circumstances brotherhood and peace were the children of liberty.

In one last argument, Castilla reminded those present that the oath-taking undertaken by residents of the capital constituted a legal act, and that it was also a requisite for establishing a government that would be aware of their needs and customs and thus be able to offer legislation that would lead to happiness. The oath-taking carried out in the plaza before authorities and the attendance at religious events such as the thanksgiving mass and the Te Deum collectively made up a complete ritual that acknowledged the Independence Act and thereby its political legitimacy.

A COMMEMORATIVE MEDAL AND MEMORIES OF INDEPENDENCE

The cabildo of Guatemala was instructed to have a medal cast "which would, down through the centuries, perpetuate the memory of the fifteenth of September of 1821, when Guatemala proclaimed its joyous independence."[46] Months later, in 1822, the

Marquis of Aycinena presented the ayuntamiento of Guatemala a proposal for the engraving of a commemorative medal.

According to the *Catálogo numismático* published by Jorge Murillo, on its obverse side the medal bears the inscription "Free and Independent Guatemala." In the center, at the foot of a pedestal is an image of a kneeling sculptor dressed in a toga, who with a chisel is engraving "September 15, 1821" and the name of Captain General Gaínza. To the right of the sculptor is a line of five elongated pyramids that probably represent the provinces of the Kingdom of Guatemala. Between the sculptor and the pedestal is a closed book resting on a surface covered with flowers.[47] These two views call to mind the book that appeared on the coin minted in 1812 for the oath-taking to the Cádiz Constitution (see Herrera, this volume), the flowers could portend a flourishing constitutional future, and a rolled-up parchment might refer to the existence and safeguarding of the history of the kingdom. On the pedestal is an elliptical shield of Guatemala City, with the image of Saint James mounted on his charger, symbol of the conquest and patron saint of Antigua Guatemala. To the side are two volcanoes, a characteristic of the landscape near the capital. The shield rests on four small spheres, one in each corner of the pedestal.

The border of the reverse side of the 1821 medal bears the inscription "A free man offers peace, but a slave never." The traditional image of the king has disappeared from the coins and in its place is a series of elements that express the presence of two sovereignties that are amicably disposed toward one another. The upper portion of the coin exhibits an angel crowned with laurels, which shows not only the presence but also the continued legitimacy of the *patronato real* in this new scenario of independence, as well as the divine origin of earthly power. This figure is given an Indian identity, with a plumed skirt and a quiver of arrows attached to a baldric, which can be interpreted as a reaffirmation, in the new political context, of the protection the Catholic Church had historically provided the Indians.

Since the sixteenth century, beginning during the reigns of Charles V and Phillip II, the extension of the empire had been represented by four spheres, referring to Europe, Asia, Africa, and America. On the coin, the angel opens a path between two spheres, using his hands to separate them. The right hand, touching the sphere with an image of Europe, holds an olive branch in the hope of peace and reconciliation with the mother country. The left hand, placed on the American sphere, holds a horn of plenty full of fruits and flowers, in hopes of a productive future. The hands extend toward one another from the center of each sphere, evidence of the desire for friendship between what were now two sovereignties. At the feet of the angel, on the ground, we see a broken chain with shackles, the symbol of liberty and independence. The border of the reverse of the coin reads "Guatemala, Free and Independent."

FINAL REFLECTIONS

The ritual or ceremony celebrated to publicly announce, swear allegiance to, and proclaim the Independence Act of the Kingdom of Guatemala followed steps established during the Spanish monarchy. Changes in these rituals are nonetheless evident, beginning with the Independence Act and the manifesto of the superior political chief that replaced the royal seal. Rather than orders emanating from Madrid, the different documents that organized the ceremonies were produced by the new authorities in Guatemala City. Changes included the symbols used in the ceremonies, such as the tricolor flag used during the proclamation instead of the royal pennant, and the commemoration medal that did not include an image of the king.

In the capital of the kingdom, the oath-taking process did not encounter problems, but in other regions of the province situations varied. There were constitutional ayuntamientos loyal to the capital and others that placed conditions on that loyalty. The areas bordering Chiapas debated their allegiance to Mexico or to Guatemala, but in at least one case they were influenced by the clergy and remained with Guatemala.

As had been the case under the former regime, the ceremony rested on two pillars crucial to the crown: the cabildo and the clergy. The former guaranteed the space and mechanisms to be used; the latter contributed to fostering obedience. It is clear, nonetheless, that the Provisional Advisory Junta, the interim government of the kingdom, held but a precarious legitimacy. Who would maintain unity in the absence of a king? To whom would the provinces give their loyalty and legitimacy? The political future was to be defined in a future congress; in the meantime, the basis of the new political system would be sustained by Cádiz constitutionalism.

NOTES

1. Salazar Baena, "Representar"; Rípodas, "Versión," 245.
2. Río, "Felipe II," 677.
3. Valenzuela, *Liturgias*, 95.
4. Ibid., 108.
5. In 1786, during the period of the Bourbon reforms, intendancies in the Kingdom of Guatemala were established in Chiapas, Honduras, San Salvador, and Nicaragua-Costa Rica. In this chapter, the "province of Guatemala" refers to the territory that included the alcaldías mayores of Sacatepéquez, Verapaz, Suchitepéquez, Chimaltenango, Totonicapán, Sololá, Escuintla, and Sonsonate, as well as the corregimientos of Chiquimula and Quetzaltenango. [Editor's note]
6. Trens, *Historia*, 218–23.
7. On September 1, 1820, the provincial council had begun to meet in Guatemala City, and that of León was revived in October of the same year. In May 1821, Spanish authorities permitted the formation of a council in every intendancy in the kingdom. In August, Chiapans took steps to organize another council, and between September and November Honduras and San Salvador did likewise. Rodríguez, *Cádiz*, 131, 142; Avendaño, *Centroamérica*, 50–51.
8. Acta de Independencia de la capitanía general de Guatemala, in *Boletín del Archivo del Gobierno de Guatemala* (hereafter *BAGG*), 1938, year 4, no. 1, 127–29. Other studies on the independence process include Vásquez, "Plan"; Gutiérrez, "Proceso"; Dym, "Actas"; Vielman, *Enigmas*; Argueta, "Centroamérica."
9. Gaínza served as an interim captain general after his predecessor, Carlos Urrutia, had been forced to give up his position because of ill health.
10. Acta de Independencia de la capitanía general de Guatemala, in *BAGG*, 1938, year 4, no. 1, 218, Article 8. After independence was declared, the provincial council became the Provisional Advisory Junta.
11. Ibid., 128, Article 7. Articles 3–6 detail the convening of a Congress. Rojas, *Documentos*; García Laguardia, "Independencia."
12. Dym, "Soberanía"; Avendaño and Hernández, *¿Independencia?*
13. Haring, *Imperio*, 237–39; Ayala, *Iglesia*.
14. The *patronato real* was an agreement between the Vatican and the Spanish monarchy that gave the latter, among other privileges, the prerogative of naming bishops and other church officials in its dominions. [Editor's note]
15. "Instrucciones para la constitución fundamental," 117–19.
16. "Constitución de Cádiz," 1.49, Article 12.
17. Acta de Independencia de la capitanía general de Guatemala, in *BAGG*, 1938, year 4, no. 1, 128, Article 2.
18. Ibid., 129, Articles 12–14.
19. Emphasis added. Bando del capitán general Gabino Gaínza, in ibid., 136.
20. The document presented by Gaínza is cited in detail here because of its usefulness for understanding social and political conditions at the time of independence.
21. Ibid., 137–38.

22. Wortman, *Government*, 182, 222; Solórzano, "Comunidades," 112–15; Piel, *Sajcabajá*, 243.
23. Acta de Independencia de la capitanía general de Guatemala, in *BAGG*, 1938, year 4, no. 1, 129, Articles 14, 15, 18, 19.
24. Emphasis added. Ceremonial de la juramentación de la independencia, in ibid., 130–32; Juramentación de la independencia en la ciudad de Guatemala, in ibid., 153–54. Other studies of the independence ceremonies include Díaz, *Fiesta*; Ortemberg, "Entrada"; Conde and Monsalvo, "Construcción"; Godoy, "Fiestas"; and Munilla, *Celebrar*.
25. The Tribunal del consulado del comercio was the body authorized by the Spanish crown to judge cases regarding commerce, and the protomedicato was similarly authorized to undertake the training of medical personnel and oversee the actions of medical professionals. [Editor's note]
26. Acta de juramentación de la ciudad de Guatemala, in *BAGG*, 1938, year 4, no. 1, 153–54. Celebrations of the independence oath-taking ceremonies are described in González, "Jura"; Monteagudo, *Relación*; and Gamio, *Municipalidad*.
27. Actas de juramentación del clero, in *BAGG*, 1938, year 4, no. 1, 192, 205–8, 223–25, 243–44.
28. Actas de juramentación de los vecinos de las parroquias del Sagrario, in *BAGG*, 1938, year 4, no. 1, 194, 196, 223–24, 226, 237. The lists with the signatures of those who participated were attached to the oath-taking acts.
29. Acta de juramentación del claustro de la Universidad de San Carlos, in ibid., 206–7; Escuadrón de Dragones, in ibid., 224–25.
30. Government employees took oaths in, among others, the following offices: accounting, treasury, mint, tobacco and gunpowder, secretary of government. These employees included, for example, officials, lawyers, doormen, tax collectors, and commissioners. Acta de juramentación de la Audiencia territorial, in ibid., 238–39; Actas de juramentación de la Contaduría Mayor, in ibid., 191–203; Acta de los subalternos de las cajas de Hacienda Pública, in ibid., 192; Acta de los empleados de la renta de correos, 20 de septiembre, in ibid., 197–98; Acta de la Casa de Moneda, in ibid., 203–4; Acta de la Contaduría de propios y comunidades, in ibid., 202; Acta de la Junta de diezmo del Arzobispado, in ibid., 204; Acta de la Dirección General de Rentas, Tabaco y Pólvora, in ibid., 204; Acta de la Secretaria de Gobierno, in ibid., 213.
31. Acta de la ciudad de Antigua, in ibid., 188. In a very brief report, the town of Cuajiniquilapa simply mentions having sworn obedience. Acta del Ayuntamiento de Cuajiniquilapa, in ibid., 256.
32. Acta del Ayuntamiento de Salamá, in ibid., 200–201, 230–31.
33. Acta del Ayuntamiento de Cahabón, in ibid., 255–56; Acta del Ayuntamiento de Cobán, in ibid., 238.
34. Acta del Ayuntamiento de Chiquimula, in ibid., 236.
35. Acta del Ayuntamiento de Zacapa, in ibid., 259.
36. Acta del Ayuntamiento de San Sebastián Tejar, in ibid., 259.
37. See Taracena, *Invención*; and Pollack, *Levantamiento*.
38. Acta del Ayuntamiento de Jacaltenango, in *BAGG*, 1938, year 4, no. 1, 245.

39. Acta del pueblo de San Marcos, in ibid., 248; Acta del pueblo de San Andrés, in ibid., 248–49; Acta del pueblo de San Antonio, in ibid., 249; Acta del pueblo de Concepción, in ibid., 250; Acta del pueblo de Santa Ana Huista, in ibid., 251–52; Acta del pueblo de Huehuetenango, in ibid., 198–99.
40. Correspondencia del pueblo de Quezaltenango al Ayuntamiento de la ciudad de Guatemala, in ibid., 217–18; Juramento de la independencia por el Ayuntamiento Constitucional y pueblo de Quezaltenango, in ibid., 220–21; Correspondencia del Corregidor de Quezaltenango sobre que el Ayuntamiento lo despojó del mando, in ibid., 252–54.
41. Acta del Ayuntamiento de Sololá, in ibid., 218–20.
42. Acta del Ayuntamiento de San Marcos, in ibid., 261–62; Acta del pueblo de Patzúm, in ibid., 229–30.
43. Acta del Ayuntamiento de Gualán, in ibid., 236; Acta del Ayuntamiento de Santa Rosa, in ibid., 242–43; Acta del Ayuntamiento de Mazatenango, in ibid., 246–47.
44. Acta del Ayuntamiento de Chimaltenango, in ibid., 227–28.
45. Sermón leído por el canónico José María Castilla, in ibid., 156–60.
46. Acta de Independencia de la capitanía general de Guatemala, in ibid., 129, Article 17.
47. Murillo, *Historia*, 120–21.

BOURBON REFORMS AND ENLIGHTENMENT IN CHIAPAS, 1758–1808

Christophe Belaubre

When Mariano Robles Domínguez wrote the first lines of his *Memoria histórica de la provincia de Chiapas* in 1813, a political process scarcely a half century old had radically transformed the discourse of the American Creole elite, embedding new ideas in all parts of colonial society. According to Robles, elected representative from Chiapas to the Courts of Cádiz, the well-being of the people must guide public actions, and colonial subjects must stop questioning, evading, or modifying laws:

> When laws do not enjoy exact and appropriate observance, which a *just government* proposes with their sanction; when persons charged with assuring their compliance are, rather than their executors, their principal violators, for vile self-interest . . . and when instead of employing the most careful attention and effort to inform themselves regarding the condition of the *people* under their care, and of the means that should be adopted to assure their *prosperity* and that of the *state*, they abandon [the people] and render them fruitless; they serve no purpose other than to exasperate the spirits of those same *people*.[1]

Those words, formulated so clearly and constructed as a prime mover, represent overwhelming proof of the scope and influence of the Enlightenment movement in the Spanish empire, of the presence of a generation of men whose minds were formed by the use and understanding of new ideas conceived in Europe and "reconfigured" in America. In fact, "change," "reform," "improve," "optimize"—words heard in most political speeches of the era—are concepts often mentioned with good intentions. This follows logically, since the essential function of politics implies managing public affairs as efficiently as possible. Yet these words also hide inevitable problems, because those who use them rarely consider how their discourse will be received or what would be the appropriate mechanisms that permit the "reform message" to reach those who would benefit from it. Everyone wants a better life, more social justice, high levels of education, a good health system for all. But how do you communicate to the majority of the population the simple idea that these goals cannot be reached without reforming individuals in their own *habitus* and mentalities, without changing society or the state as a whole? Proposals to increase taxes or open national markets to international commerce, for example, do not easily garner support among the general population.

Furthermore, the "reform" message that repeats itself incessantly on the radio, television, and internet today was not exactly what the learned men of the eighteenth century looked to spread in their society. These reformers wanted to convince their neighbors that absolute government control combined very well with the powers of reason and knowledge. Absolutism and Enlightenment, or, stated another way, "enlightened despotism," these men thought, could change the colonial system for the mutual benefit of both projects. Changing mentalities and imposing structural reforms clearly constituted a challenge, not terribly different (notwithstanding the obvious disparities) from that which the more "enlightened" politicians of Chiapas face today.[2]

Taking the previous discussion into account, in this chapter I scrutinize the late eighteenth- and early nineteenth-century history of Chiapas, considering that the inroads made by neoclassicism and the reform spirit, fed by the Enlightenment, are key elements that allow us to understand the political culture of a Creole elite that immediately interpreted the extraordinary news of the captivity of the Spanish kings in 1808 as a clear signal that they would soon be "liberated" from the tutelage of the monarchy.[3] The Creole thinking that established the bases for magnicide did not appear from nowhere but rather grew out of an ideological reform movement that expanded during the long eighteenth century, beginning with the rise to power of the first Spanish Bourbon (Philip V, Duke of Anjou, second grandson of Louis XIV, who entered Madrid in February 1701) and ending with the penetration of Napoleonic troops into same city in March 1808.

Under the ancien régime, the Catholic Church ideologically dominated all Spanish American societies, including that of Chiapas. This domination was demonstrated by strict control over primary and secondary schools, universities, and, by extension, the whole social body through a culture that was organized, and well rooted, in the fear of an all-powerful God. Sheltered by the protection offered by the *real patronato*, Chiapan "intellectuals," in the image of those studied by French medievalist Jacques Le Goff, were mainly members of the clergy. It was they who, by professional necessity, could read and write, and who became the leaders of the "crisis of consciousness" in Chiapas,[4] fomenting reform within a field of action defined by well-established limits that could not be violated; the reformers themselves assured that they would not be.

The search for means to improve agriculture, livestock production, and commerce constituted an important concern during this period in America—not unique or exclusive but undoubtedly constant. As part of that search, broad-ranging discussions about improving production characterized the Spanish American eighteenth century, although, as historian Juan Pedro Viqueira points out, rootless Chiapan Indians were not proletarianized French peasants.[5] Furthermore, the desire to increase production, and thereby the wealth of the people, was accompanied by a profound restructuring of the treasury, by a generalized and ambitious policy of freeing commercial activities, and by administrative reforms that led to the creation of intendencies and a regular army. The effects of these reforms continue to be difficult to measure.[6]

Although the diffusion of the Enlightenment in Chiapas has been discussed in a solid monograph, its impact on the population and the internal dynamics of its development are little known, and the purely Hispanic American dimension of the movement has likewise received little attention.[7] This chapter does not intend to resolve these problems fully but rather to propose possible avenues for more systematic investigation in the future. To approach this period, I employ two investigative methods. One is a social history that a group of colleagues have been developing for the past fifteen years within the framework of the *Diccionario biográfico centroamericano*, tracing the trajectory of actors in the spread of Enlightenment thought and stressing social ties among them.[8] Drawing on superficial hints extracted from exceptional or isolated sources, the second method involves using the evidential paradigm developed by the Italian historian Carlo Ginzburg to try to understand the process surrounding the spread of a new atticism and of the Enlightenment.[9] Without entering into a "chimerical search for origins," the method proposed by Ginzburg favors combing clues and accumulating a wide variety of facts, thus allowing greater insight into the thinking and the internal mobility of different groups, as well as their solidarities, their networks, and their conflicts, these latter an object of the study. Using the traces left by numerous actors to develop collective biographies, based on existing historiography and new primary sources, allows us to move from the socio-ideological to the political and to discuss how customs come to be transformed.[10]

A careful analysis of classic genealogies can be a starting point for the development of social genealogies, using the information they contain to highlight social behaviors,[11] thereby opening a path for research not based exclusively on "family history" or the history of urban elites. For the case under discussion, this type of focus avoids historicizing a single professional category, like the clergy, since although many of the actors were in fact churchmen there were also royal officials, attorneys, merchants, and even, although in lesser numbers, artisans and commoners from Ciudad Real and other parts of Chiapas.

Starting with the analysis of a group still in formation, whose very existence depended on a specific historical context, new social collectivities and social networks capable of transcending the corporative system become visible.[12] These new collectivities and networks fed into a common experience lived by the larger group, which accepted or rejected the initiatives the smaller bodies put forth.

This methodology does not attempt to create a global portrait of colonial society, favoring instead the uniqueness of the actors and of social differences;[13] it looks to consider those experiences lived by individuals that do not necessarily fit into the commonly held idea of an elitist and cultivated world of the Enlightenment. The intention is to include within this group of "propagators" of the Enlightenment in Chiapas, for example, actors like the unusual impoverished Creole Rafael José Rodríguez.[14] There are obviously limitations in this proposal due to the fragility of the corpus of information that refers to this group, but the cross-pollination of sources nonetheless helps to draw a collective portrait that is probably not far from social reality, not as "forced" as the classic social history analyses.[15] In some sense, the poorly conserved archival materials in Chiapas make qualitative analysis a near necessity.[16]

This chapter first discusses a social group strongly dominated by the upper clergy but open to others, especially royal officials and merchants of the region. In the following section, I identify the primary social and cultural networks that allowed the diffusion of a certain type of "Enlightenment," cherished and maintained within the ideological framework clearly established by the church and the absolute power of the king. The final part of the chapter analyzes how these ideas spread to the rest of society, which entails expanding the focus of observation to include all the regions of Chiapas. I consider small details of daily life, including those discourses that offer a sense that some of the "Enlightened" message permeated the middle and popular classes. This last concern is not fully developed in this chapter, and the discussion herein is necessarily of a preliminary nature.

AN "ENLIGHTENED" GROUP DOMINATED BY THE UPPER CLERGY

The study of any social group, and a fortiori that of the people involved in spreading Enlightenment thinking, implies placing each person in a precise local context, in a particular microsocial dynamic, and *that* requires reconstructing family groups and networks of close friends. Without succumbing, as Alain Corbin did, to the urge to reveal the history of the "unknown" shoemaker Louis-Francois Pinagot, every biographical work must bear in mind, as Pierre Bourdieu emphasizes, that the life path of any person implies "a collection of objective relationships that have united the agent under consideration to the set of other agents involved in the same field and facing the same space of the possible."[17] In other words, an individual moves within a "social space" that is also a space of diversity that exists because of the very diversity that creates it.[18] The inevitable gaps in the documentation sometimes make this social diversity inaccessible to the historian, and at other times information can be too plentiful, erasing important details or making access to them more difficult. Both factors frustrate attempts to sift out individual itineraries correctly, especially when referring to people who traveled through different parts of the Spanish American empire.

Additionally, biographies are by nature limited and their purpose should always be questioned. For example, the presence of a large library in the home of a cleric tells nothing of his reading practices and less about his understanding of the concepts present in these books, but it does offer information about his ability to acquire them. Without access to the writings of such a cleric, as is often the case, it is impossible to ascertain whether he was a reader or simply a collector, enamored of books as objects and hoping to impress those in his social circle. In Central American archives, and especially in Chiapas, private sources such as personal letters and memoirs are rare or difficult to access. Yet these are the sources that usually allow the greatest insight into the personalities of the actors and reveal the intensity and nature of their social relationships, at times exposing even their political convictions.[19]

Forty individuals make up the group presently under study, a number bound to increase as understandings of the social networks of each actor, and the cultural environment of Chiapas in the second half of the eighteenth and first half of the nineteenth century, are broadened and refined. Dominated by representatives of the church (more than 20 percent of the total), the group moved in a moderately urban society, saturated with Christian values.[20] Although they submitted to strict rules imposed by the church, the clergy belonged to a society that had begun a process of secularization and could not completely avoid changing along with that society. The concrete participation of the clergy and the nature of the relationships they wove with others, however, have yet to be analyzed.

Bishops were undoubtedly among the most dynamic and well-trained people in Chiapas, capable of understanding the links among local, regional, and imperial realities. The crown, ever vigilant in the recruitment of people with high prestige who could put the new policies from Madrid into place, carefully calculated the nomination of each bishop. Although their reforms had definite regalist nuances, all of the seven bishops in Chiapas between 1753 and 1808, from José Vital de Moctezuma to Ambrosio Llano, actively participated in the spread of new ideas. The prelates helped to strengthen a Bourbon state that they defended with fervor, notwithstanding the marked differences in their relative influence and in their activity levels. All were convinced of the need to stimulate effective public instruction as the only means to remedy the social ills caused by ignorance. Despite the risks involved, the bishops increased their official visits in order to be closer to their parishioners, worked to stop the severe and constant epidemics that devastated the Indian people, and supported the initiatives made by royal authorities to develop commercial activities in the region. Above all, supported by their own networks of collaborators, these men clashed with the interests of powerful families dominated by "Creole" components. Nevertheless, none ventured into the delicate terrain of political criticism or fostered in any way what has been called "Creole consciousness."[21] Happily, for the historian, the bishops usually provided dependable information on the other actors in Chiapan society. Polanco, for example, reported that alcalde mayor Juan de Oliver of Tuxtla had received an excellent education.[22]

The following paragraphs provide portraits of the bishops who introduced Enlightenment ideas into Chiapas. Although not well known, José Vital de Moctezuma, bishop between 1753 and 1766, a former provincial of the Mercedarian order in Mexico and a descendent of the Aztec emperor, physically transformed Ciudad Real. He dedicated a good part of his large fortune to the construction of church buildings and to social works.[23] Juan Manuel Vargas y Rivera, originally from Lima, succeeded Vital de Moctezuma at the end of 1770. Information about his career suggests an intellectual bent in Vargas y Rivera, who lived for a time in Spain before crossing the Atlantic a second time to take his post in Chiapas, bringing with him a chaplain, three pages, and a servant; shortly after his arrival a younger brother, who would secure a position in the cathedral chapter of Ciudad Real, joined him.[24] It is reasonable to suppose that the family of Vargas y Rivera would have maintained useful contacts in the Courts of Cádiz since a Creole family, especially acting at some distance from their social base, would normally have had a difficult time obtaining two nominations of that kind.

In 1777 the diocese received a truly "Enlightened" leader in the person of Francisco Polanco. Endowed with a strong personality, Polanco had been trained by the Jesuits in a Basque country marked by fierce internal debate. He was a man of experience—sixty years old when he crossed the Atlantic for the first time and a former canon of the cathedral of Santander—and in the good number of writings that survived him he expressed a strong desire to reform and consolidate the church.[25] In 1788, Francisco Gabriel de Olivares, who had studied at the prestigious Colegio Mayor San Ildefonso of the University of Alcalá de Henares, replaced Polanco and continued his efforts. Aided by his private secretary, Antonio Hurtado y Latorre, the new prelate implemented a variety of reforms whose intensity can be measured by the level of resistance they generated.[26]

In the period after the departure of Olivares, a group of intellectuals led by Jacobo de Villaurrutia, an audiencia judge in Guatemala City, played a dominant role in the kingdom, supporting Enlightenment thinking through the Sociedad de los Amigos del País and the *Gazeta de Guatemala*.[27] Articles printed in the October 1, 1798, issue of the *Gazeta* described the visit to Ciudad Real undertaken by the great Spanish naturalist José Mariano Mociño, whose presence in the city had surely been produced through the efforts of Bishop Fermín Fuero (1795–1800), since the two had known each other for many years and maintained friendly relations.[28] Bishop Fuero depended on his brother Juan Nepomuceno, provisor and vicar capitular, and on his private secretary, Dr. Joseph Castañares.[29] After the death of Fuero, the provisor and vicar general of the archdiocese of Guatemala, Ambrosio Llano (1802–15), arrived in Chiapas and continued the work that had been undertaken by the previous two bishops, but with a clear desire to maintain a certain level of dialogue with local elites, a wish expressed by the naming of Father Mariano Robles Domínguez as his secretary.[30]

In addition to the bishops and their retinues, priests in the monasteries, especially in Santo Domingo, as well as in the parishes made their influence felt by demonstrating a real vision for the future of the region. One such man, Dr. José de León y Goicoechea, parish priest of Tonalá, a corresponding member of the Sociedad de los Amigos del País, is mentioned in a book of ordinations as the half-brother of the famous José Antonio Goicoechea.[31] León y Goicoechea grew up in the capital of the kingdom and there, as he himself put it, he took advantage of "the favors and patronage of the good citizens of that capital." León y Goicoechea was made librarian of San Carlos University and, in approximately 1794, he was about to sit for a competitive exam the winner of which would fill a vacancy at the cathedral in Comayagua, when Olivares, then bishop of Chiapas, requested he return because of the "great need he had" of the man, that is, to take the position of provisor and vicar general.[32]

Alcaldes mayores, and later intendentes, along with their subdelegates, were among the most active lay agents promoting the Enlightenment. Few of these authorities, however, applied themselves full-time to their royal responsibilities, thus limiting their ability to promote reforms actively. These men undertook commercial activities that were normally tied to the interests of local merchants, and thus Luis de Engrava y Ovalle could not begin his period as alcalde mayor without the security bond (*fianza*) posted by merchants Sebastián de Olaechea, Salvador de Esponda, José Canales, Francisco Pérez, and George de Castillejo. The bonds, meant to assure that Indian tribute would be collected effectively by the royal officials, tied them to certain powerful families and placed them in the difficult position of permanent negotiation when it came to imposing or applying reforms.

Kinship bonds often strengthened these "professional" relationships; the first alcalde mayor of Tuxtla, Juan de Oliver, for example, married Josefa Antonia

Olaechea, daughter of the above-mentioned merchant Sebastián de Olaechea.[33] While governing, de Oliver promoted the new ideas, leaning directly on the local elite, whose support for him can be appreciated in their having permitted such an advantageous marriage. In fact, the naming of Salvador de Esponda, nephew of Sebastián de Olaechea, as lieutenant to the subdelegate of Ixtacomitán shows that the relationship between Oliver and the local elite was ongoing and substantive.[34] The various topics these different actors discussed among themselves remain unknown, but their relationships had evident social and political implications.

The Spaniard Antonio Serrano Polo, a legal advisor (*teniente letrado*) to the intendente between 1790 and 1798, stands out during this period, in part because of his unusual nature—impertinent, haughty, and disobedient, terms that may well denote an ability to promote social change; he was often the subject of complaints from his contemporaries. Above and beyond the intense conflicts created by his presence, of particular interest regarding Serrano Polo are his friendship with botanist José Mariano Mociño and his somewhat ambiguous attitude during the crisis caused by the 1813 Belén conspiracy in Guatemala City. The personal life of Serrano Polo clearly created tensions, as can be appreciated in testimony given by an accountant of the Royal Treasury who stated that he "was not afraid to present himself in public at plays given in the La Merced neighborhood with a woman known throughout Ciudad Real for her scandalous and licentious behavior."[35] Beyond the gossip so common in Hispanic American societies of the epoch, the liberal character of Serrano Polo can be appreciated, and his attitudes surely had an impact on the ideas of his contemporaries.

Although bishops and high royal functionaries led their contemporaries in the dissemination of new ideas, attorneys and doctors also made contributions, though a lack of data limits the conclusions that can be drawn about them at present. We do know that Pedro Vallinas practiced medicine in Ciudad Real during this period.[36]

Certain groups of Creoles and creolized Europeans, peninsular Spaniards among them, played roles in the spread of Enlightenment ideas. Details such as the marriage of Bonifacio Fernández Martínez, an official of the Royal Bank and native of Molina de Aragón in the peninsular province of Guadalajara, to the daughter of audiencia judge José Bernardo de Asteguieta can offer insight into how ideas flowed in the region.[37]

Several similar cases underline the intensity of the links with the capital of the Kingdom of Guatemala and with Quetzaltenango. Victoria Zebadúa Esponda, daughter of attorney Marcial Zebadúa, for example, lived in Guatemala City with her father and married a member of the powerful Pavón family.[38] The road through the highlands of Guatemala, passing through the burgeoning town of

Quetzaltenango, served as an umbilical cord that joined the capital of the Kingdom of Guatemala and Ciudad Real. The first and second marriages of Rita de la Tovilla Velasco, to Quetzaltenango merchants Juan Nepumuceno de Salazar González de Vega and José Gregorio Carrascosa Morales, demonstrate how that geography can be seen in a desire to do business, share news, and exchange symbolic and relational capital.[39]

Finally, the social networks that allowed the Enlightenment—initiated by the Spanish hierarchy and assimilated by certain Creole groups—to spread through the provinces were embodied in Chiapas by the presence of the Francophile (*afrancesado*) intendente José Mariano Valero.[40] Father of seven, married to a Spaniard, this important royal functionary had initially been named to a post in Honduras by reformer José de Gálvez and served as legal advisor to the intendente in Chiapas between 1798 and 1809. He belonged to the "Enlightened" middle class sent to America with the special mission of putting into practice the new intendencia system. Through her marriage to attorney José Cecilio del Valle, the eldest daughter of Valero established a solid alliance with one of the best-informed intellectuals of the kingdom.[41]

Locusts attacked the coastal region of Soconusco while the intendente of Chiapas was away, and Valero, acting in his stead, received information about the crisis from subdelegate José Farrera and from the alcalde mayor of neighboring Suchitepéquez, José Rossi y Rubi, two men known for their involvement with Enlightenment thought. In 1821 an inventory of Valero's library included 114 titles, including the book *Elocuencias*, by Friar Matías de Córdova, which Valero may have obtained during his years in Chiapas from Córdova himself. This is yet another detail that demonstrates the functioning of a Central American network that permitted the diffusion of Enlightenment thinking. The network and the spread of Enlightenment thinking can adequately be studied only through close attention to how local, regional, and Atlantic scales interacted.[42]

A CONSERVATIVE MOVEMENT AND ITS LIMITED SOCIAL IMPACT

The Enlightenment in Chiapas, as in many parts of the Spanish empire, has turned out to be a movement driven from above by the Count of Floridablanca, Gaspar Melchor de Jovellanos, and the Count of Campomanes. Some royal bureaucrats and certain bishops, however, tightly controlled its development. John Lynch stresses that the Enlightenment was in reality a good pretext for improving a second conquest of America after a century of inertia in which the management of American resources had gradually come to be controlled by powerful Creoles.[43] In Chiapas, Ciudad Real acted as the center of "Enlightened" thinking and action, which was intended to reform the state and the church and thereby free them from Creole power. Those active in spreading Enlightenment thought in Chiapas wanted to pull the province out of "ignorance" and increase its productive capacity.

Ciudad Real: Place of Encounters and Diffusion

The city of Ciudad Real, located in a valley "which suffers from excessive cold, a great deal of fog, abundant rain and continuing inclemency from an east wind," populated in 1748 with 534 houses, 121 of them with tiled roofs, and a little more than six thousand residents in 1776, acted as the center for receiving and spreading Enlightenment ideas in the region.[44] Without attempting to measure fully the intensity of the social and economic ties that joined the province of Chiapas to the rest of the world, the information that follows helps us understand those links.

In 1842, Emeterio Pineda stressed the importance of commerce among ladinos in the city, an activity that increased their interaction with the Creole world that dominated the importation of Spanish merchandise. Pineda described the ladinos as "much given to commerce, rather than to agriculture and industry. In general, their appearance is clean and composed and the population of San Cristóbal is noted for these characteristics."[45] Creoles or Spaniards, such as Salbador Peres Carbayo, who maintained a commercial relationship with Julián Crespo of the "Comercio de España" circle (Spaniards who resided in Guatemala City, involved in commerce through Cádiz), had a role in extending the horizons of the residents of Ciudad Real.[46] Through official correspondence, through the information carried by teamsters in their endless comings and goings between Guatemala City and New Spain, and through the constant movement by travelers of all kinds (including smugglers), residents of Ciudad Real kept in touch with news that affected Oaxaca, Villahermosa, Guatemala City, and all of the Atlantic world.[47] The commercial movement that teamsters and others made possible was vital to the local economy; three of the eight recommendations that finalize the report mentioned at the beginning of this chapter, made by representative Robles to the Cádiz congress, request concrete methods for stimulating the economy.[48]

Furthermore, although the Conception order convent benefited Ciudad Real, many nuns in the convents of the capital of the kingdom had been born in Ciudad Real, indicating continued financial and familial links.[49] In addition to the young women who traveled to Guatemala City, encouraged by a desire to distinguish their families from others in Ciudad Real, some young men, especially the most ambitious, who aspired to a university degree, made the same journey to educate themselves. The list of men from Chiapas who journeyed to Guatemala City for higher education includes José de León y Goicoechea, Marcial Zebadúa León, Mathías de Córdova, Carlos Cadena, Mariano Robles Domínguez, Diego de Salazar, and Gonzales de Vega. Other men traveled to be ordained, since the diocese of Ciudad Real often remained without a bishop for many years and, for economic reasons, they could not permit themselves what could well have been lengthy waits.[50] Additionally, friars from both the Mercedarian and Dominican orders, in fulfillment of the responsibilities that the rotating nature of their obligations required, traveled frequently to other regions in their province.

The Movement of Ideas:
Flows from Spain, Guatemala, Tabasco, and Tehuantepec

Without considering the porosity of its administrative borders, it is impossible to understand how ideas could have entered Chiapas. The new manners of thinking benefited from a combination of external influences (mainly from Spain, Guatemala, Tabasco, and Tehuantepec) and the interests of some small groups with regional influence in Chiapas who routinely used their power to affirm themselves politically in the face of interference from central authorities. The works of Clavijero, Moziño, Alzate, Gamarra, Velázquez de León, and others created an Enlightenment culture in New Spain that could not but exert influence throughout Chiapas.

Although the province of Chiapas was quite poor and isolated, the regular arrival of Spanish-born immigrants brought about an "intellectual and social regeneration." The civil servants, merchants, clerics, and dependents, such as the relatives of the bishops,[51] came to nourish the "natural" ties with the peninsular culture the Creoles maintained. In fact, the ties to the mother country did not break, since being a Spaniard was important social capital that permitted good marriages and access to public employment. It was common, as David Brading demonstrated, for a new arrival to invite a relative a few years after himself settling in.[52] Dominicans, Franciscans, and Mercedarians often went to Madrid to request boatloads of new friars or to fulfill responsibilities resulting from rotations in the more important positions of each province, which meant that many monks would necessarily pass through Chiapas. As can be seen in the examples given, an intense circulation of people brought fresh news from Europe or from other parts of the Kingdom of Guatemala.

An increasing number of Spaniards arrived during the eighteenth century, and according to historian Laura Machuca the Spanish population in the nearby villa of Tehuantepec grew notably.[53] According to Bishop Polanco the elite of Ciudad Real—a total of fifty persons who bore the title of "don" and were considered to be "men of honor"—were renovated with new arrivals. José Sánchez, native of Salamanca, and Agustín Villa Troncoso, native of Galicia, who wed the daughter of royal standard bearer Santiago González, are good examples.[54] Additionally, a great whirl of royal officials brought their own stories of the changes affecting the peninsula: Agustín de las Cuentas y Zayas and Cristóbal Ortiz de Avilés were natives of Seville, Francisco de Saavedra y Carvajal of Aragón, and Manuel Junquito Baquerizo of Córdoba.

News and men circulated even more regularly from Guatemala, via the road to the capital that passed through Quetzaltenango, acting, as has been mentioned, as an umbilical cord. It was common for clergymen to be commissioned for the defense of one interest or another in the capital. At the end of the eighteenth century, the vocal presence of the high court judge Jacobo de Villaurrutia and his secretary, don Alejandro Ramírez, as has been mentioned above, made the powerful influence of Guatemala City felt in Chiapas. Both men pressed new ideas on the captaincy general and made people believe that a new reformed society could be created by the work of the Sociedad de los Amigos del País. Their efforts resonated in Ciudad Real, where many responded to the call for subscriptions made by the editors of the *Gazeta de Guatemala*, even as they supported the newspaper with their pens and local initiatives. Bishop Fermín José de Fuero, as a founding member of the *Gazeta*, along with then-subdelegate of Soconusco Luis Antonio Pardo y Quiroga and local militia colonel José Ballesteros y Navas, sent money and reports. Parish priest Dr. José de León y Goicoechea,[55] whose family was related to Spanish-born merchant José Vives y Orts,[56] was a very active informant for the newspaper.

In the northern part of Chiapas, change came not from Ciudad Real but from the neighboring province of Tabasco, as the presence of new arrivals demonstrates. In 1814 a census of Palenque mentioned the presence of fourteen American Spaniards: six from Macuspana, five from Jalapa, one from Villahermosa, and two from Tacotalpa.[57] There were also some foreigners in northern Chiapas, such as the Frenchman Joseph Poumian, who married Petrona Josefa Sabo from Teapa under delicate circumstances and had established residency by 1781.[58]

External influences also came through specialists, such as the professor of surgery José María Conde y Muñós, who assisted the parish priest of Chapultenango, don Martín Robles, giving him "internal and external medical assistance" until his death.[59] Bishops and royal employees, such as the above-mentioned Vital de Moctezuma from México City and Royal Treasury official Bonifacio Fernández Martínez from Molina de Aragón in the province of Guadalajara, might arrive from anywhere in the empire, bringing with them different experiences and possibly new ideas.[60]

In addition to the teamsters mentioned above, any number of merchants plied the roads between New Spain and Guatemala. Pilgrims undertook the same voyage, sometimes traveling with their families, to the town of Esquipulas (in what is now eastern Guatemala) to honor the Black Christ. In short, there were thousands of opportunities to exchange ideas and compare experiences.

Reforming Church and State from Within

Although the imperial state seemed to rest on foundations built to last, realities on the ground belied that impression. The Bourbons took back government institutions weakened by a veritable culture of negotiation that had offered powerful families in Ciudad Real ample room for maneuver. Immersed in a network of local interests, the greater part of the colonial bureaucracy could not be trusted, and reform in this area represented a challenge the Bourbons managed to meet, despite some limitations, by steadily giving more power to royal officials.

According to representative Mariano Robles, "The Ayuntamiento of Ciudad Real worked on the same terms that [the conquistador] Mazariegos established, *but with their hands now tied* because the authorities left them so little room for movement that they had no freedom, not even to meet in their councils."[61] The same Robles thought that the intendente "was usually a tyrant, taking on as many powers as, or even more than, a president or a viceroy; he tried to put everything under his jurisdiction, even including the altar or sanctuary." The tone reveals the spirits of those who wielded Creole power in this period, and their reflections on the serious political challenge they had been obliged to face, from the second half of the eighteenth century onward.

The caricature described by Robles did not, however, correspond to reality. Consider the behavior of the intendente Agustín de las Quentas Zayas, who was anything but a despot. Governing does not always imply complying with the letter of the law, but rather taking into account the lived reality of the moment. That must have been what Quentas Zayas was thinking when twenty Indians appeared before him early on August 4, 1791, asking him "in the name of their people not to allow money which was theirs to be taken." In fact, the Indians knew that the intendente had come to comply with a Royal Treasury decree that ordered community funds from Ciudad Real and Tuxtla be lent to Francisco Sebastián Chamorro at an interest rate of 5 percent. The 25,000 pesos Quentas Zayas had turned over to the Santo Domingo convent, where an agent of Chamorro was staying, was a considerable sum. The intendente reflected on the short note the Indians had given him, which directly threatened "the Spaniard who is taking away our money." Fearful of an uprising, he consulted the bishop and the legal advisor. Together, the three men decided to return the funds to the royal coffers and inform the president of the audiencia, who approved their decision. Not only did the president ratify the measure, but the Council of the Indies agreed, stating that "the assets of Indian communities should be considered with great respect and are not to be withdrawn for other uses without their approval."[62]

The new central power, established with peninsular Spaniards occupying high positions in the church and state, involved an administrative modernization whose spirit could not be separated from the spread of the Enlightenment. In fact, state reforms were possibly the most visible expression of the new spirit that brought the different actors together. The flow of Enlightenment ideas can be sensed in the lines written by representative Robles when he himself denounced the nepotistic manner in which the intendente exercised his powers. Firing two shots at once, Robles stated, "Usually the proposed [subdelegate] is first of all some protégé, servant, or the recommendation of [the intendant], despite legal prohibitions."[63] Beyond the classic criticism of the colonial system, the cited text implies that the Bourbon reforms did not achieve their goals because they left lower-level royal officials in a weakened position whenever they attempted to impose authority in their jurisdictions.

Several aspects of ecclesiastical organization felt the weight of the reforming spirit, but church finances captured the most attention.[64] Between 1775 and 1795, for example, Bishops Polanco and Bishop Olivares confronted, apparently in vain, the resistance of canons opposed to the filing of reports and presenting clear accounts of how tithes were distributed. Bishop Polanco directly attacked canon Nicolás de la Barrera in a document titled "Responses to the Thirteen Warnings and Objections to Accounts" in which the influential priest was treated as a thief because of the suspicious disappearance of 59,014 pesos.[65]

For his part, Bishop Olivares began to exchange correspondence with President Bernardo Troncoso, revealing a desire to "promote the good order and government of the Cathedral of the Holy Church which it now lacks." Olivares sent master Francisco Texada to Guatemala City, along with a letter and a set of instructions containing thirteen articles, commissioning him to solve several problems present in the relationship between civil and ecclesiastical governments and to reduce friction within the government of his own diocese. For example, in Article 6 of his instructions he "requests that the bank in which the funds now held at the home of the so-called treasurer Bartolomé Gutiérrez be transferred to the appropriate offices of the Holy Church," showing just how threadbare the relations between the treasurer and the bishop had become. Article 9 even asks that the salary of 500 pesos the treasurer enjoyed be transferred to another official (the mayordomo de rentas) and that the salary of the official in charge of tithes be raised. The opposition by Olivares to the "previous practices" of the canons of his diocese is confrontational: "In that Church the annual ritual of presenting accounts is not observed, nor even the forming of tables for the distribution of tithes."[66]

These instructions express a clear will to rationalize government, implying an improvement in the manner in which knowledge of past experiences would be systematized, leading in turn to an effort to order the archives. With this goal in mind, Olivares tasked Father Manuel Mariano Chacón with the drafting of a book of the circulars (*cordilleras de oficio*) sent from the cathedral.⁶⁷

THE "ENLIGHTENED" GROUP IN ACTION
Social Customs, Education, and Agriculture

In Guatemala, Archbishop Cortés y Larraz was shocked to discover the type of Christianity the Indians professed, and bishops in Chiapas were aware of the "calamitous" state of an almost unreachable Indian world, ignorant of the most basic principles of Catholicism. Faced with the religious practices of the Indians of San Andrés Chamula, who adored a dirty image of Saint Peter dressed in Indian clothing, Bishop Olivares, an imprudent pragmatist, started an actual riot when he moved to replace it with another made by ladinos.⁶⁸ During a pastoral visit in the town of Ocozocoautla on June 26, 1792, Bishop Olivares decided to prohibit in all parishes of the diocese, under penalty of total excommunication, the "Blessing Dance" in which men and women mutually blessed each other, perceived by the bishop as an insult to Catholics.⁶⁹

Although their success was limited, almost all bishops made efforts to promote the opening of schools, and over time their insistence could influence local elites.⁷⁰ Bishop Fuero had very clear ideas about the role of public education: "We are all born with the same intellectual abilities, which form the most important part of our nature. . . . The most obvious and natural [of the rights of all] is public education, in which literacy, the practice of virtuous acts, and the incomprehensible truths of our sacred religion are simultaneously taught."⁷¹ The edicts proclaimed by the bishops sought through all means possible, including indulgences—one hundred days' pardon was common for all kinds of actions, and even more for those willing to preach in the streets—to broaden the understanding of Christian doctrine.⁷² Bishop Fuero, aware that the principal city of his diocese lacked an efficient educational system, vainly tried to convince vicars of the city convents to open elementary schools for the people who lived in the poorer neighborhoods surrounding the city center.⁷³ Efforts to establish public education did not always bring the results expected, as can be seen in the case of Huitiupán, where the bishops opened new schools. In June 1800, Capt. Marcos Montes de Oca took up his pen to denounce the attitude of the town schoolmaster, don Juan de Flores, who had been in Tila for two months under the pretext of making his confession.⁷⁴

Members of the clergy and royal officials (mainly intendentes, alcaldes mayores, and subdelegates) proposed and implemented innovative experiments in the heart of a social network composed of a small circle of actors who shared a certain vision for change, and the results were limited. Fernando Antonio Dávila, in a report written in Spain in 1813, confirms the backwardness of the province of Chiapas in terms showing that elitist initiatives did little to advance structural change:

> More than any others, the miserable province of Ciudad Real has been totally abandoned in [the field of agriculture]. Here there are no trained planters who attempt improvements to benefit their land . . . at the same time no one has knowledge of methods and manners to fertilize the soil, nor are there proper tools to work it. . . . It is unbelievable, but doubtlessly true, that in these parts a large plow with a suitable handle is unknown.[75]

Although the initiatives were few and most of them failed, the eighteenth century was more about "growth" than about "development." The most marginalized social groups suffered heavily from epidemics and agricultural crises, and in the end the Enlightenment in Chiapas seems more like a historiographical construct than a historical reality. Ideas clearly circulated, and new research paths can be explored by accepting that the values of the Enlightenment spread by capillary action and communication between different sectors, particularly among attorneys, doctors, artisans, and subaltern groups who were trying to take back, and take control of, the rules of a renovated eighteenth-century universalism.[76]

Epidemics and Vaccines

Epidemics devastated Chiapas and the rest of the Kingdom of Guatemala during the eighteenth century, sometimes leading to the disappearance of entire towns. Faced with Indian deaths resulting from the 1786 epidemic that struck the region surrounding Tuxtla, the alcalde mayor don Miguel del Pino y Martínez redoubled circulars that provided information about simple measures which, according to popular thinking, would help to eliminate the illness quickly.[77] In Tuxtla, del Pino y Martínez worked closely with a "doctor of medicine" and organized meetings with local authorities and principales throughout the town, offering instructions on the best way to fight the epidemic, specifically requesting that healers "who with their fatal medicines kill people" be excluded.[78] Of greater significance than the personal participation of the alcalde mayor in the process was the express will to spread new ideas in public meetings and, taking advantage of the critical nature of the circumstances, to break with old social practices through persuasion. The systematic use of circulars shows a clear vision regarding the importance of communication, in this case used to save lives.

Perhaps influenced by Moziño, Bishop Fuero improvised a hospital where medicine and food were offered free to the sick, and when smallpox devastated the region he recommended a prevention plan for individual homes, a measure not as lukewarm as it may initially appear since it required a use of "publicity" that would be available to the general public. Discussions focused on opening up the private sector to facilitate a solution to group problems probably fed into the idea of focusing on individual homes. A certain level of modernity, then, had begun to penetrate all layers of society in Ciudad Real, and with it attempts to implement integrated responses to the epidemics found a more positive reception.

Fuero and Moziño also dedicated time to "*tiña*, a rare form of leprosy," which they considered to be a principal cause of a notable population loss in the diocese. In a pastoral letter of August 1798, Bishop Fuero made a clear attempt to gather clinical data that would permit a better understanding of the illness; in all the parishes of the diocese each patient was to be physically examined in order to identify more clearly the symptoms presented.[79] Although certainly not implemented everywhere, the edict may well have provoked debates in locales where those suffering from the disease were usually forced out of town without pity or justification.

In July 1804, Bishop Llano published an edict assuring that his clerics would assist the teachers who had been charged with applying the vaccination.[80] Here again the efforts of the authorities—in this case the bishop—to involve the wider public in its own development deserve emphasis. Beyond vaccinating people in all the towns, the recommendations given by Llano implied an educational process and person-to-person efforts that could be carried out without occasioning public debate over the new need; everyone became a potential "vaccine giver." The proliferation of regulations offered a means to spread Enlightenment thought through the use of less visible mechanisms that allowed access to all segments of society.

The documents indicate that the movement spread through concentric circles, overcoming the bad roads and geographic isolation, to reach the most distant parts of the territory. In the hope of increasing revenue from Indian tribute, mid-eighteenth century authorities decided to divide the alcaldía mayor of Ciudad Real into two alcaldías, one with its seat still in Ciudad Real and the other with its capital in Tuxtla. The notion that better administration could create an effective response to the demographic collapse of the Indian population in Chiapas reflected an "Enlightened" manner of confronting the problem.

Friar Domingo de Gutiérrez Horna presented Bishop Francisco de Polanco with statistics covering twenty years of information on the towns of Ostuacán and Sayula, which revealed a strange number of deaths in the latter. On investigating the possible reasons for what was a notable difference between the two towns, the friar explained to Polanco that these deaths probably resulted from working in the limestone quarries in Sayula. He then asked that the quarrying activities be prohibited and argued in a clearly utilitarian manner that "the town was ending up without people and the king without tribute. All of this is attributable to the mentioned mortality rate."[81] The example of Gutiérrez Horna demonstrates the arrival of a progressive vision at the local level, though in many cases the channels through which that vision traveled can be difficult to reconstruct.

Banned Books: An Underground Culture

Opening the doors to free trade between Spain and America (1778) effectively increased the exchange of goods, including books. That decision turned out to be a challenge for the Inquisition, whose ever subtle control over the circulation of books became yet more difficult to manage.[82] It is easy to suspect that the prohibitions were also counterproductive, raising considerable curiosity in a public that could legitimately sense the manipulation implied by authorizing one book and banning another.[83]

The edicts banning books were read in public plazas like any others, but in a city like Ciudad Real, where private libraries were rare and there were no printing presses or bookstores (although one or two merchants may have sold a few books among the other products in their stores), the strange need for these laws could have provoked discussions among the residents. Some authorized books were already inciting arguments, especially the writings of Friar Benito Jerónimo Feijoo, considered a precursor of enlightened despotism in Spain and known in the ecclesiastical circles of the capitancy general for his positions in favor of the methods of experimental science.[84]

As an instrument for repression and for the control of the written word, the Inquisition was moderate, and few confiscations were actually carried out. Nevertheless, based on the lists of books seized in Guatemala, we have a sense that undesirable publications—like the popular and often confiscated *History of the People of God* by Father Isaac-Joseph Berruyer (1728–57), *Institutiones iuris ecclesiastici* by Carlo Sebastiano Berardi (published in Spanish in 1791), the morality novels of Marmontel, *Elementos de moral* by Mably (Spanish version 1799), the works of the poet Edward Young, and evidently the works of the "heretic" Voltaire or the *Social Contract* of Rousseau—could pass from hand to hand until they were denounced and ended up in the archives of the Inquisition.[85] In his *Memorias*, Miguel García Granados stated categorically: "The Spanish regime, it is true, had banned the introduction of the works of all the free thinkers, but they nonetheless continued to enter as contraband, and young people read them on the sly. Voltaire, Rousseau, Holbach and other writers of the eighteenth centuries went from hand to hand."[86]

Conserving Pre-Columbian History

The sixteenth and seventeenth centuries involved the almost systematic destruction of the symbols of Indian culture, but by the beginning of the nineteenth century shifting ideas favored rescuing pre-Colombian sites and an appreciation for Indian culture. In 1813 representative Robles, who described himself as a Spanish citizen, drew on the writings of the Dominican Remesal to describe the "ominous inhumanity of the Spaniards" during the conquest. Robles highlighted the political works of Las Casas and made reference to different aspects of indigenous culture, recognizing their importance.[87]

Canon José de Ordóñez, icon of the conservative "Enlightened" effort, showed a singular intellectual openness to the pre-Columbian period, contributing to early studies of Palenque that sparked so much interest in Madrid and Guatemala that three expeditions to explore the site were financed during the decade of the 1780s.[88] Antonio de Solis, the priest who first discovered Palenque in late 1784, did not expect to find an ancient city when he began his trip into the jungle, and his happening upon on it probably came about by chance, though the timing was excellent.

Dominican provincial friar Tomas Luis de Roca was aware that Estachería, president of the audiencia, held a favorable attitude toward studies of the pre-Columbian past and used the power of his order in Chiapas to get detailed information about Palenque. In a letter addressed to the king, Estachería adopted a notably deferential attitude toward the Indian past: "One must admire their architecture, however coarse it may be, and be amazed at the solidity and numbers of the buildings, produced by people today so little inclined to homes of any duration and permanence."[89] His interest piqued, Estachería would later ask Antonio Bernasconi to survey and map Palenque, preparing the expedition himself and composing an extensive seventeen-chapter set of instructions for the architect. Bernasconi left Guatemala City on January 29, 1785, and reached Palenque on February 25. He would write a report, draw four maps, and collect several statues—thereby beginning a long history of pillaging.[90] José Antonio Calderón, lieutenant of the town of Santo Domingo del Palenque, supported Bernasconi with zeal and intellectual openness, complementing the report with fine details that drew the attention of experts in Madrid. Calderón was well aware of the benefits of surrounding himself with Indians and ladinos, "whose age provided them with the most experience."[91]

Estacheria also made unsuccessful efforts to discover whether manuscripts in Indian languages gave any clue as to the origin of Palenque. On March 15, 1786, the audiencia president saw his efforts repaid by an order from the king, whose permission he had asked to continue investigating the ruins. This time, a captain of the Royal Artillery Force, don Antonio del Río, traveled to Palenque and gathered six crates of objects that he found to be of greatest interest, all of which were sent to Spain on the frigate *Bastanesa*.[92]

Years later the same canon, Joseph Ordóñez, personally negotiated transferring the cadaver of Bishop José Vital de Moctezuma to Ciudad Real. He knew that the remains of this direct descendent of the Aztec emperor could not remain in the small church of San Bartolomé de los Llanos. Subdelegate Joaquín Gutiérrez de Arce described the operation in terms that scarcely hide his skepticism that the bones found in the church were really those of the bishop.[93]

Regional Examples: Northern Chiapas and Tuxtla

In 1813 representative Robles defended the idea that the Courts should "propose the means for prosperity . . . for the benefit and happiness of our heroic nation, *even the towns of more reduced extension* that have the good fortune to be included within its limits."[94] Robles supposed continuity, accepting the fact that real power lay among the privileged families, and that any new policy would require negotiations in which they would have to be included. In the second half of the eighteenth century the powerful Landeros family dominated northern Chiapas, as the following examples demonstrate. Subdelegate Bernardo Landeros worked with intendente Agustín de las Cuentas Zayas in an attempt to relocate some scattered families in the highlands of Tila and Tumbalá with the idea of starting a new town.[95] Doña Ana Gorgonia Landeros married José Antonio Calderón shortly before he received a commission to visit the recently discovered archaeological site of Palenque. In January 1807, Manuel Landeros, parish priest of Palenque, died, and the naming of Bernardo Mariano Castro, native of Yucatán, as his replacement cost the family local influence.[96]

The efforts of the alcalde mayor Miguel del Pino y Martínez deserve mention since nearly all of the priests in the area mentioned his charity, efficiency, and altruism. In the parish of Tuxtla, Manuel Ruiz offered extensive details concerning the driving force that del Pino y Martínez provided in the construction of a system to bring water from the outskirts of town to its center. The alcalde mayor also established several public primary schools for Indian children, including the first public primary school in Tuxtla. Finally, del Pino y Martínez dedicated himself to the construction of the royal road that ran from Tuxtla to Ixtacomitán, completing eighteen leagues during his tenure.[97]

CONCLUSION

On September 21, 1809, the ayuntamiento of Ciudad Real suspended interim gobernador intendente José Mariano Valero from his functions and ordered his arrest, because of "grave suspicions" of disloyalty to the king. Bishop Llano did not oppose these actions and, in order to avert unrest, accepted political leadership of the region until the arrival of another intendente a short time later.[98] On October 14, the accused asked, unsuccessfully, to be freed. Valero was sent in chains to Spain, despite the opposition of Governor Antonio González y Saravia, who considered the decision to be an outrageous example of royal impotence, typical of the new period that was about to begin, a period of political autonomy, conditioned by an eighteenth century itself marked by social change and by modifications in the mentalities of society as a whole.[99]

In truth, the Enlightenment was a period of intense change in Chiapas, but not as a moment, as it has often been presented, in which a few "great men" decided that it was time to modernize society and seek other means to achieve happiness. In reality, a whole social body was in movement, on very different levels and in very different ways. Creoles, Spaniards, ladinos, blacks, and Indians took part in interchanges that would push forward the implementation of administrative reforms—even if it was to organize resistance; all were aware of the spirit of reform in the government of Charles III.

Nonetheless, the impulse for reform came from the top down, from the social strata better prepared to receive and spread the new ideas. Members of the upper clergy and, to a lesser degree, royal officials and their entourages, who had developed networks that grew from the exchange of services among themselves, tried by all available means to spread an "Enlightened" ideology restricted to specific patterns of behavior: improving how state and clerical machinery functioned, investigating pre-Columbian Indian culture, building roads, and opening schools and hospitals. The project was essentially limited, in some ways conservative, in that it looked to build an ordered society able to undertake economic activities directed toward improving the well-being of only a small segment of the population.

Nevertheless, through hidden paths that those active in spreading the Enlightenment helped to blaze, albeit at least in part unintentionally, reason progressed against faith in Chiapas, as in any other part of the world. A future with new forms of government could be imagined, public debates became more common, thanks in part to the changes bishops wished to implement in health care, and new ideas traveled to even the remoter parts of Chiapas. Perhaps what took place in Chiapas was the true meaning of "Enlightenment," which deserves to be explained in greater detail, a transformation of cultural values in a population of Africans, Indians, ladinos, and Creoles who were quite present in their own history.

NOTES

1. Emphasis added. Robles, *Memoria*, 3–4. [Editor's note: The term *pueblos* has been rendered here as "people."]
2. The present-day state of Chiapas, part of the Mexican Federation, was a peripheral part of the Kingdom of Guatemala during the colonial period. It was initially divided into two separate jurisdictions: the alcaldía mayor of Ciudad Real and the gobernación of Soconusco. In 1768 the alcaldía mayor was divided into two, forming the alcaldías mayores of Tuxtla and Ciudad Real. Finally, in 1786 the crown created the intendencia of Ciudad Real, governed by an intendente, which included both alcaldías mayores and Soconusco. The territory of the intendancy was divided into eleven subdelegations, each headed by a subdelegate, nominated by the intendente and named by the president of the audiencia of Guatemala. The subdelegations were Palenque, Ocosingo, Tila, Huixtan, Tuxtla, Comitán, Huitiupan, Simojovel, Ixtacomitán, San Andrés de las Coronas, Tapachula, and Tonalá. The latter two subdelegations had formed the territory of Soconusco prior to the 1786 reform. See Pineda, *Descripción*, 45; and Hall and Pérez, *Historical*, 32.
3. Studies on the Creole elite in Chiapas are scarce. For the sixteenth century, see Lenkersdorf, *Génesis*; and Nájera, *Formación*; on the eighteenth century, Polushin, "Bureaucratic," stands out; and for the nineteenth, see Torres, *Hombres*.
4. The author refers to the book by Paul Hazard whose original (1935) title in French was *La Crise de la conscience européene*. It has been translated into English most recently under the title *The Crisis of the European Mind, 1680–1715*. [Editor's note]
5. See Sarrailh's classic work, *España*. See also Miranda, *Ideas*; Barudio, *Época*; and Viqueira, *¿Relajados?*, 18.
6. Dym and Belaubre, *Politics*.
7. Carvalho, *Ilustración*. See also Gutiérrez, *Casa*; and Claps and Gutiérrez, *Formación*.
8. On the *Diccionario biográfico centroamericano* (hereafter *DBC*), see http://afehc-historia-centroamericana.org and the "Diccionario" link. The focus of the dictionary is on the social relations woven among the many actors represented in the dictionary, rather than on the actions of a specific few. The internet publication of the dictionary, using a unique format that involves the participation of more than forty historians, allows links to be established between the persons cited in the now more than 350 entries. Regarding the use of the biographical sketch method to discern social networks, see Bertrand, "De la familia." On social conflict as an historical object, see Belaubre, "Traslado," and "Redes."
9. The evidential method implies the right to not place all archival documents on the same level, and to attach importance to one document or one fact that is of no apparent significance. For more on the evidential method, see the public debate in the Italian journal *Quaderni di storia* 6, no. 11 (1980). Ginzburg did not invent the use of clues in historical research, which goes back to the German school at the beginning of the nineteenth century, as can be seen in the definition of history provided by Ranke as a "deciphering of sacred hieroglyphics." See Noiriel, *Sur la crise*, 160.
10. For Chiapas, the contributions made by Octavio Gordillo y Ortiz deserve mention, especially his *Diccionario biográfico de Chiapas*.

11. Daumand, "Généalogies," 10, 23. See the work undertaken on the González Batres family, following the lead of genealogist Ramiro Ordóñez Jonama. Ordóñez, "Familia"; and Belaubre, "Cuando."
12. Viguerie, *Histoire*; Croix and Prévost, *Église*.
13. Veyne, *L'inventaire*.
14. Belaubre, "Violencia."
15. On these new investigative technologies, see *Le Mouvement social. L'histoire sociale en mouvement*, no. 200 (July-September 2002).
16. For a clear idea of the archives in Chiapas, see Fenner, "Fuentes."
17. Bourdieu, "L'illusion," 72.
18. Bourdieu, "Espacio."
19. Lévi, "Usages." On the practices of reading, see Belaubre, "Entre cultura," in press.
20. Alma Margarita Carvalho has emphasized the significant percentage of religious leaders (34 percent) among the founders of the *Sociedad de los Amigos del País de Chiapas* (Society of Friends of the Country in Chiapas) in 1819. Carvalho, *Ilustración*, 244.
21. Lavallé, "De l'esprit."
22. Orozco y Jiménez, *Documentos*, vol. 2.
23. Paula, *Noticias*, 89–92; Markman, *Architecture*, 286; Aubry, "Mayorazgo," 4–5. See Christophe Belaubre, "José Vital de Moctezuma," in *DBC*, July 17, 2013.
24. Expediente de información y licencia de pasajero a Indias de Juan Manuel Vargas y Rivera, obispo de Chiapas, fraile mercedario, a Guatemala (mayo de 1770), in the Archivo General de Indias (hereafter AGI), Contratación, 5513, no. 17; Cámara de las Indias a 28 de enero de 1789 and Título de todas las presentaciones eclesiásticas hechas desde 1635 hasta la fecha de 1821, Guatemala, in AGI, Guatemala 913, obispos y prebendas de Chiapa (1633–1821).
25. See the Informe del obispo Francisco de Polanco sobre el estado de su diócesis, in AGI, Guatemala 531.
26. Carvalho, *Ilustración*, 83, 181, 190, 206–8; Christophe Belaubre, "Francisco Gabriel de Olivares y Benito," in *DBC*, July 8, 2011.
27. *Gazeta de Guatemala* 6, no. 261 (1802).
28. Libro en que se copia las cordilleras de oficio mandado hacer por el padre cura don Manual Mariano Chacon, de orden de su Sría. Yllma. Sor. Dr. don Francisco Gabriel de Olivares y Benito de 1792, Ciudad Real, 1792, in the Archivo Histórico Diocesano de San Cristóbal de las Casas (hereafter AHDSC), fol. 37v.
29. Christophe Belaubre, "Fermín José Fuero," in *DBC*, October 28, 2012.
30. Christophe Belaubre, "Ambrosio Llano," in *DBC*, December 2, 2012.
31. Libro de ordenaciones de 1781/1784, ciudad de Guatemala, in Archivo Histórico Arquidiocesano de Guatemala (hereafter AHAG), T2, 82. He was the son of Lucas de Goicoechea and María Velendis and began his ecclesiastical career on April 28, 1784. He was probably born around 1760, and we know that he died in October 1799. He had not reached his fortieth birthday at the time of his death, obviously limiting his impact in pushing forward Enlightenment ideas in Chiapas.
32. Carta al rey del doctor don Josef de León y Goicoechea, provisor de aquella diócesis,

expone su mérito presente en atención a sus circunstancias actuales, Ciudad Real, 1 de agosto de 1795, in AGI, Guatemala 921.
33. Aramoni, "Juan de Oliver," 48.
34. Gutiérrez, "Notas," 104–8. See Christophe Belaubre, "Juan Oliver," in *DBC*, October 27, 2013.
35. Sobre la conducta y procedimientos del teniente letrado y asesor ordinario don Antonio Norberto Serrano Polo: Informe del contador de la Real Hacienda don Francisco Duran, Ciudad Real, 1795, in Archivo General de Centroamérica (hereafter AGCA), sig. A1.29 (I), leg. 41, exp. 475, fol. 28.
36. Declaración del maestro de cirugía Pedro Vallinas vecino de esta ciudad, Ciudad Real, 1795, in AGCA sig. A1.29 (I), leg. 41, exp. 475. fol. 28.
37. AHAG, Sagrario, Matrimonios de Españoles, book no. 4, 1729–1821, 3rd part, 1799–1821, fol. 77.
38. AHAG, Sagrario, Matrimonios Comunes, book no. 1, 1822–1867, fol. 79.
39. Falla, "Familia," 508.
40. Christophe Belaubre, "José Mariano Valero y Ortega," in *DBC*, May 2, 2013.
41. Andrés Brillante y Ramos sobre agravios en Comayagua el 10 de septiembre de 1797, Comayagua, 1797, in AGI, Estado, 49, no. 49.
42. Libro de protocolo de José García 1821, in AGCA, sig. A1.20. leg. 3051, fols. 167–79. On the network that disseminated Enlightenment ideas in Guatemala and its Atlantic dimension, see Belaubre, *Église*.
43. Lynch, *Revoluciones*.
44. "Ciudad Real 1748."
45. Pineda, *Descripción*, 22.
46. Libro de protocolo de Antonio Santa Cruz (1771–1792), ciudad de Guatemala, 1780, in AGCA, sig. A1.20, leg. 342, fol. 2v–3. Peres Carbayo indebted himself to Crespo for slightly more than 12,500 pesos in January 1780.
47. On this subject, see Machuca, "Relaciones."
48. Requests include opening a canal in the isthmus of Tehuantepec, upgrading certain rivers for navigation, and lifting certain duties at the ports of Tonalá and Tapachula. See Robles, *Memoria*, fols. 68–71.
49. Examples are numerous in the different convents of the capital. María de la Concepción, a Capuchin novice, was born in Ciudad Real, the daughter of Domingo Miguel Reyes and Leonor Sulecio. Libro de protocolo de José Díaz González, ciudad de Guatemala, 1800, in AGCA, sig. A1.20, leg. 950. Micaela Alfonsa de la Tovilla y Velasco, whose father lived in Ciudad Real, joined the Santa Clara convent. Libro de protocolo, 1777, in AGCA, sig. A1.11, 22, leg. 5813, exp. 49089. María Manuela and Teresa Josefa de Salazar y González de Vega, who lived in Ciudad Real, entered, respectively, the Santa Catalina and Capuchina convents. AHAG, T2, 91, exp. 2712 (1802); and expediente para ingresar en el convento de Capuchinas, 1783, in AHAG, T1, 93. María Ventura de San Antonio, the daughter of royal standard-bearer Santiago González and María Antonia de Murga y Unquera, took the veil at the Santa Clara convent. Expediente para ingresar en el convento de Santa Clara, 1797, in AHAG, part 93, Convento de Santa Clara.

50. For example, Pedro José Solórzano y Villatoro, native of Comitán, legitimate son of Domingo Solórzano and Catarina Villatoro, was ordained in 1804. AHAG, T7, 43, Ordenaciones.
51. Bishop Francisco de Polanco, for example, came to Chiapas with Santiago Moreno, a cleric and secretary, native of Orillares; Manuel Antonio Quiroga, a priest and church administrator, native of Santa María de Vilabella; Antonio Becerro Polanco, prosecuting attorney (*fiscal*), originally from Villanueva, Valle de Villaescusa; José de la Carrera, page, native of Valle de Piélagos, and José Manuel Sánchez Pariente, page, originally from Vilvestre. Expediente de información y licencia de pasajero a Indias de Francisco de Polanco, electo obispo de Ciudad Real de Chiapas, a Guatemala, con las siguientes personas, Ciudad Real, 1777, in AGI, Contratación, 5522, no. 2.
52. Brading, *Mineros*.
53. Machuca, *Comercio*, 225. Fifty family heads were registered in the first half of the eighteenth century and 550 by its end.
54. AHDSC, Sección del obispo Polanco, in a cloth-bound book; Superior despacho de ruego y encargo a SS para que promueva a los vecinos de esta ciudad a que hagan postura en los oficios consejiles y expediente sobre su cumplimiento, fols. 130–44. See particularly the list of local men of honor who could enter the city cabildo, created by Polanco in 1781. On the wedding of don Agustín Villa Troncoso, see AHDSC, Informaciones matrimoniales, 1751–1803.
55. Carvalho, *Ilustración*, 244–45. De León y Goicoechea reported on damages the area had suffered from the storm that devastated the coast of Chiapas in 1794.
56. José Vives y Orts, native of Spain, was married on December 23, 1819, in Ciudad Real to Josefa de León y Goicoechea. Archivo de la curia diocesana de Ciudad Real, Sagrario, Matrimonios, no. 8, 1814–1823, fols. 85–89v. Courtesy of Udo Grub.
57. Ruz, *Tabasco*, 20. Padrón de los padres regulares asignados al convento de Santo Domingo de Tecpatan y demás habitantes del Pueblo. Año de 1813, in AHDSC, Tecpatan 4, D4, Padrones.
58. Ruz, *Tabasco*, 103.
59. Ibid., 101. He requested the large sum of 3,343 pesos for his work and was described as from "far-off lands."
60. Christophe Belaubre, "José Vital de Moctezuma," in *DBC*, July 17, 2013.
61. Robles, *Memoria*, fols. 24–25 (emphasis added).
62. Carta del intendente de Chiapas, Agustín de las Quentas Zayas al marqués de Baxamar, Ciudad Real, September 30, 1791, in AGI, Guatemala 646, Expedientes e instancias de partes.
63. Robles, *Memoria*, fol. 31.
64. The successful efforts of the intendente Quentas Zayas to increase annual tribute income by 6,375 pesos show that royal treasury officials in Chiapas implemented similar policies. Trens, *Historia*, 184.
65. AHDSC, Sección del obispo Polanco. In a clothbound book; Advertencias que hizo el Archidiácono don José de la Barrera para firmar las cuentas de 20 años y satisfacción, y reparos a dichas advertencias, fols. 43–63. This document is followed by another written

by Polanco: "Satisfacción a las trece advertencias y reparos a las cuentas," fols. 51–60. See also Trens, *Historia*, 164.

66. Correspondencia entre el capitán general Bernardo Troncoso y el obispo de Ciudad Real Francisco Gabriel de Olivares, Ciudad Real, 1790, in AHDSC. Regarding the trip undertaken by Texada to Guatemala, see ibid., fol. 46.
67. Libro en que se copian las cordilleras de oficio mandado hacer por el padre cura don Manuel Mariano Chacón, de orden de su Sría. Yllma. Sor. Dr. don Francisco Gabriel de Olivares y Benito de 1792, in AHDSC.
68. García de León, *Resistencia*, 455–56.
69. Libro en que se copian las cordilleras de oficio mandada hacer por el padre cura don Manuel Mariano Chacón, de orden de su Sría. Yllma. Sor. Dr. don Francisco Gabriel de Olivares y Benito de 1792, in AHDSC, fols, i–iv.
70. Ibid., folio 3v. See the recommendations made by Bishop Olivares when he visited the parish of Tuxtla on July 24, 1792.
71. Taracena, *Expedición*, 56.
72. [Editor's note: The document refers to *cantar la doctrina*.] Libro en que se copian las cordilleras de oficio mandado hacer por el padre cura don Manuel Mariano Chacón, de orden de su Sría. Yllma. Sor. Dr. don Francisco Gabriel de Olivares y Benito de 1792, 16 de enero de 1799, in AHDSC, fol. 42v.
73. Carvalho, *Illustración*, 189.
74. Carta de Marcos Montes de Oca al intendente don Agustín de las Quentas Zayas, Ciudad Real, 19 de junio de 1800, in AHDSC, Comitán 5, Papeles de Rafael de Tovar y Guimbarda.
75. AGI, Guatemala, 974 (1813).
76. For a more nuanced treatment of the idea of an eighteenth century of great prosperity, see Florescano, *Precios*. Berthe's expression "growth without development" is used by Juan Pedro Viqueira in the introduction of his book *¿Relajados?*, 16.
77. See the testimony of the priest of San Miguel Arcángel Copainalá, Father Melchor Hernández, in Testimonio relativo de los meritos y servicios de don Miguel del Pino y Martínez, teniente coronel de la provincia de Escuintla y alcalde mayor que fue de ella y de la de Tusta de las Chiapas en el reino de Guatemala, Ciudad Real, 1788, in AGCA, sig. A1.29, leg. 41, exp. 474, fol. 12.
78. See the testimony of don Manuel Ruiz, permanent vicar of the benefice of Tuxtla, independent ecclesiastical judge of the Zoques, Testimonio relativo de los méritos y servicios de don Miguel del Pino y Martínez, teniente coronel de la provincia de Escuintla y alcalde mayor que fue de ella y de la de Tusta de las Chiapas en el reino de Guatemala, Ciudad Real, 1788, in AGCA, sig. A1.29, leg. 41, exp. 474, fol. 16.
79. Libro en que se copian las cordilleras de oficio mandado hacer por el padre cura don Manuel Mariano Chacón, de orden de su Sría. Yllma. Sor. Dr. don Francisco Gabriel de Olivares y Benito de 1792, Ciudad Real, 1792, in AHDSC, fols. 34, 37.
80. Ibid., fols. 58–60.
81. Aramoni, *Refugios*, 231.
82. In May 1768, in a report from Floridablanca and Campomanes, the Inquisition had been

severely criticized: "The abuse in the banning of books ordered by the Holy Office [of the Inquisition] is one cause of the ignorance that reigns in a large part of the nation." Sarrailh, *España*, 294.
83. Sobre la publicación del edicto sobre libros prohibidos en las cuatro iglesias principales de la Ciudad Real de Chiapas, 1765, in AGN, Inquisición, vol. 1071, exp. 8, fols. 171–72.
84. Although notarial archives with posthumous inventories are rare in Chiapas, there is no reason to believe that the situation there would have been different than that in other parts of the kingdom where there are indications of the presence of works by Feijoo. In 1779, when an inventory was made of the library of doctor of law Manuel Bernardino Jáuregui, fourteen volumes of the works of Feijoo were found, certainly including his *Teatro crítico* written between 1726 and 1739. In 1802 the library of the priest José María Eloso y Cueva, less ample than that of Jáuregui, held fifteen volumes of Feijoo. Libro de protocolo de José Díaz González, ciudad de Guatemala, AGCA, sig. A1. 20, leg. 952, fols. 326–31.
85. Mérida, *Historia*, especially the inventory of the archive of the Inquisition, 127–50.
86. García, *Memorias*, 17.
87. Robles, *Memoria*, fols. 6–8, 24–25.
88. Poblett, *Narraciones*.
89. Carta al rey del presidente Josef Estacheria, Guatemala, 26 de agosto de 1785, in AGI, Guatemala 645, Expedientes e instancias de partes.
90. Mapa del territorio donde estaban situadas las ruinas llamadas de Palenque en la provincia de Ciudad Real de Chiapa, AGI, MP, Guatemala 257; Diseño de casas, plano y corte de las mismas, de las ruinas de una gran población en el sitio llamado de Palenque en la provincia de Ciudad Real de Chiapa, AGI, MP, Guatemala 258; Dibujos de algunas figuras y adornos de las ruinas llamadas de Palenque en la provincia de Ciudad Real de Chiapa, AGI, MP, Guatemala 259; Plano del Palacio de las ruinas llamadas de Palenque en la provincia de Ciudad Real de Chiapa, AGI, MP, Guatemala 260. See Carta de Antonio Bernasconi, Guatemala, 13 de junio de 1785, in AGI Guatemala 645, Expedientes e instancias de partes.
91. Report of José Calderón in Poblett, *Narraciones*, 19.
92. Carta al rey del presidente Josef Estacheria, Guatemala, 9 de julio de 1788, in AGI, Guatemala 645, Expedientes e instancias de partes.
93. Certificación de la exhumación de los restos del obispo Moctezuma, Ciudad Real, 1794, in AHDSC:

> The Indians were instructed to dig at a patch where lime met brick, which they kept digging at until around seven in the evening that day and we stopped for the night, marking the hole with a line in the earth that had been dug up, to continue the operation the following day. We began again at about nine in the morning and, not finding anything, the Indians continued digging and carrying off the dirt until they ran into some more rotten boards which seemed to be from a coffin, and inside them were some pieces of lining and braid assumed to be from the compartment in which the above-mentioned bishop was buried. Since from these signs it is credible that the bones

brought out were those of the body sought, and, having searched with all possible care for the relics which the mentioned document refers to, no sign of which was found, they were brought out with nothing else and wrapped in cotton.

94. Robles, *Memoria*, fol. 5.
95. "Fundación de San Fernando Guadalupe." Don Bernardo Landero of Palenque advised the intendente to found the town of Salto de Agua.
96. See AGCA, sig. A1.11, leg. 113, exp. 4805, 1807.
97. See the testimonio de don Manuel Ruiz vicario perpetuo del beneficio de Tuxtla, foráneo y juez eclesiástico de los de Zoques, 1788, Tuxtla, in AGCA, sig. A1.29, leg. 41, exp. 474; Testimonio relativo de los méritos y servicios de don Miguel del Pino y Martínez, teniente coronel de la Provincia de Escuintla y alcalde mayor que fue de ella y de la de Tusta de las Chiapas en el reino de Guatemala, fols. 13v–17.
98. Se acusa a Valero de deslealtad al rey y la patria, Ciudad Real, 14 de octubre de 1809, in AGCA, sig. A1.30, leg. 19, exp. 368. Laughlin, *Gran*, 170. Valero moved to the Indies upon receiving his nomination as legal advisor of the province of Comayagua in April 1787. After five years in Comayagua, he became embroiled in a noisy political battle that came up in a June 1793 meeting of the board of tithes. Despite the gravity of the matter, he was cleared. According to Andrés Billantes y Ramos, chief officer of the royal treasury of Comayagua, the audiencia judge Ambrosio Cerdan was involved in that decision along with the public prosecutor, don Miguel de Bataller, who, as a friend and countryman, was biased in favor of then prisoner Valero. See Payne, this volume, on the bishop of León and his ascendancy to power in that intendency a few years later.
99. Documentos que acreditan la religiosidad, patriotismo y demás circunstancias del licenciado José Mariano Valero, ex gobernador intendente de Ciudad Real, 1811, in AGCA sig. A1. 15, leg. 312, exp. 2180.

PART II
Rebellion and Repression

LOCAL POWERS AND POPULAR RESISTANCE IN NICARAGUA, 1808–1813

Elizet Payne Iglesias

In recent years, Central America has seen a series of commemorations, both official and academic, honoring social movements active in the isthmus between November 1811 and September 1821.[1] Late nineteenth- and early twentieth-century liberals began labeling these movements as events of national importance, reconstructing the incidents as independence-related, with the manifest intention of creating and strengthening patriotic traditions as a means to develop national identities. The 1911 Salvadoran centenary commemorations, under the government of Manuel Enrique Araujo, exemplify this trend, with the construction of a monument dedicated to independence era heroes and the publication of texts focused completely on this theme, among them the magazines *Próceres*, *Próceres de la Independencia*, *Patria*, *Libro Araujo*, and the *Álbum del Centenario*.[2]

Things happened differently in Nicaraguan historiography, which, although it catalogued the events of December 1811 and January 1812 in the context of independence,[3] did not characterize the movements of León, Granada, and the rest of the urban centers involved in protests as events of national importance.[4] Nevertheless, national authorities clearly made efforts to mark these dates. The conservative governments that led Nicaragua after 1910 made timid attempts toward commemorating them, and others did likewise in the 1990s with the erection of an obelisk in the historic district of Granada in memory of what were described as the "Granadan Heroes" of 1812.

Protests of different types marked late eighteenth- and early nineteenth-century Central America, from conflicts within cabildos, movements in opposition to government monopolies, taxes, and Indian tributes to actions with incipient political expressions. An explanatory model in the tradition of the *longue durée* must take several factors into account. The economic, social, ecclesiastic, military, political, and administrative impact of the Bourbon reforms ranks among the most important and most celebrated of these factors, as do later expressions of a more sociopolitical nature derived from processes begun in Europe, such as the Courts of Cádiz in the Spanish case and the seeds of independence planted in the Caribbean, New Spain, and South America.

One explanation of the protests analyzed in this chapter requires a careful look at the composition and interests of the cabildo members. José Antonio Fernández, a Costa Rican colleague, has suggested that Central American cabildos at the end of the eighteenth century and beginning of the nineteenth were "fields of conflict."[5] Their efforts to preserve or consolidate interests and privileges, particularly in the case of Nicaragua and its cities, drove them to a divisiveness that has provoked military confrontations throughout their history. Heavily swayed by pactist ideas (see Rodríguez, this volume), the juntas that had first appeared in Spain in 1808 and shortly thereafter in its American colonies influenced the cabildos. Unlike other cabildos in Spanish America, however, the Central Americans formed local rather than provincial juntas, as pointed out by historian Jordana Dym.[6]

In addition to the juntas, the Indians and *castas* (the part of the population considered to have some African heritage) participated in the protests as part of an antitax struggle, expressing their distaste for levies and tribute. The castas also tried to secure representation in local cabildos, which could indicate that they were aware of discussions underway in Cádiz regarding the political rights of African descendants.[7] In the Nicaraguan case, the cabildos fought consistently to favor the interests of local elites, which corroborates the claim that they had an enormous impact on the political life of the country, to such a degree that, in the opinion of historian Germán Romero, in this early rivalry they acted like small republics.[8]

In this chapter I analyze the origins of the protests in the province of Nicaragua between 1808 and 1813, as well as the groups that participated in them, their interests, their manner of expressing themselves, and the repression they faced from the Spanish authorities. I place emphasis on economic and social explanations and look at military actions—which were few in this period—only in their specific contexts.[9] Although each of the movements in El Salvador, Nicaragua, and Honduras between 1811 and 1814 had its own characteristics, none of them provoked major uprisings or long-lasting violent actions; they also did not produce many victims.[10] The real wars would occur years later, under the Central American Federation (1824–42).

NICARAGUA AT THE BEGINNING OF THE NINETEENTH CENTURY: INTRA-ELITE CONFLICT AND POPULAR EXPRESSION

A few days after the Salvadoran movement began, a wave of protests shook the province of Nicaragua.[11] Despite the limited documentation available regarding these events, it is clear that the movements were extremely important locally and regionally. I argue here that the movement in Nicaragua was an example of how conflict had become generalized in the isthmus, though it also demonstrates some unique aspects of the Nicaraguan events. In the particularly important Granadan case, the movement and subsequent official repression had repercussions on the conduct of leaders and civil bodies in the principal Central American cities. In addition to Granada, I consider events in the provincial capital of León, Masaya, the villa of Nicaragua or Rivas, Nueva Segovia, and other localities in the province.

Toward the second half of the eighteenth century, tax levies in the Kingdom of Guatemala, and in this case in Nicaragua, provoked reactions from the different social and ethnic groups. Sales tax (*alcabala*) was one of the major sources of income for the treasury offices in the city of León, and Miles Wortman indicates that the city of Granada provided one of the largest percentages of income received in that office. According to Wortman, "Granada, along with the port of El Realejo, Masaya, Managua, Costa Rica and other towns, consistently paid 50% of all funds collected and 75% of all the income that entered the royal coffers [in León]."[12]

For their part, León and Granada, the two most important cities of the province, each built up hinterlands of their own, so that they eventually became separate economic regions and created rival elite groups with considerable freedom of movement. This was particularly true of Granada, which, although subordinate to León, maintained a great deal of autonomy. José Antonio Fernández has found that problems inside the cabildos, and therefore among the elites of the two cities, were related to jurisdictional struggles that included conflicts over the control of the villas and towns in the surrounding regions.[13] The exaggerated regionalism in the two cities grew, in my opinion, from these power dynamics in which the city of Granada found itself obliged to struggle at all times for its autonomy and for dominion over its spacious hinterland. The city, a lake port with access to the Caribbean via the San Juan River, managed its own commerce, both legal and illegal, with Panama, Cartagena, and the Mosquito Coast.

According to Antonio Juarros, at the start of the nineteenth century the province of Nicaragua had a population of 103,943 in eighty-eight towns, villas, and cities, though Severo Martínez Peláez indicates a sum of 150,000 residents at the end of the colonial period.[14] The province concentrated most of its population, as well as its political and economic activities, on the Pacific coast. Population mixtures involving Indians, Spaniards, and blacks were so common that mestizos and mulattos eventually outnumbered Indians.[15] Nevertheless, the Indian presence was still significant on the Pacific coast, especially in the district of Granada, whose jurisdiction included the town of Masaya, where one-third of the Indian population lived; in the city of Granada, the Indians lived primarily in the old town of Jalteva.

Although most residents engaged in subsistence pursuits and commercial exchange for the internal market, leading groups in the principal cities involved themselves in economic activities such as raising cattle and mules as well as small-scale production of indigo, cacao, and gold, along with pine lumber and its derivatives, directed toward foreign markets. Ranching and indigo were most common in the northern and central parts of the Pacific coast; cacao was a monoculture in the south, and gold and resinous woods came from the north.[16] Commercial agriculture and demographic growth in the eighteenth and nineteenth centuries may have created land pressures, especially along the Nicaraguan Pacific coast, which could explain a progressive tendency toward wealth concentration and, as a consequence, social and ethnic stratification. Contraband trade with the English and with the Zambo Mosquitos (people of Indian and African heritage who lived on the Mosquito Coast) through the port of Granada and the San Juan River increased significantly during this period.

INSURGENCY IN THE CITY OF LEÓN

León had been the capital of Nicaragua since the sixteenth century, and with the Bourbon reforms it became the capital of the intendancy of León in 1787; after the call to the Courts of Cádiz and the election of representatives in 1810–12, it was immediately converted into the seat of the provincial council of León, Nicaragua. Its intendant, José Salvador, had governed the province for nearly two decades when the protests of December 1811 broke out.

There are no exact figures on the population of León in the early nineteenth century, but Guatemalan historian Severo Martínez Peláez estimated it at around 20,000 at the end of the colonial period, probably a somewhat exaggerated figure. Germán Romero, in his study of the social history of Nicaragua in the eighteenth century, suggests a population of 14,122 by 1776. In any event, it was smaller than the capital of the kingdom, more similar in size to the city of San Salvador.[17]

Social Protest in León

In a report sent from Captain General José de Bustamante y Guerra to the secretary of Gracia y Justicia dated July 20, 1812, he assured him, to some degree correctly, that "all commotions and revolutions are of the same nature, especially in these towns. A single spirit inspires them, they are focused on the same end, and spring from the same causes; the immediate effects are likewise similar. The only difference consists in the methods, in the greater or lesser audacity and ability of their promoters, and in the moral and physical resistance which opposes them."[18]

Bustamante doubtless knew very well the external expressions of the general political crisis the crown suffered at that time. His military training and participation in repressive activities in Uruguay had made him highly aware of the situation in the colonies (see Hawkins, this volume). He did not, however, understand a good many of the peculiarities of the Kingdom of Guatemala, especially those that involved the behavior of local and regional power groups.

News reporting the activities of Hidalgo and Morelos in New Spain arrived quickly in the kingdom,[19] just as in Nicaragua people were aware of the news from San Salvador and other rebellious locales. The social and political processes occurring in other regions must be considered if we are to account for the spread and impact of ideas expressed by rebels on the local level. Nonetheless, considering internal conditions is fundamental for in-depth comprehension of such events, and it is only with knowledge of them that the demands, problems, ideas, and interests of those who protested can be analyzed. In this perspective, although the actions taken by rebels in the city of León formed part of broader protests against oppressive policies such as monopolies, taxes, and tribute in the colonies, they took on nuances that reflected the moment in which they coalesced, and they were expressed in particular local forms.

A December 13 general call to action amassed crowds in front of the cabildo building in León, and between 5:00 and 7:00 in the evening events began to unfold. After a riot, at 6:00 P.M. the crowd forced intendant José Salvador to surrender his staff of command and later stripped both the militia colonel and the sales tax administrator of their offices. The records consulted indicate that a good number of rebels took part in the movement, though official numbers seem somewhat exaggerated, citing a figure of 7,000–8,000 men out of a population of 14,000. This group, armed with knives, machetes, and sticks, demanded the resignation of the governor-intendant and immediately presented a list of demands, at the same time attacking the homes of the governor-intendant and of the Spaniards loyal to the king, buildings that symbolized royal authority in the province.[20]

Once inside the ayuntamiento, activists urged authorities to organize an open city council meeting in which other actions concerning the community could be drawn up, and at the same time they indicated "that in no way did they want to be governed, commanded or occupied by any European Spaniard unless it was His Lordship [the bishop] himself."[21] Fray Nicolás García Jerez took advantage of this situation, not only converting himself into the mediator for the movement on December 14, 1811, but also organizing a junta on the same day and promptly becoming its president. García Jerez managed to neutralize the protest movement when he was named bishop-intendant of Nicaragua, strengthening a clearly pro-Spanish policy.[22] The first point approved by the junta consolidated the power of the bishop by assuming the defense of the Catholic religion under the mediation of the Virgin of Nuestra Señora de la Concepción.

What kind of demands did the demonstrators present? They were certainly strong enough to press the new authorities, since official declarations indicate that "all of what we have yielded to has been by force and to avoid the destruction and extermination of the city."[23] These demands were essentially economic and political, such as naming a new governor; abolishing the liquor monopoly; lowering the price of tobacco, stamped paper, and gunpowder; suppressing the sales tax; lowering the wagon tax and the tax on beef cattle; and, finally, freeing those under arrest in León.[24]

Horacio Cabezas adds that other demands included the abolition of slavery and the suppression of Indian labor conscriptions in the form of repartimientos.[25] Although I have not been able to confirm these two claims in original sources, from other parts of Nicaragua there are references to demands for the elimination of slavery and forced Indian labor such as repartimientos. Further, the authorities feared independence ideas and mentioned them specifically. For historians, these petitions have elicited different interpretations; some see in them indications of interest in independence, whereas others reject that hypothesis and argue that the protests had antitax and anti-Spanish goals.[26]

The junta also recognized King Ferdinand VII and its subordination to him, and promised to carry out works of justice and "look to the public good."[27] But republican influences of the period and the call to Courts should not be ignored, since they had an impact on the ideas of the activists, as can be appreciated by the fact that an election was proposed for neighborhood representatives "who would be authorized to come to an understanding with the government,"[28] clearly demonstrating the positive reception given to the idea of representation. Nevertheless, as district representatives were named, the junta demanded that they swear loyalty, and thereby complete subordination, to the bishop, which would mean the consequent neutralization of the movement.

I propose that, given the nature of these petitions, they can be attributed to the economic and social difficulties faced by the popular sectors who lived in the León neighborhoods, in particular the high cost of living, excessive taxes, and the locust plague that had damaged the indigo fields. Political demands that essentially reflected anti-Spanish feelings should be added to the mix, as they have already been established for the rest of the movements, especially those in El Salvador, Tegucigalpa, and other cities of the isthmus. In some of the protests, racial and ethnic issues became visible, not only in León but also in Granada and in the villa of Nicaragua, creating fears of violence against "white" groups, both Creoles and peninsular Spaniards.

Evidence shows that ethnic conflict stimulated discontent among the castas; for example, it was said that the "good" castas in León "despise the Creoles." It would seem that most of the León rebels formed part of this group, as Bishop García Jerez mentioned to Bustamante y Guerra: "If I had but acceded to the demands of the Mulattos, we would have seen León swimming in the blood of those who supported us and of the despicable men who followed them."[29] In the end, as the bishop-intendant testified when the movement came to a halt: "The lives, goods, and interests of the whites have been saved. There is subordination to the legitimate powers and to the high courts that govern us, and these people are calm, peaceful, and tranquil."[30]

In Guatemala, the captain general, based on reports from the bishop, described the rebel plan in León to the king: "[Prepared] in the delirium of agitated and ignorant commoners, they installed what they referred to as a governing junta whose president was the bishop, his colleagues a doctor and pharmacist, an inexperienced attorney, one resident of good repute, and another of mediocre reputation."[31] Such information, even if it does not tell us much about the ethnic and social situation of the activists, does allow us to deduce that some of them had undertaken advanced studies and that others at least had a profession or position; it also expresses "assessments" or prejudices, as the cited text demonstrates.

From my perspective, fear that a generalized movement could develop in the neighborhoods of León and the surrounding area is obvious. It is also clear that places like San Juan, San Nicolás, Laborío, and Matiare hastened to show support for the bishop, as did the Indians of Subtiava and other cities like Nueva Segovia.[32] In general, the "commoners" were judged to be a group that was easy to convince and had little capacity to discern what was correct regarding rebellious acts. Even the captain general expressed that thought in relation to the unrest during this period: "Those who form the lower classes are unfortunate wretches who blindly follow the impulses pressed upon them. They proclaim our monarch or turn against his legitimate judges. They insult their leaders and twist the laws according to the instructions of those who can influence them."[33]

Bustamante y Guerra thought those who caused protests were motivated by ambition, a desire for access to public sector employment, and commercial greed, referring to the typical concerns of the dominant Creole group, because "the unfortunate common man does not seek positions nor does he worry about commerce." He continued: "The lower class, submerged at such a great distance, cannot receive impressions or knowledge except through mediating channels."[34] Here we see the ever-present search for a "hidden hand" and the concept that common people were not capable of expressing themselves independently, a recurring failure to acknowledge the ability of all social groups to communicate their thoughts, values, and demands.[35] An opposite and equally erroneous position, adopted in some historiographical interpretations, grants the León movement a great deal of popular participation and but a minimum presence to the local Creole group.[36]

León: Between Mediation and Repression

It would be an error to think that Bishop García Jerez faced no obstacles in his mediation or that his leadership was absolute. In fact, as he himself testified while forming the junta, he found himself at first with very limited authority. In one of his letters he indicated being "without the necessary force to make [him]self obeyed and respected," and he complained to the captain general that the provincial council of León did not want to recognize him as governor-intendant of Nicaragua.[37] Initially, the impossibility of depending on the power of the militias or the León battalion—since the latter was apparently on the side of the rebels at the times of greatest activity—bothered the bishop. He reported that he controlled two hundred armed men "in appearance only. . . . The arms are in the hands of others and even the keys to the powder house."[38]

Notwithstanding this complicated panorama, the shrewd political mediation of García Jerez worked out peacefully, and he wrote a consensus document that put an end to the movement. As mentioned earlier, he exhorted those involved to "divine respect and to loyalty to the King" and put forward as patron saint the Virgin of Nuestra Señora de la Concepción. Next he issued measures regulating the presence of people in the streets of the city of León; he likewise ordered the expulsion of all outsiders or suspicious individuals and prohibited the movement of armed persons or groups.[39]

Despite all this, after the consensus document mentioned above was issued, official reprisals began when the bishop-intendant took a firm stand to ensure that the movement would not spread. This effort had little impact, since Granada and other important population centers such as Rivas and Masaya were already in the process of revolt. In a message sent to Bustamante y Guerra, the bishop wrote that the movements were occurring not only in León but also in the rest of the province, particularly in Granada, Segovia, and Nicaragua.[40]

Prior requests for arms and troops from Guatemala were now repeated with greater urgency, and although the province had both a shortage was argued. Nicaragua was well supplied with gunpowder, since in every important city there was a powder magazine. But in León some feared that a good part of the militias would join the rebels, which initially seemed to happen, causing Bustamante y Guerra to remark that there was a real danger that "the attack would be superior to the resistance,"[41] and to request troops from elsewhere in Central America. The bishop-intendant requested that five to six hundred men with a "good military leader," and arms, be dispatched. After his resignation, García Jerez proposed that leadership be vested in the hands of an intendant who was not a cleric and suggested the Guatemalan leader José María Peinado or another who was not European.[42]

Troops from the villa of San Miguel and the mulatto militias of Olancho entered the province of Nicaragua to suppress the protest movement,[43] and the Cartago battalion was ordered to do the same, as was a small company from the town of El Viejo, in northwestern Nicaragua. Clearly the fear of a generalized rebellion in the provinces of the isthmus mobilized a good number of men toward

Nicaragua, a strategic province that needed to be saved, but with troops sent in from elsewhere, to assure that they had no roots in the region.[44]

Once the process of official repression began, the fear of a new revolt rekindled and awakened any number of suspicions among the authorities. The captain general of Guatemala wrote: "I cannot say that this fire has been quenched. The combustibles remain, as do those who fan the flames. They continue to work, using the stealthiest and most ingenious methods, as well as the most depraved and immoral."[45] García Jerez and his associates did all they could to keep that flame from extending throughout the province, and especially to Granada, the villa of Nicaragua, and Nueva Segovia, at a moment when the governing junta was still being installed. In the words of the bishop:

> On the morning of December 4 in the meeting room of the ayuntamiento, at the time of this fortunate installation, I stood firm on two things. The first was that we had to erase the call for representatives from Granada, Segovia and Nicaragua. The second was that if there was no acknowledgment of submission to [the junta], not only would I not take part in that burlesque called the presidency, but I would go immediately to the plaza and allow my head to be cut off rather than fail in my duty.[46]

Despite all these precautions, the measures had no effect among dissatisfied sectors, and what happened in León, if it did not directly provoke the events of Granada, contributed to fanning the flames.

GRANADA: CREOLE RESISTANCE AND POPULAR RADICALISM

The city of Granada benefited from a significant boom during the first half of the eighteenth century, leading to the consolidation of a small local and regional elite composed of peninsular Spaniards and Creoles made rich by commerce and livestock production. Outside of the principal urban centers of the province, Granada competed economically with the provincial capital, and the power wielded by its elite influenced other locales in the hinterland such as the villa of Nicaragua, now Rivas, and such towns under its jurisdiction as Acoyapa and Chontales. The strategic location of the city and its reputed wealth led to its being sacked at least five times during the seventeenth century, and Granada continued to suffer the danger of new attacks from pirates, which meant that the city was well supplied with arms, boasting infantry, cavalry, and flag battalions, each with suitable quarters, armories, and powder magazines.[47]

The ethnic heterogeneity characterizing most population centers on the Pacific side of Nicaragua was also present in Granada. Germán Romero states that in 1776 its population totaled 8,233: 1,695 Indians in Jalteva, 4,765 mulattos, 910 mestizos, and 863 Spaniards.[48] Divided by ethnic background, they were also geographically divided in the city. The "whites" lived in the downtown area, the mulattos near the lake to the south, and Indians separated in the communally controlled territory known as the Jalteva neighborhood to the west. Despite its reputation for wealth and its location, Granada could not be considered a very large city, and its center remained quite small. The large number of stores, taverns, gaming houses, and other businesses emphasize the importance of port activities. The convents of San Francisco, San Juan de Dios, San Sebastián, and Guadalupe adorned the city, as did the San Juan de Dios hospital, established in the seventeenth century.

Factors Driving the Movement in Granada

In Granada especially, the foundations for rebellion had already been established by September 1811, several months before the protests in San Salvador and León. Without doubt, the recent incidents at the end of 1811 in the intendancy of San Salvador and the provincial capital of Nicaragua helped stir feelings already being expressed in the local cabildo by two rival factions. Information on the events in Granada is scarce, and the most important document for understanding them is the "Brief Report on Incidents in Granada, Nicaragua, between September 29, 1811 and August, 1813," written by activist leader Manuel Antonio de la Cerda during his imprisonment in Guatemala in 1813.[49] The statements made by de la Cerda are valuable because they are from a witness directly involved, though there are clear omissions, given the fact that the author wrote this text as part of his judicial defense.

Internal problems in the Granadan cabildo had become even tenser in December 1811 and were further complicated by the municipal elections of January 1, 1812. The documentation is not clear about rival factions inside the cabildo, and even less about the causes of the enmity between them. Nonetheless, the historiography shows the existence of two groups. One, represented by first mayor-elect Roberto Sacasa, was known in liberal historiography as the royalist group, and therefore pro-Spanish; the other group, led by nominated councilman Juan Argüello, was known as the rebels.

Things got worse when, after a substitution of authorities in the cabildo, Juan Argüello, a regidor, was elected mayor, provoking the immediate resignation of Sacasa, a well-known royalist who was the outgoing mayor and had been named deputy for Masaya to the same Granadan ayuntamiento, an office he also resigned. In the middle of these deliberations, rumors spread connecting the Sacasa group with the French. There were also rumors about the circulation of broadsides, as well as of death threats exchanged between the two groups.[50]

What is clear is that in January 1812 the Granadan cabildo came to be controlled by a new sector of the elite opposed to royalist interests. The new cabildo, led by Argüello and de la Cerda, was installed, initially with the approval of the bishop-intendant of León, Nicolás García Jerez. One week after the naming of the authorities, a popular movement sprang up in the city, after which members expelled from the former cabildo moved to Masaya, and from that moment on popular participation became more and more intense and in favor of the new cabildo. In Granada, community involvement determined the development of the movement, as can be appreciated in the manner that the neighborhoods demanded their own representatives or delegates. As part of this effort, the popular sectors put forward the figure of Father Benito Soto, to whom, it was said, the common people could express their sentiments.[51]

Demonstrations against the local commandant, José Sierra, forced his removal and exerted pressure for "suspicious" Spaniards and Creoles to resign from their positions in the municipal government, which they did, under the threat that "if it didn't happen, [the people] would form a junta like in León."[52] This opening up of the ayuntamiento brought certain consequences that would mark events in Granada.

Members of the new cabildo perceived danger in the possibility that popular actions might swing out of control, so they tried by all means at their disposal to reduce tensions and thereby avoid an attack on the "whites." As de la Cerda himself wrote, "The cabildo tried every means possible to keep the common people from endangering the lives of those they considered suspicious."[53] It was clear that, although people from the neighborhoods took part just as the rebel cabildo did, the former were not only responding to Creole interests but also acting on their own personal motivations.

From the point of view of Horacio Cabezas, if the situation in Granada demonstrated more popular activism, it was because of the support of Haitian militias that had taken the San Carlos fort some days earlier.[54] I have found that the popular participation in Granada corresponds to what Van Young has affirmed, that "social behaviors have latent as well as manifest functions, that is to say, social consequences that cannot be anticipated or perceived by the actors in a given situation and that cannot consciously motivate their actions, but which are nevertheless important."[55]

The first months of 1812 were hectic in the city. The safety of the "whites" was feared for, since "it came to the extreme of inflaming people to the point of wanting to knife all whites on the night of January 30 and distribute the positions of public employment among themselves." The tension was reduced through dialogue with the people and by requiring that they swear loyalty to the cabildo, all handled by a corps of volunteers "who served to rein in the disorder."[56]

The petitions of the subaltern groups in Granada, passed on to the governing junta in León by Father Soto, revolved around abolishing slavery, suppressing the tax on meat sales, lowering the price of tobacco, and ending double taxation on the resale of livestock. Clearly, most of these claims were of an antitax nature, which supports the idea that the popular sectors took part in the protest actions motivated by economic and social complaints. Still, ideas discussed in Cádiz concerning equal representation for all classes and the elimination of Indian tribute were not unfamiliar.

Horacio Cabezas maintains that the Granadan movement declared freedom of commerce via the San Juan River, a reference not found in other documents. Frances Kinloch states that traffic on the San Juan had been increasing for many years as the result of the Napoleonic invasion of Spain, which caused the regency council to permit direct commerce between Portabelo and Jamaica, thereby fostering commerce with the English.[57]

Masaya: At the Crossroads

The problems became even more difficult for Granada when the majority of councilmen who had been turned out of the cabildo struck out on their own and moved to nearby Masaya, seeking aid from forces in León, which was now under royalist control. Unfortunately, Masaya was immersed in its own problems stemming from the rivalry between Indians and ladinos and the struggle in support of Gabriel O'Horan, a local leader being held prisoner in the San Carlos fort. Unrest increased with two small migrations that occurred simultaneously: the arrival in Granada of Masaya Indians complaining about mistreatment at the hands of local authorities and ladinos, and the appearance in Masaya of cabildo members expelled from Granada. Despite attempts at mediation in which Father Soto acted as arbitrator, the conflict had become aggravated to the point that authorities opened fire, killing more than sixty Indians who had sought protection in the home of their delegate.[58]

With the deaths, the situation worsened, creating fear of an Indian invasion from Masatepe, whose residents supported the Masayans. The commandant of the villa of Masatepe requested military assistance from Granada, which the rebel cabildo denied. The Indians decided to move on to Granada and stayed there until April 1812, during which time a great deal of violence was registered in the city. Indians complained that the authorities were demanding already abolished tribute and hiding information that favored them,[59] indicating their awareness of debates concerning tribute payment in Cádiz between 1810 and 1812.

Repression and Resistance

The new Granadan cabildo held power between January and April 1812. Both this body and the ex-cabildo members who had been ousted and established themselves in Masaya were losing control of the situation, so much so that the movement, now controlled by subaltern groups, began to be repressed, initially by troops largely from Honduras and led by Commander Pedro Gutiérrez, an important figure in the royal efforts to control León. Early on the morning of April 20, these forces decided to take Granada in a surprise attack, thus beginning what would be the most violent period in the city. First, at the powder house, a sentinel charged with keeping watch over the city was killed and another injured; shortly thereafter the building was taken, along with the arms of the sentries who, according to Antonio de la Cerda, fled toward the Indian neighborhood of Jalteva. Although at a disadvantage, the Granadans resisted for some time. Nonetheless, troops surrounded the rebels in the center of the city, and the Creoles who had taken part in the first defensive efforts took refuge in the home of the adelantado of Costa Rica, Diego Montiel.

Faced with the presence of royal troops, it would be the popular sectors of the city that offered the most direct and prolonged resistance. Ayón mentioned that some four hundred men took part, among them some groups belonging to the city battalion as well as fellow countrymen or volunteers who did not form part of the militias. Artilleryman Gregorio Robledo, who made the decision to attack the royal troops, Chiso Cajina, Demetrio Peña, and the drum corps formed part of the resistance.[60]

While the Creoles and a few Spaniards sought protection in the home of the adelantado of Costa Rica, the popular sectors, with arms and a cannon, advanced on them on the night of April 23, trying to set fire to the house with the intention, it would seem, to "knife all the whites for suspicion of selling them out."[61] Intimidated, rebel cabildo members and other Spaniards protected there were put under pressure to sign a peace accord with Pedro Gutiérrez, the commander of the royal troops. The previous day, April 22, members of the cabildo had entered into conversations with representatives of the crown through the mediation of Father José Joaquín González. As it turned out, the accord signed would not be respected, but it did represent the moment in which the city of Granada formally surrendered.

The accord began with an offer of loyalty to the church and to the king (notwithstanding his absence), noting that "the residents of Granada had not broken with the principles of government which ruled in the Spanish monarchy."[62] The negotiators quickly reached several agreements: there would be a general disarmament throughout the city, and people would return to their homes; troops would be withdrawn to their quarters; the cabildo would continue to function; and there would be no reprisals against locals involved, neither personally nor in terms of their possessions.

For his part, in the capital of the kingdom, Bustamante y Guerra ordered strongly repressive actions against the insurgent cabildo of Granada. In fact, at the beginning of May the captain general named a military chief in the province "to discover the instigators or leaders and those who by force of arms made formal resistance to the royal troops on April 21, since such a horrible crime cannot be included in the general pardon issued in other places where there were popular uprisings."[63] All those who held public posts and participated actively in the rebel actions were thereby suspended.

With their reinstatement on June 8, the members of the 1811 cabildo began to imprison the rebel councilmen.[64] During the months of June, July, and August, even as the publication of the Cádiz Constitution became known in Granada, the process of imprisoning the rebels continued.[65] Doubtless, reprisals in Granada focused especially on the rebel elites, but militia members and popular-sector volunteers who had participated actively in the movement also appeared on the lists of those arrested. Once the rebel cabildo and the principal popular leaders were captured, they suffered through a long and difficult trial, which would end the following year, colored by accusations of poor judicial procedures, particularly with reference to witness statements.

In Granada, popular discontent against Spanish authorities and especially against royal troops persisted, and in March 1813 a group led by Nicolás de la Rocha, Melchor Bermúdez, Gabriel Herrera, and Cornelio Guerrero attempted to steal arms, free prisoners, remove public-sector employees (who would have been replaced by their followers), and take military installations, especially the San Carlos fort.[66] Although there is no additional information on this plan, such a development would not be surprising in a city with such staunch opposition and constant repression. Some of the prisoners arrested were sent to the fort, others to enforced military service, and the women to a women's prison (*casa de reclusion*).[67]

Women, Creoles as well as mestizas and mulattas, were active in the movement, and this participation deserves further study. Judicial authorities charged Josefa Chamorro, for example, with cooperating in the Granadan resistance and of offering hospitality to rebels Miguel Lacayo, José Telésforo Argüello, Juan y José Manuel de la Cerda, Joaquín Chamorro, and others. Charges against the same Josefa Chamorro also included hiding gunpowder and sacks of shrapnel in her home. Several other women from the popular sectors were important in the uprising, particularly the partners (*compañeras*, significant others) or family members of rebels, such as Maria Gregoria Robledo and María Ulloa, who were sentenced to a year of confinement for their actions.[68]

In July of the same year, most of those condemned for their participation in the 1812 rebellion were sent from Granada to Guatemala City, the first group in conditions ill suited to men considered to be members of the Granadan elite. In a statement made by Manuel Antonio de la Cerda, who lived through the trip, their legs were shackled and, accompanied by but two mules, they were taken to Guatemala City in the custody of two hundred Caribbean blacks.[69]

After a month of travel, the prisoners reached Guatemala City on August 14, 1813, and were deposited forthwith in the royal prison. The poor conditions in which they were held and the critical situation facing their families in Nicaragua aroused sentiments of solidarity in the capital of the kingdom and other Central American cities. In the capital, the Belén conspiracy (see Hawkins, this volume) was motivated largely by outrage at repression aimed at the "prisoners of Granada." During the January 1814 uprising, the Salvadoran Creoles expressed the same feelings of indignation.[70]

It can safely be stated that the Granadans faced the fiercest repression used in the Kingdom of Guatemala during this period, but they had also put up the strongest resistance (see Hawkins, this volume). A lack of organization and a dearth of specific plans, along with the fragmentation of the dominant sector in Granada and the fear that popular action could spiral out of control, caused the movement to fail.[71]

THE EXPANDING WAVE: MOVEMENTS IN OTHER PARTS OF NICARAGUA

As mentioned above, the generalized feeling of discontent, present after 1811, toward the Spanish authorities who governed these isthmian provinces had specific manifestations that reflected local conditions in each town. One of the first reactions to events in León and Granada took place in the villa of Nicaragua (also known as Rivas), which formed part of the district of Granada and had obtained its title as a villa in 1717, although it had originally been an old Indian settlement. In the eighteenth and nineteenth centuries the economy of Rivas drew largely on cacao production, livestock, and its geographic location in the narrow stretch of land dividing Lake Nicaragua from the Pacific Ocean, making it an important stop on the route to Nicoya, Costa Rica, and Panama. Germán Romero described it as having some 11,637 residents by 1778, including 538 Spaniards, 7,152 mulattos, 554 mestizos, and 2,664 Indians.[72]

The movement in the villa of Nicaragua began on December 23, 1811, with participation from people who lived in the neighborhoods of Potosí, Obraje, and the Indian area of San José. At 11:30 P.M. a mass of protestors demanded that the command of the city be transferred to retired lieutenant Félix Hurtado, the leader of the movement. The crowd then broke down the jailhouse doors, releasing prisoners, and formed a governing junta composed of Creoles, similar to what had occurred in the cities of San Salvador and León.

The first actions in the villa were directed against Spanish authorities, who were required to resign, but things did not stop there. Given the strong antitax sentiments that mobilized the protesters, the postmaster, the tobacco monopoly administrator, and the official in charge of the gunpowder, legal paper, and playing card (*naipe*) monopolies were also forced out, all of them symbols of royal fiscal practices. According to available information, the people in the villa made no declarations against the king but rather against his representatives. Further, they all marched under the same banner: "Religion, king and country."[73]

The Indians in Rivas demanded that tribute be charged fairly and also that forced labor be abolished. Mulattos and mestizos, who formed a majority of the population, insisted on lowering the sales tax to 2 percent, abolishing the export tax, and slicing somewhere between two and five reals from the price of tobacco. The protesters demanded that "neutral justice" be applied, and this claim was strengthened by a request that Spanish administrators in charge of all the different taxes and monopolies mentioned above provide clear reporting of their accounts.[74]

Rebels in the villa of Nicaragua also demanded the complete abolition of slavery; interestingly, this was not repeated elsewhere.[75] As of yet, there is no specific study that discusses the problem of slavery in Nicaragua, but sources indicate that as of the end of the eighteenth century and the beginning of the nineteenth the manumission of slaves had made the presence of free blacks and mulattos much more common. Another interesting petition in the case of Rivas concerns taxes and restrictions on the slaughter, supply, and price of livestock on the hoof and as meat, requesting that citizens butcher animals in previously defined locations and that the price be reduced to three reals for three pounds.[76]

On a political plane, just as in León, a priest, vicar Rafael de la Fuente, named president of the rebel junta, backed the demands of the people at the moment of greatest fervor, although the actual application of the agreements reached there is not clear. Rebel action in Rivas ended with an invitation to a religious ceremony in which the president of the junta neutralized the movement. Nicaraguan bishop García Jerez showed his confidence in de la Fuente through a letter in which he indicated that "the villa of Rivas has lived up to my hopes."[77] The movement in Rivas influenced the unrest that began days later in Nicoya and Cartago, a subject not treated in this work.

It was no coincidence that on January 8, 1812, when the situation in Granada was worsening, fifty-nine militiamen rebelled against Commander José Anselmo Barrios in the San Carlos fort, located at the point at which the San Juan River empties into Lake Nicaragua. Although this mutiny is rarely mentioned, it is significant in that it took place at the Spanish garrison where the Masayan leader, Gabriel O'Horan, was imprisoned. The fort was captured for only two hours, and with help of troops from the Castillo, located on the San Juan halfway between Lake Nicaragua and the Atlantic, the rebels were neutralized. Even though they were unable to maintain control of the fort, it is notable that the leadership came from Granada, whose dominant sectors, given their commercial activities, would have had the greatest interest in taking over the route from Lake Nicaragua down the San Juan. Also, authorities suspected that communication from the Caribbean via the San Juan River would have had a great deal of influence on these movements, but as of yet the sources provide limited support for that claim.

There were also protests in Nueva Segovia, an old mining and lumbering district in northern Nicaragua, just south of Honduras. This population served as a buffer zone along the border with Honduras and particularly with the Mosquito Coast; as the bishop wrote, it "resists strong temptations and . . . serves as a dam against neighboring areas."[78]

Located in a mountainous area with little population, far from the principal centers of the province, Nueva Segovia was described as in "general ruin" as early as 1780. As of the end of the eighteenth century, its population maintained the old dichotomy between whites and Indians—although there were ladinos, they were less important numerically—with the whites living in the center of town and, of course, filling the prominent public posts. News of the events in the province reached Nueva Segovia, whose cabildo "of Spaniards has been the first to recognize the government of the reverend bishop,"[79] submitting themselves thus to the decisions in León.

Residents of Nueva Segovia put forward their own petitions, including the opening of a *casa de rescate*, given the number of mines in the area, and the granting of permission to raise tobacco, since soil conditions were suitable for its cultivation.[80] The cabildo asked that ladinos be prohibited from living in Indian towns and that marriage between social classes (e.g., Indians, Spaniards, mestizos, mulattos) not be allowed, this latter an old concern from centuries past.

Finally, evidence shows insubordination in towns in the area of Chontales, east of Lake Nicaragua, including Teustepe, Acoyapa, and Juigalpa. In Teustepe, townsmen attempted to raise a militia in support of the Granadan rebels in their resistance against the royal troops. Records indicate a fragmenting of local governing groups, possibly related to matters in Granada, since the city was influential on the eastern side of Lake Nicaragua, which fell under its jurisdiction. Granadan elites had spread toward Chontales in search of land to use for raising livestock, and the region had become a crucial point for contraband trade with Zambo Mosquitos and Englishmen established on the Caribbean coast.

CONCLUSIONS

The spreading waves of protests generated in Central America, provoking rebellions of different intensities, definitely reached the towns and forts of Nicaragua. The phenomenon had extended from its principal urban centers, the small and stately city of León and the no less attractive Granada, toward the small villas and Indian towns, all the way to the borders with the Mosquito Coast, in the small forts of San Carlos and El Castillo de la Inmaculada Concepción.

In León, the movement of December 13, 1811, was an immediate consequence of the events in San Salvador, so much so that their demands were very similar. The importance of local conditions in León and the specificity of Leonese antitax and anti-Spanish demands should nonetheless not be underestimated in attempts to understand the events there. In Granada, motives for revolt came from within the dominant Creole group, which had splintered into factions, and from the popular sectors who had their own concerns. The latter expressed themselves with greater autonomy owing partly to the fragmentation of the Creoles but also to political, ideological, and tactical contributions provided by French blacks and from the Cádiz experience. All this allowed popular sectors to defend their rights and raise their own petitions against taxes and monopolies, and in favor of better representation in the local cabildo. The weakness of Creole leadership in the last stage of the confrontation also gave popular sectors a unique defensive role at the time of Spanish repression in the city.

The demand to abolish slavery is one of the specificities in Nicaragua, perhaps related to the mulatto and mestizo majority there, distinguishing it from El Salvador. As we have seen in León as well as in Granada and in the villa of Nicaragua, ethnic and social problems had an impact on the different movements, as can be seen in the fear Creoles showed about a general attack against "whites." This suggests that subaltern sectors were aware not only of debates in Cádiz but also of events in the Caribbean during the previous years, most obviously the slave revolt that led to Haitian independence. Although precise information is lacking, we can infer that news passed orally and secretly from person to person, thereby avoiding the suspicions of the authorities. This work also demonstrates that both Indians and castas made clear in their petitions that they were aware of the abolition of Indian tribute and of debates in favor of and against the participation of castas in elections for the provincial councils.

It can be inferred that when struggles within the elite moved beyond the institutional framework of the cabildo, which then lost control of subaltern groups, these latter expressed their discontent in the streets, demonstrating economic and social concerns more than political ends. With this in mind, comparing the case of Metapán in El Salvador with Granada, notwithstanding their differences, offers important insights.[81] In fact, although all the movements under discussion originated, to some degree, in the internal problems of local elites, in these two cities there were valid conditions for comparison. Though Granada had a cabildo and Metapán did not, both were prosperous localities in the eighteenth and nineteenth centuries, with similar ethnic makeups and dominant groups whose power had a great deal of influence on the events in the broader community.

In both Metapán and Granada, struggles among the elites created problems that could not be resolved within the formal set of rules normally used to resolve conflicts, pushing the subaltern sectors, allied with one elite group or another, to take their concerns to the streets. In both cases, the popular sectors took active roles in the movements, and in the end the subaltern groups were able to organize themselves autonomously. In Metapán they attacked and sacked all the symbols of taxation, and in Granada they first demanded their own representative, vocalized their own claims, and finally offered resistance to troops that invaded the city. Also, in both locales official repression was much heavier than in the provincial capitals such as San Salvador and León. Examples would include the long trial carried out against Juan de Dios Mayorga, at that time a leader in Metapán, and the prolonged repression suffered by the "prisoners of Granada" in Guatemala City jails.

The failure and consequent repression of social movements in the province of Nicaragua do not imply that the territory was completely pacified. The following years, from 1813 to 1821, would be significant from a political as well as social and economic points of view. The 1812 Cádiz Constitution would promote significant changes in the political environment and was received with great public festivities (see Herrera, this volume) and high hopes by the population in general, especially by Creoles. In 1814 new intendant Juan Bautista Gual was received in León, and in the same year the provincial council of León, formed of people who had participated in earlier movements, was installed. Among them were Joaquín Arrechavala, Domingo Galarza, Pedro Chamorro, Vicente Agüero, José Carmen Salazar, and attorney Juan Francisco Aguilar.

The existence of the new council favored Nicaragua, since it gave the province more autonomy on the local level. Nicaragua was thus able to propose that it be given simultaneously the categories of captaincy general and audiencia, a request it brought before the Courts in March, only a few months before the abolition of the constitution by Ferdinand VII in May 1814. This request follows from the establishment of an intendancy in the province at the end of the eighteenth century, opening the gates for an escape from Guatemalan control. Petitions regarding economic and social conditions did not disappear. Both in the Courts, through their representative Antonio López de la Plata, and in the kingdom itself, residents of Nicaragua proposed improved commercial conditions for their products and especially, with reference to fiscal concerns, fewer taxes and other surcharges.

This chapter confirms the importance of the expressions and demands made by the different social groups that became involved in the Nicaraguan conflict. In my opinion, vindicating the participation of subaltern groups is of particular importance since, generally, their actions have been analyzed as if they were conditioned by those of the Creoles. This study shows that the popular sectors—Indians and castas—had their own socioeconomic and, albeit incipient, political interests, and that by promoting them they hoped to improve their living conditions. Notwithstanding, this story did not end on a positive note since neither the Creoles nor the Indians and castas obtained the benefits that had been negotiated, nor did they manage to unify their goals, since their agendas were pronouncedly different.

NOTES

1. See Payne, "Sediciosos," 79–108, and an abbreviated version of the same text published in Payne, "¡No hay rey!"
2. Corpeño, *Patria*; Corpeño and Turcios, *Libro*. I thank Salvadoran historian Carlos Gregorio López Bernal for his generosity in providing this information.
3. Ayón, *Historia*, 3.443.
4. Gutiérrez, "Historiografía"; Payne, "Historia."
5. Fernández Molina, "De tenues."
6. Dym, "Soberanía."
7. The importance of the Bourbon reforms and the Courts of Cádiz , both necessary for understanding the moment, can be appreciated in the issues provoking these protests.
8. Romero, "Estado," 220.
9. With the implementation of the Militia Regulations (*Reglamento de milicias*) in 1765 and the intendancy reforms in 1787, the number of Spanish troops and local militias grew, particularly along the Caribbean coast; in the forts of Omoa, Trujillo, El Castillo, and Matina; and in the capital cities of Guatemala, San Salvador, Comayagua, León, and Cartago.
10. A series of antitax and anti-Spaniard movements took shape between 1808 and 1814 in the principal cites of the kingdom. In Guatemala City an 1808 movement led to the arrest of the poet Simón Villegas y Bergaño, Agustín Vílchez, and Pablo Alvarado, and their legal cases were not resolved until 1820. The Spanish authorities tenaciously pursued French spies and any of their possible followers who might be found in the kingdom. In the provinces, movements began in San Salvador, as well as in villas and Indian towns at the end of 1811. These spread to León in Nicaragua in December 1811 and to Tegucigalpa in January 1812. As is discussed in this chapter, that same month unrest became visible in Granada and the nearby villas of Masaya and Nicaragua, ending with court cases opened against their leaders in 1813. Repression in Granada was the most virulent in the territory, generating support for resistance to repressive Spanish policies. Mérida, "Historia," 56–68; Payne, "Sediciosos," "¡No hay rey!," and "Negros," 69–76; and Hawkins, this volume.
11. These movements appeared initially on November 5 in San Salvador and later spread to Sensuntepeque, the Nonualcos, Zacatecoluca, Usulután, Chalatenango, Cojutepeque, Santa Ana, Metapán, and other towns of the province.
12. Wortman, "Rentas," 254.
13. Fernández, "Dinámica," 132.
14. "Memoria del estado político," 49; Martínez, *Centroamérica*, 8.
15. Romero, *Estructuras*, 242.
16. Ibid., 251.
17. Martínez, *Centroamérica*, 8; Romero, *Estructuras*, 174. León had few neighborhoods: downtown, the mulatto area of San Felipe, the Indian quarters of San Juan and San Nicolás Laborío, and the nearby Indian town of Subtiava in the southwest. The San Francisco, La Merced, and San Juan de Dios churches, each with its respective convent, dotted the city and, along with the cathedral, seat of the bishopric, rounded out the principal religious architecture.

18. Informe del capitán general de Guatemala al secretario de Gracia y Justicia, in *Revista de los Archivos Nacionales de Costa Rica* (hereafter *RAN*), 1938, 640.
19. It seems that the movement begun by Hidalgo did not spread to the south with enough strength to create the same type of serious impacts it had in New Spain. Nonetheless, it should not be assumed that the ideals promoted by Mexican revolutionaries regarding Indian and American rights and their anti-Spanish cause did not make waves in the Kingdom of Guatemala. On the contrary, the ideas of Hidalgo and Morelos promoted political participation and emancipatory notions in the isthmus.
20. Carta de la Junta Gubernativa de León de Nicaragua al capitán general de Guatemala, in *RAN*, 1938, 633–34.
21. Ibid., 633.
22. García Jerez is central to an understanding of the unfolding of the events in León. In effect, the bishop emerged as the supreme mediator by ordering that no act of violence be carried out by either side; he also began to hear and pronounce brief resolutions favoring the insurgents. García Jerez ordered Mariano Murillo, a merchant whose attempt to leave the city had previously been impeded by rioters who believed him to be traveling to advise royal authorities about the growing movement, to remain in León. Later an agreement was reached that assured the activists that there would be no recriminations or reprisals against them.
23. Carta de la Junta Gubernativa de León de Nicaragua al capitán general de Guatemala, in *RAN*, 1938, 633.
24. Ayón, *Historia*, 3.444.
25. Cabezas, "Carácter," 17–18.
26. Among them, the Guatemalan Julio Pinto Soria maintains that in the city of León participants were in fact thinking of independence and of forming a type of republic with other cities and towns of the isthmus. Pinto, *Centroamérica*, 114. On the other hand, Costa Rican Rafael Obregón Loría prefers to refer to these protests as antitax and anti-Spaniard. Obregón, *Nuestra*.
27. Obregón, 56.
28. Carta de la Junta Gubernativa de León de Nicaragua al capitán general de Guatemala, in *RAN*, 1938, 635.
29. Informe del capitán general de Guatemala al secretario de Gracia y Justicia, con documentos anexos, in Fernández Bonilla, *Documentos*, 44.
30. Carta de fray Nicolás García Jerez, obispo de Nicaragua y Costa Rica a José Bernardo de Astegrieta y Sarralde, 1811, in *RAN*, 1938, 632.
31. Informe del capitán general de Guatemala al secretario de Gracia y Justicia, in *RAN*, 1938, 637.
32. Archivo Nacional de Costa Rica (hereafter ANCR), Complementario colonial, no. 1981, fol. 4, 1812.
33. Informe del capitán general de Guatemala al consejo de regencia, in Fernández Bonilla, *Documentos*, 53.
34. Ibid., 89.
35. These ideas were proposed by late nineteenth-century authors such as Le Bon and Taine. The former wrote that a crowd lowers its sane and rational elements to an animal level,

and, in turn, the crowd attracts degenerate criminals and persons with destructive instincts. Rudé, *Multitud.*
36. Pinto, *Centroamérica*, 114.
37. Informe del capitán general de Guatemala al secretario de Gracia y Justicia, con documentos anexos, in *RAN*, 1938, 646; Zelaya, *Nicaragua*, 59.
38. Informe del capitán general de Guatemala al secretario de Gracia y Justicia, con documentos anexos, in *RAN*, 1938, 648.
39. García Jerez also took public measures against the presence of vagabonds and minors, as well as illegal games. Ayón, *Historia*, 3.470–72. The bishop named priests as mediators in the principal neighborhoods of the city. In San Felipe Apóstol, he named Pedro Caballero and the minor order priest José María Guerrero; in the San Juan de Dios neighborhood, he placed Licenciado don Manuel López de la Plata. Pedro Solis was named for the Jesús neighborhood, Francisco Chavería in San Sebastián, Gregorio Quadra in San Francisco, Juan Delgado and, provisionally, friar Francisco Miguelena in San Juan. In Laborío, the bishop named bachelor Pascual López. Archivo General de Centroamérica (hereafter AGCA) sig. B 638, leg. 24 (1811).
40. Informe del capitán general de Guatemala al secretario de Gracia y Justicia, con documentos anexos, in Fernández Bonilla, *Documentos*, 38.
41. Ibid., 26.
42. Informe del capitán general de Guatemala al secretario de Gracia y Justicia, con documentos anexos, in Fernández Bonilla, *Documentos*, 37–38. [Editor's note: Bustamante had sent Peinado to keep the peace in San Salvador in December 1811 shortly after the unrest there.]
43. Originally, the mulatto militias in Olancho had resisted recruitment, but the Olancho battalion would play an important role in the repression of the cities of León and Granada, especially the latter. Under the command of Pedro Gutiérrez, the troops left their base for Nicaragua via Nueva Segovia, where they complied with orders to recruit as many men as possible so as to bring the battalion to full strength, 1,000–1,200 men.
44. The rest of the armed forces, from San Miguel, Cartago, the Yoro battalion, and El Viejo militias, played a less important role, although they were on the alert for any seditious act. For example, the interim governor of Comayagua requested the support of the Yoro battalion so as not to remain defenseless without the Olancho battalion. The Fícaro company, Nueva Segovia squadron, was added to this latter. Some elements from San Miguel were sent to Nicaragua, even though a good number would remain in their villa for "observation and reserve." All of these armed forces were ordered "not to use arms unless it was absolutely necessary." Informe del capitán general, in Fernández Bonilla, *Documentos*, 47–48.
45. Informe del capitán general de Guatemala al secretario de Gracia y Justicia, in *RAN*, 1938, 641.
46. Ibid., 643–52.
47. It was attacked by the pirate David in 1665, by Morgan in 1665, Mansfield in 1666, Gallardillo in 1670, and Escalante in 1685 or 1686. Arellano, "Granada," 50.
48. Romero, *Estructuras*, 176–77.
49. Cerda, "Sucinto."

50. The story went around that a spy or French emissary was hiding out at the home of the commandant of Granada, José Sierra. This was the seed of the unrest, according to de la Cerda himself: "The people were incited to rebellion, largely fed by the rumor that the city was being surrendered to the French by the group called 'royalists.'" The group that has traditionally been considered royalist was made up of Creoles like Roberto Sacasa, Francisco Crespo, Esteban Cordeviola, Eduardo Arana, Pedro Chamorro, Agustín Alfaro, Adrián Zavala, Luis Blanco, and others. The other belligerent group has been designated the "rebel cabildo," formed by a Creole majority that included Juan Argüello, Manuel Antonio de la Cerda, Miguel Lacayo, and others bearing the last names Cordero, Espinoza, Molina, and Vargas. See ibid., 235–38.
51. Ibid., 236–37.
52. Ibid., 237.
53. Ibid., 238–39.
54. Cabezas, *Independencia*, 56.
55. Van Young, *Crisis*, 281.
56. Cerda, "Sucinto," 239.
57. Cabezas, *Independencia*, 18. Kinloch maintains that, although tensions existed between Guatemalan and Nicaraguan merchants, the argument that this set the stage for the uprisings of 1811 and 1812 is controversial. Kinloch, "Independencia," 25.
58. Cerda, "Sucinto," 240. Although Ayón refers to nine dead and several more wounded, Gámez indicates that, whereas non-Indians mentioned nine deaths, Indians insisted that there were sixty. Gámez, *Historia de Nicaragua*, 91; Ayón, *Historia*, 3.469.
59. Barboza, *Historia*, 52.
60. Ayón, *Historia*, 3. 476; Cerda, "Sucinto," 248.
61. Cerda, "Sucinto," 248.
62. Ayón, *Historia*, 3.477.
63. Cerda, "Sucinto," 257.
64. These prisoners were not all jailed at the same time. Some leaders fled to their haciendas, others hid in different places, and others, alleging health problems, stayed in their homes under strict guard. In July, property seizures began, notwithstanding the agreement made by Commandant Gutiérrez.
65. A series of earthquakes starting June 29 in Granada worsened the situation of the prisoners, and several of them were accused of attempting to escape. Some of the people who managed to get away participated in the March 1813 uprising, discussed below, led by the mulatto Gregorio Robledo (who had given the order to attack the Spanish troops in April 1812), and some say they were trying to assassinate Commandant Palomar and other guards. Notwithstanding the repression that followed, a few days later Robledo managed to escape to the mountains of Boaco.
66. Ayón, *Historia*, 3.487–88.
67. Nicolás de la Rocha, Melchor Bermúdez, Pedro Guerrero, Blas Mora, Gabriel Herrera, Cornelio Guerrero, Manuel Castillo, Feliciano Borge, María Gregoria Robledo, and María Ulloa are listed.
68. Ayón, *Historia*, 3.485–86.

69. Cerda, "Sucinto," 270–71. The rebels sent to Guatemala traveled in two groups. One group included Miguel Lacayo, Juan Argüello, Juan Espinoza, the adelantado of Costa Rica, Manuel Antonio de la Cerda, José Telésforo Argüello, Joaquín Chamorro, Pío Argüello, León Molinar, Juan Cerda, Francisco Vargas, Francisco Cordero, the priest Benito Soto, and Narciso Hernández. The other included Juan Ignacio Marenco, attorney José Manuel Cerda, Cleto Bendaña, Vicente Carrillo, José Cruz Mesa, Leandro Cuadra, Juan Pío Núñez, Feliciano Bendaña, Mariano Marenco, Eduardo Montiel, Ignacio Ugarte, and Juan Marín Solórzano.
70. Payne, "Sediciosos."
71. The legal situation of the prisoners was controversial at that time, since their crimes were considered to be of a military nature.
72. Romero, *Estructuras*, 180.
73. They also petitioned that Europeans be prohibited from being tavern keepers (*pulperos*). Ayón, *Historia*, 3.456.
74. They asked that Indians not pay more than four reals as tribute for single men and two for married men, and that they be reimbursed for any balances remaining or any increases they had paid during the past seven years when the tax had been raised to fourteen, eighteen, and twenty-one reals. Ibid., 3.455.
75. Ibid., 3.456; Gámez, *Historia de Nicaragua*, 87; Cabezas, "Carácter," 17–18.
76. Ayón, *Historia*, 3.456.
77. León Fernández, *Documentos*, 41.
78. Ibid., p. 28.
79. Informe del capitán general de Guatemala al secretario de Gracia y Justicia in Fernández, *Documentos*, 20.
80. Ibid. [Editor's note: The *casa de rescate* was an institution in which miners sold their gold and silver for money, after paying whatever fiscal obligations were owed to the crown.]
81. Payne, "¡No hay rey!"

TOTONICAPÁN, 1820
One of the Tips of the Iceberg?

Aaron Pollack

By April 1820, a rebellious group of Indians in the Totonicapán district had taken control of several towns in the Western Highlands of Guatemala, through a slow process in which the Spanish alcalde mayor had slowly abandoned his authority. The movement had grown from a refusal to pay tribute after its reestablishment in 1816, following several years in which the head tax had been eliminated, per order of the Courts of Cádiz. As a result, when late in the spring of 1820 news arrived in Guatemala that the 1812 Cádiz Constitution would be reestablished, the people of the region celebrated what they assumed to be their vindication.

Orders arrived that the restoration of the constitution would be celebrated on July 9, 1820, and the rebels ordered bullfights, drums, and fireworks in its honor. In the same celebration, the parcialidades and religious brotherhoods (*cofradías*) installed the primer principal of the town, Atanasio Tzul, as governor, officially recognizing the de facto Indian political dominance in the region.[1] With this, the seat of the alcaldía mayor of Totonicapán accompanied King Ferdinand VII, who in the first session of the reinstalled Spanish Courts swore allegiance to the Cádiz charter, six years after having abolished it. Totonicapán followed instructions that called for the publication and oath-taking in "at least the capitals" of the provinces,[2] which Carlos Urrutia, captain general of the Kingdom of Guatemala, had issued with the consent of the ayuntamiento of Guatemala City.[3] The neighboring town of San Cristóbal Totonicapán celebrated as well, notwithstanding the resistance of its Indian mayor.[4] Unlike Madrid and Guatemala City, in San Miguel Totonicapán there were no Spanish authorities among the organizers of the festivities, since the alcalde mayor, José Manuel de Lara y Arrese, did not attend the ceremonies.

In addition to Atanasio Tzul, Lucas Aguilar (or Akiral),[5] alcalde of the brotherhood of the Santísimo Sacramento, the most important cofradía in the town, a number of others, both "nobles" (*principales*) and commoners (*maceguales*), actively led the rebellion. After the July 9 ceremonies, Indians of San Miguel Totonicapán extended their influence to nearby towns and, upon the departure of the alcalde mayor a few days later, took complete control of the provincial seat and maintained it until the August 3 arrival of one thousand ladino and Spanish militiamen from surrounding towns put an end to this brief experiment in autonomous Indian government.[6]

The Totonicapán movement was one of the political proposals that K'iche' leaders developed when faced by a novel situation in which the weakness of Spanish authorities and their changing policies favored the strengthening of other powers in the region—both that of ladinos and Creoles, who focused their efforts in the city of Quetzaltenango, and that of Indians, who made up a large majority in the Guatemalan highland towns.[7] These examples of political organization made the weakness of the colonial government visible and showed just how strong regional and local actors had become, particularly since the beginning of the century, when policies implemented by Charles IV and his minister Godoy, initiated to fill the royal coffers in wartime, combined ominously with a locust plague and a debilitating economic crisis related to drops in indigo production and commerce.[8]

One could argue that the local or regional powers that came to be important during this period did not fully submit to a central government until the consolidation of the Guatemalan republic under Carrera starting around 1850, which represented a new hegemony, partially based on support negotiated and declared by certain peasant and Indian sectors, who made demands on the government in return for their cooperation.[9] The local and regional powers creating this new hegemony and benefiting from it would have favored, as can be extrapolated from the reflections sketched out here, those sectors within the towns themselves that could assure stability in the rural, often principally Indian, population.

Through the arguments developed in this chapter, I place the 1819–20 movement in the Central American context of the epoch. This is a context conditioned by a notoriously difficult economic situation, a political reality marked by the recent experience of the *vacatio regis*, social unrest in urban as well as rural areas (see Payne, this volume), and the liberally tinged measures put forward by the Spanish government and partially implemented by kingdom authorities (see Hawkins, this volume). I also discuss the movement as part of the sociopolitical uniqueness of the Guatemalan highlands, and of the internal dynamics of the towns themselves, with the goal of understanding how local affairs are thoroughly and inevitably entangled in much larger processes.

In this case, I argue, Cádiz policies that eliminated the existing systems for expropriating surpluses produced in the Indian towns—both tribute and the personal services and rations provided to priests—had a greater influence on the movements and later developments than did reforms to the political system.[10] Additionally, although documentary evidence that supports this hypothesis is weaker, I believe that the elimination of the estates, which effectively had both economic and political implications, also influenced the growth of the movement in Totonicapán.

During the period between 1811 and 1814, I would further maintain, protests carried out in the Guatemalan highlands resembled the uprisings in San Salvador, León, Granada, and Tegucigalpa. Participation by the popular sectors in all of the unrest grew primarily from economic problems, but, unlike the more urban movements, leaders in Indian towns during this period showed no interest in political autonomy from Spain, nor did their actions permit any interpretation that could link them to a desire for independence. I point out not only the absence of references to ideas of autonomy and independence but also a lack of ties to the autonomy-seeking Creoles who showed interest in independence and later participated in the republican networks activated during the period of Mexican annexation.

It may well be that fear among the Creoles regarding the possibility of a peasant and Indian uprising like that which destabilized New Spain during this period inhibited the formation of alliances between Indians and those who sought autonomy and independence. Along these same lines, I propose that this same fear would have pushed the Spanish authorities to accede to the demands of protesting towns, avoiding the use of violence and the possibility of eruptions that could overturn the existing government and social hierarchy.

The movement of the Totonicapán Indians in July and August 1820, with its eagerness to launch itself throughout the province, was similar to what had happened in the above-mentioned Central American cities in their uprisings of 1811–14 (see Payne and Hawkins, this volume), as were the "coups" that municipal governments in the provincial seats of Quetzaltenango (see Avendaño, this volume), Sololá, and Chimaltenango undertook against Spanish provincial authorities when these locales declared their independence in September 1821. Unlike what was happening in the rest of Central America—where such movements, born in larger towns in provinces with wider territorial pretensions, would have an impact on the formation of the different nation-states of Central America—the Totonicapán movement was rather a precursor or example of Indian mobilization that would, among other causes, be fundamental to the fall of the sixth state of the Central American Federation, the State of Los Altos.

TOTONICAPÁN DISTRICT

The alcaldía mayor of Totonicapán was divided into two districts. Totonicapán included San Miguel Totonicapán and the nearby K'iche' towns of Santa María Chiquimula, Momostenango, San Bartolomé Aguacaliente, San Francisco el Alto, San Cristóbal Totonicapán, and San Andrés Xecul, as well as two ladino towns (*valles*), San Carlos Sija and Salcajá, officially founded as such in the second half of the eighteenth century. The largest part of the alcaldía mayor, the district of Huehuetenango, which included forty-four towns, was much less densely populated.[11] It included the territory that corresponds to the present-day department of Huehuetenango, some towns in the north of what is now the department of El Quiché,[12] and important extensions on the other side of the present border with Chiapas, Mexico, both to the southwest and to the north, where it included a good part of the Lacandón jungle.

By 1820, San Miguel Totonicapán had lost its leading position in western Guatemala, known as Los Altos, to the economic and political vigor of nearby Quetzaltenango, an Indian town that had been granted a Spanish ayuntamiento in 1805. San Miguel Totonicapán was nonetheless important because of its extensive territory and the relatively large population of the alcaldía mayor. Although it did not have great expanses of land in areas suitable for raising indigo, cacao, cotton, or other agricultural crops with greater commercial value, San Miguel Totonicapán produced significant quantities of corn and wheat that were sent to Guatemala City. It also produced large quantities of cotton and wool textiles, marketed both in the main regional marketplace, Quetzaltenango, and in nearby provinces. San Miguel Totonicapán and other towns in the district produced part of the local textiles (*ropa de la tierra*) sent from Quetzaltenango to supply territories of the Kingdom of Guatemala, parts of New Spain, and Peru.[13] The town was the capital of an alcaldía mayor providing a great deal of Indian tribute which, though progressively losing fiscal importance relative to alcabala and the tobacco monopoly, continued to be one of the three principal revenue sources for the government of the kingdom until 1820.[14] San Miguel Totonicapán, like the Totonicapán district, showed considerable variation in its interior. It was a complex space, full of agriculturalists, day laborers, and weavers as well as merchants and travelers with many contacts in other provinces of the kingdom and in neighboring New Spain.

In the Indian towns of San Miguel Totonicapán, Momostenango, and San Cristóbal Totonicapán, between 3 percent and 10 percent of the population were classified as ladino and Spanish.[15] In these three parochial seats, as in several others in the alcaldía mayor and in the neighboring corregimiento of Quetzaltenango, "alcaldías of Spaniards and ladinos" had been established in 1802, so that in each town there were two separate cabildos, each responsible for its "class" to the alcalde mayor. Additionally, as of 1792, San Miguel Totonicapán had a separate cabildo for the 578 caciques who lived in the town,[16] that is, a third municipal government.[17] The other towns in the district were governed by Indian cabildos.

Ladinos and Indians took part in the principal economic activities of the district, growing corn and wheat as well as weaving textiles for domestic use and trade.

In the mid-size population centers many had other work,[18] as can be confirmed in the general census of 1825 undertaken in San Miguel Totonicapán and the census surveys of ladinos and Spaniards in the alcaldía mayor of Totonicipán undertaken in 1810.[19] According to Veblen, people had become merchants and artisans at least partly because of the very real scarcity of arable lands the district faced in the last decades of the eighteenth century, an effect of Indian demographic recovery and the overgrazing that had been common in previous centuries, in part resulting from the need to pay tribute, often provided in woolen textiles. In addition to broadening their economic activities, says the same author, this situation drove the Totonicapenses to land conflicts, both within towns and between neighboring populations. Unlike other regions, Veblen also notes, the inhabitants of the Totonicapán district could not depend on large lowland tracts to increase the acreage under cultivation.[20]

Until a few years earlier, the alcalde mayor had been the main axis of the regional economy, his importance stemming from the distribution of goods, and especially of credit, uniting the local economy to that of the kingdom and the Atlantic.[21] Combining the roles of tax collector and regional impresario, the alcalde mayor extracted surplus production from the rural economy and at the same time assured the basis for a good part of the textile production by distributing cotton to the women in the region, who spun and wove it, receiving in exchange a payment probably equal to the amount due for tribute obligations. By the second decade of the nineteenth century, however, perhaps partly because of the general economic crisis, the alcalde mayor seems to have lost this function as well as that of assigning workers in the forced labor system known as the *repartimiento de labor*.[22]

CONTEXT

Since the middle of the eighteenth century, Indian tribute had officially been converted from payment in kind to cash, but the rates applied as a result of this conversion varied notably from town to town throughout the kingdom. After 1800 efforts began to standardize tribute payment at two pesos per Indian tributary, and by 1802 initial attempts had been made to apply the new rate in parts of the kingdom, such that some towns perceived a notable increase.[23] In 1803 the imposition of the new tribute rate caused an uprising in the large Kekchí town of Cobán in the alcaldía mayor of Verapaz, the province most negatively impacted by the new rates.[24]

Although their actions were unrelated to any tribute increase, Indians from three towns in the alcaldía mayor of Totonicapán carried out protests against different forms of extraction of surplus production during these same years. In 1802 inhabitants of Santa María Chiquimula, in the Totonicapán district, rebelled against the Indian mayor and the repartimientos he implemented;[25] as punishment, the primary organizers of the uprising were executed, their bodies publicly exposed until the middle of 1812.[26] In Momostenango, the seat of the parish in which Santa María Chiquimula is located, resistance had broken out in opposition to tribute payments and to the community fund contributions in 1804, as well as against new charges decreed by royal edict in April of that year that assessed each religious brotherhood five pesos as a one-time contribution and an additional annual charge of one peso each.[27] In 1803 the Chujs of San Mateo Ixtatán, a town bordering the intendancy of Ciudad Real, opposed the payment of prebends, threatening the priest in the process.[28]

In 1805 several Spanish authorities, perhaps because of the above-mentioned actions, became worried at rumors of an Indian uprising encouraged by the Kekchís of Cobán through a "convocation" that came to include San Pedro Sacatepéquez, located in the corregimiento of Quetzaltenango. Whatever the source of their fears, correspondence among then-alcalde mayor Prudencio Cozar, the priest of San Pedro Francisco Franco, and Francisco del Castillo Aguayo described Spanish concerns and the clear memory of Indian rebellions in the neighboring provinces of Ciudad Real and Yucatán.

Cozar explained his worries in a letter addressed to Father Franco: "Several serious occurrences in the towns under my jurisdiction, which the high courts are aware of, have me in a state of the utmost vigilance regarding the possibility that the Indians of this area are planning a disturbance. I have come to understand that a call has come to members of your parish from the people of Cobán, and it appears that they have not agreed."[29] Father Franco replied that he had heard this rumor two years earlier and again in recent months, but, after consulting with some Indian leaders whom he trusted, the priest felt that for the moment there was no danger. Castillo reflected that "if the Province of Yucatán and that of Zendales in Ciudad Real of this Kingdom had not looked with indifference in the last century on some voices and warnings that preceded the catastrophe, so much blood of innocent priests would not have been shed in either place."[30]

Although it is unclear whether there was any real basis for Cozar's worries—there is, after all, a reference to Prester John in this report—the fear is revealing, as is the reference to two important rebellions in nearby provinces some forty and one hundred year earlier.[31] The concerns also indicate the fragility of the political and social systems at this particular moment. In the ensuing years, after the abdications of Bayonne in 1808, the already fragile reality of domination by Spaniards and (more variably) ladinos over Indians, if not so much (or not necessarily) that of colonial dominion,[32] became even weaker, especially in the light of decisions by the regency council and the Courts of Cádiz, as well as the autonomist-tinged rebellions in other provinces of the kingdom.

In September 1810, the enormous rebellion led by Hidalgo broke out in the intendancy of Guanajuato, New Spain. The impression it must have made on Guatemalan Creoles should be stressed, considering the Indian and peasant nature of this rebellion (setting aside the objectives and the contacts of Hidalgo himself), as well as the often brutal violence the rebels directed against Spaniards. According to Mario Rodríguez, members of the ayuntamiento of Guatemala City feared "that an Indian uprising might stir up the Castas and thus upset a society dominated by a white elite."[33] This same body suggested moderate policies in response to the uprising in San Salvador at the beginning of November 1811, which the captain general of the kingdom, José Bustamante y Guerra, implemented (see Hawkins, this volume).

A few weeks after the Hidalgo uprising, the recently arrived viceroy of New Spain made public, with the clear intention of reducing support for the revolutionary priest, a regency council decree of May 1810 that abolished Indian tribute in New Spain.[34] Its publication also had a notable impact in the neighboring Kingdom of Guatemala, where a few months later, on January 9, 1811, the subdelegate of Simojovel, in the northern part of the Ciudad Real intendancy, stated that Indians of that district, especially those of Amatán, were asking if the travelers moving between Ciudad Real and the New Spanish territory of Tabasco as well as Indians living in the latter province had spoken the truth when they claimed that tribute had in fact been abolished. The decree published in New Spain was reflected, at least somewhat, in the decision made in April 1811 by recently installed Captain General Bustamante, to eliminate the standardization of tribute payment that had begun in 1801, returning the rates to their previous levels.

During 1811 a certain uneasiness could be perceived in several Indian towns, quite in harmony with events in several cities of the kingdom. Things came to a head in Patzicía, a Kakchiquel town of five thousand in the alcaldía mayor of Chimaltenango, possibly one of the few negatively affected by the return of the tribute rate to its former level. In October 1811, the townspeople of Patzicía protested after receiving contradictory information regarding the possible tribute reduction.[35] In Momostenango as well, residents organized protests to manifest their disagreement with statements made by the alcalde mayor to the effect that the elimination of standardized tribute payments, that is, their reduction, had never occurred.[36] In the same month, San Miguelito, a village in Santa Catarina Ixtahuacán just south of San Miguel Totonicapán in the alcaldía mayor of Sololá, organized a protest caused by tensions between the town seat and the village, as well as by economic demands made by the priest. Even earlier, in September of the same year, the assistant (*juez preventivo*) to the alcalde mayor stated that Indians in the parish of Nebaj, in Huehuetenango district, had begun to ignore and disobey him, to such an extent that the mayor of Chajul "was insolently pressuring other towns [Nebaj and Cotzal] to rise up against the priest and against [him]."[37]

These acts, in combination with much more troublesome uprisings in San Salvador, León, and Granada at the end of 1811 (see Payne and Hawkins, this volume),[38] the latter episode lasting until April of the following year, pushed Bustamante to eliminate Indian tribute on January 3, 1812, thereby putting into effect a decision approved by the Courts of Cádiz in March 1811.[39] Explaining the decree at least partially as a counterinsurgency measure, as had occurred in New Spain, the captain general indicated that it would not apply to "all those who have committed or may commit offenses and crimes against the King and against the legitimate authority of his ministers and judges, denying them the respect and obedience that is their due."[40] Bustamante immediately replaced tribute with a request for voluntary contributions of two pesos per person, an amount that equaled the official rate in force after the standardization partially implemented after 1801, prior to the 1811 reduction.

Despite the elimination of tribute, social instability continued in 1812, as demonstrated by protests in Indian towns. Uncertainty over the "voluntary" nature of the donation and over the payment of tribute due at Christmas 1811 combined with a power struggle between the former Indian governor and his new ladino replacement to cause a May 1812 protest in the town of Comalapa in the alcaldía mayor of Chimaltenango.[41] In March of the same year, residents of the small town of San Andrés Xecul, in the Totonicapán district, organized in opposition to the intervention of the priest in their elections.[42]

The tensions in 1811–12 in many Indian towns of the Guatemalan highlands, including some of the largest, can be compared to those felt in the cities of San Salvador, León, and Granada during the same period. In the Indian towns, unlike in the cities, these anxieties, mainly economic, did not translate into the autonomist demands linked to Creoles, who, as has been pointed out by many authors, coordinated their actions with the popular sectors principally to promote their own political and economic interests.[43] In the highland Guatemalan towns, even when matters of local politics provoked discussions and protests, no one linked their actions to any kind of economic or political separation from Guatemalan or Spanish authorities. Despite the presence of plans for autonomy from Guatemala City shared by Creoles and ladinos in the highlands, the towns operated separately from that aim and Indians did not put forward a similar plan of their own until 1820.

The Creole and ladino plan for autonomy in the west was clearly seen in the instructions drawn up by the ayuntamiento of Quetzaltenango in 1810 and sent to the only American member of the regency council, Miguel de Lardizábal y Uribe; in the new instructions drawn up in 1813 for José Cleto Montiel, representative to the Courts of Cádiz; in the efforts undertaken before and during Mexican annexation; and in the tensions during the republican period that finally led to establishment of the Los Altos state (1838–40).[44] But this plan, unlike those of the cities mentioned, was based on a sharp division between Indians and everyone else, that is, ladinos and Spaniards. The fear felt by Spaniards (and probably many ladinos) toward Indians in the highlands of both Guatemala and Chiapas on the one hand inhibited an alliance between Indians and those working toward regional autonomy and on the other made it expedient for colonial authorities, hoping to avoid further acts of rebellion, to acquiesce to demands from Indian towns.

Political reforms from Cádiz, rather than those of an *economic* nature (which I address later), have made the Courts of Cádiz famous: the establishment of universal citizenship (in civil matters if not completely in the political realm), the separation of powers, and the creation of three levels of representative government. In the towns under discussion, these reforms allowed the election of representatives to the Courts and later to the provincial council, but it seems that constitutional ayuntamientos that should have been elected in 1813 and 1814 were not formed.[45]

At the end of 1812, the elections of mayors and councilmen for constitutional ayuntamientos were carried out only in those places where ayuntamientos had already existed.[46] Elections in towns which up until then had been governed by Indian cabildos began only after the delayed installation of the provincial council, at the beginning of September 1813, when Bustamante ordered the establishment of new constitutional ayuntamientos.[47] It would seem that elections were not carried out in most of the towns, since records indicate that relatively few constitutional ayuntamientos were formed outside of cities and villas. In San Miguel Totonicapán, upon Bustamante's order elections were not carried out, purportedly because of the absence of a proper census. But, as is mentioned later, some Totonicapenses believed that these elections did in fact occur.[48]

1813

The political stability of the audiencia of Guatemala came under threat in 1813 (see the Introduction to this volume). In Totonicapán district, some of the principales and many of the K'iche' commoners of San Miguel Totonicapán, accompanied by Indians and apparently ladinos from other nearby towns, rose up in support of alcalde mayor Narciso Mallol prior to his ouster in October.

According to local observers, the first constitutional period (1812–14) in particular, as well as the previous presence of "Enlightened" priests in Totonicapán, were the main causes of the 1820 rebellion. Prudencio Cozar, then quartermaster of the royal armies (*comisario ordenador de los reales ejércitos*) and previously corregidor of Quetzaltenango (1786–1802) and alcalde mayor of Totonicapán (1802–11), opined:

In 1811 when the man named by the Cortes took control, he circulated those Republican maxims which were of course expressed at that meeting; and even with the rusticity of the Indians, it had the terrible effect, well-known in that jurisdiction, and especially in its district capital Totonicapán. The abolition of tribute increased their arrogance, the title of citizen did so even more, so that they thought themselves to be superior to the Spaniards and ladinos, based on the numbers of individuals, since there are very few persons of these classes [Spaniards and ladinos]. From those beginnings came the present occurrences as well as the countless incidents which have taken place in that jurisdiction.[49]

Throughout 1813 an unusual alliance developed between alcalde mayor Mallol, named by the regency council in August 1810, and the principales and maceguales of San Miguel Totonicapán. This alliance and its immediate implications have been described in other places, and a brief mention of the actors and events of particular interest for this study suffices here.[50] Mallol supported the town of San Miguel Totonicapán in two conflicts over land: one with Gregorio Francisco Pinillos Urbina, heir to the enormous Urbina hacienda located in the Totonicapán valley, bordering Salcajá and Quetzaltenango; the other with the parcialidades of the Garcías, Ávilas, and Mendozas, that is, the caciques from San Miguel itself. In the first case, Mallol faced the corregidor of Quetzaltenango as well as Pinillos, who had twice been first mayor of Quetzaltenango and clearly acted as a power broker in the region. In the second, he was apparently the victim of an imbroglio organized by the Totonicapán caciques, who misled a group of Indians from nearby Chichicastenango, inciting them to ambush and seriously wound the alcalde mayor.

At the same time, when news arrived that the Courts had issued a decree eliminating the provision of rations and personal service the Indians had owed the priests, Mallol immediately implemented it, receiving the support of many of the town principales. After this decision, Mallol found himself in conflict with the archbishop and Franciscan friars charged with the parish in San Miguel Totonicapán.[51]

In spite of the fact that Bustamante had clearly ordered that elections not be held for a single (constitutional) ayuntamiento, the man elected mayor of the alcaldía of Spaniards and ladinos, Santiago González, tried to have himself recognized as constitutional mayor, which would have implied the elimination of the Indian cabildo. In this case, Mallol, here in agreement with Bustamante, found himself in the position of defending the Indian cabildo against pressure from ladinos and Spaniards.

As a result of the conflicts, at the end of July 1813 the Indian governor, Juan Cruz Soch, traveled to the capital of the kingdom with Estanislao Argueta, legal representative (*síndico*) of the alcaldía of Spaniards and ladinos—or of the constitutional ayuntamiento, depending on who described it—to lodge their respective complaints against the alcalde mayor. Soch presented himself in the court documents as representing not only himself but also other town caciques and principales and succeeded in bringing Mallol to trial, to be judged by the corregidor of Quetzaltenango, Miguel Carrillo de Albornoz. When Carrillo reached Totonicapán, Governor Soch formally requested that he order Mallol and his closest aides, who were also under accusation, out of the provincial seat during the trial, and Carrillo agreed. As a result, despite working to postpone his departure, on October 11 Mallol retreated to San Carlos Sija, a ladino town several leagues distant from San Miguel Totonicapán.

During the days that followed, if not the same eleventh of October, a group of "principales of the commons of *calpules* who make up the governance of the town," among them Francisco [Atanasio] Tzul, almost all ex-officials of the cabildo or of the five parcialidades, asked then-judge Carrillo de Albornoz to desist from his judicial investigations, stating in their request that Mallol "looks on us as his children in a way that no one has looked on us until this time."[52] The principales were not successful, and in ensuing days the trial began. It ended unexpectedly when Mallol returned to San Miguel Totonicapán on October 28 from San Francisco el Alto, but only after issuing Carrillo a passport that would allow him to leave the alcaldía mayor of Totonicapán, as long as he did so no later than the twenty-seventh. The group of principales accompanied Mallol as a part of an "army of Indians," as Bustamante would describe it.[53] The "constitutional" ayuntamiento estimated their number as four thousand, and Mallol depicted them as "the officials and principales so [illegible] of ladinos as well as Indians of the towns of Salcajá, San Cristóbal, San Francisco [el Alto], [San Carlos] Sija and Momostenango, in addition to a great multitude from [San Miguel] Totonicapán, so many that they obstructed our progress."[54]

In their description of Mallol's entrance, members of the "ayuntamiento" of Totonicapán, who had escaped to Quetzaltenango with Carrillo, were interested in frightening the authorities of the kingdom. According to this body, "In one voice [the Indians] said to him, *Long Live Our Prince Narciso Our King and Liberator and Death to the Corregidor of Quesaltenango and all his Allies with Mendoza*." As if this were not enough, they claimed in the same report that Mallol had said that "in the middle of the plaza he would remove and do away with the vestments of the priest, cut off his head, and present it on a plate to the Indians, whom he had ordered to apprehend any ladinos they found and give them fifty lashes."[55] Neither members of the ayuntamiento nor anyone else repeated those accusations, and it seems that this was a poorly disguised attempt to imply that Mallol and his followers had imitated the peasant movement in New Spain, whose troops had entered Chiapas scarcely six months before.[56] A short time later, Bustamante relieved Mallol of his post, and on December 15 of the same year several K'iche's asked the superior political chief to reinstate him, a request that landed six of the principales in jail, probably at least in part because of the fear that they might somehow be tied to the Belén conspiracy, which Bustamante brought to its end just a few days later, on December 21.[57]

TRIBUTE

Indian protests in the highlands continued during the first liberal period and after the reapplication of tribute (now officially known as a "contribution") in 1816, one result of the return of Ferdinand VII in March 1814 and his repeal of the constitution and of the other measures legislated by the Courts of Cádiz. Two further violent protests occurred in Santa Catarina Ixtahuacán, in the parish of San Miguel Totonicapán, in May 1813 and November 1814, related, like that of 1812 mentioned above, to problems within the town and also, at least in 1813, to rations paid to the priest.[58] In April 1815, the commoners of Quetzaltenango participated in an uprising for reasons related not only to tribute but also to the rejection of health policies imposed in response to a smallpox epidemic.[59] Two weeks later, on May 1, a riot broke out in the nearby Mam town of San Juan Ostuncalco, with the support of neighboring San Martín Sacatepéquez and Concepción Chiquirichapa, demanding the removal of the Spanish and ladino alcalde, who persecuted "idolatry" and supported the application of smallpox vaccines.[60]

This same smallpox epidemic affected the Totonicapán district during 1815, and its impact became magnified by a July 1816 earthquake that affected a region extending from Ciudad Real in Chiapas to Guatemala City, and ravaged a smaller, but still quite significant area between Soloma in northern Huehuetenango and the alcaldía mayor of Verapaz, including Totonicapán district.[61] The two events impoverished the region, reducing both the disposition and the ability to pay tribute, so that only eleven of the forty-nine towns of the alcaldía mayor of Totonicapán paid the amount due for 1816 and eighteen made no payment prior to that due in the second half of 1817.[62]

In 1821 the people of the town of Sacapulas, located in a part of Huehuetenango that bordered Totonicapán district, remembered: "The year 1817 this town suffered greatly, very terribly, from hunger: we sold our hatchets, hoes, millstones, and absolutely everything, because we had nothing to eat and some died of hunger. Many went away to the lowlands near the coast and to other towns: corn very expensive. . . . Many people, just to keep going, ate cottonseed and leather."[63]

Different towns in the Totonicapán district used a variety of mechanisms to avoid their tribute payments in 1816. Momostenango insisted on the need to take a new census because of the epidemics of typhoid in 1811–12 and of smallpox in 1815. San Cristóbal Totonicapán indicated that it had not been informed that tribute payments had begun anew, then argued that it had been informed of only one of the two annual payment dates, and that in any event the emigration that resulted from grain scarcity in the region made tribute collection impossible. Santa María Chiquimula and San Miguel Totonicapán simply refused to pay, without excuses. San Miguel Totonicapán, or at least its first mayor, Atanasio Tzul, made the decision to collect what was owed for the community fund and other contributions but refused to collect tribute. Also, the towns of San Antonio Ilotenango, San Pedro Jocopilas, Santa Cruz del Quiché, and San Sebastián Lemoa, in the alcaldía mayor of Sololá, just east of Santa María Chiquimula and San Miguel Totonicapán, joined forces to request a two-year grace period.[64]

The specific situations of the towns clearly showed the difficulties they were facing, and in some cases the Spanish authorities not only postponed tribute payment but also permitted the use of community funds to buy grain. As time passed, faced with the refusal of many towns to pay tribute in both the Totonicapán and Huehuetenango districts, the authorities of the kingdom increased their pressure on the alcalde mayor, José Manuel Lara. By 1817 interim attorney general (*fiscal*) José Cecilio del Valle, concerned by the risk that resistance to payment could set an example for the rest of the kingdom, causing a shortage in the royal coffers, considered the situation "like what happened in the period of the . . . Courts, which deprived the treasury of tribute income without considering at the same time any effective measures to fill the vacuum." Valle, still under the command of Bustamante, proposed that the alcalde mayor implement methods "of rigorous justice which the same laws that hold him responsible also authorize him to take."[65]

But although the "laws" permitted it, the authorities of the captaincy general did not show a willingness to apply "rigorous justice." They reflected in their actions what had been proposed when tribute was reinstated: the American context of active subversion called for the application of mild measures to assure collection while avoiding the use of force. With this in mind, they left Lara, who by August 1818 owed 12,000 pesos in tribute, without means to guarantee collection in the future. Authorities did not apply any new policy in their rejection of violence in these towns but instead maintained the same procedures that had been in force under the Courts of Cádiz. One possible interpretation is that the Spanish authorities were losing their ability to impose their will, but even if that were the case the same men made strategic decisions concerning in what towns and with what people repressive tactics should be applied. It would seem that, beginning in the Cádiz period, efforts had been made to avoid the use of violence in the densely populated Indian highlands, despite their monetary and symbolic importance, out of fear of an Indian uprising that would call to mind not only Hidalgo and Morelos but also Cancuc and Cisteil.

MOVEMENT

In September 1818, the alcalde mayor feared the possibility of a revolt in the towns of San Miguel Totonicapán and Santa María Chiquimula, a reflection of how much the control Lara exercised in his province had deteriorated. This was perhaps owing to the arrival of Carlos de Urrutia, who had replaced Bustamante as captain general in March of the same year.[66] To prevent the possibility of a revolt, Lara assured the presence of militiamen from Salcajá during Michaelmas festivities, celebrating the patron saint of San Miguel Totonicapán, and requested even more reinforcements to intimidate the people of Chiquimula.[67] Lara avoided even greater difficulties, apparently through the intervention of the priest Eulogio Gálvez, who managed to quiet discontent in Chiquimula.[68]

Lara and the Spanish authorities faced a problem in that they did not want to, or perhaps could not, use force to assure tribute payment, as can be seen in the comment of Quartermaster General Cozar, written in September 1818: "I have had several orders from superiors never to use armed force against the Indians."[69] This situation, analyzed from a standpoint that considers both coercion and consent as the components necessary for the maintenance of hegemony, implies that to the degree that Lara did not use coercion—evidently afraid of Indian rebellion and its possible consequences—the existing hegemony began to unravel; that is, the problem for Spanish authorities with refusing to use violence was that it put in check the exercise of colonial as well as "ethnic" power in Totonicapán, an obvious weakening of central authority symptomatic of the epoch.[70]

As this power was diluted, other possible hegemonies began to develop, clearly based on existing experience. For the principales and maceguales of Totonicapán, these new proposals did not refer to Voltaire, Rousseau, Bentham, and others who had influenced the "Enlightened" residents of the capital.[71] The new hegemonies simmering in Totonicapán were evidently drawn from their own experiences, which did include, though they were not limited to, the years under constitutional government (clearly influenced by the intellectual lights of the epoch), and surely *did not* consider the possibility of an estrangement from the Spanish monarchy. But neither, in the end, did they differ greatly from those brief experiments in autonomy already mentioned, which had been led by provincial seats in these same years, in different parts of the kingdom.

Lara clearly communicated his weakness in an edict he sent to the towns in June 1819, explaining to them that if they did not pay their contributions it would be the audiencia that would "dictate such measures of severe punishment as it might be pleased to impose," implying that the alcalde mayor would not be the one making the decisions in this regard.[72] On July 10, with several responses to his edict in hand, among them one from the curate of Soloma revealing the very precarious position of Spanish authorities in his parish, Lara asked Captain General Urrutia his permission to abandon those gentle measures that had not proven effective, particularly in the "provincial seat, which is the perfect example of insubordination and rebellion."[73]

A few days later, Lucas Aguilar, then alcalde of the powerful Santísimo Sacramento religious brotherhood, proved Lara correct. In a meeting the alcalde mayor had called with town priests, the cabildo, and brotherhood members in the hope of convincing these latter to support tribute payment, Aguilar voiced his rejection of this proposal and hit one or more cabildo members. According to then-governor Nicolás Bulux, from that moment forward Aguilar, Atanasio Tzul, and the others became more recalcitrant in their positions.[74]

By October, Father Gálvez of Momostenango, the same man who had calmed the people of Chiquimula the year before and who at that time supported the use of gentle measures, had come to the point of suggesting the use of "rigor" in the treatment of those in revolt.[75] Gálvez simply recognized the strength the movement exhibited and the risks it implied for authorities.

The group leading the movement had at its center Aguilar—a macegual, potato and apple grower, and leader of the religious brotherhoods—and Tzul—a principal, soap maker, ex-alcalde, and "first principal"—who then began to consolidate their power in the town of San Miguel Totonicapán. After December 1819, the group began to structure itself as a movement through large meetings *en calpul* in which the leaders, principales, and commoners together discussed tribute in the homes of Dionisio Sapón and the merchant Francisco Magarin.[76] Should this collection of maceguales and principales, with their meetings that broke traditional caste barriers to discuss together the future policies of their town, be understood as an example of the Habermasian public sphere, interpreted by many as an important step toward political modernity?[77] During the months that followed, the group accelerated its activity with a plan to seek support in other towns and to consolidate the movement within San Miguel, continuing to meet until the beginning of August 1820, when Spanish and ladino militias quashed the rebellion.[78]

In January 1820, rebels in Santa María Chiquimula again took center stage when recently elected mayors began to return tribute collected by their predecessors, and in February they rose up against the priest, Father José Patricio Villatoro, rejecting his attempts to collect rations. The situation became so serious that Villatoro had to send a plea to alcalde mayor Lara to come "with soldiers to get [him] out of this vile town."[79] On the fourth Friday of Lent, March 17, some two hundred men and women from Santa María Chiquimula traveled to San Miguel Totonicapán and, with the support of the Totonicapenses, demanded they be given a document that supposedly confirmed the elimination of tribute and which, according to those present, the authorities held in their power. The large crowd, including many women, became enraged and a handful of people, among them Aguilar, Tzul, and María Zapón, Aguilar's wife, attacked the second mayor; Tzul snatched away his ceremonial staff.[80] The demonstrators threatened to destroy the home of Lieutenant Collado, who fled town shortly thereafter.

Two weeks later, on April 2, Easter Sunday, another demonstration left the home of Lucas Aguilar for the main plaza, where a proclamation eliminating tribute, issued in January 1812, was read.[81] Demonstrators listened while the movement leaders explained that they had held onto that proclamation since 1812 but had never made it public, implying that tribute had never been reestablished in 1816; such a claim ignored and negated a fiscal practice that had been in place for more than four years, not only in Totonicapán but throughout the kingdom.

On both March 17 and April 2, in the hopes of strengthening their movement, leaders made references that they apparently knew were false. Their actions, like other similar ones in which the arrival of some "document" was awaited to confirm the stand taken by leaders of Indian movements, protests, or uprisings, are often interpreted as proof of ignorance rather than as examples of the manipulations that many political leaders use to strengthen their own positions.

During the ensuing months, the real power in several towns in Totonicapán district rested in the hands of movement leaders. Spanish authorities made no attempt to impose their decisions on them, and Indian authorities feared them in the face of pressure to return collected tribute and threats against their persons. This power was to be strengthened by an event unforeseen by all the actors involved: the news that, at the beginning of March, Ferdinand VII, under strong pressures from some segments of the Spanish army, had decided to reinstate the 1812 constitution.

News of this decision reached the hands of Captain General Urrutia on May 4, 1820, via Havana.[82] Although it was kept secret until the end of June, it must be noted that after May 3 militia officials in Totonicapán began sending reports to Quartermaster General Cozar indicating that movement participants had begun opening mailbags in search of a document. So it is very possible that the same news had been communicated informally to the Totonicapán movement leaders, a notion strengthened by the confirmation by the principales in an undated report sent to the lieutenant alcalde mayor, Ambrosio Collado, that they had searched three times for "our letter that reached the Real Audiencia, which we have known came on May 5, 1820, [that is] our paper in the Real Audiencia."[83] What is clear from the documentation is that on approximately June 24 the people of Totonicapán, through some informal means, brought the news of the reinstatement of the constitution and that movement leaders claimed that this information was proof of their successful efforts before the authorities, strengthening their position in the region.

As mentioned at the beginning of this chapter, on July 9 rebels from Totonicapán invited towns in the district to extensive festivities planned to celebrate what to them meant the elimination of tribute, as well as the establishment of universal citizenship and the elimination of distinctions among the different "classes": Indians, Spaniards, ladinos, maceguales, principales, and caciques. The Indians celebrated without the alcalde mayor or any other Spanish authority, and several days later Lara fled to Quetzaltenango in fear of his life.

During the ensuing weeks, until August 3, the movement controlled San Miguel Totonicapán and the nearby towns of San Francisco el Alto, San Cristóbal Totonicapán, and San Andrés Xecul, demanding the return of collected tribute, charging taxes, dispensing justice, and placing sentinels at the borders of its territory. This effort to establish a regional government had the support of Indians, especially the maceguales, from the towns mentioned, who took turns guarding the homes of Tzul and Aguilar.[84]

In San Cristóbal Totonicapán, San Francisco el Alto, and San Andrés Xecul, some maceguales, under instruction from Aguilar and Tzul, insisted violently that mayors return tribute that had been collected, repeating what had begun in San Miguel Totonicapán and Santa María Chiquimula. In the decades that followed, the maceguales of San Francisco el Alto and especially of San Cristóbal Totonicapán maintained a power struggle with the principales in their respective towns. The maceguales participated fully in town politics, demonstrating the divisions between Indian "classes." An analysis of their behavior, and that of the principales (who often argued among themselves), opens an important window on the richness of local politics in the Indian towns.[85]

After April 1, when Cozar accepted a request to involve himself in weakening the movement, he began to communicate with the principales of the three most important towns in the district (Momostenango, Santa María Chiquimula, and San Miguel Totonicapán) in the hope of convincing them to desist from their rebellious acts. But it seems that Cozar was acting to pacify the territory, preferably with the support of clergy members, without using violence or applying pressure for tribute payment, which also demonstrates that for the authorities the matter had taken on a much different and more threatening aspect.[86] In the case of San Miguel

Totonicapán, although Cozar maintained good communication with the mayors and the Indian governor, and even with previous authorities, he failed to convince movement leaders that they visit him in Quetzaltenango, let alone that they desist in their activities. In Santa María Chiquimula he reminded the town leaders of the violent repression that he himself had inflicted on the town almost two decades before. He was able to divide the principales in Momostenango, in part through the arrest and the negotiated release of an activist who had first organized against tribute nearly a decade before.[87]

When the militias were finally mobilized under orders from Cozar on August 3, the movement, which could count on considerable support from San Francisco el Alto, San Cristóbal Totonicapán, and San Andrés Xecul, had to face one thousand militiamen without the presence of their greatest (potential) allies, Momostenango and Santa María Chiquimula. The militias came from Santa Cruz del Quiché, San Carlos Sija, Salcajá, Momostenango, and mainly Quetzaltenango. The rearguard of the latter was attacked by a group of Indians from San Cristóbal Totonicapán and San Francisco el Alto, the only direct confrontation during the suppression of the movement, resulting in the death of one Indian from San Francisco and some forty injured militiamen. When the militias reached San Miguel Totonicapán, they were faced with a "shower of stones." The following day, under orders from Cozar, who acted *ad terrorem*, faced with a hillside full of people who had left the town center, the soldiers raised a gallows and flogged several of the movement participants.[88]

With no further significant resistance, the movement lost the territorial control it had achieved, but this defeat did not constitute its complete collapse, nor did it imply the adoption of a fearful or submissive attitude toward Spanish authorities. On the contrary, leaders constantly questioned the actions of Cozar and the militias, as well as the jailings and treatment received. Their repeated petitions, combined with demonstrations carried out by the wives and families of those arrested, both in Quetzaltenango and in the capital, resulted in a pardon for Atanasio Tzul, Lucas Aguilar, and the majority of the prisoners on March 1, 1821.[89]

One month later, movement leaders, Tzul and Aguilar among them, appeared in court to demand freedom for their comrades from San Francisco el Alto, who remained in prison for having taken part in the August 3 rearguard attack on the militia. The position of the rebels was strengthened by the efforts of the captain general and the provincial council to assure that prisoners received treatment that did not violate the reinstated constitution. Nevertheless, their complaints, petitions, public demonstrations, and legal appeals demonstrate that, although suppression of the movement had ensured territorial control, it had not led to the absolute subordination of the men and women who had brought it into being.

IMPLICATIONS

The 1819–20 movement in Totonicapán, initiated as a rejection of tribute payment, was above all a demonstration of great local power, in this case Indian power, which consistently limited central government pretensions throughout the first half of the nineteenth century, at least in the mainly Indian areas of what would later be Guatemala, if not in the rest of Central America. It is then, following the model established by Jordana Dym and Xiomara Avendaño, a demonstration of the importance of municipal governments as political structures maintained throughout the process of transition from colonial life to the establishment of the new nation-states of Central America.[90]

But the movement also demonstrates the importance of the first Spanish liberalism to the process of independence, as the same authors indicate. It was nurtured by the fiscal reforms implemented in Cádiz, which effectively eliminated mechanisms for the confiscation of agricultural and artisanal surplus (Indian tribute and ecclesiastical taxes) as well as, albeit to a lesser extent, abolishing social "classes." Political reforms enacted, in the best of cases only partially in the Totonicapán district during the first constitutional period, seem to have had little impact.

The Totonicapán movement cannot be analyzed separately from the competition between that town and nearby Quetzaltenango, as is the case in the interregional rivalries between Comayagua and Tegucigalpa or León and Granada, but in the case of Los Altos regional proposals involved clearly different notions concerning relations among social groups.[91] The "alcaldías of Spaniards and ladinos," formed in 1802, demonstrated the existing relationships among these groups, and through them the colonial government established, or perhaps confirmed (more research on this idea is needed), that in the corregimiento of Quetzaltenango and the alcaldía mayor of Totonicapán the most important barrier dividing social groups was that between Indians and non-Indians. Although it appears that this barrier was not rigid or insurmountable in terms of daily life, relationships between the two groups in the two provincial capitals were different. There is no doubt that Indians dominated positions of political leadership in the town of San Miguel Totonicapán, and for the most part in its district as well, whereas in Quetzaltenango those positions were in the hands of Spaniards and ladinos. It should be noted that the social categories of the epoch in Quetzaltenango did not distinguish between Creoles and peninsular Spaniards, which seemed to be important in other cities in the kingdom, underlining that the important distinction lay elsewhere.[92]

In addition to the legal and conceptual base offered by the elimination of Indian tribute, ecclesiastical taxes, and caste privileges, the movement provided the people of Totonicapán with an experience of political organization *on a regional scale*, which allowed them to deal with the levies and demands of Spanish, Mexican, Central American, *altense* (from Los Altos), and Guatemalan governments during the succeeding decades. Although there were other causes for the instability of the various regimes in these years, the political organization of these subordinate groups—ladinos (especially in the east) and Indians—profoundly marked Guatemalan history in this period.

As the most obvious means of expropriating surpluses produced by farmers, artisans, and merchants who formed the bulk of the Indian as well as the ladino population in the Kingdom of Guatemala at the beginning of the nineteenth century, and even under the liberal governments of the Central American Federation, fiscal policies were one of the main points of contention between these groups and the governments that implemented them. In the conflicts both in the intendancy of León and in San Salvador between 1811 and 1814, fiscal concerns were a primary motivating factor, and they continued to be in ensuing decades.[93] In Indian towns in what is now Guatemala, tribute payment continued to be a point of conflict in the years after 1820. In 1822 leaders from Quetzaltenango tried to bring the Indian towns of Los Altos into their regional project, and thereby into the Mexican Empire, with the argument that Iturbide had eliminated tribute.[94] Resistance to the head tax (in part a revamped and reduced form of tribute) in Santa Catarina Ixtahuacán, and the repression that the state of Los Altos applied in order to collect it, offered Rafael Carrera a pretext for military intervention, putting an end to the sixth state of the Central American Federation in 1840. Resistance to the poll tax had in fact been one of several motives that provoked the regional uprising that carried Carrera to power.[95]

In contrast to popular/autonomist movements in San Salvador, León, and Granada, the numerous protests, demonstrations, and riots in the Guatemalan highlands did not involve autonomist concerns until 1820, perhaps due to a failure of awareness or interest on the part of Indian leaders, but also because of a lack of ties between these towns and promoters of autonomy or independence in Guatemala City and Quetzaltenango.[96] K'iche' leaders probably saw little future in allying themselves with Creoles from these cities, and the Creoles themselves would have kept their distance from that possibility upon glimpsing the specter of an Indian uprising with anti-Spaniard or anti-ladino tinges. But the movements also provoked fear among authorities of the Spanish government, so that they either acceded to the demands of the Indians or responded with "gentle" measures. The movement of 1820, perhaps precisely because it had autonomist tinges insomuch as it sought provincial control, could not be ignored by Spanish authorities.

The study of this movement invites us to delve into the machinations inside different towns and municipal governments and their alliances with other actors, in the hope of understanding conflicts that would create different formations on a regional as well as Central American scale. It involves penetrating into the struggles between maceguales and principales in the towns of the Totonicapán district, which possibly reflect conflicts existing in the cities of the kingdom, and later of the federation. It drives us to remove the very "special" status that often colors the history of Indian towns. Or, at the very least, it offers ideas for reconsidering in their historical context the distinctive relationships between Indians and the state and between Indians and non-Indians that existed during the first half of the nineteenth century.

This study also invites us to analyze more carefully the category of "Indian," which, whether used to justify exploitation and repression or the need for "civilization," hides a notable heterogeneity that can scarcely be seen in the documents of the era. In the Central American case at least, the notions held about Indians—like the conservative/liberal dichotomy or the absolutism/liberalism binary that Rodríguez discusses in this volume—need to be revisited with a critical eye toward the nineteenth-century constructions that still color research agendas and interpretations.

NOTES

Research for this chapter was carried out in part thanks to a Fulbright Hays Dissertation Enhancement Fellowship.

1. The first principal was the most important representative of the five parcialidades, the "common," which included everyone but the caciques, ladinos, and Spaniards. The post went to a leader of the "Lincaj" parcialidad. It is my belief that at that time the five parcialidades together were the real power behind, or at times in opposition to, the official Indian cabildo.
2. 28 de junio de 1820, in Archivo General de Centroamérica (hereafter AGCA), sig. A1, leg. 6930, exp. 57192.
3. Rodríguez, *Cádiz*, 131.
4. El común todo el pueblo de San Cristóbal al señor juez de letras y jefe político de Totonicapán, August 3, 1824, in AGCA, sig. A1, leg. 6094, exp. 55403.
5. In San Miguel Totonicapán, the Spanish surname Aguilar corresponds to Akiral in K'iche.' I am grateful to Nicolás Aguilar for his kindness in pointing out this usage.
6. The militiamen arrived from San Carlos Sija, Salcajá, Quetzaltenango, Momostenango, and Santa Cruz del Quiché. The movement has been discussed earlier in Contreras, *Rebelión*; McCreery, "Atanasio Tzul"; Bricker, *Cristo*, 153–67; Portillo, *Crisis*, 245–50, and the work on which this chapter is based, Pollack, *Levantamiento*.
7. Given the strong political bias of studies on the independence period and the tendency to understand politics only in terms of the actions of dominant groups—that is, Creoles and, only recently, ladinos—little study has been made of the alcaldías mayores and corregimientos of what would later be Guatemala, except for Quetzaltenango and, in part, Totonicapán. Taracena, *Invención*; Pollack, *Levantamiento*; González, *Experiencia*. Study is needed of the alcaldías mayores of Chimaltenango, Escuintla, Sololá, Suchitepéquez, and Verapaz, as well as the corregimiento of Chiquimula.
8. See Belzunegui, *Pensamiento*, 161–203; and Arrioja, "Guatemala," for a discussion of the devastating impacts of the crisis on the kingdom and the efforts of the government to confront them.
9. Woodward "Changes"; Carmack, *Rebels*, 128–34; Taracena, *Invención*, 311–23; García, *Acción*, 130–42. I thank Brian Connaughton for suggesting the interpretation of the consolidation under Carrera as a "new hegemony."
10. In addition to their initial counterinsurgency goals (during the crisis of the Spanish monarchy), fiscal policies of the first liberal epoch in Spanish America initially sought to include a much broader segment of the population in direct, usually somewhat proportional, tax systems. But as seen during the first half of the nineteenth century in many regions with high percentages of Indian population, these attempts failed because of resistance among nearly all groups affected by the changes. Thurner, *From Two Republics*, 20–53; Guerrero, "Proceso"; Morelli, *Territorio*, 159–90; Pollack, "De la contribución."
11. Van Oss has calculated the population density of the Totonicapán district at 29.53 persons per square kilometer in 1800, about equal to the most densely populated region in the kingdom, Sacatepéquez (30.20 per square kilometer), which included at that time

both New and Old Guatemala, that is, Guatemala City and Antigua. None of the other provinces in the kingdom maintained a population density greater than 20 persons per square kilometer. Van Oss, "Población," 306.

12. Cunén, Sacapulas, Uspantán, Nebaj, Cotzal, and Chajul.
13. Taracena, *Invención*, 32–42.
14. "Informe del Ministro Tesorero"; Wortman, *Government*, 153, tab. 7.5.
15. Pollack, *Levantamiento*, 238, tab. 3. The term *ladino*, as used in the highlands at the beginning of the nineteenth century, could refer to mestizos, castas (mulattos, *pardos*), or persons of Indian background who officially or, presumably, unofficially had changed category. In popular speech, at least part of the time, it meant anyone who was not Indian, even if legally a Spaniard.
16. Juarros, *Compendio*, 38.
17. The story of the caciques of Totonicapán is long and complicated. They were part, according to Fuentes y Guzmán, of a mixture of the local K'iche' nobility with the Indian conquistadors who accompanied Pedro de Alvarado when he invaded from Mexico. Fuentes y Guzmán, *Recordación*, 47–48. Although they enjoyed a significant share of power in the town, the caciques can better be understood as a clan, or perhaps like a separate estate, rather than a leadership group. For the purposes of this chapter, it may suffice to stress that their status as caciques exempted them from the payment of tribute and also from the provision of personal service and rations to priests. At times they served as a local militia in the repression of Indian towns in the region. See Chaclán, *Caciques*; and Pollack, *Levantamiento*, 38–41.
18. Juarros (ca. 1800) calculated the populations of Momostenango at 5,420, Santa María Chiqimula at 6,000, San Francisco el Alto at 5,300, San Cristóbal at 3,580, and San Miguel Totonicapán at 6,849. Juarros, *Compendio*, 40.
19. Padrón general del pueblo de Totonicapán, 1825, in AGCA, sig. B, leg. 1135, exp. 26029; Pollack, *Levantamiento*, 244–46, tab. 7.
20. Veblen, "Ecological," 350–55, 359. Stefania Gallini does not deny the possibility that the lands in the Guatemalan highlands, a territory much larger than the Totonicapán district, could have become unable to support the local population by the end of the eighteenth century. Nonetheless, she argues that the existence of land conflicts does not prove such an assertion. Gallini, *Historia*, 49–51 and n57.
21. Patch, "Imperial," and *Indians*; Pollack, *Levantamiento*, 48–55.
22. McCreery, *Rural*, 111, and on labor assessments, 93–112.
23. For an excellent discussion of Indian tribute during the last decades of the colony, especially the changes in the amounts charged during the first decades of the nineteenth century, see Fernández Molina, *Tributos*. The standardizing of tribute rates was carried out with many inconsistencies throughout the kingdom, depending on the previous tribute rates, local resistance, and the fear it provoked. These conclusions are based on ongoing research. See also Ayón, *Historia*, 3.350–60, on the application of the standardization policy in the León intendancy.
24. By 1800, Juarros estimated the population of Cobán at more than 12,000 people. Juarros, *Compendio*, 25.
25. Martínez, *Motines*, 86, 103, 204, 256; Gutiérrez, "Racismo."

26. Alcalde mayor Narciso Mallol to the audiencia of Guatemala, June 3, 1812, in AGCA, sig. A1, leg. 5478, exp. 47116.
27. Juan López natural del Pueblo de Momostenango quejándose contra su alcalde mayor don Prudencio Cozar por agravios que dice le infiere, March, 1804, in AGCA, sig. A1, leg. 192, exp. 3927, and sig. A3, leg. 2535, exp. 37083, fol. 160.
28. Van Oss, *Catholic*, 85; Lovell, *Conquest*, 113, tab. 8; Oficio de los señores de la Real Audiencia pasando a esta superioridad los avisos sobre las amenazas que los yndios de San Mateo Yxtatan hicieron a su cura don José María Orellana, September 25, 1803, in AGCA, sig. A1, leg. 192, exp. 3923.
29. Prudencio Cozar to Father Francisco Franco, June 7, 1805, in AGCA, sig. A1, leg. 6109, exp. 56025.
30. Francisco del Castillo Aguayo to Prudencio Cozar, June 9, 1805, in ibid.
31. It should be noted that, unlike New Spain and the Andean regions, in the intendancy of Ciudad Real, in the provinces that would later form Guatemala and in the intendancy of Yucatán, all of which were demographically dominated by Indians, there is no record of social violence tied to a desire for autonomy or independence during the independence period. Ruz and Taracena, "Pueblos."
32. This distinction perhaps helps explain the later successes of the movement of Carrera and of Indians and ladinos—but not Creoles—who supported him; or at least it may help distinguish between colonialism sensu stricto and internal colonialism.
33. Rodríguez, *Cádiz*, 104.
34. Número 70. Bando del virrey, publicando el de la Regencia de la Isla de León, libertando del tributo a los indios, in Hernández, *Colección*, vol. 2. The decree refers only to the Viceroyalty of New Spain, and it was not until March 1811 that the Courts extended it to the rest of the American territories. The new viceroy, Venegas, took the initiative by eliminating tribute paid by those mulattos and blacks who remained loyal to the king and took part in the suppression of the Hidalgo movement.
35. Pollack, "Protesta."
36. These tensions continued for the next few months and exploded during a riot in 1812. Carmack, *Rebels*, 118–20. Criminal contra varios Yndios del Pueblos de Totonicapán por Principales motores en el alzamiento que hubo. "Alcalde mayor de Totonicapán to el Comisionado en el pueblo de Momostenango," 30 October 1811, in AGCA sig. A1, leg. 5478, exp. 47123, fol. 10.
37. Hawkins, *José de Bustamante*, 92; Hermegildo López to Narciso Mallol alcalde mayor of Totonicapán, September 21, 1811, in AGCA, sig. A1, leg. 113, exp. 56194.
38. The mobilizations in Tegucigalpa began the first two days of January 1812, so they would not have influenced the decision made by Bustamante.
39. Manuel Fernández Molina pointed out the relationship between the elimination of tribute and the political needs of Bustamante in the face of the uprisings of San Salvador, León, and Granada as early as 1974. Fernández Molina, *Tributos*, 33–34.
40. In the same decree, Bustamante argued that he had not received official notification, but that he found out about the abolition of tribute from the *Gaceta de Lima*. Ibid., 33.
41. At that time Comalapa had a population of "between 7,000 and 8,000 Indians." Juarros, *Compendio*, 46.

42. These were not elections for a constitutional ayuntamiento but simply annual elections of the mayors of the Indian town.
43. Marroquín, *Apreciación*; Peccorini, *Voluntad*; Pinto, *Centroamérica*; Martínez, *Patria*, 338–41, Hawkins, *José de Bustamante*; López, "Noviembre." I understand autonomy here to mean the real or intended destitution of municipal or provincial authorities and the seating of new authorities.
44. González, "History"; Taracena, *Invención*.
45. There is partial documentation referring to the elections carried out in January 1813 and January 1814, with the participation of parish electors to select district electors for the Totonicapán district. In 1813, among the parish electors were included Juan Menchú, probably a cacique of San Miguel Totonicapán, and Manuel Vicente, almost certainly a cacique from Momostenango. Among all the parish electors listed for both elections, they were the only Indians. January 9, 1814, in AGCA, sig. A1, leg. 6117, exp. 56602, and January 17, 1813, in AGCA, sig. A1, leg. 6116, exp. 56514.
46. On how in the Ecuadoran case these ayuntamientos could be elected by other methods while formally complying with constitutional requirement, and also on how much practical impact the limitation on the participation of voters of African descent could have had, see Morelli, *Territorio*, especially 91–130.
47. See Hawkins, this volume; and Hawkins, *José de Bustamante*, 166.
48. But see Hawkins, *José de Bustamante*, 166–67; Dym, *From Sovereign*, 128–29; and Avendaño, *Centroamérica*, 34n42. González Alzate mentions that in the corregimiento of Quetzaltenango elections often turned violent in those towns with a significant ladino presence. González, "History," 211.
49. Prudencio Cozar to Captain General Carlos Urrutia, April 1, 1820, in AGCA, sig. A1, leg. 193, exp. 3942, fol. 27.
50. Pollack, "Cortes."
51. In 1820 some people from Totonicapán referred to the 1813 conflict as a riot against Father Moreno, which underlines the importance of personal service and rations as a motive for the conflict. Testimony of First Mayor Lucas Méndez, August 13, 1820, in AGCA, sig. A1, leg. 5480, exp. 74155, fol. 19v; Testimony of Second Mayor Domingo Yxchal, August 13, 1820, in ibid., fol. 20; Testimony of ex-Governor Nicolás Bulux, August 13, 1820, in ibid., fol. 23. It should be noted that the parish of San Miguel Totonicapán, which included the towns of San Francisco el Alto and Santa Catarina Ixtahuacán, had a population of 13,604 in 1800, so that if it was not *the* largest parish in terms of number of Indians (the only ones who provided rations and personal services) in the Kingdom of Guatemala, it was surely one of them. See Van Oss, "Población."
52. Principales of Totonicapán to the corregidor of Quetzaltenango, ca. October 11, 1813, in AGCA, sig. A1, leg. 4772, exp. 41186. Despite all the problems involved in interpreting a document of this nature, even reading against the grain, I stress some relevant points: (1) the names of the different principales and their respective parcialidades are listed, in addition to the names of the alcaldes of the religious brotherhoods; (2) the syntax of the document does not seem to be that of an author whose native tongue is Spanish; and (3) the content of the cited phrase does not commonly appear in documents of this nature.

53. Bustamante to the attorney general (*fiscal general*), Juan Gualberto González Bravo, February 22, 1814, in ibid.
54. Constitutional ayuntamiento of Totonicapán to Francisco Berdugo, Scribe of the cámara del crimen, October 29, 1813, in AGCA, sig. A1, leg. 5479, exp. 47139, fol. 41. Mallol to the real audiencia of Guatemala, October 30, 1813, in ibid., fols. 51v–52.
55. Ayuntamiento constitucional de Totonicapán to Francisco Berdugo, escribano de la cámara del crimen, October 29, 1813, in ibid., fol. 41 (particularly strident underscoring in the original). Anselmo Mendoza was one of the leaders of the group of Spaniards and ladinos in the town and had close ties to Prudencio Cozar, the quartermaster general of the royal armies mentioned above.
56. Early in September, royal soldiers traveled through Momostenango and San Bartolomé Aguacaliente, and probably San Miguel Totonicapán, en route to Chiapas, so at this time the Mexican uprising would have seemed very near. Comisionado José María Montiel to alcalde mayor Narciso Mallol, September 12, 1813, in AGCA, sig. A1, leg. 6116, exp. 56470.
57. "Extracto de la Conspiración de Belén"; Rodríguez, *Conspiración*.
58. Lo actuado en la causa criminal contra el comun de yndios de naguala por insurrectos, resistencia a la justicia, y hechos atrozes, in AGCA, sig. A1, leg. 204, exp. 4130; Contra Fran.co Xcapta Diego Mai, Mig.l Tziquin, Diego Xcaptña, Melchor [Xinata], Domingo Coti and Pascual Xocol p.r autores de alboroto el 2 de Nbre en Xtahuacan, in AGCA, sig. A1, leg. 5529, exp. 47766; Martínez, *Motines*, 154–55. According to an 1829 report signed by the mayor of Jacaltenango, a town on the Royal Road in the district of Huehuetenango and one of the last towns before the border with the intendencia of Ciudad Real, in an 1813 uprising the Indians drove priests and ladinos out of the area. The alcalde mayor and thirty militiamen arrived to calm the situation. Manuel Camposeco to the Jefe Político de Totonicapán, Juan José Gorris, July 14, 1829, in AGCA, sig. A1, leg. 6116, exp. 56761.
59. Grandin, *Blood*, 72–76. In 1813 the principales presented a petition indicating that the maceguales preferred tribute payment to charges that would result from the new tax system. Grandin questions the truth of whether the proposal actually originated among the maceguales, since one of the causes of the 1815 uprising was that tribute continued to be charged, notwithstanding its legal abolition.
60. Ibid., 76. Grandin notes this same uneasiness over vaccinations in several towns in the Quetzaltenango corregimiento.
61. White, "Guatemala."
62. Razón circunstanciada que a virtud de comisión el exmo. señor presidente gobernador capitán general de este reino he tomado yo el abajo firmado comisario ordenador honorario de los reales ejércitos y actualm.te encargado de este corregimiento de Quetzaltenango del tributo q.e han pagado los pueblos de la alcaldía mayor de Totonicapán, al presente alcalde mayor, y al anterior don Francisco Pacheco, perteneciente a los tercios de San Juan de 1816 primero desde su restablecimiento hasta la fecha, con expresión de la de los recibos, y demás que sigue, December 15, 1818, in AGCA, sig. A3, leg. 2569, exp. 37711, fols. 6–9v.
63. Común de Sacapulas to the President of the audiencia of Guatemala, February 28, 1821, in AGCA, sig. A3 16, leg. 254, exp. 5229.

64. Carmack, *Quiché Mayas*, 333.
65. Cecilio del Valle to the Real Junta Superior, July 30, 1817, in AGCA, sig. A1, leg. 252, exp. 5163; Fernández, *Tributos*, 37.
66. Also in 1818, the Indian governor of Totonicapán, Nicolás Bulux, in response to pressure from Lara over tribute, simply told him that the people did not wish to pay. Lara imprisoned him, but that same afternoon he felt obliged to release the governor in the face of strong rumors that the arrest had upset the townspeople. Written communication signed by Manuel José Lara, September 2, 1818, in AGCA, sig. A3 16, leg. 2901, exp. 43269. That same month, the town of Santa María Chiquimula rose up in opposition to the taking of a census, forcing the precipitated flight of the alcalde mayor. Diligencias instruidas sobre el motín del pueblo de Sta. Maria Chiquimula, n.d., in AGCA, sig. A1, leg. 193, exp. 3940.
67. Lara to Cozar, September 21, 1818, in AGCA, sig. A1, leg. 6118, exp. 56715. The quartermaster general, Cozar, who stated that he had received repeated instructions not to use force against the Indians, blocked the dispatch of the Quetzaltenango militia. Cozar to Lara, September 21, 1818, in ibid., exp. 56725; Cozar to Lara, September 22, 1818, in AGCA, sig. A1, leg. 193, exp. 3940, fol. 34.
68. Padre Eulogio Gálvez to Bishop Ramón Casaús y Torres, in AGCA, sig. A1, leg. 193, exp. 3940, fol. 42.
69. Cozar to Lara, September 22, 1818, in ibid., fol. 34.
70. I do not refer to hegemony understood as a process, a complicated negotiation necessary among the different actors in a society that produces and reproduces it, but rather the concept of hegemony outlined by Gramsci in which, in addition to the consensus existing among the different classes and groups of society, the state maintains at its disposal the possible use of coercion. Gramsci, *Selections*, 12. On hegemony as a negotiated and constructed long-term process, see particularly Joseph and Nugent, *Everyday*.
71. It should be mentioned that neither these authors nor other eighteenth-century luminaries were especially influential outside of fairly small circles in Guatemala City and some of the larger cities of the kingdom. See Belaubre, this volume.
72. Circular from Lara to the local authorities in the parishes of Chiantla, Soloma and Jacaltenango, June 15, 1819, in AGCA, sig. A3 16, leg. 2901, exp. 43272.
73. Lara to Urrutia, July 10, 1819, in AGCA, sig. A3 16, leg. 254, exp. 2511.
74. Testimony of the ex-Governor (1819) Nicolás Bulux, August 13, 1820, in AGCA, sig. A1, leg. 5480, exp. 74155, fol. 23.
75. Father Elogio Gálvez to Lara, October 6, 1819, in AGCA, sig. A1, leg. 6118, exp. 56751.
76. Testimony of Rufina León, Spaniard, March 20, 1820, in AGCA, sig. A1, leg. 193, exp. 3942, fol. 79v; Testimony of José Víctor Torres, Spaniard, April 8, 1820, in ibid., fols. 81v–82.
77. See Herrera "Escenarios," on these spaces in San Salvador in 1811; and Guerra and Lempérière, *Espacios*, for a broader discussion of Latin America.
78. The documents refer to efforts by leaders of Totonicapán and Chiquimula to contact the following towns: San Cristóbal Totonicapán and Momostenango in Totonicapán district; Cunén and Sacapulas in Huehuetenango district; San Antonio Ilotenango and Santa Catarina Ixtahuacán in the alcaldía mayor of Sololá; Santa María de Jesús,

Olintepeque, and San Pedro Sacatepéquez in the corregimiento of Quetzaltenango. See Pollack, *Levantamiento*, 141–42, for more information on these relationships. Uncertainty as to how real some of these contacts were and what they might have involved must be stressed.

79. Collado to Lara, February 20, 1820, in AGCA, sig. A1, leg. 193, exp. 3942, fol. 2v; Collado to the audiencia of Guatemala, February 21, 1820, in ibid., fol. 4.
80. Testimony of Martín Cobocah, Indian of Totonicapán, cabildo scribe, March 20, 1820, in ibid., fol. 77v (among various testimonies in the same document). This action, with its strong symbolic weight, was in some ways a revocation by the five parcialidades, the unofficial Indian government, of the power vested in the mayor. This interpretation is strengthened if we consider that the action was undertaken before the general public present at the demonstration.
81. A few days earlier, on March 28, in Sacapulas, a town in the Huehuetenango district, the alcalde mayor gave permission for residents to send a commission to the capital to find out if tribute still in fact existed. Lara had to flee after a confusing incident in which he used a knife to defend himself. Pollack, *Levantamiento*, 138–39.
82. Urrutia to señor regente don Francisco Paula Vilches, July 15, 1820, in AGCA, sig. A1, leg. 6930, exps. 57127 and 57187; Rodríguez, *Cádiz*, 131.
83. Principales de San Miguel Totonicapán to Ambrosio Collado, n.d., in AGCA, sig. A1, leg. 193, exp. 3942, fol. 50.
84. Men from Momostenango came as well to take shifts, but in this town there was no demand for the return of collected tribute, reflecting a lack of cohesion regarding the movement among the townspeople.
85. It would be worthwhile to question whether this participation had previously existed or was the manifestation of a new "public sphere."
86. Draft of a document addressed to Cozar, probably written at the end of March 1820, in AGCA, sig. A1, leg. 193, exp. 3942, fols. 18–20.
87. Carmack, *Rebels*, 119; written communication from Ambrosio Collado, May 8, 1820, in AGCA, sig. A1, leg. 193, exp. 3942, fols. 44–45; Pedro Regalado de León to Ambrosio Collado, April 27, 1820, in ibid., fol. 55; Pedro Regalado de León to Ambrosio Collado, in ibid., fol. 57.
88. Cozar to the audiencia of Guatemala, May 7, 1821, in ibid., exp. 3946, fols. 10–11. Martínez Peláez notes the use by Cozar of the phrase *ad terrorem*. Martínez, *Motines*, 259. Portillo cites a document from the provincial council that mentions rumors about many Indians deaths. Portillo, *Crisis*, 246–47.
89. Severo Martínez Peláez believes this pardon was the result of a 2,000-peso payment made to the appropriate authorities. Martínez, *Motines*, 91.
90. Dym, *From Sovereign*; Avendaño, *Centroamérica*.
91. Pollack, "Modelos."
92. The argument here is not that the category "ladino" was indistinguishable from that of "Spaniard" but rather that the distinction was relatively less important than that between Indians and non-Indians.
93. It should be noted that, in the uprisings of 1811 in the León intendancy, popular sectors demanded the elimination of forced labor drafts in the form of repartimientos and

slavery. The absence of these claims in the conflicts of Totonicapán makes one think either that they did not exist or that they had little importance for the townspeople. See Payne, this volume.

94. Pollack, *Levantamiento*, 170–76.
95. This was one of the six points in the original Carrera manifesto. Woodward, *Rafael Carrera*, 65; also see 62, 63, 67, 86, 90, and 407 for more references on the importance of the resistance to the tax during this period, and 90, 137, and 407 on its reduction and elimination by the government of Mariano Rivera Paz in 1838. I am presently working to discover whether the poll tax was applied to the ladino population to the same extent that it was to Indians, which could have incited resistance among the former, who during the colonial period had been exempt. In Ecuador, "Blancos-mestizos" opposed a tax of this nature. Guerrero, "Proceso."
96. The most obvious exception to this was the presence of Indians Tomás Ruiz, his brother Saturnino, and especially Manuel Tot in the Belén conspiracy of 1813.

THE MYTH OF BUSTAMANTINE TERROR

Timothy Hawkins

To nineteenth-century nationalist historians, the epoch of independence in Spanish America represented a unique opportunity to view the birth of their respective nations from the perspective of a dramatic, turbulent, and heroic transformation from the colonial regimen to a nation-state.[1] Through their works, deeds such as Miguel Hidalgo's 1810 Grito de Dolores, José de San Martín's 1817 trans-Andean expedition, and Simón Bolívar's 1813 Admirable Campaign etched themselves into national consciences and exemplified the power of popular unity. More than simply recording the transition from one epoch to another, these histories sought to promote and diffuse a sense of national identity in the new Latin American republics.

Unlike most other Spanish colonies, Central America did not experience a sustained or generalized independence movement between 1810 and 1821. Instead, the Kingdom of Guatemala preserved the colonial order while rebellions and revolutions devastated much of the rest of the empire. During the independence decade, no great leader emerged whose actions resonated beyond the provincial level. When separation from Spain finally happened in 1821, it occurred within the framework of Agustín de Iturbide's Plan de Iguala, an outcome that was disorganized but peaceful. Thus, the isthmus first joined the Mexican Empire, before embarking on the path of an independent republic in 1823. By 1840, after years of political turmoil, the nation that had been a consequence rather than the objective of independence had fragmented into five scarcely viable countries.

It is not surprising that this history has been problematic for those interested in understanding Central America according to norms established by Mexican and South American historians. Without liberators, without a violent struggle or clear examples of public unity in support of independence, and above all without a unified nation, Central American historians created an interpretive framework for their independence based on a collection of failed conspiracies and local uprisings, the patriotic posture assumed by the ayuntamiento of Guatemala City, and the martyrdom of a few revolutionaries.

Lacking a hero of independence, these historians constructed the figure of an arch-villain and argued that the passivity of the Kingdom of Guatemala during the 1810s resulted from the brutal and oppressive rule of Captain General José de Bustamante y Guerra (1811–18). In this narrative, Bustamante personified Spanish absolutism. He imposed a reign of terror that crushed opposition to the colonial system and stifled all dissidence. Ironically, according to this paradigm, these actions proved counterproductive, for they intensified the sentiments for independence among Central Americans. For regional historians, this unexpected but welcome result finally propelled the great liberation movement of the early 1820s.[2]

Considering the fact that contemporary scholarship has presented more complete, nuanced, and ultimately persuasive accounts of independence in other parts of the Spanish empire, the long-term persistence among Central American historians of such a partisan interpretation of independence movements in the isthmus is distinctive. This paradigm emerged to satisfy the need to tell a cohesive national history of the region. It was based on certain theories as to the nature of the liberation of Spanish America that did not necessarily fit the experience of the isthmus. Therefore, it has tended to distort both the role of Bustamante and the support for independence in the Kingdom of Guatemala for the purposes of better conforming to the traditional model.

The case in favor of a Bustamantine terror rests on the affirmation that the captain general governed the kingdom in an arbitrary and despotic manner. It maintains that he violently snuffed out dissension and ignored local sentiment, subverted orders from the crown and the constitutional government, persecuted the elite families, and terrified the local population to achieve its submission. Those charges rest largely on six perceived examples of misconduct: Bustamante's crackdown after the 1811–12 uprisings in El Salvador and Nicaragua; his disdain for the Constitution of 1812; his treatment of accused traitors and revolutionaries; his strong dependence on military justice; his frequent confrontations with the ayuntamiento of Guatemala City and the Aycinena oligarchy; and his enthusiastic embrace of absolutism after the restoration of Ferdinand VII. This argument also assumes that there was substantive opposition to the crown in Central America, that Bustamante needed all the coercive instruments of Spanish power to preserve colonial order, and that the captain general governed for many years without any institutional supervision.

Nevertheless, before history can judge the validity of this thesis, Bustamante's actions must be placed in the proper context. If one sets aside the dictates of official history and examines the conditions at the time, it is possible to conclude that the Kingdom of Guatemala witnessed the appearance of its first counterinsurgency state during this period, but not a reign of terror. Such an alternative interpretation of the period rests on multiple counterarguments. These include the limited flexibility of colonial administrators, the frequent communication between Bustamante and Spain, the impact of viceregal decisions on his policies, the nature of the struggle for power between the government of the captaincy general and the local oligarchy, and the degree to which the captain general maintained both the active and passive support of the majority of the population. My objective in this chapter is the reconsideration within this framework of some of Bustamante's most controversial acts with the intention of undermining the concept of Bustamantine terror and even the historiographical myth of Central American independence.

Between 1808 and 1811, the colonial administration in the Kingdom of Guatemala struggled to preserve Spanish dominion over the isthmus in the face of multiple challenges: the fall of the Bourbon monarchy; concerns about possible French intervention; the questionable legitimacy of the Spanish loyalist governments; the growing support for autonomy among many American subjects; and the emergence of independence movements in other parts of the empire. Between 1812 and the restoration of Ferdinand VII in 1814, that is, the two years after the outbreak of the first rebellions in Central America, the government of Captain General José de Bustamante was also beset by the quixotic imperial policies of the Spanish Cortes and its liberal constitution. Consequently, building from the precedents set by those who came before him as well as other colonial governors of Spanish America, Bustamante undertook the construction of a counterinsurgency state on the isthmus that helped reaffirm Spanish sovereignty there for the remainder of the decade. This obsessive concentration on preventing rebellion also led to a significant erosion of the legitimacy of Spanish dominion among a small but important segment of the population.

Only eight months after Bustamante arrived in Guatemala in March 1811, the first rebellion against the imperial order broke out in San Salvador. Between November 1811 and March 1812, the government worked to resolve both this crisis and contemporaneous unrest in Nicaragua through a strategy Bustamante called "prudent conciliation," which often depended on the participation of local elites to work toward eliminating the motives behind the agitation.[3] In the Salvadoran case, for example, Bustamante diffused the provincial unrest by nominating the Guatemalan José de Aycinena as interim intendant. In April 1812, only the Nicaraguan city of Granada refused to negotiate an end to its rebellion, despite a series of amnesty offers made by Bustamante. As a result, the forces of the monarchy mustered outside of Granada during the third week of April.

Bustamante made one final attempt to pacify the Granadans with the offer of an official pardon. When this effort failed, on April 21 combat began. After two days of skirmishes, the royalist commander entered into negotiations with rebel leaders and proposed an amnesty in exchange for an immediate cessation of hostilities and the peaceful occupation of the city by the royalist army. Under this promise, Granada surrendered on April 25 (see Payne, this volume).[4]

Even before the news of the capitulation reached Bustamante, he was aware that the insurgents had fired on soldiers of the king. The implications of this act were not lost on the captain general, and in what became the first controversial decision of his administration he rejected the terms of the truce. Arguing that the Granadans forfeited their pardon when they refused his second amnesty proposal, Bustamante ordered the interim intendant to imprison all those implicated in the revolt.[5]

Events in Granada had a profound impact on Bustamante's attitude toward insurrection. Until this military confrontation, the captain general could maintain that disturbances in the kingdom had come about from a combination of persistent injustices and the unstable times in which they were living. Therefore, according to Bustamante, his policy of prudent conciliation was an appropriate response to reasonable political demands. However, Granada convinced him that unprecedented revolutionary sentiment now infected the isthmus. To contain it, Bustamante concluded that the official response to rebellion must be more forceful than before.

Critics of his administration have described this new period as the beginnings of Bustamantine terror. However, instead of marking an arbitrary metamorphosis of Bustamante from prudent conciliator into hard-line tyrant, these policy changes paralleled the adoption of new counterinsurgency methods in New Spain under Viceroy Francisco Javier Venegas and the commander of royalist forces, Félix María Calleja. Mindful of the heavy-handed, often brutal, but also successful responses to the nearly two-year-old rebellion there, Bustamante sought to apply some of those same counterinsurgent tactics in Central America once the political situation in the isthmus began to deteriorate.[6]

After the uprisings in San Salvador and Nicaragua, when Bustamante had reason to doubt the continued value of prudent conciliation, he found in the neighboring viceroyalty an officially sanctioned, alternate model for dealing with social discontent. Guided by the Venegas/Calleja precedents, the captain general concentrated his counterinsurgency efforts in four areas: increasing police and judicial authority over insurgents; improving military readiness within the kingdom; developing new instruments of propaganda and civil control; and suppressing reforms decreed by the new constitutional government in Spain.

It is not surprising that such policies found little support among the local Creole elite, especially when a counterinsurgency state in Central America developed just as a liberal constitution for the empire was adopted. In principle, Creoles now claimed a vastly expanded political role at the imperial, regional, and local levels. In practice, this meant that Bustamante's priorities would all be quickly challenged by a Creole community of uncertain loyalty to the crown. Politically energized and legitimized by the Cádiz Constitution, the Guatemalan elites refused to stand aside while the captain general unilaterally implemented measures that he regarded as fundamental to the preservation of order among a rebellious population and an important part of his discretionary authority as the highest-ranking colonial official on the isthmus.

Bustamante was aware that his new counterinsurgency state threatened to change the long-existing balance of power among the institutions that maintained the colonial system, given that his strategy affected well-established jurisdictions, norms, and rulings. Therefore, he tried to explain his actions by appealing to the unprecedented crisis in which the empire was enmeshed. In the fourth provision of the decree establishing a superintendency of police, the captain general inserted an anonymous maxim on "political prudence" that could have served as the guiding philosophy of his administration in the face of rebellion: "There are cases in which scrupulous justice would be the most sovereign injustice; where the Magistrate, servant of the Law, should proceed in one manner, and the Government, obligated to conserve the public peace, in another much different manner. And the Prince or his representative should always do what must be done, so long as he is attending to and considering the welfare and security of the people."[7]

The audiencia, however, did not accept this argument. When they received the decree, the oidores expressed their concern that similar actions in other colonies had generated great public opposition, and that, keeping in mind the current state of the kingdom, establishing a police superintendency would be unwise. They recognized that a comparable reform had functioned well in suppressing the insurrection in New Spain but maintained that the situation there was much worse than in Central America. Given that Bustamante had begun his command with conciliatory efforts, the audiencia recommended that this policy continue. Thus, underlining the limits on Bustamante's authority as governor, in the meeting of the real acuerdo of January 27, 1812, his proposal to establish a police superintendent was refused.[8]

Despite this setback, by the summer of 1812 the captain general was already far from the conciliatory policies that had characterized his first year in the isthmus. With broad support from provincial officials, the military, and the church, he was able to lay a strong foundation for a counterinsurgency state in the Kingdom of Guatemala. First, Bustamante directed his attention to the judicial system in an effort to strengthen his authority over the prosecution and punishment of subversives. This element of his counterinsurgency strategy, however, had unwanted consequences. More than any other controversial issue during this period, the debate among the captain general, the audiencia, and the ayuntamiento of Guatemala

City concerning the treatment of those suspected of *infidencia* (disloyalty/treason) divided the Central American governing elites and precipitated a period of open hostility that would persist until the end of Bustamante's tenure in 1818.

The term *infidencia* covered a variety of crimes associated with sedition. These included thoughts, words, and deeds that endangered public security, undermined the authority of the state, or challenged the legitimacy of the sovereign (*lesa majestad*, high treason). During the imperial crisis, most individuals suspected of any kind of subversion were accused of this offense. The adjudication of such cases was, however, less straightforward. The audiencia, later supported by the ayuntamiento, argued that infidencia traditionally fell under civil jurisdiction and that, after the abolition of fueros by the royalist government in Spain,[9] the criminal court (*sala del crimen*) should continue to try suspects.[10]

At first, Bustamante did not seem to have problems with the position of the oidores, an attitude that explains his decision in 1811 to dissolve the Tribunal of Loyalty (*Tribunal de Fidelidad*) established by his predecessor to investigate cases of infidencia. He changed his mind, however, with the arrival of a new royal decree in March 1812.[11] By that date, conditions in Central America had devolved. Prisons in the capital and provinces were now full of presumed subversives from the many revolts in the kingdom. Recent warnings about French espionage received widespread distribution (and were met with widespread concern) across the isthmus. The administration feared new challenges to Spanish rule at any moment. Reports from New Spain indicated that its own security committee (*junta de seguridad*) had begun to judge cases of infidencia. And, in response to this climate of insecurity, Bustamante had already begun to increase the military presence in the colony.

With this new decree the regency council sought to recognize the negative impact of a state of war on normal judicial functions and procedures. The council decided to return authority over certain types of infidencia to generals and military governors, as defined by the general ordinances of the army. In his position as captain general, Bustamante was a military governor, and he appreciated the argument that military justice was a better and more efficient manner to deal with subversion. The arrival of this decree gave him opportunity and authority to concentrate cases of infidencia under the jurisdiction of the captaincy general. As a result, Bustamante published a decree on April 13, 1812, that mandated military trials for all crimes of a subversive nature.[12]

The immediate consequence of this order was the creation of war councils to investigate and judge the cases of Manuel Antonio Gordón, Mateo Antonio Marure, Francisco Cordón, Juan de Dios Mayorga, and other less prominent figures imprisoned for a variety of subversive acts. The establishment of these military tribunals provoked immediate opposition from the audiencia and members of the

Creole elite. Responding to an investigation by the audiencia into the Marure trial, which became the emblematic case in the jurisdictional tug-of-war, Bustamante simply identified the corresponding section of the army ordinances that gave military tribunals authority over subjects accused of espionage or conspiracy against the forces of the king, "in whatever form it is attempted or executed."[13]

Frustrated by the administration's stance, in July oidores began to debate the real meaning of the regency decree concerning infidencia. Once the audiencia declared itself in opposition to the use of military tribunals in cases of subversion, the accused and their families began to ask for the protection of civil jurisdiction. Although the oidores agreed that all such cases should be considered by the sala del crimen, their only recourse at the moment, since the captain general stood firm in his conviction and had imprisoned the suspects in military prisons, was an appeal to the crown.[14] A summary of the legal dispute was sent to Spain for review on November 18. However, within two weeks colonial authorities received a letter from the regency council, dated July 2, that did nothing to constrain the captain general. This decree gave Bustamante the authority to govern as he deemed appropriate to suppress rebellion, provided that his policies were made in concert with other colonial authorities. It also charged the colonial authorities with promoting "the greatest exactitude in the pursuit and quick substantiation of cases of infidencia, and in the application of the corresponding punishments." The crown, it appeared, wanted results.[15]

Since the colonial administration continued to insist on order and security, the Creole elite found themselves worried that the liberal promise inherent in the Constitution of 1812, which reached the colony in September, would go unfulfilled. To the great delight of this elite, a series of royal decrees that accompanied the constitution required that elections be held for positions in two new political institutions. First, constitutional ayuntamientos were to replace the old municipal councils in all towns with more than one thousand inhabitants. Second, provincial councils (*diputaciones provinciales*) were established as regional assemblies for Guatemala and Nicaragua.[16] At the same time, imperial reforms resulted in the demotion of the governor to the position of superior political chief (*jefe político superior*) and of the audiencia to the category of a supreme court. Quite rightly, the Creoles expected to dominate these new liberal institutions and the elections for representatives to the Cortes in Spain, to the exclusion of the tiny peninsular Spanish community and the lower classes. Such an outcome would give them an unprecedented level of power in the colony.

The confrontation between the captain general and the Creole elite concerning the implementation of the Constitution of 1812 began at once and persisted until the summer of 1814, when the news of Ferdinand VII's decision to revoke the charter arrived in Guatemala. This result vindicated Bustamante, left Creoles deeply bitter, and consequently gave impetus to a series of recriminations and acts of vengeance that permanently soured the remaining years of Bustamante's mandate. Within the context of this constitutional experiment, Bustamante's actions have been classified as hypocritical at best, tyrannical at worst. And though many of his policies were obstructionist and contrary to the spirit of the Cádiz reforms, it must be recognized that the conditions Bustamante faced at that moment were extraordinary. Put bluntly, he had received orders from a government of doubtful legitimacy to apply a new political system without delay in a very traditional society faced with external and internal subversion. Prudence, a common word in Bustamante's vocabulary, dictated that local authorities show moderation during this process. The ayuntamiento of Guatemala City was not, however, disposed to accept this position, preferring instead to press and threaten the captain general at every opportunity, seeking to acquire for itself all the power it could.

Despite the optimism of imperial reformers in Spain and the enthusiasm of the Creole elite in Central America, by January 1813, when the first full year of the new constitutional order began, the Kingdom of Guatemala was not a suitable place for political experimentation. Even without overt opposition to Spanish authorities or clear signs of subversion, accusations and detentions never stopped, and disruptive rumors ran unchecked through rural areas in the absence of good communication and trustworthy news sources.

In this climate of uncertainty, it would have been extraordinary for a governor such as Bustamante, with his military background and mentality, to accept the power sharing and political reforms established by the Constitution of 1812. Even if the captain general had not been ideologically opposed to the complete deconstruction of the system of enlightened despotism that had governed the empire during the Bourbon epoch, his experience in colonial administration would have made him cautious about the viability of liberal reform during such a difficult moment in the history of the kingdom.

In a report to the regency council in March 1813, Bustamante presented his analysis of political tendencies in Central America.[17] According to the captain general, the greatest challenge to the preservation of the colony, other than the foreign threat presented by the Morelos rebellion in neighboring New Spain, was the growing pretentions of the Creole elite for political power. In his opinion, the autonomy the Creoles demanded and the constitution seemed to offer was in reality a subterfuge for seeking independence. Therefore, a rapid and complete implementation of the new system, with constitutional ayuntamientos and provincial assemblies, would only provide stimulus to a process of rupture between Guatemala and Spain.

Bustamante argued that Spanish authorities found themselves faced with a concentrated and coordinated attack by Creoles through their own political organ, the ayuntamiento. According to him, the first serious challenge to Spanish dominion had taken place in 1809, when the municipal council of Ciudad Real ousted the interim intendant of Chiapas, José Mariano Valero, and installed one of their own in the post (see Belaubre, this volume). In his opinion, the reaction of then-captain general Antonio González Saravia had been too conciliatory, since it contributed to the growing belief that political power "should be in the ayuntamientos or in juntas made up of individuals elected by them."[18] By the end of 1810, the ayuntamiento of Guatemala City had codified this perspective in the instructions it wrote for Cortes representative Antonio Larrazábal, a document distributed throughout the colony with great success, which, according to Bustamante, urged that local institutions assume important powers that belonged exclusively to the colonial state and its functionaries.[19]

According to Bustamante, Creole elites, excited by the promise of autonomy and hoping to take advantage of the weakness of the imperial system, had been behind the San Salvador and Nicaragua uprisings at the end of 1811 and the Tegucigalpa revolt in January 1812. Even though he had been able to suppress these disturbances, Bustamante described himself as confronted by an ayuntamiento in the capital that was increasingly recalcitrant. The Guatemalan city council, he declared, intended to achieve its objectives by pushing the Cádiz reforms and blaming official counterinsurgency measures for having originated the political unrest in the kingdom, even though these disturbances had already begun before the policies were implemented.

The first conflict of the constitutional period resulted from a dispute over the implementation of the Cádiz reforms. In a letter dated January 3, the ayuntamiento fulfilled its threat to send a complaint to Spain accusing the colonial administration of delaying elections for a Cortes representative and for the provincial councils. The councilmen indicated that the elections of the previous December to form the first constitutional ayuntamientos had been a great success. According to them, it was essential that the electoral process advance so that the provincial councils could convene as soon as possible and the representatives to the Cortes could reach Spain in time for its opening. Challenging the captain general's position that instability in the provinces had influenced his decision regarding the continued implementation of the reforms, the ayuntamiento sought to put his good faith in doubt. In their complaint before the crown, they went out of their way to criticize Bustamante's inflexible nature and rude behavior.[20]

The emotional character of this denunciation by the ayuntamiento shows how the instability and uncertainty of the years after the fall of the monarchy gave rise to partisan perspectives. In reality, the captain general was not a tyrant, and the councilmen were not promoters of independence. However, at that time the Creole elite in Central America did see before them a great opportunity to acquire more political power in their search for autonomy within the imperial framework. But Bustamante, a proud and reserved naval officer and crown official, believed it was his duty to preserve the authority of Ferdinand VII intact in the Kingdom of Guatemala during a period in which the empire was facing grave existential threats from both revolutionaries and liberal politicians who were trying to limit the power of the king. As long as Ferdinand remained in exile and the outcome of the wars in Spain and America was not clear, the interests of the captain general and the Creole elite simply could not be reconciled.

Such considerations did not seem to weigh heavily on the Creole elite, for they continued hoping for a rapid and substantive implementation of constitutional reforms. From their perspective, Bustamante had become an obstacle to the new order. Accordingly, the only legitimate action they could take to express their growing opposition to his policies was the series of brusquely written complaints the ayuntamiento began to send to the Cortes after 1812. Unfortunately, the councilmen could not expect the imperial government to respond favorably to these expressions of colonial frustration. In fact, some of their protests were actually counterproductive. On March 4, 1813, for example, in a reply to its complaint about the publication of the constitution the ayuntamiento was instructed to work with the captain general in the interests of peace.[21]

In September, Bustamante sent the ayuntamiento a response from the Cortes concerning the accusations made against him in January regarding presumed delays in elections of representatives to that body and the provincial councils. After examining the case, the crown had declared that there was absolutely no reason to punish the acts of the captain general.[22] It was not until José de Aycinena, a leading member of the most important local family and former intendant of San Salvador, took his seat on the council of state in Spain (an imperial leadership role rarely achieved by an American, much less a Central American) in August 1813 that the Creole oligarchy acquired the necessary influence at the highest levels of government to enable them to undermine Bustamante's position.[23]

Meanwhile the ayuntamiento, invigorated by the constitution, continued to defy the authority of the captain general. Its strategy obliged Bustamante to take public positions on sensitive questions and accommodate its elevated position on every ceremonial occasion. During the spring of 1813, the councilmen claimed their right to adjudicate charges of infidencia and to oversee the treatment of prisoners in the captaincy general. This incursion into the legal dispute between Bustamante and the audiencia did not derail efforts made by the colonial administration to judge subversion in military tribunals. However, the ayuntamiento persisted in its commitment to this issue and discovered that it could serve as a constitutional defender of individual rights, acting as a thorn in Bustamante's side by taking advantage of its power to undertake unrestricted visits to prisons and publicize the condition of the prisoners in their cells.[24]

The apparently cruel treatment of those accused of infidencia by the captain general and his obsession with punishing subversives are pillars of the Bustamantine myth that appear in many national histories of the nineteenth century. It is reasonable to suspect that Bustamante did not intend to give the benefit of the doubt to those suspected of such crimes, and he definitely wanted swift and effective punishment applied to those convicted. In large part, however, the charges against Bustamante concerning the handling of prisoners tend to include areas beyond the governor's control. Spanish justice was slow, independent of the jurisdiction, as was the appeals process. Conditions inside Spanish colonial prisons, whether civil or military, were poor and often unhealthy. Unfortunately, the combination of these factors frequently caused prisoners to experience sustained misery and even death during the adjudication of their cases due to neglect, medical ignorance, as well as active mistreatment.

Bustamante was inflexible in his decision to detain suspects until the end of preliminary investigations, which caused some to languish in prison. When these individuals were acquitted of the accusations drawn up against them, they were set free. When they were given light punishment, they received it; when there was a hard sentence, it was always imposed without hope of pardon. Since there was little money to make major improvements in the prisons of the kingdom, there was little hope that reforms could alleviate the suffering of the prisoners; given the low motivation to improve the living conditions of those accused of crimes against the crown, the captain general focused on other priorities.

The Guatemala City ayuntamiento did not give up hope that more important reforms would occur once the constitutional system was fully implemented. With or without the obstructionism of Bustamante, the council would have to overcome many obstacles before the ideals of Cádiz could be fulfilled in Central America. Between February and May 1813, elections were held for the provincial council of Guatemala in the seven districts that composed this new political entity: Sacatepéquez, Chimaltenango, Quetzaltenango, Sonsonate, Ciudad Real, Comayagua, and San Salvador. After the completion of this step, the city council wrote to all the newly elected provincial representatives and asked them to travel to the capital as soon as they could to inaugurate the assembly on July 1. Unfortunately, when the day came three members had not yet arrived.[25]

Concerned about the consequences of an extended delay, on July 20 the ayuntamiento asked Bustamante to authorize the provincial council to begin its work with four members and two alternates. The captain general, however, had no inclination to make the establishment of a political institution dominated by Creoles any easier. Of greater practical concern, he had real reason to distrust the new delegates. Two of the members, José Matías Delgado and José Cañas, had been involved in the Salvadoran uprising of 1811, and of the others only Bruno Medina rose to the standard of loyalty required by Bustamante. Therefore, the provincial council did not begin work until September 2, and the captain general, who served as its president in his new position as superior political chief, didn't pay it much heed.[26]

The other two pillars of the constitutional system, American representation at the Spanish Cortes and the establishment of constitutional ayuntamientos across the isthmus, also faced significant obstacles. Although Cortes delegates were chosen in March 1813, budget problems prevented many from making the trip to Spain in time to serve. Even as late as November, José Cleto Montiel, the representative from Quetzaltenango and Totonicapán, was still in the capital presenting a request to the provincial council for payment of his travel expenses. At this stage of its existence, the assembly had trouble disbursing public funds, especially when its jurisdiction over the treasury remained uncertain. Evidence of active obstructionism on the part of Bustamante is difficult to establish beyond a reasonable doubt. The delayed selection of a representative for Guatemala City and Sacatepéquez, for example, resulted from the decision of the first candidate chosen, José María Peinado, who had been elected in February, to decline the post in favor of maintaining his position as intendant of San Salvador. In any case, when the new Cortes opened its doors in October 1813, the Kingdom of Guatemala was insufficiently represented.[27]

After the seating of the provincial council, Bustamante ordered his subordinates to establish ayuntamientos in towns that previously had not had municipal representation but whose size or influence now called for them. Soon after, the captain general began to receive reports from his alcaldes mayores and corregidores suggesting that these reforms had stalled.[28] In multiple cases, the enthusiasm of the constitutionalists was undermined by local prejudices, administrative incompetence, and personal ambition, factors far beyond the influence of Bustamante.

But even when provincial functionaries made an effort to implement the constitution, complications ensued. For example, the establishment of constitutional ayuntamientos was delayed in the alcaldía mayor of Totonicapán because of the lack of a suitable provincial census. Bustamante had no reason to block reform at this level, but neither could he make it easier. Once he issued the necessary orders from the capital, local and provincial forces determined the success or failure of the process. From the perspective of the Creole elite, nevertheless, Bustamante shouldered the responsibility for the failures of the Cádiz experiment. By the end of the summer of 1813, they had concluded that only a new captain general could put it back on track.

The August arrival in the capital of the prisoners taken during the Granada campaign exacerbated the hostility of the Guatemalan elite toward Bustamante (see Payne, this volume). Many of those detained were prominent residents of the Nicaraguan city, a group that included members of its ayuntamiento, as well as military officers and rich landholders. All had much in common with their Guatemalan counterparts. Mindful of these bonds, the Guatemalan oligarchy became a stubborn defender of the well-being of these prisoners. The most important families in the capital requested that colonial authorities transfer the Granadans from the public jail to a different site to avoid their mixing with common criminals. The Creole elite also organized the delivery of food and other supplies to the Nicaraguans during their confinement.[29]

Bustamante was not impressed by this show of support for people he considered traitors. In response, he argued, "The prison is sufficiently comfortable and decent, in proportion to the distinguished subjects to be found there, but not comparable to the enormity of the crime attributed to them." Not surprisingly, many of the Granadans fell ill with diarrhea, dysentery, and other sicknesses shortly after their arrival. Seeking a balance between "humanity" and "indispensable security," the captain general ordered the construction of a special hospital and arranged for improved ventilation inside the prison. Still, the Nicaraguans continued to accuse the colonial government of poor treatment for as long as they remained incarcerated.[30]

Emboldened by recent crown decisions exonerating him from blame in constitutional controversies with the Guatemala City ayuntamiento, Bustamante received further good news from Spain in late November 1813. On the twenty-third of that month, he forwarded to council members the new "Instructions for the Economic and Political Government of the Provinces." In this decree, the peninsular authorities again revised the balance of power between the governor, the provincial councils, and the constitutional ayuntamientos. Municipal councils now learned that their functions would be limited to local public welfare. Rather than an autonomous regional legislature, the provincial council was to be restricted to advisory and supervisory authority. Most important, the crown returned to the colonial governor "supreme authority" to preserve peace and order on the isthmus. Not surprisingly, the Guatemalan Creole elite were appalled by this news, because the Instructions profoundly weakened those political institutions the oligarchy sought as a counterbalance to the colonial bureaucracy peninsular Spaniards had long dominated.[31]

The impact of these changes was immediate. Feeling justified in his limited use of the provincial council, Bustamante proclaimed his right to convene the next annual round of local elections, a decision that sparked yet more conflict with the Guatemala City ayuntamiento in late November 1813.[32] Although the oligarchy found multiple reasons to complain to the crown at this time, their own motivations were rather straightforward. Despite their liberal vocabulary, which alluded to individual political and economic freedoms, the Guatemalan elites were most interested in replacing a peninsular political oligarchy with one headed by Creoles. From this perspective, the 1813 political war between Bustamante and the Guatemala City ayuntamiento should be understood as a dispute over contradictory interpretations of a new but undefined constitutional system, one that seemed to imply greater home rule while failing to break outright with the traditional order. Without precedents to follow, each combatant tried to secure the best possible position and the strongest allies. But, with Spanish politicians mired in similar struggles in the Cortes and sending conflicting messages to the colonies, it is not surprising that few reforms were implemented effectively. In the end, this standstill convinced the more radical among the isthmian elite that political reform would result from force of arms only.

Between October 28 and December 21, 1813, a group of well-connected Creoles used the convent of Belén in Guatemala City to plan a coup against the colonial government.[33] By drawing on their military contacts, they believed they could convince the militia companies of the capital to overthrow the captain general and other Spanish authorities. With Bustamante in prison, the conspirators intended to free all political prisoners and take possession of the public treasury. The ultimate objective of the uprising, which was set for December 24, remains unclear, although it seems to have been independence. In any case, José de la Llana and Macario Sánchez, two officers who had been invited to the convent for one of the meetings, denounced the conspirators to the authorities. The colonial government deposed some twenty-four witnesses to confirm the meetings and afterward received the unsolicited testimony of Joaquín Yúdice, one of the original members of the plot, who filled in many details and denounced the leaders. On December 21, the conspiracy collapsed after the arrest of most of those accused.

No proof exists to suggest that the planned coup had generalized support or that it reflected popular sentiments. However, the fact that members of the Guatemala City ayuntamiento, most notably José Francisco Barrundia, were reputedly involved confirmed Bustamante's concerns about the loyalty of the Creole elite. One month after the failure of the Belén conspiracy, a more significant challenge to Spanish authority developed in San Salvador. Although this second Salvadoran uprising was suppressed quickly, the captain general again had reason to believe that a network of Creole subversives was threatening the colonial order. In the wake of these disturbances, the government discovered a letter that rebel leaders had purportedly sent in May 1813 to José María Morelos, demonstrating that at least some members of the Creole elite were in direct contact with Mexican insurgents.[34] After imposing martial law in the Salvadoran city and transferring several military units to the province, Bustamante ordered an in-depth investigation of the revolt with the goal of prosecuting all those involved.

This latest experience with insurrection disillusioned the captain general, who concluded that most Spanish American subjects were not ready for the type of political reform conceived by the new constitution. In his view, the Cortes should have undertaken a careful, measured application of the new charter's rights and liberties. Instead, it overwhelmed the empire with a complicated tangle of modern laws and institutions that turned out to be ineffective. In his opinion, the only segment of society capable of operating in this climate was the "Enlightened" group of "priests and attorneys" of high society, who intended to exploit the political confusion to reinforce the Creole-dominated oligarchies. By presenting the masses with manipulated and poorly elaborated interpretations of constitutional reforms, these subversives hoped to alienate unlettered "common people" and foster support for autonomy or independence. The captain general determined that the subversives and any other subject corrupted by these sentiments would have to be exiled if the established order were to be maintained.[35]

Bustamante believed that he had indulged discontented Creoles too long. He did not repudiate his initial policies of conciliation. In fact, he argued, "The system of prudent moderation that I adopted was useful, because it will make the system of justice which I intend to promote in the future stand out even more."[36] Writing to the regency council, the captain general then recommended certain measures he considered critical to the survival of Spanish authority on the isthmus and elsewhere. Given the fact that he was fighting what he considered a "war of intrigue," he asked the crown to confirm that the Laws of the Indies empowered overseas governors to sidestep normal judicial procedures in times of crisis. Notably, he sought permission to exile anyone who might represent a threat to public order. He also asked for streamlined infidencia trials, arguing that court formalities delayed justice. Although the viceroys Venegas and Calleja had implemented similar extrajudicial policies in New Spain, it is worth emphasizing that the captain general sought authorization from Spain first. In fact, the crown declined to endorse his proposals.

The Creole elite lost their battle (though not the war) with Bustamante on August 19, 1814, when the captain general published the royal decree of May 4 that abolished the constitution and annulled the legislation adopted by the junta central and the Cortes while Ferdinand was in exile. This declaration reestablished an absolute monarchy throughout the empire, a process that began on the isthmus three weeks later, when Bustamante announced that the crown had restored the traditional powers of the captain general and eliminated the position of superior political chief. Shortly thereafter, the provincial councils ceased to function, while the ayuntamiento of Guatemala City persisted in a state of political limbo until the beginning of December. In the end, authorized by a subsequent royal decree, the captain general ordered the municipal council to reconvene in its 1808 form, that is, with its preconstitutional powers and membership. That Bustamante proved to be an enthusiastic accomplice in the dismantling of the constitution should not come as a surprise. The restoration of absolutism in the Spanish empire confirmed him as captain general and legitimized his counterinsurgency policies. Moreover, it foretold a difficult future for his Creole antagonists.[37]

In August 1814, six years after the overthrow of the Spanish monarchy precipitated an imperial crisis, the traditional order was restored to the Kingdom of Guatemala. Of course, nothing could erase the impact of the recent constitutional experiments in Central America. Some colonial elites benefited enormously from the Cádiz reforms or at least recognized their inherent potential. Others had become permanently radicalized. During the last half of Bustamante's tenure in office, however, most Central Americans expressed no opposition to the return of absolutism. Having overcome the ripples of unrest that once imperiled the colonial establishment, the kingdom appeared ready to reclaim its place within the empire of Ferdinand VII.

The apparent end of this chapter of crisis in the Spanish monarchy heralded the possibility of reconciliation between unhappy Creoles and the crown. Nevertheless, Bustamante and the Guatemalan oligarchy fought constantly during his final years as captain general. Supporters of the concept of a Bustamantine terror recognize this period as the culmination of Bustamante's efforts to impose a military dictatorship and wreak vengeance on his enemies. That perspective rests on a particular interpretation of the events that dominated colonial politics between 1815 and 1818: Bustamante's campaign against those who signed the Instructions of 1810; his deteriorated relationship with the audiencia; two deaths that resulted from his efforts to combat subversion; and his persecution of the Aycinena and Beltranena houses.

It is not necessary to turn to stale tropes of Spanish oppression to understand the motivations behind the behavior of Bustamante at this time. As a monarchist, he held political views that were widespread throughout the isthmus. Central Americans did not require a reign of terror to accept a political tradition that the majority of them understood better than liberal constitutionalism. Thus, acting now with the full support of the crown, the captain general tried to govern for the first time within the parameters of Bourbon enlightened absolutism. This meant a frontal attack on the Creole oligarchy, which in his opinion was the most dangerous and destabilizing group in the colony. There is little doubt that personal animosity shaped this campaign. However, Bustamante also made a rational evaluation of the main threat to the Spanish colonial regime. Unfortunately for him, the segment of society he hoped to disempower was deeply entrenched and had good connections at the Cádiz Cortes. When the crown concluded that it could not dispense with the Guatemalan oligarchy, the captain general himself became expendable.

Personal factors also help explain the visceral hatred that members of the Creole elite felt toward Bustamante. His military detachment, Spartan lifestyle, disgust at ostentation, and scruples at accepting gifts or bribes reflected his firm conviction that close association with local families was unprofessional and constituted a threat to his honor and reputation. Many perceived this attitude as arrogance and interpreted his reserve as contempt for Creole society. Invariably, Bustamante contrasted poorly with other colonial officials. In part due to the longer nature of their mandate, members of the audiencia often entered into mutually beneficial alliances with the local elite. During Bustamante's last years in the kingdom, the Creole oligarchy made every effort to seize upon this positive relationship with the tribunal to gain advantage in their continuing disputes with the captain general.

Describing this period as the Bustamantine terror requires one to argue that Bustamante had no justification for the continued application of counterinsurgency measures. Although the isthmus had exhibited no signs of unrest since the uprising in San Salvador in 1814, active rebellion persisted to the north and south. Critically, the crown did not give any indication that it would abandon the use of force as the preferable solution to rebellion. In the spring of 1815, a Spanish expeditionary force led by General Pablo Morillo disembarked in New Granada and fought insurgents in a brutal war that lasted until 1820. In New Spain, Viceroy Félix Calleja continued his counterinsurgency campaign with equal ferocity until the arrival of his replacement in September 1816. In this crisis environment, the captain general had no incentive to moderate his policies.

In his view, Bustamante believed that his principle duty was to prevent social disturbance. This mindset led him to make a series of controversial decisions, which his enemies used against him to good effect. On April 27, 1815, the real acuerdo met to discuss a list of complaints regarding mail security that had accumulated over the past two years. The oidores expressed concern that many residents of the capital had lost confidence in the mail because of unnecessary delays, evidence of tampering, and a new requirement for delivering the post at night. This had caused people to consider alternative means of sending their correspondence, a solution with dangerous implications for future postal revenue. As early as May 1813, Bustamante had admitted to the Guatemala City ayuntamiento that security concerns compelled his administration to open certain letters, especially those sent to and from areas in conflict. However, in 1815 the audiencia refused to accept this justification and decided to order an investigation.[38]

Such extralegal security procedures received careful scrutiny by anti-Bustamante factions in the kingdom. But the Creole elite had other reasons to proclaim the existence of a reign of terror at this time as well. In particular, the tragic fates of two victims of the counterinsurgency state suggested the brutal nature of the colonial regime. The first case resulted from Bustamante's unsuccessful efforts to capture José Francisco Barrundia, a former member of the Guatemala City ayuntamiento who had been implicated in the Belén conspiracy. Convinced that Barrundia had escaped to the Yucatán, the captain general intercepted a letter to the Campechan José Mariano Argüelles from José Francisco Córdova, another councilman suspected of subversion. Believing that Argüelles was either an alias or that he was part of a larger conspiracy to hide the fugitive, Bustamante asked the authorities in Campeche to send the young man to Guatemala City for interrogation. Argüelles was duly arrested. He then fell ill on the road and died.[39]

The second controversy that enraged the antagonists of the captain general began on July 20, 1815. On that date, Bustamante informed the audiencia that he had launched an investigation of José Francisco Alfaro, captain of the schooner *María*, whom he suspected of being a French spy. Although most of the evidence against Alfaro was circumstantial, his name was on a list of Napoleonic emissaries the Spanish ambassador to the United States had publicized in 1810. When his personal possessions were searched, authorities found a partially encoded letter, together with the key to the code. Based on this evidence, Bustamante decided to arrest the captain, a move approved by the audiencia. Unfortunately, the investigation ended abruptly on August 20 when Alfaro committed suicide.[40]

In short order, the Creole elite proceeded to make both cases into emblematic examples of the arbitrary justice practiced by the captain general. Although it is clear that counterinsurgency measures devised in 1812 were still in force after the restoration of Ferdinand VII and that such strategies contributed to the deaths of Argüelles and Alfaro, those tragedies do not support the myth of indiscriminate terror. A review of previous investigations into subversive activities by Bustamante suggests that Alfaro would have been released if the evidence found among his belongings had been as innocent as others later claimed it was. The month the Alfaro inquiry lasted was simply not enough time for the kind of exhaustive examination that cases of infidencia received in the Spanish judicial system. In similar fashion, if Argüelles had been mistaken for Barrundia, his arrival in Guatemala would have resolved the confusion immediately. At any rate, if Bustamante needed to question him to complete his investigation of the Belén conspiracy, he was certainly acting within the law to request his presence.

On August 22, 1815, an event took place that brought the conflict between the Creole elite and Bustamante out into the open. In one of his rare appearances before the Guatemala City ayuntamiento, the captain general declared that a royal order dated March 31 had recognized the council's Instructions of 1810 as "seditious and disruptive of order." This required the administration to issue provisions for the punishment of its authors and for the destruction of all extant copies of the document in the kingdom.[41] In accordance with the king's wishes, Bustamante proceeded to relieve most of the leading members of the Guatemalan Creole oligarchy of their public positions, leaving them without hope of obtaining another position of responsibility and stigmatized by royal disfavor. This sanction was in fact one of the strongest the crown could have imposed on these individuals, because it signified the loss of privilege, power, position, and titles, all of which served as the metrics of status in the colony. The inevitable result was an avalanche of requests for mercy sent by those affected to the audiencia.[42]

Antioligarchic measures pushed by Bustamante had support among certain segments of the population and reflected his continuing interest in promoting the well-being of the kingdom in accordance with the Bourbon absolutist model. As a counterweight to the alliance between the ayuntamiento and the audiencia, the captain general sought support from the consulado de comercio of Guatemala City. Composed of peninsulars and Creoles, the consulado represented the more conservative, royalist, and mercantilist segment of the commercial elite, men like José and Gregorio de Urruela who remained outside the Aycinena family orbit. For this community, the policies of the administration promised to increase their participation in isthmian commerce. The more traditional artisanal class, who suffered from volume imports of cheap foreign goods, as well as provincial entrepreneurs who felt constrained by the economic dominance of Guatemala City, also recognized the advantages of Bustamante's position.

Since opposition to the captain general was so public, organized, and ultimately effective, it has dominated post-independence impressions of public sentiment in the kingdom. Still, the evidence suggests that the governor and his policies divided rather than united colonial society. Most of the population remained royalist to one degree or another, with many holding no firm political position at all. Although a Bustamante party may not have formed, despite the claims of radical politicians who sought to smear their opponents during the run-up to independence, the captain general had his partisans. Segments of the Creole elite did suffer political repression during the Bustamante era, but the rest of society did not necessarily share this experience.

Even if large segments of colonial society had supported Bustamante, these groups could not defend him as his position began to be undermined in Spain. By 1816 imperial politics had moderated, and Spanish officials began to seek improved relations with local elites. With rebel forces in retreat throughout the Americas, the crown found itself well positioned to seek accommodation with those colonies that had demonstrated particular loyalty. The counterinsurgency state in Guatemala, however, threatened to derail this political shift.[43]

During this critical time, the Guatemalan oligarchy was fortunate to have two strong advocates on the Council of the Indies itself. These men, José de Aycinena and Juan Gualberto González Bravo, understood the political situation in Central America well and were able to mount a determined campaign for the removal of Bustamante. The crown finally agreed to dismiss the captain general in 1817. For good measure, it also ordered the restoration of the blacklisted councilmen and granted pardons to those imprisoned for infidencia. Under the shadow of this stinging royal rebuke, Bustamante stepped down from his post on March 28, 1818.[44]

For the Kingdom of Guatemala, the spring of 1818 completed a decade of unprecedented local, regional, and imperial unrest. Notably, the colony marked this anniversary without significant changes in its economic, political, and social infrastructure. As in April 1808, a peninsular-dominated bureaucracy administered the isthmus on behalf of an absolutist monarch. As in 1808, this government cooperated with an entrenched Creole oligarchy that monopolized most economic and social power. As in 1808, the colony still suffered from the economic crisis caused by the collapse of its traditional export markets during the Napoleonic wars. Even so, as in 1808, the kingdom appeared comfortable with its position as part of the Spanish empire.

Although the Creole-led ouster of Captain General Bustamante did not suggest any inherent weakness in the traditional colonial order, the first signs of the sociopolitical divisions that would facilitate independence in 1821 and then disrupt much of the nineteenth century had begun to emerge. During the 1810s, however, although examples of frustration with Spanish rule were not uncommon and in specific cases led to the outbreak of armed insurrection, a broad-based consensus in favor of independence did not exist. In most cases, the crown easily resolved the demands presented by those with grievances. The rebellions in San Salvador and Nicaragua were more complicated, but these movements unraveled quickly because of conflicts of interests and expectations on the part of the participants. Colonial society was notoriously fragmented. This characteristic contributed enormously to the preservation of Spanish rule, because the crown cultivated its role as mediator between social groups and as guarantor of peace. Thus, the Kingdom of Guatemala, unlike Haiti, New Spain, and Venezuela, avoided devastating civil wars during the independence period.

Surprisingly cohesive, the Creole elite of Guatemala City continued to dominate colonial society, jealously protecting their sources of power and influence. Although it encouraged reforms that reinforced its position, the oligarchy was mainly a conservative force and defender of the colonial order, so long as Spain remained sensitive to its interests. Support for the constitution caused the elite to suffer at the hands of Bustamante. Notably, however, the Creoles showed no signs of wholesale desertion of the crown during this tumultuous period. Instead, they worked within the system to remove the controversial captain general. With the arrival of a new Spanish governor, the more moderate and flexible Carlos de Urrutia, the oligarchy recovered its privileged position.

Much of the credit for preserving Central America as part of the Spanish empire during this decade belongs without doubt to José de Bustamante. Despite the enormous challenges facing a colonial governor in the period of independence, the captain general maintained Spanish dominion on the isthmus by strategically applying authoritarian tactics within a counterinsurgency-based government. At the same time, sensitive to the fragile nature of his position, he also included compromise, negotiation, and the consolidation of alliances as administrative priorities. The rapid succession of revolts between November 1811 and April 1812, however, combined with the chaos of constitutional experimentation, forced him to emphasize more repressive solutions to what he considered the primary sources of instability in the kingdom. Evidence indicates that he arrived at this conclusion carefully and that he stayed within the framework defined by his viceregal counterparts in New Spain and later by the restored absolutist government of Ferdinand VII. In the end, the crown's decision to seek allies among the Creole elite during the last stages of the wars of independence fatally undermined his position. Though his career as a colonial governor ended in controversy, Bustamante served the crown as a productive imperial official for the remaining five years of his life.

Seen from this perspective, Bustamante's tenure as captain general should be considered an example of a relatively successful short-term campaign to preserve the Spanish empire and not a depraved case of Spanish oppression during the wars for independence. After the "shock" of Bayonne, colonial officials across Spanish America struggled to maintain their positions as legitimate representatives of the sovereign. In fact, only isolated parts of the distant Viceroyalty of the Río de la Plata succeeded in breaking permanently with Spain in the first years after 1808.

In the rest of the empire, the struggle for independence languished for more than a decade. Like Bustamante, Viceroys Venegas and Calleja of New Spain, Viceroy Abascal of Peru, and Captain General Morillo of Venezuela were able to resist pressures for independence for several years. And Cuba, which resembled Central America in many ways, remained a Spanish colony until 1898. As a colonial official, José de Bustamante was obligated to preserve the Kingdom of Guatemala for the Spanish crown. For seven years he fought stubbornly and effectively to comply with that duty.

NOTES

This chapter has been adapted and summarized from my book, *José de Bustamante and Central American Independence: Colonial Administration in an Age of Imperial Crisis* (Tuscaloosa: University of Alabama Press, 2004). I thank the University of Alabama Press for granting permission to include this updated and condensed version in this essay collection.

1. For example, in Mexico, see the words of friar Servando Teresa de Mier and Carlos María Bustamante. Mier, *Historia*; Bustamante, *Cuadro*. In South America, see the independence histories of Benjamín Vicuña MacKenna, Miguel Luis Amunátegui, and Bartolomé Mitre, among others. Amunátegui, *Precursores*; Mitre, *Historia*; Vicuña, *Independencia*.
2. Suggested for the first time by Alejandro Marure in his *Bosquejo histórico de las revoluciones de Centro-América*, published in 1837, this characterization rapidly established itself in liberal nineteenth-century Central American historiography. Incorporated into the national histories of writers like Rafael Aguirre Cinta and Agustín Gómez Carillo, it entered the education systems and helped provide official explanations for regional independence. Revitalized by Ramón Salazar in early 1900s, the negative vision of Bustamante managed to influence local and foreign scholars through the end of the twentieth century.
3. Bustamante to the regency council, March 3, 1813, in *Revista* 55 (1972): 59; Informe del capitán general de Guatemala al secretario de Gracia y Justicia, January 30, 1812, in León, *Documentos*, 17.
4. Salazar, *Historia*, 155; Zelaya, *Nicaragua*, 63–64.
5. Contra las tropas del Batallón fixo del Reyno de Guatemala, Guatemala, November 17, 1812, in Archivo General de Centroamérica (hereafter AGCA), sig. A2, leg. 72, exp. 1484.
6. Hamill, "Royalist," 479, 483–84; Anna, *Fall*, 66, 77–81; Rodríguez, *Cádiz*, 104.
7. Establecimiento de superintendentes de Policía, Guatemala, January 16, 1812, in AGCA, sig. B1, leg. 7, exp. 290.
8. Ibid.; Informe del oidor fiscal sobre el establecimiento de superintendentes, Guatemala, January 21, 1812, in ibid.
9. *Fueros* are special jurisdictions, managed outside of the normal judicial system, such as military courts. [Editor's note]
10. To support their position, the oidores referred to the royal order issued in Cádiz, August 25, 1811, in AGCA, sig. B1, leg. 5, exp. 190, and to the royal decree also issued in Cádiz, February, 1811, in ibid., exp. 177.
11. Real decreto, Guatemala, October 6, 1811, in AGCA, sig. A1, leg. 6090, exp. 55243.
12. Under the new rules, Bustamante decided to apply military jurisdiction to the following crimes, independent of the civil condition of the accused:

    contributing to desertion of the king's troops; burning quarters, warehouses, and other military structures; espionage; insulting sentinels or guards; *conspiracy against a military commandant, officials, or troops, in any form attempted or executed*; initiating any form of sedition, conspiracy, or uprising, or inducing others to commit such crimes against persons in royal service and against fortified positions; giving or writing anything which could incite sedition or rebellion; communicating with the enemy in time of war, whether verbally or in writing; and trying to steal arms or ammunition" (Proclama de 6 octubre 1811 sobre infidencia y Jurisdicción Militar, Guatemala, AGCA, sig. A1, leg. 6090, exp. 55243, emphasis in original).

13. Sobre que se juzgue en Consejo de Guerra don Antonio Marure, Guatemala, June 27, 1812, in AGCA, sig. B2, leg. 32, exp. 788.
14. Guatemala, October 5, 1812, in AGCA, sig. A1, leg. 6922, exp. 56936.
15. Carta acordada del consejo de regencia, July 2, 1812, in AGCA, sig. B1, leg. 6, exp. 243.
16. AGCA sig. B1, leg. 6, exps. 246–48.
17. José de Bustamante to the regency council, March 3, 1813, in *Revista* 55 (1972): 56–63.
18. Ibid., 57.
19. See "Instrucciones para la constitución fundamental." For a broader review of the implementation of the Constitution of 1812 in Central America, see Dym, "Central America."
20. In this communique, the Creole elite in Guatemala City painted Bustamante as an unreconstructed absolutist, a slow-witted autocrat who tried to maintain his authority at the expense of constitutional reforms. From their perspective, the political problem in the Americas was easy to understand: the empire was governed by functionaries who did not want to adjust to the new political order. Actas capitulares del Ayuntamiento de Guatemala, Guatemala, 1812–1813, in AGCA, sig. A1, leg. 2190, exp. 15739, fols. 19–21.
21. El secretario de Estado to the Ayuntamiento de Guatemala, Cádiz, March 4, 1813, in AGCA, sig. B1, leg. 496, exp. 8476.
22. El secretario de Estado to Bustamante, Cádiz, June 30, 1813, in AGCA, sig. B1, leg. 7, exp. 316.
23. José de Aycinena to the Ayuntamiento of Guatemala, September 14, 1813, in AGCA, sig. B1, leg. 496, exp. 8478.
24. Actas capitulares de Guatemala, Guatemala, 1812–1813, in AGCA, sig. A1, leg. 2190, exp. 15739, fols. 97–98, 103v; March 22, 1813, in AGCA, sig. B1, leg. 8, exp. 332.
25. The representative from Comayagua, Bruno Medina, was delayed on the way. Sonsonate did not elect its representative, José Cañas, until July. José María Pérez, a priest from Quetzaltenango, refused to leave his parish until a suitable replacement could be found. Actas capitulares de Guatemala, Guatemala, 1812–1813, in AGCA, sig. A1, leg. 2190, exp. 15739, fols. 144v, 155, 177v; El diputado de Quetzaltenango to the Diputación Provincial de Guatemala, Huehuetenango, June 11, 1813, in AGCA, sig. B1, leg. 9, exp. 357; La Diputación Provincial de Nicaragua y Costa Rica al Ayuntamiento de Guatemala, León, November 29, 1813, in AGCA, sig. B1, leg. 9, exp. 365.
26. Baumgartner, *José de Valle*, 67n43; Rodríguez, *Cádiz*, 121.
27. See the documents included in Mariano Bujano to Bustamante, Sonsonate, December 8, 1813, in AGCA, sig. A1, leg. 6923, exp. 56966; Huehuetenango, November 29, 1813, in AGCA, sig. A1, leg. 6923, exps. 56963, 56964, 56967; Actas capitulares de Guatemala, Guatemala, 1812–1813, in AGCA, sig. A1, leg. 2190, exp. 15739, fols. 62, 80.
28. Alcalde mayor de Verapaz to Bustamante, Salamá, October 14, 1813, in AGCA, sig. A1, leg. 6923, exp. 56968; José del Barrio to Bustamante, Chimaltenango, October 20, 1813, in AGCA, sig. A1, leg. 222, exp. 5230.

29. Actas capitulares de Guatemala, Guatemala, 1812–1813, in AGCA, sig. A1, leg. 2190, exp. 15739, fol. 197.
30. Ibid., fols. 209, 258v. See the complaints in the Colección de escritos particulares presentados por los reos presos en esta capital, remitidos por la Comisión de Granada, Guatemala, 1813, in AGCA, sig. B2, leg. 25, exp. 707.
31. Instrucción para el gobierno económico-político de las provincias, June 23, 1813, Actas capitulares de Guatemala, 1812–13, in AGCA, sig. A1, leg. 2190, exp. 15739, fol. 263.
32. Actas capitulares de Guatemala, Guatemala, 1812–13, in AGCA, sig. A1, leg. 2190, exp. 15739, fols. 273–77.
33. Documentos vinculados a la conspiración de Belén, 1814–1818, in AGCA, sig. B1, leg. 29, exp. 742–59; "Relación de los autos pasados por la Capitanía General"; Rodríguez, *Conspiración*.
34. Causa contra Miguel Delgado, in AGCA, sig. B1, leg. 30, exp. 760.
35. José de Bustamante to the consejo de regencia, May 18, 1814, in León, *Colección*, 10.482–84.
36. Ibid., 10.486.
37. Actas capitulares de Guatemala, Guatemala, 1814, in AGCA, sig. A1, leg. 2191, exp. 15741, fols. 155, 168, 182, 185v, 187v, 188v.
38. Acuerdo ordinario, April 27, 1815, Libro de acuerdos, 1811–1818, in AGCA, sig. A1, leg. 4663, exp. 39952, fol. 76.
39. Residencia de José de Bustamante, cargo 17, Guatemala, 1820, in AGCA, sig. A1, leg. 1739, exp. 11581; Salazar, *Historia*, 177–78; Rodríguez, *Cádiz*, 127–28.
40. Libro de acuerdos, Guatemala, 1811–1818, in AGCA, sig. A1, leg. 4663, exp. 39952, fol. 83; Residencia de José de Bustamante, cargo 16, Guatemala, 1820, in AGCA, sig. A1, leg. 1739, exp. 11581; Autos para determinar la causa del fallecimiento de Alfaro, Guatemala, 1816, in AGCA, sig. A1, leg. 144, exp. 2786.
41. Bustamante did not leave the hall without criticizing the council for the portraits of José de Aycinena, Manuel Pavón, and Antonio de Larrazábal, which were hanging there in direct violation of the royal will that required the elimination of all signs of the constitutional period. Actas capitulares de Guatemala, Guatemala, 1815, in AGCA, sig. A1, leg. 2191, exp. 15741, fol. 38; Real orden, Madrid, March 31, 1815, in AGCA, sig. B1, leg. 12, exp. 427.
42. Documentos presentados por varios individuos comprendidos en la inhabilitación que por pena ha impuesto su majestad en real orden de 31 de marzo de 1815 a los que aprobaron las instrucciones dadas al ex diputado don Antonio Larrazábal in AGCA, Audiencia indiferente, 1815; Documentos presentados por don Lorenzo Moreno, AGCA, sig. B1, leg. 12, exp. 420; Documentos presentados por José María Peinado, in AGCA, sig. B1, leg. 12, exp. 415; Documentos presentados por don Luis Francisco Barrutia, in AGCA, sig. B1, leg. 12, exp. 419; Documentos presentados por José María Peinado, in AGCA, sig. B1, leg. 12, exp. 420; Documentos presentados por la señora marquesa de Aycinena, don José Antonio Batres, don Lorenzo Moreno, don Luis Barrutia, don Miguel Asturias, y don Francisco Arrevillaga, in AGCA, sig. B1, leg. 12, exp. 423.
43. Report from the fiscal of Perú to the Consejo de Indias, August 19, 1816, in León, *Documentos*, 97–121.

44. Real cédula, Madrid, January 21, 1817, in AGCA, sig. A1, leg. 29, exp. 859; Real orden, Madrid, March 18, 1817, Actas capitulares de Guatemala, 1817, in AGCA, sig. A1, leg. 2192, exp. 15743, fol. 90; Real orden, Madrid, April 1, 1817, in AGCA, sig. A1, leg. 6927, exp. 57053; "Real cédula de 13 de junio de 1817."

GLOSSARY

The following definitions refer to usage in Spanish America, and more particularly the Kingdom of Guatemala, in the early nineteenth century, unless otherwise noted.

adelantado. Spanish captain charged with military conquest who unified political, military, and judicial powers under his jurisdiction. In the Central American isthmus, they were replaced by governors during the sixteenth century. In the early nineteenth century, the title *adelantado de Costa Rica* continued to be current, though it implied no political, military, or judicial power.

afrancesado. Term used to describe individuals accused of having sympathies for the French after the Napoleonic invasion of Spain in 1808.

alcabala. Internal customs duty. Often somewhat inappropriately referred to as a sales tax. Charges were applied to goods transported from one city to another for commercial purposes.

alcalde. In towns and cities, largely equivalent to a mayor or local magistrate. In Indian towns, their responsibilities included the resolution of minor judicial problems, tribute collection, and, when these were applied, the administration of forced labor drafts. Other bodies, such as *cofradías* (religious brotherhoods) were led by officials with the same title. See *alcalde mayor*.

alcalde mayor. Principal magistrate, with administrative responsibilities, in an alcaldía mayor.

alcaldía of Spaniards and ladinos. Created at the turn of the nineteenth century in the corregimiento de Quetzaltenango and the alcaldía mayor de Totonicapán (and perhaps elsewhere) to provide partial self-government for Spaniards and ladinos who lived in Indian towns with relatively large non-Indian populations or in the non-Indian dominated valles. In the Indian towns, it was effectively a parallel municipal government.

alcaldía mayor. In Spanish America, royal territorial division within the viceroyalties and captaincies general. In those regions in which intendancies were established after 1780, the alcaldías mayores were eliminated.

alférez. Royal standard-bearer or ensign who formed part of colonial municipal governments as the symbolic representative of the monarch.

asesor letrado. See *teniente letrado*.

audiencia (real). Large judicial territorial divisions and the high court that held jurisdiction over them.

ayuntamiento. Municipal council which, prior to the Cádiz Constitution, existed only in Spanish cities and villas.

ayuntamiento constitucional. Indirectly elected city and town councils implemented by the Cádiz Constitution.

cabildo. Town or city council, or the building in which it operated. At times, the governing body of other corporate entities.

cabildo eclesiástico. Corporate body, including different church authorities, that sustains the work of the bishop.

cacique. Indian noble.

calpul. 1. Divisions of people within an Indian town, synonym of *parcialidad.* 2. Assemblies in which Indians met to discuss issues among themselves.

capitán general. Captain general. Chief military officer in a capitanía general.

capitanía general. Captaincy general. Large territorial division of the Spanish empire in regions considered to be of military importance and administered by a military officer, the captain general.

casta. Person considered to be, at least in part, of African origin.

Chuj. Indigenous people living in the Cuchumatán Mountains in what is now northwestern Guatemala; also, the language they speak.

ciudad. City chartered by the Spanish crown with a government controlled by Spaniards through their ayuntamiento.

cofradía. Religious sodality.

comisario ordenador de los reales ejércitos. Quartermaster of the royal armies. Chief military commander of a region, in charge of organizing militias.

consejo de regencia. Regency council that rules a monarchy in the name of the king or queen when he or she is impeded from governing. Five-member council that governed the Spanish monarchy between January and September 1810, after the dissolution of the Suprema Central Junta and before the establishment of the Courts of Cádiz.

consulado de comercio. Commercial consulate. Merchant organization in principal cities, authorized by the crown.

cordilleras de oficio. Circulars sent out to different bureaucrats or municipal authorities in distant towns or cities.

corregidor. Spanish official responsible for political, administrative, and judicial control of a corregimiento.

corregimiento. Territorial division within the viceroyalties and captaincies general in Spanish America. By the eighteenth century they were effectively indistinguishable from alcaldías mayors, and in the latter part of that century they were eliminated in those territories where intendancies were established.

criollo. Creole. American-born Spaniard.

cuadrante. Table with information about church accounts, such as sources of income in a parish.

diputaciones provinciales. Provincial councils. Indirectly elected regional government organs created by the Courts of Cádiz.

efemérides. Important historical events, at times considered worthy of annual celebrations.

estancos. State monopolies (e.g., tobacco, liquor), at times managed directly by Spanish authorities and at times farmed out to private individuals.

fianza. Bond.

fiebres. Political grouping active in Central America around the time of independence that was identified with more radically liberal policies.

fiscal. Royal prosecutor.

fueros. Specific legal jurisdictions, applicable to certain groups, such as churchmen or members of the military.

gobernación. Territorial division within viceroyalties and captaincies general.

gobernador intendente. See *intendente*.

infidencia. Treason and other acts of disloyalty.

intendencia. Intendancy. Territorial division of the viceroyalties and captaincies general, initially established in most parts of Spanish America during the 1780s.

intendente. Spanish official in charge of an intendencia.

jefe político. Principal political and administrative authority of the provinces identified under the Cádiz Constitution, replacing the intendentes, corregidores, and alcaldes mayores.

jefe político superior. Principal political and administrative authorities of the territorial divisions established under the Cádiz Constitution who had previously been, in America, viceroys or governors.

juez preventivo. Assistant to the alcalde mayor.

juicio de residencia. Legal review; formal required legal examinations of outgoing Spanish officials in which actions they took while in office were scrutinized to consider their legality.

junta. Civil deliberative or administrative council.

jurar. To take an oath; swear to.

ladino. Non-Indian who was not a Spaniard. At times, any non-Indian.

macegual. Indian commoner.

mandamiento. Forced labor draft.

municipio. Municipality.

oidor. Judge, member of the audiencia.

pactismo. Pactism. The idea that an unwritten "pact" between a monarch and the people legitimizes government by the former.

parcialidad. Division of people within an Indian town, often with prehispanic origins; synonym of *calpul*.

pardo. Person of partial African ancestry.

patronato real. Agreement between the Vatican and the Spanish monarchy that gave the latter, among other privileges, the prerogative of naming bishops and other church officials in its dominions.

potestad regia. The expression of the will of the king.

principal. High-ranking Indian, at times of noble status, whose privileges distinguished his condition from that of the *maceguales* (commoners). This condition may have been a birthright or acquired through economic gain.

protomedicato. Royal board made up of doctors and examiners to investigate the qualifications of those wishing to become doctors and to grant medical licenses.

pueblo de indios. Indian town, governed by the members of the Indian cabildo.

real acuerdo. Highest consultative body in Spanish American viceroyalties and captaincies general, made up of the viceroy or captain general and members of the audiencia.

real patronato. See *patronato real*.

Real Sociedad Económica de los Amantes del País de Guatemala. Royal Economic Society of the Lovers of the Country of Guatemala. One of many similar societies formed toward the end of the eighteenth century in Spanish America dedicated to promoting trade, production, and enlightened thinking. Also known as the *Real Sociedad de los Amigos del País*, a much more common name for these societies.

regidor. Member of town or city council, of lesser importance than the alcalde.

repartimiento de bienes. Generally understood as the forced sale of goods to Indians and others at above-market prices; forced labor in spinning cotton or weaving cloth; (forced?) provision of credit.

repartimiento de labor. Forced labor draft.

ropa de la tierra. Textiles produced in America.

sala de crimen. Criminal court.

síndico. Syndic. A member of the municipal council, with particular responsibilities related to the judicial system.

situados. Funds sent from one Spanish colonial treasury to another or to a province outside its own territory, usually for military purposes; used, for example, to finance much of the Spanish Caribbean defense from New Spain.

subdelegaciones. Subdelegations. Territorial divisions within intendancies, administered by subdelegates.

subdelegados. Subdelegates. Spanish officials in charge of subdelegaciones who were responsible to the intendentes.

superintendencia hacendaria. Unified treasury authority.

teniente letrado. Chief magistrate of an intendancy and chief assistant to the intendente in all matters.

tercio de San Juan. Mid-year tribute payment. Along with the *tercio de navidad*, due at Christmas, one of the two annual tribute payments.

tierra realenga. Crown land. Generally referred to unclaimed land that technically belonged to the crown.

tiña. Skin disease, considered at times to be a form of leprosy.

tribunal de fidelidad. Loyalty tribunal. Established to try cases of treason or disloyalty.

túmulo funerario. Catafalque, used in royal funerals to represent the body of the monarch.

valle. Settlement of ladinos or of Spaniards and ladinos, usually located in regions demographically dominated by Indians.

villa. Chartered Spanish settlement less important than a ciudad, governed by an ayuntamiento made up of Spaniards.

Zoques. Indigenous people who live in what is now western Chiapas, and the name of a province in that region.

BIBLIOGRAPHY

ARCHIVES

Archivo General de Centroamérica, Guatemala City, Guatemala
Archivo General de Indias, Seville, Spain
Archivo Histórico del Arzobispado de Guatemala, Guatemala City, Guatemala
Archivo Histórico Diocesano de San Cristóbal de las Casas, San Cristóbal de las Casas, Chiapas, Mexico
Archivo Nacional de Costa Rica, San José, Costa Rica
Public Record Office. The National Archives, London, United Kingdom

BOOKS, ARTICLES, AND DISSERTATIONS

Acuña Ortega, Víctor Hugo. "Historia del vocabulario político en Costa Rica. Estado, república, nación y democracia (1821–1849)." In *Identidades nacionales y Estado moderno en Centroamérica*, edited by Arturo Taracena and Jean Piel, 63–74. Costa Rica: Centro de Estudios Mexicanos y Centroamericanos/FLACSO, 1995.

———. "Historia económica del tabaco: época colonial." Doctoral dissertation, Universidad de Costa Rica, San José, 1974.

———. "La invención de la diferencia costarricense 1810–1870." *Revista de Historia*, no. 45 (January–June 2002): 191–228.

———. "El liberalismo en Centroamérica en tiempos de la independencia (1810–1850)." In *La aurora de la libertad. Primeros liberalismos en el mundo iberoamericano*, edited by Javier Fernández Sebastián, 117–45. Madrid: Marcial Pons Historia, 2012.

Adelman, Jeremy. "Independence in Latin America." In *The Oxford Handbook of Latin American History*, edited by José C. Moya, 153–80. Oxford: Oxford University Press, 2011.

Álvarez Cuartero, Izaskún, and Julio Sánchez Gómez. *Visiones y revisiones de la independencia americana. Subalternidad e independencias*, Salamanca, Ediciones Universidad de Salamanca, 2012.

Amunátegui, Miguel Luis. *Los precursores de la independencia de Chile. Memoria histórica presentada a la Universidad de Chile en cumplimiento del artículo 28 de la ley de 19 de noviembre de 1842*. 3 vols. Santiago de Chile, Imprenta Barcelona, 1909–1910.

Andrien, Kenneth J. "Economic Crisis, Taxes and the Quito Insurrection of 1765." *Past and Present* 129 (1990): 104–31.

Anna, Timothy E. *The Fall of the Royal Government in Mexico City*. Lincoln, University of Nebraska Press, 1978.

Annino, Antonio. "Prácticas criollas y liberalismo en la crisis del espacio urbano colonial." *Secuencia*, no. 24 (1992): 121–58.

——. "Voto, tierra, soberanía. Cádiz y los orígenes del municipalismo mexicano." In *Las revoluciones hispánicas. Independencias americanas y liberalismo español*, coord. by François-Xavier Guerra, 269–92. Madrid, Editorial Complutense, 1995.

"Apuntes instructivos que el señor don Antonio Larrazábal, diputado a las Cortes extraordinarias de la nación española por el cabildo de la ciudad de Guatemala, dieron sus regidores (1811)." In *La génesis del constitucionalismo guatemalteco*, edited by Jorge Mario García Laguardia, 191–271. Guatemala City, Editorial Universitaria, 1971.

Aquino, Tomás de. *Comentario a la* Ética a Nicómaco *de Aristóteles*. Navarra, Universidad de Navarra, 2010.

Aramoni Calderón, Dolores. "Juan de Oliver, primer alcalde mayor de Tuxtla." *Revista de la Universidad Autónoma de Chiapas*, no. 1 (April 1985): 46–62.

——. *Los refugios de lo sagrado, religiosidad, conflicto y resistencia entre los zoques de Chiapas*. Mexico City, CNCA, 1992.

Archer, Christian I. "En busca de una victoria definitiva: el ejército realista en Nueva España, 1810–1821." In *Las guerras de independencia en la América española*, edited by Marta Terán and José Antonio Serrano, 423–38. Zamora, Michoacán, El Colegio de Michoacán/Instituto Nacional de Antropología e Historia/Universidad Michoacana de San Nicolás de Hidalgo, 2010.

Arellano, Jorge Eduardo. "Granada. La llave de Centroamérica y los piratas." *Revista Conservadora del Pensamiento Centroamericano*, no. 77 (February 1967): 50–56.

Argueta, Mario. "Centroamérica: dos independencias, dos actas." *Diario El heraldo* (Tegucigalpa), Opinión, April 7, 2014. www.elheraldo.hn/opinion/615902-210/centroamérica-dos-independencias-dos-actas.

Aristóteles. *Ética nicomáquea*. Barcelona, Editorial Planeta, 1995.

Armitage, David. "Declaraciones de independencia, 1776–2011. Del derecho natural al derecho internacional." In *Las declaraciones de Independencia. Textos fundamentales de las independencias de América*, edited by Alfredo Ávila, Jordana Dym, Aurora Gómez, and Érika Pani, 19–40. Mexico City, El Colegio de México/UNAM, 2013.

Arrioja Díaz Viruell, Luis Alberto. "Guatemala y Nueva España: historia de una plaga compartida, 1798–1807." *Revista de Historia Moderna y Contemporánea*, no. 33 (2015): 309–23.

Artola, Miguel. *Los orígenes de la España contemporánea*. 2 vols. Madrid, Instituto de Estudios Políticos, 1959.

Aubry, Andrés. "Mayorazgo y despojo de los Moctezuma o el mareo del dinero." *Boletín del Archivo Histórico Diocesano* 3 (December 1986): 1–58.

Avendaño Rojas, Xiomara. *Centroamérica entre lo antiguo y lo moderno. Institucionalidad, ciudadanía y representación política, 1810–1838*. Castello de la Plana, Universitat Jaume I, 2009.

——. "La independencia en Guatemala y El Salvador. Una nueva visión sobre los actores." In *Debates sobre las independencias iberoamericanas*, edited by Manuel Chust and José Antonio Serrano, 237–54. Madrid/Frankfurt, Iberoamericana/Vervuert, 2007.

Avendaño Rojas, Xiomara, and Norma Hernández Sánchez. *¿Independencia o autogobierno? El Salvador y Nicaragua, 1786–1811*. Managua, Grupo Editorial Lea, 2014.

Ávila, Alfredo. *En nombre de la nación. La formación del gobierno representativo en México (1808–1824)*. Mexico City, Taurus/Centro de Investigación y Docencia Económicas (CIDE), 2002.

Ávila, Alfredo, and Pedro Pérez Herrero, eds. *Las experiencias de 1808 en Iberoamérica*. Madrid, Universidad de Alcalá, 2008.
Ayala Benítez, Luis Ernesto. *La iglesia y la independencia política de Centroamérica: el caso del estado de El Salvador, 1808–1832*. San Salvador, Editorial Universitaria Don Bosco, 2011.
Ayón, Tomás. *Historia de Nicaragua desde los tiempos más remotos hasta el año de 1852*. 3 vols. Madrid, Escuela Profesional de Artes Gráficas, 1956.
Barboza, Francisco. *Historia militar de Nicaragua (antes del siglo XV al XXI)*. Managua, Hispamer, 2010.
Barcellos Guazzelli, Cesar Augusto. "Textos e lenços: representações de federalismo na república rio-grandense (1836–1845)." *Almanack Braziliense*, no. 1 (May 2005): 54–66.
Barudio, Günter. *La época del absolutismo y la Ilustración, 1648–1779*. Mexico City, Siglo XXI Editores, 1983.
Baumgartner, Louis E. *José del Valle of Central America*. Durham, N.C., Duke University Press, 1963.
Belaubre, Christophe. "Al cruce de la historia social y política: un acercamiento crítico a la 'conjuración de Belén,' Guatemala (1813)." In *Revoluciones, guerras y revoluciones políticas en la América Hispano-portuguesa, 1808–1824*, edited by Sajid Herrera, 9–29. San Salvador, Universidad Centroamericana, 2013.
———. "Cuando los curas estaban en el corazón de las estrategias familiares: el caso de los González Batres en la capitanía general de Guatemala." *Anuario de Estudios Bolivarianos*, nos. 7–8 (1999): 119–50.
———. *Église et Lumières au Guatemala: la dimension atlantique*. Paris, L'Harmattan, 2015.
———. *Élus de Dieu et élus du monde dans le royaume du Guatemala (1753–1808). Église, familles de pouvoir et réformateurs bourbons*. Paris, L'Harmattan, 2012.
———. "Entre cultura tradicional y moderna: las prácticas de lectura en Centroamérica (1750–1808)." In *Historia de las literaturas centroamericanas*, edited by Patricia Fumero, Verónica Ríos, and Werner Mackenbach. Guatemala City, F&G Editores, in press.
———. "Redes sociales y conflictos en la provincia franciscana de San Jorge de Nicaragua a inicios del siglo xix." *Cuadernos de Literatura* 14, no. 28 (July–December 2010): 30–259.
———. "El traslado de la capital del reino de Guatemala (1773–1779): conflicto de poder y juegos sociales." *Revista de Historia*, nos. 57–58 (2008): 23–61.
———. "Violencia social y justicia inquisitorial: el juicio de don Rafael Crisanto Gil Rodríguez, oriundo de San Salvador (1775–1805)." In *Violencia y poder en El Salvador*, edited by Sajid Alfredo Herrera Mena y Ana Margarita Gómez, 79–116. San Salvador, UCA Editores, 2007.
Belzunegui Ormazábal, Bernardo. *Pensamiento económico y reforma agraria en el reino de Guatemala*. Guatemala City, Afanes, 1992.
Bertrand, Michel. "De la familia a la red de sociabilidad." *Revista Mexicana de Sociología* 61, no. 2 (April–June 1999): 107–35.
Bonilla Bonilla, Adolfo. *Ideas económicas en la Centroamérica ilustrada, 1793–1838*. San Salvador, FLACSO-El Salvador, 1999.
Bourdieu, Pierre. "Espacio social y espacio simbólico." In Pierre Bourdieu, *Razones prácticas. Sobre la teoria de la acción*, trans. from French by Thomas Kauf, 11–26. Barcelona, Anagrama, 1997.

———. "L'illusion biographique." *Actes de la Recherche en Sciences Sociales*, nos. 62–63 (June 1986): 69–72.

Brading, David A. "La España de los Borbones y su imperio americano." In *Historia de América Latina*, 16 vols., edited by Leslie Bethell, 2:85–126. Barcelona, Editorial Crítica, 1990.

———. *Mineros y comerciantes en el México borbónico (1763–1810)*. Mexico City, Fondo de Cultura Económica, 1984.

Breña, Roberto, ed. "The Emancipation Process in New Spain." In *The Rise of Constitutional Government in the Iberian Atlantic World: The Impact of the Cádiz Constitution of 1812*, edited by Scott Eastman and Natalia Sobrevilla Perea, 42–62. Tuscaloosa, University of Alabama Press, 2015.

———. *En el umbral de las revoluciones hispánicas: el bienio 1808–1810*. Mexico City, Centro de Estudios Políticos y Constitucionales-COLMEX, 2010.

———. "Introducción." In *Cádiz a debate: actualidad, contexto y legado*, edited by Roberto Breña, 11–23. Mexico City, El Colegio de México, 2014.

———. *El primer liberalismo español y los procesos de liberación de América, 1808–1824. Una revisión historiográfica del liberalismo hispánico*. Mexico City, Centro de Estudios Internacionales-COLMEX, 2006.

Brenes Tencio, Guillermo. "La fidelidad, el amor y el gozo. La jura del rey Fernando VII (Cartago, 1809)." *Revista de Ciencias Sociales*, no. 119 (2008): 55–81.

———. "¡Viva nuestro rey Fernando! Teatro, poder y fiesta en la ciudad colonial de Cartago, Provincia de Costa Rica (1809): una contribución documental." *Historia Caribe*, no. 16 (2010): 75–104.

Bricker, Victoria Reifler. *El Cristo indígena, el rey nativo: el sustrato histórico de la mitología del ritual de los mayas*. Mexico City, FCE, 1989.

Bridikhina, Eugenia. *Theatrum mundi. Entramados del poder en Charcas colonial*. La Paz, Plural Editores/Instituto Francés de Estudios Andinos, 2007.

Bustamante, Carlos María de. *Cuadro histórico de la revolución mexicana*. 8 vols. Mexico City, Instituto Cultural Helénico, 1985.

Cabat, Geoffrey A. "The Consolidation of 1804 in Guatemala." *Americas* 29, no. 1 (1971): 20–38.

Cabezas Carcache, Horacio. "El carácter de la independencia centroamericana." *Lateinamerika*, no. 21 (1986): 5–31.

———. *Independencia centroamericana. Gestión y ocaso del "Plan Pacífico."* Guatemala City, Editorial Universitaria, Universidad San Carlos de Guatemala, 2010.

Cadavid Guerrero, Iván Andrés. "La concordia o amistad civil: un presupuesto de la virtud política en Aristóteles." *Revista Ratio Juris* 6, no. 12 (January–June 2011): 63–72.

Calderón, Manuel. "Las fuerzas sociales en la formación del poder político en Costa Rica 1821–849." Master's thesis, San José, Universidad de Costa Rica, 1993.

Calvo, Joaquín Bernardo. *Apuntamientos geográficos, estadísticos e históricos*. San José, Costa Rica, Imprenta Nacional, 1887.

Calvo, Thomas. "La jura de Fernando VI en Guadalajara (1747): de la religión real a la festividad." *Takwa. Revista de Historia*, no. 8 (Fall 2005): 69–92.

Cañeque, Alejandro. "Imaging the Spanish Empire: The Visual Construction of Imperial

Authority in Habsburg New Spain." *Colonial Latin American Review* 19, no. 1 (2010): 29–68.

Cañizares Esguerra, Jorge. *Cómo escribir la historia del Nuevo Mundo. Historiografías, epistemologías e identidades en el mundo del Atlántico del siglo XVIII*. Mexico City, FCE, 2007.

Cárdenas, Salvador. "Razón de Estado y emblemática política en los impresos novohispanos de los siglos XVII y XVIII." *Relaciones. Estudios de Historia y Sociedad* 18, no. 71 (Summer 1997): 63–99.

Carmack, Robert M. *The Quiché Mayas of Utatlan: The Evolution of a Highland Guatemalan Kingdom*. Norman, University of Oklahoma Press, 1981.

———. *Rebels of Highland Guatemala: The Quiche Mayas of Momostenango*. Norman, University of Oklahoma Press, 1995.

Carrillo, Ana Lorena. *Árbol de historias. Configuraciones del pasado en Severo Martínez Peláez y Luis Cardoza y Aragón*. Guatemala City, Ediciones del Pensativo/Instituto de Ciencias Sociales y Humanidades "Alfonso Vélez Pliego" Benemérita Universidad Autónoma de Puebla, 2009.

"Carta de José Santos Lombardo," *Actas del Ayuntamiento de Cartago 1820–1821*, 250–51. San José, Comisión del Sesquicentenario de Centroamérica, 1972.

Carvalho, Alma Margarita. *La Ilustración del despotismo en Chiapas, 1774–1821*. Mexico City, CNCA, 1994.

Cerda, Manuel Antonio de la. "Sucinto relato de lo ocurrido en Granada de Nicaragua, desde 29 de septiembre de 1811 hasta 18 de agosto de 1813." *Próceres. Documentos y Datos Históricos* 1, no. 7 (1911): 235–71.

Cerdas, Matilde, and Yamileth González. "La actitud de Heredia en el momento de la independencia." *Revista de la Universidad de Costa Rica*, no. 31 (September 1971): 141–49.

Cerdas, Rodolfo. *Formación del Estado en Costa Rica*. San José, Costa Rica, Editorial de la Universidad de Costa Rica, 1978.

Chaclán, José. *Los caciques de Chwi Miq'ina'(Totonicapán). Origen, presente y futuro*. Guatemala City, Fondo Editorial PAJ-FGS, 2008.

Chacón Hidalgo, Manuel. "El cacao como moneda en Costa Rica en el siglo XVIII." *Revista Diálogos*, special number (2008): 734–37.

Chafuen, Alejandro A. "Justicia distributiva en la escolástica tardía." *Estudios Políticos*, no. 18 (1985): 5–20.

Chiaramonte, José Carlos. "En torno a los orígenes de la nación argentina." In *Para una historia de América II. Los nudos (1)*, coord. by Marcello Carmagnani, Alicia Hernández Chávez, and Ruggiero Romano, 286–317. Mexico City, COLMEX, 1999.

———. *Fundamentos intelectuales y políticos de las independencias. Notas para una historia intelectual de Iberoamérica*. Buenos Aires, Teseo, 2010.

———. *Nación y Estado en Iberoamérica (el lenguaje político en tiempos de la independencia)*. Buenos Aires, Editorial Sudamericana, 2003.

———. "Principle of Consent in Latin and Anglo-American Independence." *Journal of Latin American Studies* 36, no. 3 (August 2004): 563–86.

Chinchilla, Oswaldo. "Nacionalismo y arqueología en la Guatemala de la independencia." In *VII Simposio de investigaciones arqueológicas en Guatemala*, edited by Juan Pedro Laporte and Héctor Escobedo, 3–11. Guatemala City, Instituto de Arqueología e Historia, 1994.

Chust Calero, Manuel, and José Antonio Serrano. "Un debate actual, una revisión necesaria." In *Debates sobre las independencias iberoamericanas*, edited by Manuel Chust and José Antonio Serrano, 9–25. Madrid, Iberoamericana/Vervuert, 2007.

"Ciudad Real 1748; Plano del obispado de Chiapa, de los pueblos y parajes y sitios que en él hay, formado por el ilmo. y rmo sor. maestro don fr. Joseph Cubero Ramires de Arrellano del Consejo de su majestad y obispo de este obispado." *Boletín del Archivo General del Gobierno*, no. 3 (April 1936): 209–12.

Claps Arenas, María Eugenia, and Sergio Nicolás Gutiérrez Cruz, eds. *Formación y gestión del Estado en Chiapas. Algunas aproximaciones históricas*. Tuxtla Gutiérrez, Universidad de Ciencias y Artes de Chiapas, 2013.

Conde Calderón, Jorge, and Edwin Monsalvo Mendoza. "La construcción del orden político y las celebraciones republicanas en la Nueva Granada (Colombia, 1810–1832)." *Historia y Espacio*, no. 35 (July–August 2010): 71–96.

Connaughton, Brian F. "Introducción." In *Poder y legitimidad en México en el siglo XIX. Instituciones y cultura política*, coord. by Brian F. Connaughton, 7–27. Universidad Autónoma Metropolitana—Iztapalapa/Miguel Ángel Porrúa, 2003.

"Constitución de Cádiz (19 de Marzo de 1812)." In *Las constituciones políticas y sus reformas en la historia de Nicaragua*, 2 vols., edited by Antonio Esgueva Gómez, 47–98. Managua, Editorial Instituto de Historia de Nicaragua y Centroamérica, Universidad Centroamericana, 2000.

Contreras R., Daniel J. *Una rebelión indígena en el partido de Totonicapán. El indio y la independencia*. Guatemala City, Imprenta Universitaria, 1951.

Corpeño, José Dolores. *Patria*. San Salvador, Imprenta Nacional, 1914.

Corpeño, José Dolores, and Salvador Turcios. *Libro Araujo*. Imprenta Nacional/Biblioteca del Ateneo de El Salvador, 1914.

Crespo, Victoria. "Sobre Guillermo Palacios (coord.), Ensayos sobre la nueva historia política de América Latina, siglo XIX." *Historia Mexicana* 58, no. 1 (July–September 2008): 523–34.

Croix, Alain, André Lespagnol, and Georges Prévost, eds. *Église, Éducation, Lumières... histoires culturelles de la France (1500–1830)*. Rennes, Presses Universitaires de Rennes, 1999.

Cuadriello, Jaime. "El trono vacío o la monarquía lactante." In *Visiones de la monarquía hispánica*, edited by Víctor Mínguez, 191–226. Castelló de la Plana, Publicacions de la Universitat Jaume I, 2007.

Dachner Trujillo, Yolanda. "De la individualidad política a la predestinación singular: Costa Rica en la obra de Osejo, Molina y Peralta." *Anuario de Estudios Centroamericanos* 22, no. 2 (1996): 105–128.

Daumard, Adeline. "Les Généalogies sociales: un des fondements de l'histoire sociale comparative et quantitative." *Annales de Démographie Historique*, 1984, 9–23.

Demélas, Marie-Danielle. "Pactismo y constitucionalismo en los Andes." In *Inventando la nación. Iberoamérica, siglo XIX*, edited by Antonio Annino and François-Xavier Guerra, 593–612. Mexico City, FCE, 2003.

Díaz Arias, David. "Comunidad política, identidades, ritos y rituales en la celebración del día de independencia en Costa Rica, 1824–1921." Final course report, Culturas e Identidades en América Latina y el Caribe, Programa Regional de Becas CLASCO, 2001.

———. *Construcción de un Estado moderno: política, Estado e identidad nacional en Costa Rica 1821–1914*. San José, Editorial de la Universidad de Costa Rica, 2005 (Serie de Cuadernos de Historia de las Instituciones).

———. *La fiesta de la Independencia en Costa Rica, 1821–1921*. San José, Editorial UCR, 2007.

———. "Jura y conjura en el naciente Estado costarricense: las representaciones del poder en la jura de la Constitución de 1844 y la rebelión de las autoridades militares en San José y Alajuela." *Boletín AFEHC*, no. 44 (March 4, 2010).

Diccionario de la lengua castellana, en que se explica el verdadero sentido de las voces, su naturaleza calidad, con las phrases o modos de hablar, los proverbios o refranes, y otras cosas convenientes al uso de la lengua. Dedicado al rey nuestro señor don Phelipe V (que Dios guarde), Vol. 3. Madrid, Editorial Gredos, 1976 (facsimilar edition of the 1732 original).

Diccionario de la lengua Castellana por la Real Academia Española, 5th ed. Madrid, Imprenta Real, 1817.

Diego-Fernández Sotelo, Rafael, María Pilar Gutiérrez Lorenzo, and Luis Alberto Arrioja Díaz Viruell, coords. *De reinos y subdelegaciones. Nuevo escenarios para un nuevo orden en la América borbónica*. Zamora, Michoacán, El Colegio de Michoacán/Universidad de Guadalajara/El Colegio Mexiquense, 2014.

Di Meglio, Gabriel. "La participación popular en la revoluciones hispanoamericanas, 1808–1816. Un ensayo sobre sus rasgos y causas." In *Rebeldes con causa. Conflicto y movilización popular en la Argentina del siglo XIX*, comp. by Daniel Santilli, Jorge Daniel Gelman, and Raúl Osvaldo Fradkin, 19–54. Buenos Aires, Prometeo Libros, 2013.

———. *¡Viva el bajo pueblo! La plebe urbana de Buenos Aires y la política entre la Revolución de Mayo y el rosismo*, 4th ed. Buenos Aires, Prometeo Libros, 2016.

Discurso preliminar leído en las Cortes al presentar la Comisión de Constitución el proyecto de ella. Cádiz, Imprenta Tormentaria, 1812.

Domínguez, Juan. "La América española y Napoleón en el estatuto de Bayona." *Revista Internacional de Estudios Vascos*, no. 4 (2009): 315–46.

Domínguez Sosa, Julio Alberto. *Ensayo histórico sobre las tribus nonualcas y su caudillo Anastasio Aquino*. San Salvador, Ministerio de Educación Nacional, 1962.

Dym, Jordana. "Actas de Independencia: de la Capitanía General de Guatemala a la República Federal de Centroamérica." In *Independencia, Estados y política (s) en la Centroamérica del siglo XIX*, edited by David Díaz Arias and Ronny Viales Hurtado, 3–24. San José, Centro de Investigaciones Históricas de América Central, 2012.

———. "Central America and Cádiz: A Complex Relationship." In *The Rise of Constitutional Government in the Iberian Atlantic World: The Impact of the Cádiz Constitution of 1812*, edited by Scott Eastman and Natalia Sobrevilla Perea, 63–90. Tuscaloosa, University of Alabama Press, 2015.

———. *From Sovereign Villages to Nation States: City, States, and Federation in Central America, 1759–1839*. Albuquerque, University of New Mexico Press, 2006.

———. "Soberanía transitiva y adhesión condicional: lealtad e insurrección en el reino de Guatemala, 1808–1811." In *1808: La eclosión juntera en el mundo hispano*, coord. by Manuel Chust, 105–36. Mexico City, FCE/COLMEX, 2007.

Dym, Jordana, and Christophe Belaubre, eds. *Politics, Economy, and Society in Bourbon Central America, 1759–1821*. Boulder, University Press of Colorado, 2007.

Dym, Jordana, and Sajid Herrera Mena, coords. *Centroamérica durante las revoluciones atlánticas: El vocabulario político, 1750–1850*. San Salvador, IEESFORD Editores, 2014.

Eastman, Scott, and Natalia Sobrevilla Perea, eds. *The Rise of Constitutional Government in the Iberian Atlantic World: The Impact of the Cádiz Constitution of 1812*. Tuscaloosa, University of Alabama Press, 2015.

"Extracto de la Conspiración de Belén en el año de 1813." *Anales de la Academia de Geografía e Historia de Guatemala* 36, nos. 1–4 (1963): 564–76.

Facio, Rodrigo. "Esquema social de la independencia." In *Rodrigo Facio*, by Eugenio Rodríguez Vega. San José, Costa Rica, Editorial de la Universidad Estatal a Distancia, 2006 (original article, 1937).

Fajardo, Marta. "La jura del rey Carlos IV en la Nueva Granada." *Anales del Instituto de Investigaciones Estéticas* 21, nos. 74–75 (Spring 1999): 195–209.

Falla Sánchez, Juan José. "La familia Velasco en Chiapas." *Revista de la Academia Guatemalteca de Estudios Genealógicos, Heráldicos e Históricos*, no. 9 (1987): 463–522.

Fenner, Justus. "Fuentes primarias para el Chiapas decimonónico." In *Chiapas: de la Independencia a la Revolución*, coord. by Mercedes Olivera Bustamante and María Dolores Palomo Infante, 385–436. Mexico City, Centro de Investigaciones y Estudios Superiores en Antropología Social/Consejo de Ciencia y Tecnología del Estado de Chiapas, 2005.

Fernández Bonilla, León. *Documentos relativos a los movimientos de independencia en el reino de Guatemala*. San Salvador, Talleres Tipográficos del Ministerio de Instrucción Pública, 1929.

Fernández Guardia, Ricardo. *La independencia y otros episodios*. San José, Trejos Hermanos, 1928.

Fernández Hernández, Bernabé. *El gobierno del intendente Anguiano en Honduras (1796–1812)*. Sevilla, Universidad de Sevilla, 1997.

———. *El reino de Guatemala durante el gobierno de Antonio González Saravia, 1801–1811*. Guatemala City, Comisión Interuniversitaria Guatemalteca de Conmemoración del Quinto Centenario del Descubrimiento de América, 1993.

Fernández Molina, José Antonio. "De tenues lazos a pesadas cadenas. Los cabildos coloniales de El Salvador como arenas de conflicto." In *Mestizaje, poder y sociedad. Ensayos de historia colonial de las provincias de San Salvador y Sonsonate*, edited by Margarita Gómez and Sajid A. Herrera, 73–96. San Salvador, FLACSO-El Salvador, 2003.

———. "La dinámica de las sociedades coloniales centroamericanas (1524–1792)." In *Encuentros con la historia*, edited by Margarita Vannini, 101–44. Managua, Instituto de Historia de Nicaragua/Instituto Francés de Estudios Mexicanos y Centroamericanos, 1995.

Fernández Molina, Manuel. *Los tributos en el reino de Guatemala: 1786–1821*, 2nd. ed. Guatemala City, Universidad de San Carlos de Guatemala, 2000.

Fernández Sebastián, Javier, dir. *Diccionario político y social del mundo iberoamericano. La era de las revoluciones, 1750–1850 [Iberconceptos-I]*. Madrid, Fundación Carolina/Sociedad Estatal de Conmemoraciones Culturales/Centro de Estudios Políticos y Constitucionales, 2009.

Feros, Antonio. "Clientelismo y poder monárquico en la España de los siglos XVI y XVII." *Revista Relaciones*, no. 73 (Winter 1998): 15–49.

Florescano, Enrique. *Precios del maíz y crisis agrícolas en México (1708–1810)*. Mexico City, El Colegio de México, 1969.

Floyd, Troy. "The Indigo Merchant: Promoter of Central American Economic Development, 1750–1808." *Business History Review* 39, no. 4 (1965): 466–88.

Fonseca, Elizabeth. *Costa Rica colonial. El hombre y la tierra*. San José, Editorial Universitaria Centroamericana, 1997.

Fradkin, Raúl O., ed. "Paradigmas en discusión. Independencia y revolución en Hispanoamérica y en el Río de La Plata," en Rogelio Altez y Manuel Chust (eds.), *Las revoluciones en el largo siglo XIX latinoamericano*, Madrid, Vervuert/Iberoamericana, 2015, pp. 87–107.

———. *¿Y el pueblo dónde está? Contribuciones para una historia popular de la Revolución de Independencia en el Río de la Plata*. Buenos Aires, Prometeo Libros, 2015.

Fradkin, Raúl, and Gabriel Di Meglio, comps. *Hacer política. La participación popular en el siglo XIX rioplatense*. Buenos Aires, Prometeo Libros, 2013.

Frasquet, Ivana. "Alteza *versus* majestad: el poder de la legitimidad en el Estado nación mexicano: 1810–1824." In *El imperio sublevado. Monarquía y naciones en España e Hispanoamérica*, edited by Víctor Mínguez and Manuel Chust, 255–76. Madrid, Consejo Superior de Investigaciones Científicas, 2004.

Fuentes y Guzmán, Francisco Antonio de. *Recordación Florida*. Guatemala City, Sociedad de Geografía e Historia de Guatemala, 1933.

"Fundación de San Fernando Guadalupe (Salto de Agua), 1790–1802." Boletín 7 del Archivo Histórico del Estado, 64–65. Documentos Históricos de Chiapas, 1936.

Gallini, Stefania. *Una historia ambiental del café en Guatemala. La Costa Cuca entre 1830 y 1902*. Guatemala City, AVANCSO, 2009 (Serie Autores Invitados, 19).

Gamboa, Francisco. *Costa Rica, ensayo histórico*, 5th ed. San José, Imprenta y Litografía Elena, 1974.

Gámez, José Dolores. *Historia de Nicaragua desde los tiempos prehispánicos hasta 1860 en sus relaciones con España, México y Centro América*. Managua, Tipografía El País, 1889.

———. *Historia moderna de Nicaragua. Complemento a mi historia de Nicaragua*. Managua, Fondo de Promoción Cultural/BANIC, 1993 (original edition 1889 Tipografía "El País").

Gamio Palacio, Fernando. *La municipalidad de Lima y la emancipación, 1821*, 2nd ed. Lima, Municipalidad Metropolitana de Lima, 2005.

Garavaglia, Juan Carlos. "El *Teatro del poder:* ceremonias, tensiones y conflictos en el estado colonial." *Boletín del Instituto de Historia Argentina y Americana*, no. 14 (July–December 1996): 7–30.

García, Miguel Ángel. *Diccionario histórico enciclopédico de la República de El Salvador*. 13 vols. San Salvador, Tipografía La Salvadoreña, 1932.

García de León, Antonio. *Resistencia y utopía: memorial de agravios y crónicas de revueltas y profecías acaecidas en la provincia de Chiapas durante los últimos quinientos años de su historia*. Mexico City, Ediciones Era, 1997.

García Delgado, Daniel R. "Las raíces escolásticas de la Emancipación de la América Española. Comentario del libro de Carlos Stoetzer." *Revista Sociedad y Religión*, no. 2 (1986): 67–73.

García Granados, Miguel. *Memorias del general Miguel García Granados*. Guatemala City, Encuadernación y Tipografía "Nacional," 1893.

García Laguardia, Jorge Mario. "La independencia de la Capitanía General de Guatemala. El dilema del nuevo régimen: Monarquía Constitucional o República." In *Historia comparada de las Américas. Sus procesos Independentistas*, edited by Patricia Galeana, 441–68. Mexico City, Siglo XXI Editores, 2010.

———. *Orígenes de la democracia constitucional en Centroamérica*, San José, Editorial Universitaria Centroamericana, 1971.

García Vettorazzi, María Victoria. *Acción subalterna, desigualdades socioespaciales y modernización. La formación de actores y circuitos del comercio indígena en Guatemala, siglos XIX y XX*. Louvain, Presses Universitaire de Louvain, 2010.

Gavidia, Francisco. *Historia moderna de El Salvador*, 2nd. ed. San Salvador, Ministerio de Cultura, 1958.

Gayol, Víctor. "El retrato del escondido. Notas sobre un retrato de jura de Fernando VII en Guadalajara." *Revista Relaciones*, no. 83 (Summer 2000): 149–82.

Giménez Fernández, Manuel. "Las doctrinas populistas en la independencia de Hispanoamérica." *Anuario de Estudios Americanos* 3, no. 16 (1946): 519–665.

Godoy Arellana, Milton. "Fiestas, construcción del estado nacional y resignificación del espacio público en Chile, Norte Chico, 1800–1840." *Cuaderno de Historia*, no. 37 (December 2012): 51–73.

Gómez, Ana Margarita. "De máquina imperial a control interno: el rol cambiante del ejército Borbón en la Guatemala colonial, 1762–1808." In *Los rostros de la violencia. Guatemala y El Salvador, siglos XVIII y XIX*, edited by Ana Margarita Gómez and Sajid Alfredo Herrera, 123–58. San Salvador, UCA Editores, 2007.

González, José María. *Metáforas del poder*. Madrid, Alianza Editorial, 1998.

González, Yamileth. "Continuidad y cambio en la historia agraria de Costa Rica (1821–1880)." Doctoral dissertation, Lovaina, Université Catholique de Louvain, 1983.

González Alzate, Jorge H. *La experiencia colonial y transición a la independencia en el occidente de Guatemala. Quetzaltenango: de pueblo indígena a ciudad multiétnica, 1520–1825*. Mérida, Centro Peninsular en Humanidades y en Ciencias Sociales, 2015.

———. "A History of Los Altos, Guatemala: A Study of Regional Conflict and National Integration." Doctoral dissertation, New Orleans, Tulane University, 1994.

———. "State Reform, Popular Resistance, and Negotiation of Rule in Late Bourbon Guatemala: The Quetzaltenango Aguardiente Monopoly, 1785–1807." In *Politics, Economy, and Society in Bourbon Central America, 1759–1821*, edited by Jordana Dym and Christophe Belaubre, 129–55. Boulder, University Press of Colorado, 2007.

González Obregón, Luis. "La Jura de la Independencia." In *Episodios históricos de la guerra de Independencia*, 2:309–15. Mexico City, Imprenta de "El Tiempo," de Victoriano Agüeros, 1910.

Gordillo y Ortiz, Octavio. *Diccionario biográfico de Chiapas*. Mexico City, B. Costa-AMIC Editor, 1977.

Grafenstein, Johanna von. "El situado novohispano al circuncaribe, un análisis de su composición, distribución y modalidades de envío, 1791–1808." In *El secreto del imperio español: los situados coloniales en el siglo XVIII*, coord. by Carlos Marichal and Johanna von Grafenstein, 143–69. Mexico City, El Colegio de México/Instituto Mora, 2012.

Gramsci, Antonio. *Selections from the Prison Notebooks*. New York, International, 1973.

Granados, Luis Fernando. *En el espejo haitiano. Los indios del Bajío y el colapso del orden colonial en América Latina*. Mexico City, Ediciones Era, 2016.

Grandin, Greg. *The Blood of Guatemala: A History of Race and Nation*. Durham, N.C., Duke University Press, 2000.

Gruzinski, Serge. *La guerra de las imágenes. De Cristóbal Colón a "Blade Runner" (1492–2019)*. Trans. from French by Juan José Utrilla. Mexico City, FCE, 1995.

Gudmundson, Lowell. "Campesino, granjero, propietario: formación de clase en una economía cafetalera de pequeños propietarios 1850–1950." *Revista de Historia*, nos. 21–22 (1990): 151–205.

———. *Hacendados, políticos y precaristas: la ganadería y el latifundio guanacasteco, 1800–1850*. San José, Editorial Costa Rica, 1983.

Guedea, Virginia, ed. *Textos insurgentes, 1808–1821*. Mexico City, UNAM, 2007.

Guerra, François-Xavier. *Modernidad e independencias. Ensayos sobre las revoluciones hispánicas*. Madrid, Fundación MAPFRE, 1992.

Guerra, François-Xavier, and Annick Lempérière, coords. *Los espacios públicos en Iberoamérica: ambigüedades y problemas, siglos XVIII–XIX*. Mexico City, CEMCA/FCE, 1998.

Guerrero, Andrés. "El proceso de identificación: sentido común ciudadano, ventriloquia y transescritura." In *Pueblos, comunidades y municipios frente a los proyectos modernizadores en América Latina, siglo XIX*, edited by Antonio Escobar Ohmstede, Romana Falcón, and Raymond Buve, 29–63. San Luis Potosí, Colegio de San Luis/CEDLA, 2002.

Guha, Ranajit. "The Prose of Counterinsurgency." In *Selected Subaltern Studies*, edited by Ranajit Guha and Gayatri Chakravorty Spivak, 45–84. Oxford, Oxford University Press, 1988.

Gutiérrez Álvarez, Coralia. "La historiografía contemporánea sobre la independencia en Centroamérica," *Nuevo Mundo Mundos Nuevos*, Debates, March 2, 2009, http://nuevomundo.revues.org/54642.

———. "Pueblo/Pueblos." In *Centroamérica durante las revoluciones atlánticas: El vocabulario político, 1750–1850*, coord. by Jordana Dym y Sajid Alfredo Herrera Mena, 249–64. San Salvador, IEESFORD, 2014.

———. "Racismo y sociedad en la crisis del Imperio Español. Los pueblos de los altos de Guatemala." In *Cultura y sociedad en Guatemala colonial*, edited by Stephen Webre and Robinson A. Herrera, 249–77. Woodstock, Vt., Plumsock Mesoamerican Studies, 2014.

Gutiérrez Cruz, Sergio Nicolás. *Casa, crisol y altar. De la hidalguía vasconavarra a la hacienda chiapaneca: los Esponda y Olaechea, 1731–1821*. Tuxtla Gutiérrez, Universidad de Ciencias y Artes de Chiapas, 2009.

———. "De la intendencia de Ciudad Real al estado federal chiapaneco, 1786–1835." In *Formación y gestión del estado en Chiapas. Algunas aproximaciones históricas*, coord. by María Eugenia Claps Arenas and Sergio Nicolás Gutiérrez Cruz, 19–41. Tuxtla Gutiérrez, Centro de Estudios Superiores de México y Centroamérica, Universidad de Ciencias y Artes de Chiapas, 2011.

———. "Notas preliminares acerca de una familia de la época colonial en la región zoque: los Esponda y Olaechea (1750–1821)." In *Cultura y etnicidad zoque*, edited by Dolores Aramoni Calderón, Thomas A. Lee, and Miguel Lisbona, 104–42. Tuxtla Gutiérrez, Universidad Autónoma de Chiapas/Universidad de Ciencias y Artes de Chiapas, 1998.

———. "El proceso de independencia de la provincia chiapaneca. Una visión desde las conformaciones territoriales y los nacionalismos." In *Estado Nación en México: Independencia y Revolución*, edited by Esaú Márquez Espinosa, Rafael de J. Araujo González, and María del Rocío Ortiz Herrera, 201–10. Tuxtla Gutiérrez, Universidad de Ciencias y Artes de Chiapas, 2011.

Guzmán, Moisés. "El imaginario imperial de la insurgencia mexicana." In *Guerra e imaginarios políticos en la época de las independencias*, edited by Moisés Guzmán, 169–89. Morelia, IIH-Universidad Michoacana de San Nicolás de Hidalgo, 2007.

Hale, Charles. "José María Luis Mora and the Structure of Mexican Liberalism." *Hispanic American Historical Review* 45, no. 2 (May 1965): 196–227.

Hall, Carolyn, and Héctor Pérez Brignoli. *Historical Atlas of Central America*. Norman, University of Oklahoma Press, 2003.

Hamill, Hugh M. "Royalist Counterinsurgency in the Mexican War for Independence: The Lessons of 1811." *Hispanic American Historical Review*, no. 53 (August 1973): 470–89.

Hamnett, Brian R. "Royalist Counterinsurgency and the Continuity of Rebellion: Guanajuato and Michoacán, 1813–1820." *Hispanic American Historical Review* 62, no. 1 (February 1982): 19–48.

Haring, C. H. *El imperio español en América*. Mexico City, Alianza Editorial Mexicana, 1990.

Hawkins, Timothy. "Fighting Napoleon in Totonicapán." *Latin Americanist* 61, no. 4, (December 2017): 490–510.

———. *José de Bustamante and Central American Independence: Colonial Administration in an Age of Imperial Crisis*. Tuscaloosa, University of Alabama Press, 2004.

———. "To Insure Domestic Tranquility: José de Bustamante and the Preservation of Empire in Central America, 1811–1818." Doctoral dissertation, New Orleans, Tulane University, 1999.

Hazard, Paul. *The Crisis of the European Mind, 1680–1715*. Trans. from French by J. Lewis May. New York, New York Review, 2013.

Henao, Ana María. "Ceremonias reales y representación del rey: un acercamiento a las formas de legitimación y propaganda del poder regio en la sociedad neogranadina. Cali, siglo XVIII." *Historia y Espacio*, no. 32 (January–June 2009): 5–20.

Hensel, Silke. "¿Cambios políticos mediante nuevos procedimientos? El impacto de los procesos electorales en los pueblos indios de Oaxaca bajo el sistema liberal." *Signos históricos*, no. 20 (2008): 126–63.

Hernández y Davalos, Juan. "Bando del virrey, publicando el de la Regencia de la Isla de León, libertando del tributo a los indios." Vol. 2, no. 70 in *Colección de documentos para la historia de la guerra de Independencia de México de 1808 a 1821*. 6 vols. Mexico City, UNAM, 2007. www.pim.unam.mx/catalogos/hyd/HYDII/HYDII070.pdf.

Hernández Pérez, José Santos. *La Gaceta de Guatemala: un espacio para la difusión del conocimiento científico (1797–1804)*. Mexico City, Universidad Autónoma Metropolitana-Iztapalapa/Universidad Nacional, 2015.

Herrera Mena, Sajid Alfredo. "Constitución." In *Centroamérica durante las revoluciones atlánticas: el vocabulario político, 1750–1850*, edited by Jordana Dym and Sajid Alfredo Herrera Mena, 77–93. San Salvador, IEESFORD, 2014.

———. *El ejercicio de gobernar. Del cabildo borbónico al ayuntamiento liberal: El Salvador colonial, 1750–1821.* Castelló de la Plana, Universitat Jaume I, 2013.

———. "Escenarios de lealtad e infidencia durante el régimen constitucional gaditano: San Salvador, 1811–1814." *Mesoamérica*, no. 53 (2011): 200–210.

———. "La herencia gaditana: bases tardío coloniales de las municipalidades salvadoreñas 1808–1823." Doctoral dissertation, Seville, Universidad Pablo de Olavide, 2005.

Iglesias, Francisco María. *Documentos relativos a la independencia.* 4 vols. San José, Imprenta Nacional, 1899–1902, 1921.

Inda, Angélica, and Andrés Aubry. *Los insurgentes y el obispo de Chiapas, 1810–1815. Correspondencia de Ambrosio Llano.* Mexico City, Apoyo al Desarrollo de Archivos y Bibliotecas de México, 2010.

"Informe del Ministro Tesorero de las Reales Cajas de Guatemala." In *Economía de Guatemala en los siglos XVIII y XIX*, 71–112. Guatemala City, Editorial Universitaria, 1974 [1824].

"Instrucciones para la constitución fundamental de la monarquía española y su gobierno de que ha de tratarse en las próximas Cortes generales de la nación (1811)." In *La génesis del constitucionalismo guatemalteco*, edited by Jorge Mario García Laguardia, 105–190. Guatemala City, Editorial Universitaria, 1971.

Jefferson, Ann. "Nuestra América: la visión de la gente parda del distrito de Mita, 1837." In *Repensando Guatemala en la época de Rafael Carrera. El país, el hombre y las coordenadas de su/ tiempo*, coord. by Brian Connaughton, 113–49. Mexico City, Universidad Autónoma Metropolitana-Iztapalapa, 2015.

Jiménez, Manuel de Jesús. "El año 23." In *"Doña Ana de Cortabarría" y otras noticias de antaño*, 19–42. San José, Editorial Costa Rica, 1981.

Joseph, Gilbert M., and Daniel Nugent, eds. *Everyday Forms of State Formation: Revolution and the Negotiation of Rule in Modern Mexico.* Durham, N.C., Duke University Press, 1994.

Juarros, Domingo. *Compendio de la historia del reino de Guatemala, 1500–1800.* Guatemala City, Editorial Piedra Santa, 1981.

Karpinsky, Rose Marie. "La dimensión económica de la independencia de Costa Rica a través de la gestión material de su primer jefe de Estado." *Revista de Costa Rica*, no. 3 (1973): 23–25.

Kinloch Tijerino, Frances. "La independencia en la historiografía didáctica nicaragüense," *Revista de Historia* 22 (2007): 9–34.

"La promulgación de la Constitución de 1812." *Revista Próceres* 7, pt. 1 (1911): 273–78.

Lanning, John Tate. *The University in the Kingdom of Guatemala.* Ithaca, N.Y., Cornell University Press, 1955.

Lasso, Marixa. "Revisiting Independence Day: Afro-Colombian Politics and Creole Patriot Narratives, Cartagena, 1809–1815." In *After Spanish Rule: Post-colonial Predicaments of the Americas*, edited by Mark Thurner and Andrés Guerrero, 223–47. Durham, N.C., Duke University Press, 2003.

Laughlin, Robert M. *La gran serpiente cornuda, ¡Indios de Chiapa, no escuchen a Napoleón!, Ensayo 1.* Chiapas, Mexico, Programa de Investigaciones Multidisciplinarias sobre Mesoamérica y el Sureste-UNAM, 2001.

Lavallé, Bernard. "De l'esprit colon à la revendication créole." In *Esprit Créole et Conscience nationale. Essais sur la formation des consciences nationales en Amérique Latine*, by Maurice Birckel, Bernard Lavallé, and Joseph Pérez, 8–36. Paris, CNRS, 1980.

Leal Curiel, Carole. *El discurso de la fidelidad. Construcción social del espacio como símbolo de poder regio (Venezuela, siglo XVIII).* Caracas, Academia Nacional de la Historia, 1990.

Lenkersdorf, Gudrun. *Génesis histórica de Chiapas 1522–1532. El conflicto entre Portocarrero y Mazariegos.* Mexico City, UNAM, 1993.

León Cázares, María del Carmen. *Un levantamiento en nombre del rey nuestro señor.* Mexico City, UNAM, 1988.

León Fernández, D. *Colección de documentos para la historia de Costa Rica.* 10 vols. Barcelona, Imprenta Viuda de Luis Tasso, 1907.

———. *Documentos relativos a los movimientos de independencia en el reino de Guatemala.* San Salvador, Publicación del Ministerio de Instrucción Pública, 1929.

León-Portilla, Miguel, and Alicia Mayer. *Los indígenas en la independencia y en la revolución mexicana.* IIH-UNAM-INAH/ Fideicomiso Teixidor, 2010.

Lévano, Diego. "Por la salud pública y la felicidad de la nación. Movilización militar, rogativas públicas y contribuciones patrióticas para la preservación de la monarquía hispánica en Perú, 1793–1810." In *Los dominios ibéricos en la América meridional a principios del siglo XIX*, edited by Héctor Hernández and Sara Ortelli, 104–41. Mexico City, UNAM, 2009.

Levi, Giovanni. "Les usages de la biographie," *Annales Économies, Sociétés, Civilisations* 44, no. 6 (November–December 1989): 1325–36.

Lindo Fuentes, Héctor. "Economía y sociedad (1810–1870)." In *De la Ilustración al Liberalismo*, vol. 3 of *Historia general de Centroamérica*, edited by Héctor Pérez Brignoli, 141–201. San José Costa Rica, FLACSO, 1994.

———. "Los límites del poder en la era de Barrios." In *Identidades nacionales y estado moderno en Centroamérica*, edited by Arturo Taracena and Jean Piel, 87–96. San José, Editorial de la Universidad de Costa Rica, 1995.

———. *Weak Foundations. The Economy of El Salvador in the Nineteenth Century.* Berkeley, University of California Press, 1990.

López, Roberto. "Hablar a la imaginación. Las ceremonias de proclamación y jura de la constitución de 1812 en el noroeste peninsular." *Obradoiro de Historia Moderna*, no. 20 (2011): 141–73.

López Velásquez, Eugenia. "Noviembre de 1811: revueltas populares en la provincia de San Salvador." *Cuadernos de Ciencias Sociales* 2, no. 4 (2011): 7–27.

———. "Poderes intermedios y el gobierno de pueblos de indios, ladinos y castas de San Salvador y Sonsonate en tiempos de las reformas y de las transiciones políticas (1743–1841)." In *Diálogo Historiográfico Centroamérica-México, siglos XVIII–XIX*, coord. by Brian Connaughton, 113–75. Mexico City: Universidad Autónoma Metropolitana-Iztapalapa, 2017.

Lovell, W. George. *Conquest and Survival in Colonial Guatemala: A Historical Geography of the Cuchumatán Highlands, 1500–1821*, 3rd ed. Montreal, McGill-Queens University Press, 2005.

Lucena Giraldo, Manuel. *Naciones de rebeldes. Las revoluciones de independencia latinoamericanas.* Madrid, Taurus, 2010.

Lujan Muñoz, Jorge. "El establecimiento del estanco del tabaco en el reino de Guatemala." *Mesoamérica*, no. 41 (2001): 99–136.

Lynch, John. *Las revoluciones hispanoamericanas, 1818–1826*, 8th. ed. Barcelona, Editorial Ariel, 2001.

Machuca Gallegos, Laura. *Comercio de sal y redes de poder en Tehuantepec durante la época colonial*, Mexico City, Centro de Investigaciones y Estudios Superiores en Antropología Social, 2007.

———. "Relaciones de comercio entre Tehuantepec y Chiapas (siglo XVII)." *Boletín de la AFEHC*, no. 17 (February 2006), www.afehc-historia-centroamericana.org/index_action_fi_aff_id_368.html.

Madrigal, Eduardo. "Cartago república urbana: elites y poderes en la Costa Rica colonial, 1564–1718." Doctoral dissertation, University of Toulouse, 2006.

———. "Poderes y redes sociales en la Cartago colonial, 1600–1718." *TRAMA. Revista de Ciencias Sociales y Humanidades* 2, no. 1 (July 2009): 39–62.

Marichal, Carlos. "La Iglesia y la Corona: La bancarrota del gobierno de Carlos IV y la consolidación de vales reales en la Nueva España." In *Iglesia, Estado y Economía. Siglos XVI al XIX*, coord. by María del Pilar Martínez López-Cano, 241–61. Mexico City, UNAM/Instituto de Investigaciones Dr. José María Luis Mora, 1995.

Markman, Sidney David, *Architecture and Urbanization in Colonial Chiapas*, Philadelphia, American Philosophical Society, 1984.

Marroquín, Alejandro D. *Apreciación sociológica de la independencia salvadoreña*. San Salvador, Instituto de Investigaciones Económicas/Facultad de Ciencias Económicas/Universidad de El Salvador, 1964.

Martínez Peláez, Severo. *Centroamérica en los años de la independencia. El país y los habitantes*. Guatemala City, Universidad de San Carlos de Guatemala, 1982.

———. *Motines de indios. La violencia colonial en Centroamérica y Chiapas*. Guatemala City, F&G Editores, 2011.

———. *La patria del criollo. Ensayo de interpretación de la realidad colonial guatemalteca*, 13th. ed. Mexico City, Ediciones En Marcha, 1994.

Marure, Alejandro. *Bosquejo histórico de las revoluciones de Centroamérica desde 1811 hasta 1834*. 2 vols. Mexico City, Librería de la Viuda de Ch. Bouret, 1913.

McCreery, David J. "Atanasio Tzul, Lucas Aguilar, and the Indian Kingdom of Totonicapán." In *The Human Tradition in Latin America: The Nineteenth Century*, edited by Judith Ewell and William H. Beezley, 39–58. Wilmington, Scholarly Resources, 1989.

———. *Rural Guatemala, 1760–1940*. Stanford, Calif., Stanford University Press, 1994.

Meléndez Chaverri, Carlos. *La Ilustración en el antiguo reino de Guatemala*, 2nd ed. San José, Editorial Universitaria Centroamericana, 1974.

———. "Rasgos fundamentales de la geopolítica centroamericana en la independencia." *Revista de la Universidad de Costa Rica*, no. 31 (1971): 7–23.

"Memoria del estado político y eclesiástico de la Capitanía General de Guatemala y proyectos de división en ocho provincias para otras tantas Diputaciones Provinciales, Gefes Políticos, Intendentes y Obispos, presentada á las Cortes por el Doctor D. José Mariano Méndez." In *Textos fundamentales de la Independencia centroamericana*, edited by Carlos Meléndez Chaverri, 37–52. San José, Editorial Universitaria Centroamericana, 1971.

Mérida, Martín. *Historia crítica de la Inquisición en Guatemala*. Guatemala City, 1895.

———. "Historia crítica de la inquisición en Guatemala." *Boletín del Archivo General del Gobierno* 3, no. 1 (October 1937): 4–156.

Mier, José Servando Teresa de. *Historia de la revolución de Nueva España antiguamente Anáhuac, o Verdadero origen y causas de ella, con la relación de sus progresos hasta el presente año de 1813*. Londres, G. Glindon Press, 1813.

Mínguez, Víctor. "La ceremonia de jura en la Nueva España. Proclamaciones fernandinas en 1747 y 1808." *Varia Historia* 23, no. 38 (July–December 2007): 273–92.

Miranda, José. *Las ideas y las instituciones mexicanas, primera parte, 1521–1820*. Mexico City, UNAM, 1978.

Mitre, Bartolomé. *Historia de San Martín y de la emancipación sudamericana*. 3 vols. Buenos Aires, Editorial Universitaria, 1968.

Molina Bedoya, Felipe. *República de Costa Rica. Apuntamientos para su historia*. New York, Imprenta de S. W. Benedict, 1851.

Molina Jiménez, Iván. *Costa Rica (1800–1850)*. San José, Costa Rica, Editorial de la Universidad de Costa Rica, 1998.

———. "Habilitadores y habilitados en el Valle Central de Costa Rica. El financiamiento de la producción cafetalera en los inicios de su expansión." *Revista de Historia*, no. 16 (1987): 85–127.

———. *Revolucionar el pasado. La historiografía costarricense del siglo XIX al XXI*. San José, Costa Rica, Editorial Universidad Estatal a Distancia, 2012.

———. "El Valle Central de Costa Rica en la independencia." *Revista de Historia*, no. 14 (July–December 1986): 85–114.

Molina Martínez, Miguel. "Los cabildos y el pactismo en los orígenes de la independencia de Hispanoamérica." In *Homenaje a Alberto de la Hera*, edited by José Luis Soberanes Fernández and Rosa María Martínez de Codes, 567–91. Mexico City, UNAM, 2008.

———. "Pactismo e independencia en Iberoamérica." *Revista de Estudios Colombinos*, no. 4 (April 2008): 61–74.

Monge Alfaro, Carlos. *Conceptos sobre la evolución de Costa Rica en el siglo XVIII*. San José, Costa Rica, Editorial de la Universidad Estatal a Distancia, 2007.

———. *Historia de Costa Rica*. San José, Costa Rica, Editorial Hermanos Trejos, 1947.

Monteagudo, Bernardo de. *Relación de la gran fiesta cívica celebrada en Chile el 12 de febrero de 1818*. 3rd ed. Compiled and with an Introduction by Hugo Rodolfo E. Ramírez Rivera. Santiago de Chile, Biblioteca del Instituto O'Higginiano de Chile, 1987.

Montero Barrantes, Francisco. *Elementos de historia de Costa Rica*. 2 vols. San José, Tipografía Nacional, 1892.

Montúfar, Manuel. *Memorias para la historia de la revolución de Centro-América*. Jalapa, Aburto y Blanco at the Oficina del Gobierno, 1832.

Montúfar y Rivera, Lorenzo. *Reseña histórica de Centro-América*. 7 vols. Guatemala City, Tipografía de "El Progreso," 1878.

Morelli, Federica. *Territorio o nación. Reforma y disolución del espacio imperial en Ecuador, 1765–1830*. Translated from French by Antonio Hermosa Andujar. Madrid, Centro de Estudios Políticos y Constitucionales, 2005.

Morón, Guillermo. *Historia de Venezuela*. 5 vols. Caracas, Italgráfica, 1971.

Munilla Lacasa, María Lía. *Celebrar y Gobernar. Un estudio de las fiestas cívicas en Buenos Aires, 1810–1835*. Buenos Aires, Miño y Dávila, 2013.

Murillo, Jorge. *Historia de las monedas de Costa Rica. Catálogo numismático*. San José, Editorial Universidad Estatal a Distancia/Banco Central de Costa Rica, 2005.

Nájera Coronado, Martha Illia. *La formación de la oligarquía criolla en Ciudad Real de Chiapa. El caso Ortés de Velasco*. Mexico City, UNAM, 1993.

Noiriel, Gerard. *Sur la crise de l'Histoire*. Paris, Belin, 1996.

Obregón, Clotilde, ed. *Las constituciones de Costa Rica*. 5 vols. San José, Editorial de la Universidad de Costa Rica, 2007.

———. *El proceso electoral y el poder ejecutivo en Costa Rica*. San José, Editorial de la Universidad de Costa Rica, 2008.

———. *El río San Juan en la lucha de las potencias (1821–1860)*. San José, Costa Rica, Editorial de la Universidad Estatal a Distancia, 1993.

Obregón Loría, Rafael. *Costa Rica en la independencia y en la Federación*. San José, Editorial Costa Rica, 1977.

———. *De nuestra historia patria, movimientos anti españolistas en Centro América*. San José, Universidad de Costa Rica, 1970.

O'Phelan Godoy, Scarlett. "El vestido como identidad étnica e indicador social de una cultura material." In *El barroco peruano*, by Ramón Mujica Pinilla, 99–133. Lima, Banco de Crédito, 2003.

Ordóñez Jonama, Ramiro. "La familia Batres y el Ayuntamiento de Guatemala." *Anales de la Academia de Geografía e Historia de Guatemala*, no. 67 (1993): 2–59.

Orozco y Jiménez, Francisco. *Documentos inéditos de la historia de la Iglesia de Chiapas*. 2 vols. Tuxtla Gutiérrez, Consejo Estatal para la Cultura y las Artes, 1999.

Ortemberg, Pablo. "Cádiz en Lima: de las fiestas absolutistas a las fiestas constitucionalistas en la fundación simbólica de una nueva era." *Historia* 2, no. 45 (July–December 2012): 455–83.

———. "La entrada de José de San Martín en Lima." *Histórica* 33, no. 2 (2009): 65–108.

Osejo, Rafael Francisco. *Lecciones de geografía en forma de catecismo. Comprendiendo una adición del Estado Libre de Costa-Rica*. San José, Imprenta Merced, 1833.

Osorio, Alejandra. "Courtly Ceremonies and a Cultural Urban Geography of Power in the Hapsburg Spanish Empire." In *Cities and the Circulation of Culture in the Atlantic World: From the Early Modern to Modernism*, edited by Leonard von Morzé, 37–72. New York, Palgrave Macmillan, 2017.

———. "El rey ausente: poder imperial y simulacro real en la ciudad de los reyes, Lima." In *La sociedad monárquica en la América hispánica*, edited by Magalí Carrillo and Isidro Vanegas, 83–118. Bogotá, Ediciones Plural, 2009.

Palacios, Guillermo. "Entre una 'nueva historia' y una 'nueva historiografía' para la historia política de América Latina en el siglo XIX." In *Ensayos sobre la nueva historia política de América Latina, s. XIX*, coord. by Guillermo Palacios, 9–18. Mexico City, El Colegio de México, 2007.

Palma Murga, Gustavo. "Es necesario que todo cambie para que todo siga igual. Estrategias de supervivencia económica de la élite guatemalteca en las postrimerías del periodo colonial." *Trace*, no. 37 (June 2000): 55–73.

———. "Núcleos de poder local y relaciones familiares en Guatemala a finales del siglo XVIII." *Mesoamérica* 12 (1986): 241–308.

Palmer, Steven. "Sociedad anónima, cultura oficial: inventando la nación en Costa Rica (1848–1900)." In *Héroes al gusto y libros de moda. Sociedad y cambio cultural en Costa Rica (1750–1900)*, edited by Iván Molina and Steven Palmer, 257–323. San José, PMS/Editorial Porvenir, 1992.

Palti, Elias. *El tiempo de la política. El siglo XIX reconsiderado*. Buenos Aires, Siglo XXI Editores, 2007.

Paquette, Gabriel. "The Dissolution of the Spanish Atlantic Monarchy." *Historical Journal* 52, no. 1 (2009): 175–212.

Pardo, J. Joaquín. "Independencia." *Anales de la Sociedad de Geografía e Historia de Guatemala* 4 (1981): 195–205.

Patch, Robert W. "Imperial Politics and Local Economy in Colonial Central America, 1670–1770." *Past and Present*, no. 143 (1994): 77–107.

———. *Indians and the Political Economy of Colonial Central America, 1670–1810*. Norman, University of Oklahoma Press, 2013.

Paula Andrade, Vicente de. *Noticias biográficas de los ilmos. sres. obispos de Chiapas*. Mexico City, Imprenta Guadalupana de Reyes Velasco, 1907.

Payne Iglesias, Elizet. "La historia oficial, orígenes de la historiografía liberal en Centroamérica, (1852–1930)." *Avances de investigación* (San José, Centro de Investigaciones Históricas de América Central), no. 12 (1994).

———. "Los negros franceses de Santo Domingo en Truxillo: segregación y adaptación, 1796–1821." In *Haití, revolución y emancipación*, by Rina Cáceres Gómez and Paul E. Lovejoy, 69–76. San José, Universidad de Costa Rica, 2008.

———. "¡No hay rey, no se pagan tributos! La protesta comunal en El Salvador, 1811." *Cuadernos Inter.c.a.mbio sobre Centroamérica y el Caribe* 4, no. 5 (2007): 15–43.

———. "'Sediciosos, subversivos, falaces.' Los movimientos sociales en El Salvador (1811–1814)." Master's thesis, San José, Universidad de Costa Rica, 1999.

Peccorini Letona, Francisco. *La voluntad del pueblo en la emancipación de El Salvador. Un estudio sobre las relaciones del pueblo con los próceres en la independencia y en la anexión a México*. San Salvador, Ministerio de Educación, 1972.

Peralta, Hernán. *Las constituciones de Costa Rica*. Madrid, Instituto de Estudios Políticos/Instituto de Cultura Hispana, 1962.

———. *El Pacto de Concordia. Los orígenes del derecho constitucional de Costa Rica*. San José, Imprenta Atenea, 1952.

Pérez Brignoli, Héctor. *Breve historia contemporánea de Costa Rica*. Mexico City, FCE, 1997.

———. *La población de Costa Rica 1750–2000. Una historia experimental*. San José, Editorial de la Universidad de Costa Rica, 2010.

Pérez Brignoli, Héctor, and Ciro F. S. Cardoso. *Centroamérica y la economía occidental (1520–1930)*. San José, Editorial de la Universidad de Costa Rica, 1977.

Pérez Vejo, Tomás. *Elegía Criolla. Una reinterpretación de las guerras de independencia hispanoamericanas*. Mexico City, Tusquets, 2010.

Pérez Zeledón, Pedro. "Gregorio José Ramírez." In *Gregorio José Ramírez y otros ensayos*, 145–65. San José, Editorial Costa Rica, 1971.

Piccato, Pablo. "Public Sphere in Latin America: A Map of the Historiography." *Social History* 35, no. 2 (2010): 165–92.

Piel, Jean, *Sajcabajá. Muerte y resurrección de un pueblo de Guatemala*. Guatemala City, Centro de Estudios Urbanos y Regionales/Universidad de San Carlos de Guatemala, 1989.
Pineda, Emeterio. *Descripción geográfica del Departamento de Chiapas y Soconusco*. Mexico City, Imprenta de Ignacio Cumplido, 1845.
Pinto Soria, Julio César. *Centroamérica, de la colonia al Estado nacional (1800–1840)*. Guatemala City, Editorial Universitaria, 1986.
———. "La independencia y la federación (1810–1840)." In *Historia general de Centroamérica, de la Ilustración al liberalismo*, edited by Héctor Pérez Brignoli, 73–140. Madrid, FLACSO, 1993.
Piqueras, José. "Ilustración y revolución." In *Cambio político y cultural en la España de entresiglos*, edited by Alberto Ramos and Alberto Romero,19–40. Cádiz, Universidad de Cádiz, 2008.
Poblett, Martha. *Narraciones chiapanecas, viajeros extranjeros en Palenque, siglos XVIII–XIX*. Tuxtla Gutiérrez, Consejo Estatal para la Cultura y las Artes de Chiapas, 1999.
Pollack, Aaron. "Centroamérica, 1811–1814. Iniciando una época de movilización política." *Realidad*, no. 130 (2011): 529–49.
———. "De la contribución directa proporcional a la capitación en la Hispanoamérica republicana: Los límites impuestos por la constitución fiscal." *Araucaria. Revista Iberoamericana de Filosofía, Política y Humanidades* 18, no. 36 (2016): 59–86.
———. "Las Cortes de Cádiz en Totonicapán: una alianza insólita en un año insólito, 1813." *Revista Studia Histórica. Historia Contemporánea* 27 (2009): 207–34.
———. *Levantamiento k'iche' en Totonicapán, 1820. Los lugares de la política subalterna*. Guatemala City, Asociación para el Avance de las Ciencias Sociales en Guatemala, 2008.
———. "Modelos opuestos de región: Los Altos de Guatemala en la primera mitad del siglo XIX." *Scripta Nova: Revista Electrónica de Geografía y Ciencias Sociales* 10, no. 218 (August 1, 2006), www.ub.edu/geocrit/sn/sn-218-36.htm.
———. "Protesta en Patzicía. Los pueblos de indios y la *vacatio regis* en el reino de Guatemala." *Revista de Indias* 78, no. 272 (2018): 147–73.
Polushin, Michael A. "Bureaucratic Conquest, Bureaucratic Culture: Town and Office in Chiapas, 1780–1832." Doctoral dissertation, New Orleans, Tulane University, 1999.
———. "'Por la patria, el Estado y la Religión.' La expulsión del intendente accidente de Ciudad Real, Chiapas (1809)." In *La independencia en el sur de México*, coord. by Ana Carolina Ibarra, Mexico City, UNAM, 2004.
Portillo, Geraldina. "Revisión de algunas opiniones en la historia agraria de El Salvador." Report of the V Congreso Centroamericano de Historia, Universidad de El Salvador, July 18–21, 2000.
Portillo Valdés, José María. "Constitucionalismo antes de la Constitución. La economía política y los orígenes del constitucionalismo en España," *Nuevo Mundo, Mundos Nuevos*, secc. Coloquios, January 28, 2007, http//:nuevomundo.revues.org/index4160.html.
———. *Crisis Atlántica. Autonomía e independencia en la crisis de la monarquía hispana*. Madrid, Fundación Carolina/Centro de Estudios Hispánicos e Iberoamericanos/Marcial Pons, 2006.
Quesada Camacho, Juan Rafael. *Educación y ciudadanía en Costa Rica de 1810 a 1821*. San José, Editorial de la Universidad de Costa Rica, 2007.

———. *Historia de la historiografía costarricense, 1821–1940*. San José, Editorial de la Universidad de Costa Rica, 2002.

———. "Independencia e historia." *Revista de Ciencias Sociales*, no. 36 (1987): 87–90.

Quijada, Mónica. "Las 'dos tradiciones.' Soberanía popular e imaginarios compartidos en el mundo hispánico en la época de las grandes revoluciones atlánticas." In *Revolución, independencia y las nuevas naciones de América*, coord. by Jaime E. Rodríguez O., 61–86. Madrid, Fundación MAPFRE-Tavera, 2005.

Quijada, Mónica. "La caja de Pandora. El sujeto político indígena en la construcción del orden liberal." *Historia Contemporánea* 33 (2006): 605–37.

Rabinovich, Alejandro M. "La máquina de guerra y el Estado: el Ejército de los Andes tras la caída del Estado central del Río de la Plata en 1820." Presented at the War, Violence and State Building Workshop, State Building in Latin America Group, CIAPA, San José, August 16–17, 2011.

Ramos, Frances. "Arte efímero, espectáculo y la reafirmación de la autoridad en Puebla durante el siglo XVIII: la celebración en honor del Hércules borbónico." *Revista Relaciones*, no. 97 (Winter 2004): 178–218.

"Real cédula de 13 de junio de 1817, derogando la Real órden de 31 de Marzo de 1815 y desaprobando todo lo hecho por el ex Capitán General don José de Bustamante." *Boletín del Archivo General del Gobierno* 4, no. 1 (October 1938): 37–39.

Reales exequias, por el señor don Carlos III. Rey de las Españas, y Américas. Y Real proclamación de su augusto hijo el señor D. Carlos IV. Por la muy noble, y muy leal ciudad de Granada, provincia de Nicaragua, reyno de Guatemala. Edited by Manuel Ignacio Pérez. Mexico City, Editorial Jus, 1974.

"Relación de los autos pasados por la Capitanía General relativos al proyecto de Conspiración que se formulaba en el Convento de Belén." *Anales de la Sociedad de Geografía e Historia* 11, no. 1 (1934): 13–27.

Revista de la Academia Hondureña de Geografía e Historia. Honduras, Academia Hondureña de Geografía e Historia, 1972.

Reyero, Carlos. *Alegoría, nación y libertad. El olimpo constitucional de 1812*. Madrid, Siglo XXI, 2010.

Rico Aldave, Jesús. "La renta de tabaco y su influencia en el desarrollo del campesinado en el Valle Central Occidental (1766 -1825)." Master's thesis, San José, Universidad de Costa Rica, 1988.

Río Barredo, María José del. "Felipe II y la configuración del sistema ceremonial de la monarquía católica." In *Congreso Internacional "Felipe II (1598–1998), Europa dividida, la monarquía católica de Felipe II,"* 5 vols., 1:677–703. Madrid, Parteluz, 1998.

Rípodas Ardanaz, Daisy. "Versión de la monarquía de derecho divino en las celebraciones reales de la América borbónica." *Revista de Historia del Derecho*, no. 34 (2006): 241–67.

Robles Domínguez, Mariano. *Memoria histórica de la provincia de Chiapas una de las de Guatemala presentada al Augusto Congreso por el Br. Mariano Robles Dominguez de Mazariegos, canónigo de la santa iglesia catedral de Ciudad Real de Chiapa, diputado en Cortés por su provincia*. Cádiz, 1813.

Rodríguez, Eugenio. *Biografía de Costa Rica*. San José, Editorial de Costa Rica, 1981.

———. *Rodrigo Facio*. San José, Editorial de la Universidad Estatal a Distancia, 2006.

Rodríguez, Mario. *The Cádiz Experiment in Central America, 1808 to 1826*. Berkeley, University of California Press, 1978.

———. *La conspiración de Belén en nueva perspectiva*. Guatemala City, Centro Editorial "José de Pineda Ibarra"/Ministerio de Educación, 1965.

Rodríguez Moya, Inmaculada, and Víctor Mínguez. "Cultura simbólica y fiestas borbónicas en Nueva Granada. De las exequias de Luis I (1724) a la proclamación de Fernando VII (1808)." *Revista CS*, no. 9 (2012): 115–43.

Rodríguez O., Jaime E. *La independencia de la América española*, 2nd ed. Mexico City, COLMEX/FCE, 2005.

Rodríguez Solano, Pablo. *La cuestión fiscal y la formación del Estado de Costa Rica 1821–1859*. San José, Editorial de la Universidad de Costa Rica, 2017.

———. "Derecho natural en Costa Rica (1821–1823). Una revisión crítica del proceso de independencia y formación de los estados en Centroamérica." *Illes i imperis*, no. 15 (2013): 55–73.

———. "Estado, colonización y políticas agrarias: las comunidades campesinas de Costa Rica entre 1750 y 1850." In *Mensurar la tierra, controlar el territorio. América Latina, siglos XVIII y XIX*, edited by Juan Carlos Garavaglia y Pierre Gautreau, 151–86. Rosario, Prohistoria Editores/State Building in Latin America, 2011.

———. "Estado, fiscalidad y organización burocrática en Costa Rica, 1821–1848." Master's thesis, Barcelona, Universidad Pompeu Fabra, 2010.

Rojas, Beatriz, comp. *Documentos para el estudio de la cultura política de la transición: juras, poderes e instrucciones. Nueva España y la Capitanía General de Guatemala, 1808–1820*. Mexico City, Instituto Mora, 2005.

Romero, Germán. "Estado y sociedad en Nicaragua colonial." In *Encuentros con la historia*, by Margarita Vannini, 213–29. Managua, Instituto de Historia de Nicaragua/Centro Francés de Estudios Mexicanos y Centroamericanos, 1995.

———. *Las estructuras sociales de Nicaragua en el siglo xvii*. Managua, Vanguardia, 1988.

Romero, Matías. *Bosquejo histórico de la agregación a México de Chiapas y Soconusco, y las negociaciones sobre límites entabladas por México con Centro América y Guatemala*. Mexico City, Imprenta del Gobierno en Palacio, 1877.

Roover, Raymond de. "Economía escolástica." *Estudios Públicos*, no. 9 (1983): 89–121.

Rubio Sánchez, Manuel. *Gabino Gaínza*. Guatemala City, Ministerio de Educación, 1985.

Rudé, George. *La multitud en la historia. Los disturbios populares en Francia e Inglaterra, 1730–1848*. Madrid, Siglo XXI Editores, 1979.

Ruz, Mario Humberto. *Tabasco en Chiapas, documentos para la historia tabasqueña en el archivo diocesano de San Cristóbal de las Casas*. Mexico City, UNAM, 1994.

Ruz, Mario Humberto, and Arturo Taracena Arriola. "Los pueblos mayas y el movimiento de independencia." In *Los indígenas en la independencia y en la revolución mexicana*, edited by Miguel León-Portilla and Alicia Mayer, 369–402. Mexico City, Instituto de Investigaciones Históricas-UNAM, 2010.

Sagastume Paiz, Tania. *Trabajo urbano y tiempo libre en la ciudad de Guatemala, 1776–1840*. Guatemala City, Universidad de San Carlos/Municipalidad de la Ciudad de Guatemala, 2008.

Sala i Vila, Nuria. "'Derecho, poder y libertad' a propósito de las batallas por la autonomía jurisdiccional entre las Audiencias del Cusco y Charcas (1820–1825)." *Revista de Indias* 76, no. 266 (2016): 51–82.

———. "El Trienio Liberal en el Virreinato peruano: los ayuntamientos constitucionales de Arequipa, Cusco y Huamanga, 1820–1824." *Revista de Indias* 71, no. 253 (2011): 693–728.

———. "Justicia conciliatoria durante el liberalismo hispano en el Perú: el caso de Huamanga." *Anuario de Estudios Americanos* 69, no. 2 (July–December 2012): 423–50.

Salazar, Ramón A. *Historia de veintiún años. La independencia de Guatemala*. Guatemala City, Secretaría de Educación Pública, 1928.

Salazar Baena, Verónica. "Representar al rey ausente. Ceremonias reales en Nueva Granada, 1760–1810." *Instituto Colombiano de Antropología e Historia*, November 2010. www.icanh .gov.co./?idcategoria=6488.

Samayoa Guevara, Héctor Humberto. "Proceso contra el peluquero Vilches." *Revista Antropología e Historia de Guatemala* 6, no. 1 (1954): 49–61.

Samper Kutchbach, Mario. "La especialización mercantil campesina en el noroeste del Valle Central, 1850–1900. Elementos microanalíticos para un modelo." *Revista de Historia*, no. 1, special (1985): 49–87.

———. *Producción cafetalera y poder político en Centroamérica*. San José, Editorial Universitaria Centroamericana, 1998.

———. "Los productores directos en el siglo del café." *Revista de Historia*, no. 7 (July–December 1978): 123–217.

Santilli, Daniel, Jorge Daniel Gelman, and Raúl Osvaldo Fradkin, comps. *Rebeldes con causa. Conflicto y movilización popular en la Argentina del siglo XIX*. Buenos Aires, Prometeo Libros, 2013.

Sarazúa, Juan Carlos. "Territorialidad, comercio y conflicto al este de Guatemala: Santa Rosa, 1750–1851." Bachelor's thesis, Guatemala City, Universidad de San Carlos de Guatemala, 2007.

Sarrailh, Jean. *La España ilustrada de la segunda mitad del siglo XVIII*. Mexico City, Fondo de Cultura Económica, 1974.

Serrano Ortega, Jorge Antonio, coord. *El sexenio absolutista, los últimos años insurgentes. Nueva España (1814–1820)*. Zamora Michoacán, El Colegio de Michoacán, 2014.

Serulnikov, Sergio. *Conflictos sociales e insurrección en el mundo colonial andino. El norte de Potosí en el siglo XVIII*. Buenos Aires, Fondo de Cultura Económica, 2006.

———. "Nuevas formas de hacer política: los sectores plebeyos urbanos y la debacle de la sociedad de Indias en el Alto Perú." In *Hacer política. La participación popular en el siglo XIX rioplatense*, edited by Raúl O. Fradkin and Gabriel Di Meglio, 15–47. Buenos Aires, Prometeo Libros, 2013.

Sibaja, Luis Fernando. *Del Cañas-Jerez al Chamorro-Bryan: las relaciones limítrofes entre Costa Rica y Nicaragua en la perspectiva histórica, 1858–1916*. Alajuela, Costa Rica, Museo Histórico Cultural Juan Santamaría, 2006.

Smith, Robert S. "Indigo Production and Trade in Colonial Guatemala." *Hispanic American Historical Review* 39, no. 2 (1959): 181–211.

Solórzano Fonseca, Juan Carlos. "El comercio de Costa Rica durante el declive del comercio español y el desarrollo del comercio de contrabando inglés: periodo 1690–1750." *Anuario de Estudios Centroamericanos* 20, no. 2 (1994): 27–39.

———. "Las comunidades indígenas en Guatemala, El Salvador y Chiapas (siglo XVIII)." *Anuario de Estudios Centroamericanos* 11, no. 2 (1985): 93–130.

———. "Los años finales de la dominación española (1750–1821)." In *De la Ilustración al Liberalismo*, edited by Héctor Pérez Brignoli, 13–71, vol. 3 of *Historia general de Centroamérica*. San José Costa Rica, FLACSO, 1994.

Solórzano Fonseca, Juan Carlos, Patricia Alvarenga, and Elizabeth Fonseca. *Costa Rica en el siglo XVIII*. San José, Editorial de la Universidad de Costa Rica, 2003.

Soto, Willy. "Costa Rica y la federación centroamericana. Fundamentos históricos del aislacionismo." *Anuario de Estudios Centroamericanos* 17, no. 2 (1991): 15–30.

Stoetzer, Carlos. *Las raíces escolásticas de la emancipación de la América española*. Madrid, Centro de Estudios Constitucionales, 1982.

Stone, Samuel. *La dinastía de los conquistadores. La crisis de poder en la Costa Rica contemporánea*. San José, Editorial Universitaria Centroamericana, 1975.

Tanzi, Héctor José. "Fuentes ideológicas de las juntas de gobierno americanas." *Boletín Histórico*, no. 31 (1973): 25–42.

Taracena Arriola, Arturo. *Estado de Los Altos, indígenas y régimen conservador en Guatemala, 1838–1851*. San José, Editorial de la Universidad de Costa Rica, 1993.

———. *La expedición científica al reino de Guatemala*. Guatemala City, Editorial Universitaria, 1988.

———. *Invención criolla, sueño ladino, pesadilla indígena. Los Altos de Guatemala: de región a Estado, 1740–1871*. Antigua Guatemala, Editorial El Porvenir/Centro de Investigaciones Regionales de Mesoamérica, 1999.

———, ed. *La primera guerra federal centroamericana, 1826–1829. Nación y estados, republicanismo y violencia*. Guatemala, Universidad Autónoma Metropolitana-Iztapalapa/UNAM/Cara Parens/Universidad Rafael Landívar, 2015.

Taracena Arriola, Arturo, Enrique Gordillo Castillo, Tania Sagastume Paiz, et al. *Etnicidad, Estado y nación en Guatemala, 1944–1985*. 2 vols. Guatemala City, Centro de Investigaciones Regionales de Mesoamérica, 2004.

TePaske, John J. *La real hacienda de Nueva España: la real caja de México (1576–1816)*, Mexico City, INAH, 1976.

TePaske, John J., and Herbert Klein. "The Seventeenth-Century Crisis in New Spain: Myth or Reality?" *Past and Present*, no. 90 (February 1981): 116–35.

Thibaud, Clement. "Formas de guerra y mutación del ejército durante la guerra de independencia en Colombia y Venezuela." In *Revolución, independencia y las nuevas naciones de América*, coord. by Jaime E. Rodríguez, 339–364. Madrid, Fundación MAPFRE TAVERA, 2005.

Thurner, Mark. *From Two Republics to One Divided: Contradictions of Postcolonial Nationmaking in Andean Peru*. Durham, N.C., Duke University Press, 1997.

Torres Freyermuth, Amanda Úrsula. *Los hombres de bien. Una historia de la elite chiapaneca, 1824–1825*. San Cristóbal de las Casas, Centro de Investigaciones Multidisciplinarias sobre Chiapas y la Frontera Sur (CIMSUR)-UNAM, 2018.

Torres Freyermuth, Amanda Úrsula, and Aquiles Omar Ávila Quijas. "El ayuntamiento de Ciudad Real y el asesor letrado José Mariano Valero. Conflicto político en vísperas de la independencia, 1804–1809." *Signos Históricos* 19, no. 38 (2017): 88–137.

Trens, Manuel B. *Historia de Chiapas, desde los tiempos más remotos hasta el gobierno del general Carlos A. Vidal (¿ . . . 1927)*. Mexico City, La Impresora, 1942.

———. *Historia de Chiapas, desde los tiempos más remotos hasta la caída del segundo imperio (¿... 1867)*. Tuxtla Gutiérrez, Consejo Estatal para la Cultura y las Artes de Chiapas, 1999.

Valenzuela, Jaime. "Entre campanas y cañones: perspectivas sobre la sonoridad política en el Santiago borbónico." *Revista de Historia Iberoamericana* 3, no. 1 (2010): 69–83.

———. *Las liturgias del poder. Celebraciones públicas y estrategias persuasivas en Chile colonial (1609–1709)*. Santiago, Centro de Investigaciones Diego Barros Arana/DIBAM/LOM Editores, 2001.

Van Oss, Adriaan C. *Catholic Colonialism: A Parish History of Guatemala, 1524–1821*. Cambridge, Cambridge University Press, 2002.

———. "La población de América Central hacia 1800." *Anales de la Academia de Geografía e Historia de Guatemala* 15 (1980): 291–311.

Van Young, Eric. *La crisis del orden colonial. Estructura agraria y rebeliones populares de la Nueva España, 1750–1821*. Mexico City, Alianza, 1992.

———. *The Other Rebellion. Popular Violence, Ideology, and the Mexican Struggle for Independence, 1810–1821*. Stanford, Calif., Stanford University Press, 2002.

Varela Suanzes-Carpegna, Joaquín. *La teoría del Estado en los orígenes del constitucionalismo hispánico (Las Cortes de Cádiz)*. Madrid, Centro de Estudios Constitucionales, 1983.

Vázquez Olivera, Mario. *El imperio mexicano y el reino de Guatemala. Proyecto político y campaña militar*. FCE/CIALC-UNAM, 2009.

———. "El Plan de Iguala y la independencia de Guatemala." In *La independencia en el sur de México*, edited by Ana Carolina Ibarra, 395–430. Mexico City, FFYL-UNAM, 2004.

———. "El Plan de Iguala y la independencia de San Salvador." In *Historia comparada de las Américas. Sus procesos Independentistas*, edited by Patricia Galeana, 399–467. Mexico City, Siglo XXI Editores, 2010.

Veblen, Thomas T. "The Ecological, Cultural, and Historical Bases of Forest Preservation in Totonicapán, Guatemala." Doctoral dissertation, Berkeley, University of California, 1975.

Vega Carballo, José Luis. "Etapas y procesos de la evolución sociopolítica de Costa Rica." *Estudios Sociales Centroamericanos*, no. 1 (January–April 1972): 45–72.

———. *Orden y Progreso. La formación del Estado nacional en Costa Rica*. San José, Instituto Centroamericano de Administración Pública, 1981.

Velasco, Julián Andrei, "Fiesta y poder: persistencias y significaciones de las representaciones sobre el poder en la ciudad de Panamá a través de las juras, 1747–1812," in *Boletín AFEHC*, no. 48, 2011, https://www.academia.edu/1753838/Fiesta_y_poder:_Persistencias_y_significaciones_de_las_representaciones_sobre_el_poder_en_la_ciudad_de_Panam%C3%A1_a_trav%C3%A9s_de_las_juras_1747-1812.

Veyne, Paul. *L'inventaire des différences. Leçon inaugurale au collège de France*. Paris, Le Seuil, 1976.

Vicuña MacKenna, Benjamín. *La independencia en el Perú*. Buenos Aires, Editorial Francisco de Aguirre, 1971.

Vielman, Julio. *Los enigmas de la Independencia, 1808–1823*, vol. 1. Guatemala City, Centro Editorial Vile, 2013.

Viguerie, Jean. *Histoire et dictionnaire du temps des Lumières (1715–1789)*. Paris, Éditions Robert Laffont, 1995.

Viqueira, Juan Pedro. *¿Relajados o reprimidos? Diversiones públicas y vida social en la ciudad de México durante el Siglo de las Luces.* Mexico City, Fondo de Cultura Económica, 1987.

Vives, Pedro. "El ámbito del imperio en la ciudad colonial: ¿una función desestructuradora?" In *Historia y futuro de la ciudad iberoamericana,* edited by Francisco Solano, 47–74. Madrid, CSIC, 1986.

Vogel, Robert C. "Rebel without a Cause: The Adventures of Louis Aury." *Laffite Society Chronicles* 8, no. 1 (February 2002): 2–12.

White, Randall, A. "The Guatemala Earthquake of 1816 on the Chixoy-Polochic Fault." *Bulletin of the Seismological Society of America* 75, no. 2 (1985): 455–73.

Wobeser, Gisela von. "Gestación y contenido del Real Decreto de Consolidación de Vales Reales para América." *Historia Mexicana* 51, no. 4 (2002): 787–827.

Woodward, Ralph Lee, Jr. "Changes in the Nineteenth-Century Guatemalan State and Its Indian Policies." In *Guatemalan Indians and the State: 1540 to 1988,* edited by Carol A. Smith, 52–71. Austin, University of Texas Press, 1990.

———. "Economic and Social Origins of the Guatemalan Political Parties (1773–1823)." *Hispanic American Historical Review* 45, no. 4 (1965): 544–66.

———. *Rafael Carrera and the Emergence of the Republic of Guatemala, 1821–1871.* Athens, University of Georgia Press, 1993.

Wortman, Miles L. *Government and Society in Central America, 1680–1840.* New York, Columbia University Press, 1982.

———. "Government Revenue and Economic Trends in Central America, 1787–1819." *Hispanic American Historical Review,* no. 55 (May 1975): 251–86.

———. "Rentas públicas y tendencias económicas en Centroamérica, 1787–1819." In *Lecturas de historia de Centroamérica,* by Luis René Cáceres, 245–86. San José, Publicación del Banco Centroamericano de Integración Económica, 1989.

Zelaya Goodman, Chester. *Nicaragua en la Independencia.* Managua, Fundación Vida, 2004 (Colección Cultural de Centroamérica, no. 16).

CONTRIBUTORS

Xiomara Avendaño Rojas received her doctorate in history from El Colegio de México and is professor at the Universidad de El Salvador, where she coordinates the undergraduate program in history. She has authored numerous articles and chapters published in journals and collective volumes, as well as *Centroamérica entre lo antiguo y lo moderno: institucionalidad, ciudadanía y representación política, 1810–1838* (Castelló de la Plana, Universitat Jaume I, 2009); *Elecciones indirectas y disputa del poder en Nicaragua: el lento camino hacia la modernidad* (Managua, LEA-Grupo Editorial, 2007); and, with Norma Hernández Sánchez, *¿Independencia o Autogobierno? El Salvador y Nicaragua, 1786–1811* (Managua, LEA-Grupo Editorial-Sophie Ediciones, 2014). She also coordinated the collective volume *Historia electoral en Centroamérica: elecciones, organizaciones políticas y ciudadanía (siglos XIX y XX)*, published in Managua by LEA-Grupo Editorial (2011).

Christophe Belaubre, a French specialist in the history of the Catholic Church in Central America during the colonial period, has been professor at the Universidad Industrial de Santander in Colombia and is presently research associate in the "France, Americas, Spain: Societies, Powers, Actors" (FRAMESPA) research project, which is supported by the Centre national de recherche scientifique. He acted as editor of the journal *Mesoamérica* for a five-year period and is presently editor of the *Boletín de la Asociación para el Fomento de los Estudios Históricos en Centroamérica* (AFEHC). His published works include books and articles about Central American history, most recently *Église et Lumières au Guatemala: la dimension atlantique (1779–1808)*, published by L'Harmattan (Paris, 2015).

Timothy Hawkins received his Ph.D. from Tulane University in 1999 and currently serves as professor of history at Indiana State University. His scholarly work, including *José de Bustamante and Central American Independence: Colonial Administration in an Age of Imperial Crisis* (Tuscaloosa, University of Alabama, 2004) and *A Great Fear: Luis de Onís and the Shadow War against Napoleon in Spanish America, 1808–1812* (Tuscaloosa, University of Alabama, 2019), focuses on the reaction of colonial officials to the wars of independence. He has also contributed to edited collections such as *Napoleon's Atlantic: The Impact of Napoleonic Empire in the Atlantic World* and *Politics, Economy, and Society in Bourbon Central America, 1759–1821*, as well as journals including *Colonial Latin American Historical Review* and *Latin Americanist*.

The Salvadoran ***Sajid Alfredo Herrera Mena*** holds a doctorate in the history of America from the Universidad Pablo de Olavide in Seville and an undergraduate degree in philosophy from the Universidad Centroamericana José Simeón Cañas (UCA) in El Salvador. He is presently director of the university press at the UCA. His research interests include local governments, subaltern resistance, public opinion, and political thinking, which can be appreciated in his articles and book chapters that have been published in Colombia, Costa Rica, El Salvador, Ecuador, Germany, Mexico, Nicaragua, Spain, the United States of America, and Venezuela. His works include *El ejercicio de gobernar. Del cabildo borbónico al ayuntamiento liberal. El Salvador colonial, 1750–1821* (Castelló de la Plana, Valencia, 2013) and the collective volumes *Mestizaje, poder y sociedad. Ensayos de historia colonial de las provincias de San Salvador y Sonsonate*, coordinated with Ana Margarita Gómez (San Salvador, Facultad Latinoamericana de Ciencias Sociales, 2003), *Los rostros de la violencia. Guatemala y El Salvador, siglos XVIII–XIX*, coordinated with Ana Margarita Gómez, (San Salvador, UCA Editores 2007), and *Centroamérica durante las revoluciones atlánticas. El vocabulario político, 1750–1850*, coordinated with Jordana Dym (San Salvador, Instituto Especializado de Educación Superior para la Formación Diplomática, 2014). His present research focuses on Indian town finances in the Central American provinces of San Salvador and Sonsonate during the Bourbon reforms (1776–1808).

Elizet Payne Iglesias is professor at the Escuela de Historia in the Universidad de Costa Rica and researcher at the Centro de Investigaciones Históricas de la América Central (CIHAC) in the same university. She holds a doctorate in history and is a specialist in the colonial history of Central America. She is author of *El siglo XVII en Costa Rica: origen y crisis de una colonia marginal* (San José, Editorial Universidad Estatal a Distancia, 1990), *El puerto de Truxillo. Viaje hacia el melancólico abandono* (Tegucigalpa, Editorial Guaymaras, 2007), and, with Eugenia Ibarra, *Costa Rica en el siglo XVI: de las sociedades cacicales a la sociedad colonial* (San José, EUNED, 1990). Her published articles include "Identidad y Nación: El caso de la Costa Norte e Islas de la Bahía en Honduras, 1876–1930," *Mesoamérica*, 2001. Payne has undertaken research on antitax and anti-Spanish social movements in Central America, particularly in El Salvador, between 1811 and 1814. She is presently researching pearl and shell dye production on the Pacific coast and the Caribbean ports of Central America. She coordinates the research project "Central American Societies between the Colonial World and Modernity" at the CIHAC. She was awarded the 2008 Silvio Zavala Colonial History Prize by the Pan-American Institute of Geography.

Aaron Pollack received his doctorate in geography from Clark University (2005) and held positions as professor in the Universidad Cultural del Estado de México and as professor/researcher at the Instituto de Investigaciones Dr. José María Luis Mora prior to joining the Centro de Investigaciones y Estudios Superiores en Antropología Social (CIESAS)-Sureste as professor/researcher. He has published *Levantamiento K'iche' en Totonicapán, 1820. Los lugares de la política subalterna* (Guatemala City, Asociación para el Avances de las Ciencias Sociales, 2008) and articles in journals such as *Araucaria*, *Historia Mexicana*, and *Revista de Indias*. His research interests center on Central America and the Mexican state of Chiapas during the first half of the nineteenth century and he is presently focused on the relationship between fiscal policies and the societies in which they develop.

Pablo Rodríguez Solano received his undergraduate degree from the University of Costa Rica, where he also studied in the Central American Master's Program in History. In 2009 he joined the "State Building in Latin America" research project, funded by the European Research Council, led by Juan Carlos Garavaglia and headquartered in the Universitat Pompeu Fabra (UPF) in Barcelona. He received his master's and doctoral degrees (2013) from the UPF while participating in that project. Rodríguez Solano has worked in the Museo Nacional de Costa Rica, where he undertook research about Limón province. He is presently professor in the Escuela de Estudios Generales at the Universidad de Costa Rica and researcher in the Centro de Investigaciones en Identidad y Cultura Latinoamericanas (CIICLA) located in the same university. He also forms part of the research group "Empires, Metropolis and Extra-European Societies" at the UPF and the "Transcultural Convergences in Central America and the Caribbean" research network. His research focuses on how fiscality, land, and migration relate to the conformation of institutional structures in the construction and consolidation of Latin American states.

INDEX

abdications of Bayonne, effects of, 7–8, 16, 19, 45, 60, 159, 163
absolutism/liberalism binary, 52–53, 58, 63–64, 66–71, 176
Acta de los nublados ("Clouds Act"), 57, 61
Acuña, Víctor Hugo, 63, 71
Africans/African descendants, 2, 23, 24, 134, 138–39, 148
agriculture: cacao industry, 59, 136; crises and plagues, 118, 138, 159; indigo production and commerce, 5, 6, 136, 159; modernization efforts, 104–5, 118; and trade, 59, 161
Aguilar (Akiral), Lucas, 158, 172, 174, 175
Alajuela, Costa Rica, 59, 60, 69
alcabala (sales tax), 26n10, 135, 161
Alfaro, José Francisco, 204–5
Antigua Guatemala, 91
Argüelles, José Mariano, 204–5
Argüello, Juan, 142–43
Aristotelian thought, 65
armed conflicts, 144, 145, 175, 177, 189–90. *See also* military actions
artillery fire in ritual/ceremony, 39–40, 47–48, 89
artisans and craftsmen, 161–62, 205
autonomist movements: Creole elites and partial autonomy, 6, 8–9, 165–66 (*see also* Bustamante/Creole contention); evolution of, 8–13, 177
Avendaño Rojas, Xiomara, 72, 81, 176
Aycinena, José de, 189, 196, 206
ayuntamiento constitucional. See constitutional ayuntamientos, establishment of

ayuntamientos, pre-constitutional, 3. *See also* constitutional ayuntamientos, establishment of

Barrios, Gerardo, 51–52
Barrundia, José Francisco, 13, 200, 204–5
Belaubre, Christophe, 103
Belén conspiracy, 13, 110, 147, 169, 200, 204
bells in ritual/ceremony, examples of, 39, 89, 90
Beltranena proposal, 10, 13
Bernasconi, Antonio, 121
bishops, Enlightenment era profiles, 106–9
Black Christ, 114
Bonaparte, Joseph, 7, 45
Bonaparte, Napoleon, 5, 45, 60, 144. *See also* abdications of Bayonne, effects of
Bonilla, Adolfo, 21, 63, 71
books, and Inquisitional repression, 120
Bourbon reforms, impact of, overviews, 3–6, 133. *See also* Enlightenment thought, influence and spread of
Bourdieu, Pierre, 106
Bridikhina, Eugenia, 43
Bulux, Nicolás, 172, 184n66
Bustamante/Creole contention: antioligarchic (Creole) strategies, 202–3, 204–6; counterinsurgency strategies of Bustamante, 165, 190–95, 196–97, 199–200; Creole campaigns against tyranny of, 194–95, 200–206; on Creoles and nature of rebels in Nicaragua, 139
Bustamante y Guerra, José de: arch-villain narrative and myth of tyranny, 24, 55–56n42, 187–88, 197; captain general tenure, overview, 190–91, 206–8;

247

Bustamante y Guerra, José de (*cont.*)
dismissal of, 206; and Granadan rebellion, 145–47, 189–90; on insurgencies, nature of, 136; liberal constitutional policies, opposition to, 194–95; and presentation of constitution, 48; on weakness of Cortes of Cádiz, 201. *See also* Bustamante/Creole contention

Cabezas Carache, Horacio, 31n71, 138, 143, 144
cacao industry, 59, 136
Cádiz Constitution. *See* Constitution of Cádiz
Cahabón, Guatemala, 92
Calderón, José Antonio, 121, 122
Calleja, Félix María, 190, 203
Calvo, Joaquín Bernardo, 67, 68
Cañas, José, 198
Cañas, Juan Manuel de, 61
cannons, firing of. *See* artillery fire in ritual/ceremony
Carrera, Rafael, 159, 177
Carrillo de Albornoz, Miguel, 168
Cartago, Costa Rica, 59, 62, 68, 69–70, 140
Casaús y Torres, Ramón Francisco, 48, 90
castas (people of partial African descent), 2, 23, 24, 134, 138–39
Castilla, José María, 96–97
Castillo, Florencio del, 60
Castillo Aguayo, Francisco del, 163
Catálogo numismático, 98
Catholic Church: dominance of, Enlightenment era, 104, 106–9; God and legitimization of monarchical authority, 42, 45, 46; *patronato real*, 84–85, 98, 104; reformation of, Enlightenment era, 115–17; relationship with independent government, 97; religious ceremonies as political rituals, 37–39; resurrection symbolism, 40; and royal authority, ratification of, 42. *See also* clergy, roles and influence of

Central American Federation, 17–18, 22, 134, 160, 177
Central American independence, analysis and comparisons: abdications of Bayonne, impact of, 7–8; causes and origins, analysis, 10; comparison to other Spanish American movements, 8–11; historiographic analysis, 18–24, 66–73; overview, 6; subaltern politics, focus on, 6–7. *See also* independence movements, dynamics analysis
Cerda, Manuel Antonio de la, 142–43, 145
Cerdas, Rodolfo, 69
ceremonies and rituals, 81–82, 87–88. *See also* oath-taking ceremonies
Chacón, Manuel Mariano, 117
Chamorro, Francisco Sebastián, 115
Chamorro, Josefa, 146
Charles III, 39
Charles IV, 38, 40–45, 159. *See also* abdications of Bayonne, effects of
Chiapas, province of: civic, social, and familial networks, 109–11; clergy, dominance of and Enlightenment era, 106–9; conservatism, impact of, 111–17; declaration of independence and support for Plan de Iguala, 82; Enlightenment initiatives, 117–22; and Enlightenment reform, overview, 103–6; Guatemala, relationship and cross-cultural ties, 111, 112–13, 114
Chimaltenango, Guatemala, 164
Chiquimula, Guatemala, 92, 171
Chontales area insurgencies, 149
citizenship rights and concepts, 24, 78n46, 167, 174
Ciudad Real, Chiapas: and Guatemala, relationship with, 111, 112–13; and Jose Vital de Moctezuma, 108, 121–22; and ousting of Valero, 4, 122, 195; role in spread of Enlightenment, 23, 109–13
civic and social influences, Enlightenment era profiles, 109–11
classism, 136, 139, 148–49, 174, 176

clergy, roles and influence of: dominance of and Enlightenment era, 106–11; ecclesiastical taxes, 159, 162–63, 176–77; Enlightenment era, 109; and loyalty to sovereignty of nation, 51–52; and support of independence, 92, 93, 96–97. *See also* Catholic Church
Cleto Montiel, José, 198
"Clouds Act," 75n1
Cobán, Guatemala, 4, 92, 162, 163
coffee industry, 59, 70
cofradías (brotherhoods), 158
coins/medallions, giving of in rituals, 41, 48, 50, 88, 97–98
Collado, Ambrosio, 173
College of Attorneys, 46
Comayagua, ayuntamiento of, 8
Comayagua province (Honduras), 8, 16, 46–47, 130n98
"Comercio de España," 112
commemorations of social movements, 133
community funds, 115, 135, 163, 170
concord, definitions and concepts, 65–66
Concordia Compact (Pacto de Concordia), 58, 61–62, 64–65
conservatism, impact of, 111–17. *See also* absolutism/liberalism binary
constitutional ayuntamientos: establishment of, 193, 195, 198–99; failures to elect, 166, 167–68, 198; loyalty gestures, 91
constitutional monarchy, 50–52, 82, 83–84
Constitution of Cádiz: contention between Creoles and Bustamante, 193–94; impact on ritual symbolism, 38; liberal policies of, 189; presentation of and oath-taking ceremonies, 47–52; promulgation, 47; reinstatement of 1820, 13–14, 60–61, 158, 173–74; revocation of (1814) by Ferdinand VII, 13, 151, 193–94, 201–2; on ties to Catholic Church, 85
constitutions, ideology of, 64
contraband trade, 5, 75n9, 136, 149

Córdoba treaties, 61, 63, 71
Córdova, José Francisco, 204
Cortes. *See* Courts of Cádiz
Costa Rican independence and perspectives on: approach and method, 57–58; Concordia Compact (Pacto de Concordia), 58, 61–62, 64–65; declaration of, 61; dynamic analysis, 64–72, 73–74, 79n76; period of, overview, 61–63; pre-independence profile, 58–61
counterinsurgency strategies: Bustamante, 165, 190–95, 196–97, 199–200, 202–3, 204–6; Spanish crown, 203, 206
Courts of Cádiz: and elimination of tributes, 93, 144, 158, 164, 165; impact of, overview, 60–61, 166; and importance of representation, 84, 103, 122, 198; instructions to Larrazabal (1810), 11, 51, 84, 195, 202, 205; political reforms, overviews, 166; and sovereignty of nation, 38, 47, 50. *See also* constitutional ayuntamientos
Cozar, Prudencio, 163, 166–67, 171, 173, 174–75
Creoles: autonomy (partial), desire for, 6, 8–9, 165–66, 200, 207; Belén conspiracy, 110, 147, 169, 200, 204; friction with castas, 138–39; and Hidalgo conspiracy, 9; and insurgency in Granada, 141–47, 150–52; and loyalty rituals, 43–44; and Mexican independence movements, 82, 164; political culture, evolution of, 103; resistance to reform in Ciudad Real, 111–13; and spread of Enlightenment, 110. *See also* Bustamante/Creole contention
criollos. See Creoles

dancing and ceremony, 95
Dávila, Fernando Antonio, 117–18
decoration and adornments in ritual: coins/medallions, 41, 48, 50, 88, 97–98; dress

decoration and adornments in ritual (*cont.*) and costume, 39, 41, 44; pennants (royal/political) and ritual symbolism, 42, 43, 88–89, 95–96; portraiture (royal) and ritual symbolism, 40, 41, 42, 43, 48. *See also* imagery in ceremony and ritual

Delgado, José Matías, 198

del Pino y Martínez, Miguel, 118, 122

democracy, conceptual analysis, 68–70

demographic data: Costa Rica, 58–59; Granada, 141–42; Kingdom of Guatemala overview, 3; Nicaragua, 135, 136; Rivas, 147; Totonicapán district, 161–62

Diccionario de la lengua castellana, 38

Di Meglio, Gabriel, 7

Dios Mayorga, Juan de, 45, 151, 192

disease. *See* health and medicine

distributive justice concepts, 64–66

dramatizations in ritual ceremony, 43–44

dress in ritual ceremony, 39, 41, 44

Dym, Jordana, 45, 71–72, 134, 176

earthquakes, 156n65, 169

ecclesiastical taxes, 159, 162–63, 176–77. *See also* rations and personal service tribute to priests

economic issues: church finances and reformation era, 116–17; and Costa Rican independence, 59–60; and independence movements, 68–69, 177; Napoleonic wars, 206

education issues, 107–8, 117, 120, 128–29n82

ejidos (common lands), 76n30

El Salvador, 51–52. *See also* San Salvador (El Salvador)

English, trade with, 2, 4, 136, 144

Enlightenment thought, influence and spread of: Bourbon reforms, impact of, overviews, 3–6, 133; and Catholic dominance, 106–9; and Catholic reformation, 115–17; Chiapas analysis, 23, 106–13, 117–22; and church/state reformation, 115–17; civic, social, and familial networks, 109–15; and dominance of the church, 104; goals of reform, 103–5, 123; initiatives for change, examples, 117–22; overviews, 3–6, 133; recommendations for further investigation, 105; social dynamics and geneaologies, study of, 105–6, 107. *See also* independence movements, dynamics analysis

epidemics, 108, 118–20, 169, 170

Estachería, Josef, 121

estanco (monopoly), 94

ethnic conflicts and insurgencies, 138–39, 143, 144, 148–49, 150, 164

evidential method, 124n9

Facio, Rodrigo, 68–69, 70

familial bonds and spread of Enlightenment, 109–11, 122

Ferdinand/Fernando VII: loyalty pledges, 138, 140; revocation of Constitution of Cádiz, 13, 151, 193–94, 201–2. *See also* abdications of Bayonne, effects of

Fernández, José Antonio, 134, 135

fireworks and ceremony, 88, 90

First Political Statute of the Province of Costa Rica, 62

fiscal concerns: *alcabala*, 26n10, 135, 161; Bourbon fiscal reforms, 4, 5; tax levies and protests against, 26n10, 135, 137–38, 144, 148, 150; tobacco production and regulation, 26n10, 58, 59, 60, 138, 144, 148, 149. *See also* tribute payments

flags in ceremonies. *See* pennants (royal) and ritual symbolism

Fradkin, Raúl, 7

Franco, Francisco, 163

French espionage, fears of, 142, 192, 204

French Revolution, 5

Fuente, Rafael de la, 148

Fuero, Fermín José de, 109, 117, 118–19

Gaínza, Gabino, 83, 85–87, 91, 98

Gálvez, Eulogio, 171, 172
Gamboa, Francisco, 69
Garavaglia, Juan Carlos, 37
García Granados, Miguel, 120
García Jerez, Nicolás, 137, 138–41, 143, 148
Gazeta de Guatemala, 5, 39, 46, 48, 109, 114
Ginzburg, Carlo, 105
God and legitimization of monarchical authority, 42, 45, 46
Goicoechea, José Antonio, 109
González Bravo, Juan Gualberto, 206
González Saravia, Antonio, 7, 28n29, 122–23, 195
Granada, Nicaragua, insurgency in: early 1800s profile, 135–36, 141–42; evolution of, 142–44, 150–51; repression and reprisals, 145–47; resistance actions, 144–45, 189–90
Greek symbolism in Spanish ritual, 42
Gualán, Guatemala, 95
Guatemala, Kingdom of. *See* Kingdom of Guatemala
Guatemala, "province" of: Independence Act, impact of and regional tensions, 90–96; independence and loyalty issues, 83–87; oath-taking ceremonies, 87–89, 97–98; terminology and territories, 100n5. *See also* Guatemala City
Guatemala City: Belén conspiracy, 13, 110, 147, 169, 200, 204; and Chiapas, relationship and cross-cultural ties, 111, 112, 114; elite response to abdications of Bayonne, 8; Granadan prisoners in, 146–47, 151, 199; oath-taking ceremony to Independence Act, 96–98; unrest of 1766, 4
Guatemalan highlands, 158
Gutiérrez, Pedro, 145, 155n43
Gutiérrez Horna, Domingo de, 119–20

Hapsburg dynasty, influence of, 37–38
Hawkins, Timothy, 187
health and medicine: Enlightenment initiatives, 118–20; epidemics, 108, 118–20, 169, 170; prisoners, 199, 204; vaccination programs, 119, 169
Heredia, Costa Rica, 59, 60, 62, 69
Herrera Mena, Sajid Alfredo, 20–21, 37
Hidalgo rebellion, 6, 9–10, 9–11, 137, 164
historiography of Central America: on Costa Rican independence, 66–73; current analysis and synopsis of content, 18–24; integration of subaltern politics, 6–7
Huehuetenango district, 161

imagery in ceremony and ritual: and Cádiz era changes in, 49–53; coins/medallions and symbolism, 41, 48, 50, 88, 97–98; dress and costume, 39, 41, 44; pennants (royal/political) and symbolism, 42, 43, 88–89, 95–96; portraiture (royal) symbolism, 40, 41, 42, 43, 48; as representation of political culture, 52–53. *See also* symbolism in ceremony and ritual
Independence Act of the Kingdom of Guatemala: Costa Rican support of, 57; edict of Provisional Advisory Junta, 85–87; oath-taking ceremonies, 81–82, 89–91, 91–96, 99; overview, 14–18; and relationship with Catholic Church, 84–85; and support for constitutional monarchy, 82–84
independence movements, dynamics analysis: and absolutism/liberalism binary, 66–70, 71; colonial devolution, 70–73; natural law and distributive justice concepts, 63–66, 67; overview, 73–74. *See also* Central American independence, analysis and comparisons; Mexican independence movement, influence of
Indians: cultural restrictions/injunctions, 117; ethnic conflicts, 144, 149; fealty demonstrations, 46–47, 95; fear of rebellion by, 160, 163, 166, 171; history,

Indians (*cont.*)
    preservation of, 120–22; subordination of and symbolism, 41, 42, 43, 46–47, 95; and vaccination programs, 119. *See also* native cultures; tribute payment
indigo production and commerce, 5, 6, 136, 159
infidencia (disloyalty/treason) enforcement, 192–94
Inquisition, 120
"Instructions for the Economic and Political Government of the Provinces," 199
instructions to Larrazabal (1810), 11, 51, 84, 195, 202, 205
intellectualism and Enlightenment era, 5–6, 8, 111
intendancy system defined, 2–3
Interim Fundamental Social Pact of the Province of Costa Rica. *See* Concordia Compact (Pacto de Concordia)
Iturbide, Agustín de, 14–15, 62

Jacaltenango, Guatemala, 92
Jalteva, Nicaragua, 135, 145
Jovellanos, Gaspar Melchor de, 111
juntas, formation of: Guatemalan reticence to, 9, 11; in León, 137–39; local *vs.* regional, 134; Provisional Advisory Junta, 83–84, 85–87; in response to abdications, 7; in South America, 8–9; superior governmental junta *(junta superior gobernativa)* (Costa Rica), 61–62; Supreme Central Junta, 7, 8, 46
jurar (oath taking), 38

K'iche' leaders, 159. *See also* Totonicapán rebellion
Kingdom of Guatemala: colonial era political organization, 2–3; demographic overview, 3; and Enlightenment reforms, overview, 3–6; geographical profile, 2; independence declared, 61; independence period overviews, 7–8, 206–7; terminology and territories, 100n5. *See also* Guatemala, province of; Independence Act of the Kingdom of Guatemala

labor conscription, 138, 148, 162
ladino, definition, 26n4
Lake Nicaragua, 135, 136, 148
land, privatization of, 76n30, 77n38
Landeros family, 122
Lara, José Manuel, 170, 171, 172, 173, 174, 184n66
Larrave, Mariano, 89
Larrazábal, Antonio, 11, 51, 84, 195, 202, 205
León, Nicaragua: early 1800s profile, 135, 136–37; insurgency and repression in, 137–41, 150, 151; and provincial council, 60–61
León y Goicoechea, José de, 109, 114
leprosy, 119
liberalism: and Constitution of Cádiz, 20, 49, 50, 63–64, 189; and evolution of independence, 20–22; and nation/state concepts, 64–66; and protest, 176. *See also* absolutism/liberalism binary
limestone quarries, 119
liquor regulation, 4, 86, 87, 94, 138
Llano, Ambrosio, 107, 109, 119, 122
localism and devolution of power, 70, 72
locust plagues, 111, 138, 159
Lombardo, José Santos, 73
Los Altos, State of, 18, 64, 160, 166, 177
Los Altos region, 80n80, 161, 176
loyalty pledges. *See* oath-taking ceremonies

maceguales (Indian commoners), 158
mail service issues, 203–4
Mallol, Narciso, 166, 167–69
maps, xiii–xxi
Mariano Valero. *See* Valero, José Mariano
Martínez Peláez, Severo, 135, 136
Marure, Alejandro, 21, 63, 209n2
Marure, Mateo Antonio, 192–93
Masaya, Nicaragua, 135, 144, 173

Matina, Costa Rica, 59, 75n9
Mazatenango, Guatemala, 95
medals, commemorative, 97–98. *See also* coins/medallions, giving of in rituals
Medina, Bruno, 198
Memoria histórica de la provincia de Chiapas (Robles Domínguez), 103
Memorias (García Granados), 120
mestizo population, 3, 23, 58, 59, 148, 150
Metapán, revolt of 1811, 45, 150–51
Mexican Empire, annexation proposals/movements, 11, 14–15, 62, 72, 82, 93, 187
Mexican independence movement, influence of: Central American overviews, 14–16, 187; on Chiapas independence, 82; on Costa Rican independence, 57–58, 61, 62, 71–73; on San Salvadoran insurgents, 201. *See also* Mexican Empire, annexation proposals/movements
militarization symbolism, 41
military actions, 134, 140–41, 172, 175, 177
military tribunals under Bustamante, 192–93, 203
mining industry, 59, 75n9
Mociño, José Mariano, 109, 110, 113, 118, 119
modernization and Enlightenment era reform, 4, 104–5, 107–8, 116, 117–18, 118–20
Molina, Felipe, 66–67
Molina, Iván, 59, 70
Momostenango, Guatemala, 161, 162, 164, 170, 174–75
monarchical power. *See* sovereignty and source of power
Monarchy of the North *(Septentrión)*, 84
Monge, Carlos, 68, 70
Montiel, Diego, 145
Montiel, José Cleto, 165, 198
Morelos, José María, 10, 137, 201
Morillo, Pablo, 203
Mosquito Coast, 136, 149
Moziño, José Mariano. *See* Mociño, José Mariano

mulatto population, 3, 23, 58, 138–39, 140, 148, 150
Murillo, Jorge, 98
music and ceremony, 88, 89, 94, 95
mythological symbolism, 42, 82

Napoleon (Bonaparte). *See* Bonaparte, Napoleon
national identity, 69, 187–88
nation/state, concepts of, 46, 50, 64–67. *See also* sovereignty; state formation, concepts of
native cultures, subordination of and symbolism, 41, 42, 43, 46–47, 95
natural law and civil rights, 37, 63–66
"new Latin American political history," 7, 19, 20
New Spain. *See* Hidalgo rebellion; Mexican independence movement, influence of; Plan de Iguala, influence of
Nicaragua, province of: Chontales area insurgencies, 149; and Costa Rica, administrative ties to, 58, 60–61; early 1800s profile, 134–36; insurgencies, evolution and consequences of, 149–52; Jalteva, 135, 145; Masaya, 135, 144, 173; Nueva Segovia unrest, 149; Rivas (villa of Nicaragua) revolt, 147–48; San Carlos fort rebellion, 148–49. *See also* Bustamante y Guerra, José de; Granada, Nicaragua, insurgency in; León, Nicaragua
Nicoya, 75n14, 76n19, 147, 148
Nueva Granada, 2, 149
Nueva Guatemala, 3. *See also* Guatemala City
Nueva Segovia unrest, 149
nuns, 112

oath-taking ceremonies: artillery fire, 39–40, 47–48, 89; bells, ringing of, 39, 89, 90; Cádiz era evolution of, 52–53; ceremonies and rituals, examples, 81–82, 87–91; to Charles IV

oath-taking ceremonies (*cont.*)
    in Granada, 40–45; coins/medallions, giving of in rituals, 41, 48, 50, 88, 97–98; conditional demands, examples of, 93–94; to Constitution of Cádiz, 47–52, 98; definitions and historical perspective, 37–39; to Ferdinand VII, 138, 140; Independence Act of the Kingdom of Guatemala, 81–82, 89–91, 91–96, 99; music and dance, 88, 89, 94, 95; Totonicapán district, 158. *See also* symbolism in ceremony and ritual
obedience, oaths of. *See* oath-taking ceremonies
Ochomogo, battle of, 62, 69
O'Horan, Gabriel, 144, 148
Olaechea, Sebastián de (and family), 109–10
Olancho, Honduras, 140
Olivares, Francisco Gabriel de, 108, 109, 116–17
Oliver, Juan de, 109–10
Ordóñez, José de, 121–22
Oreamuno, Joaquín, 62
Osejo, Rafael Francisco de, 67
Osorio, Alejandra, 43

pactism, 38, 44–45. *See also* sovereignty and source of power
pactum translationis, 44, 77n36
Palavicini, José, 40
Palenque (Mayan archeological site), 121, 122
Palti, Elias, 20
patronato real, 84–85, 98, 104
Patzúm, Guatemala, 94
Payne Iglesias, Elizet, 133
Peinado, José María, 28n29, 140, 198
peninsular culture, 113–14
pennants (royal/political) and ritual symbolism, 42, 43, 88–89, 95–96
"people" and independence analysis, 67–70
Peralta, Hernán, 68, 69
Pérez Brignoli, Héctor, 70

Pineda, Emeterio, 112
Pinillos Urbina, Gregorio Francisco, 167
Pino y Martínez, Miguel del, 118, 122
Pinto Soria, Julio César, 79n76
Plan de Iguala, influence of, 14–15, 61, 82. *See also* Mexican independence movement, influence of
Polanco, Francisco, 108, 113, 116, 119–20
Pollack, Aaron, 158
portraiture (royal) and ritual symbolism, 40, 41, 42, 43, 48
pre-Columbian history, preservation of, 120–22
priests. *See* clergy, roles and influence of
principales (Indian nobles), 158
procession/promenade, symbolism of, 41, 47–48, 88–89
provincial councils *(diputaciones provinciales)*, 12–16, 83, 166, 193, 195–200; of Nicaragua y Costa Rica (of León), 60–61, 75n11, 136, 140, 151
Provisional Advisory Junta, 83–84, 85–87
"prudent conciliation" strategy of Bustamante, 189–91, 201
Puntarenas, Costa Rica, 59

Quentas Zayas, Agustín de las, 115
Quetzaltenango, Guatemala: and Chiapas, relationship and cross-cultural ties, 110–11, 114; and commerce of Totonicapán district, 161; oath-taking in, 93; regionalism and classism in, 176; tribute protests in, 169

Rabinovich, Alejandro M., 64
racial conflicts and insurgencies. *See* ethnic conflicts and insurgencies
rations and personal service tribute to priests, 159, 167, 169, 173. *See also* ecclesiastical taxes
Real Sociedad Económica de Amantes de la Patria de Guatemala (Royal Economic Society of Lovers of the Homeland of Guatemala), 4, 5

regency council formation, 8–9, 46
regionalism, 72, 135, 176. *See also* localism and devolution of power
religious ceremonies as political rituals, 37–39
repartimientos, 138, 162
repression by force, 140–41, 144, 172. *See also* military actions
republicanism, 67–69, 83–84
rituals. *See* oath-taking ceremonies
Rivas (villa of Nicaragua) revolt, 147–48
Robledo, Gregorio, 145, 156n65
Robles Domínguez, Mariano, 103, 115, 121, 122
Rodríguez, Mario, 20, 71, 79n76, 164
Rodríguez Solano, Pablo Augusto, 21, 57, 72
Romero, Germán, 134, 136, 141–42
ropa de la tierra (local textiles), 161
Royal Economic Society of Lovers of the Homeland of Guatemala, 4, 5
"rural democracy," 68

Sacasa, Roberto, 142
Salamá, Guatemala, 91–92
Salvador, José, 136, 137
San Carlos fort (Nicaragua), 143, 144, 148–49
San Cristóbal Totonicapán, Guatemala, 158, 160, 170
San José, Costa Rica, 59, 60, 62, 68, 69–70
San Juan River, 135, 136, 144, 148
San Marcos, Guatemala, 94
San Miguel, El Salvador, 140
San Miguel Totonicapán Guatemala, 158–59, 160, 161–62, 166–69, 170, 171–75
San Salvador (El Salvador), 45, 150–51, 189, 200–201
San Sebastián el Tejar, Guatemala, 92
Santa Catarina Ixtahuacán, Guatemala, 169
Santa María Chiquimula, Guatemala, 162–63, 170, 171–75
Santa Rosa, Guatemala, 95

Santiago de Guatemala, 3
Santísimo Sacramento brotherhood, 172
scholasticism, 64–66, 67
Second Political Statute of the Province of Costa Rica, 62
secularizing policies and religious ritual, 49, 107
separatism. *See* autonomist movements
Serrano Polo, Antonio, 110
ship symbolism, 42
Sierra, José, 143, 156n50
silver mining, 75n9
slavery, protests against, 138, 144, 148, 150
smallpox, 118–19, 169, 170
Soch, Juan Cruz, 168
social/class hierarchies, 41, 48, 49, 136. *See also* classism
social commerce and spread of Enlightenment thinking, 109–11, 113–15
social democratic thought, 68
Sociedad de los Amigos del País, 109, 114
Sololá, Guatemala, 94
Soto, Benito, 143, 144
South America, independence era effects and comparisons, 8–11
sovereignty and source of power, 42–46, 50–53, 64–67. *See also* symbolism in ceremony and ritual
state formation, concepts of, 65–67. *See also* nation/state, concepts of
subversion, acts of, and jurisdictional disputes, 192–94
sugar cane industry, 59
sun, symbolism of, 41, 50
superior governmental junta *(junta superior gobernativa)* (Costa Rica), 61–62
Supreme Central Junta, 7, 8, 46
symbolism in ceremony and ritual: artillery fire, 39–40, 47–48, 89; bells, ringing of, 39, 89, 90; funeral rituals, 39–40; militarization, 41; overview, 23; procession/promenade, 41, 47–48, 88–89; resurrection symbolism, 40;

symbolism in ceremony and ritual (*cont.*)
  ship symbolism, 42; subordination of native cultures, 41, 42, 43, 46–47, 95. *See also* imagery in ceremony and ritual; oath-taking ceremonies
syncretism, and ritual symbolism, 41–42

Tabasco province (New Spain), 114
tax levies and protests against, 26n10, 135, 137–38, 144, 148, 150, 161. *See also* ecclesiastical taxes; tribute payment
Tehuantepec, Oaxaca (New Spain), 113–14
terminology, 26n4, 100n5, 124n1, 180n15
textile crafts, 161, 162
Thomism, 64, 65
Three Guarantees *(Tres garantías)*. *See* Plan de Iguala, influence of
tiña (skin disease), 119
tithes, distribution of, 116–17
tobacco production and regulation, 26n10, 58, 59–60, 138, 144, 148, 149
Totonicapán rebellion: 1818–1820 protest movement, 171–75; continued protests, 169–71; historical context and evolution of unrest, 162–66; impact and effects of, 176–78; Mallol incident 1813, 166–69; overview, 24, 158–60; regional civic/political profile, 160–62
trade and market development: agricultural, 59, 161; contraband, 5, 75n9, 136, 149; and Napoleonic wars, 206; Nicaraguan profile, 135–36
translatio imperii concept, 64
Tribunal of Loyalty *(Tribunal de Fidelidad)*, 192
tribute payments: elimination of, 93, 144, 158, 164, 165; and Indian mortality, 119; protests against, 4, 134, 144, 148, 162–63; standardization/destandardization of, 27–28n20, 162, 164; "voluntary" donations, 165. *See also* community funds; ecclesiastical taxes; Totonicapán rebellion
Tzul, Atanasio (Francisco), 158, 168, 172, 174

Urrutia, Carlos Luis de, 158, 171, 172, 173, 175

vacatio regis (absence of the sovereign). *See* abdications of Bayonne, effects of
vaccination programs, 119, 169
Valero, José Mariano, 4, 111, 122–23, 130n98, 195
Valle, José Cecilio del, 96, 170
Van Young, Eric, 143
Vargas y Rivera, Juan Manuel, 108
Vásquez, Mario, 72
Vega Carballo, José Luis, 69, 71
Venegas, Francisco Javier, 190
Verapaz (alcaldía mayor) of Guatemala, 91–92, 169
villa of Nicaragua (Rivas) insurgency, 147–48
Villatoro, José Patricio, 172–73
Villaurrutia, Jacobo de, 108–9, 114
Virgin of Nuestra Señora de la Concepción, 137, 140
Vital de Moctezuma, José, 108, 114, 121–22

Western Highlands of Guatemala, 30n51, 158. *See also* Los Altos region
wood, markets in, 59, 136
Wortman, Miles, 135

Ximena, Pedro, 38–42

Zacapa, Guatemala, 92
Zambo Mosquito people, 136, 149

www.ingramcontent.com/pod-product-compliance
Lightning Source LLC
Chambersburg PA
CBHW021342230426
43666CB00006B/371